William Walton

Muse of Fire

O for a Muse of fire, that would ascend
The brightest heaven of invention. . . .

The Life of Henry the Fifth (Prologue)
William Shakespeare

William Walton

Muse of Fire

Stephen Lloyd

THE BOYDELL PRESS

First published 2001
The Boydell Press, Woodbridge

ISBN 0 85115 803 X

The Boydell Press is an imprint of Boydell & Brewer Ltd
PO Box 9, Woodbridge, Suffolk IP12 3DF, UK
and of Boydell & Brewer Inc.
PO Box 41026, Rochester, NY 14604–4126, USA
website: http://www.boydell.co.uk

A catalogue record for this book is available
from the British Library

Library of Congress Cataloging-in-Publication Data
Lloyd, Stephen, 1944–
    William Walton : muse of fire / Stephen Lloyd.
        p. cm.
    Includes bibliographical references and index.
    ISBN 0–85115–803–X (alk. paper)
    1. Walton, William, 1902–   2. Composers – England – Biography.
    I. Title.
    ML410.W292 L56 2001
    780'.92 – dc21   00–051947

This publication is printed on acid-free paper

Printed in Great Britain by
St Edmundsbury Press Ltd, Bury St Edmunds, Suffolk

Contents

Illustrations

13. Siegfried Sassoon with Stephen Tennant in 1929.
    Reproduced from Penelope Middleboe, *Edith Olivier: from her Journals 1924–48* (London, Weidenfeld and Nicolson, London, 1989)

14. Dressing-up: Zita Jungman, Walton, Cecil Beaton, Stephen Tennant, Georgia Sitwell, Baby Jungman and Rex Whistler in 1927.
    Reproduced by permission of Sotheby's Picture Library

15. Walton with Hubert Foss in 1932.
    Reproduced from Duncan Hinnells, *An Extraordinary Performance: Hubert Foss, Music Publishing and the Oxford University Press* (Oxford–New York, OUP, 1998), by permission of Diana Sparkes

16. Hyam 'Bumps' Greenbaum.
    Photograph supplied by Sidonie Goossens and Kyla Greenbaum

17. *La Mortella*, Walton's home and water gardens in Ischia.
    Photo: Author

18. Walton rehearsing the BBC Symphony Orchestra in 1941 at the Corn Exchange, Bedford.
    Reproduced from Gerald Jackson, *First Flute* (London, Dent, 1968)

19. Walton with the Sitwells on the occasion of Dame Edith's seventy-fifth birthday concert at the Royal Festival Hall in 1962.
    Reproduced from Elizabeth Salter, *Edith Sitwell* (London, Oresko Books, 1979)

20. Walton at rehearsal, conducting the London Symphony Orchestra.
    Reproduced from Humphrey Searle and Robert Layton, *Twentieth Century Composers Vol. III – Britain, Scandinavia and the Netherlands* (New York, Chicago, San Francisco, Holt, Rinehart and Winston, 1972)

21. Walton at Aldeburgh in 1966.
    Photo: Lionel Carley

22. Sir William Walton. A portrait in later life.
    Reproduced from Frank Howes, *The Music of William Walton* (London, OUP, 1974)
    © Douglas Glass

Text Figures

Introduction and Acknowledgements

Anyone investigating the life and music of William Walton is indebted to certain writers whose books have become standard works of reference on the composer. Michael Kennedy's penetrating *Portrait of Walton* (OUP 1989, revised 1998) and Lady Susana Walton's more personal and gossipy portrait of her husband, *William Walton: Behind the Facade* (OUP 1988), are two that come immediately to mind. Nor can anyone wanting to examine the music overlook Frank Howes' *The Music of William Walton* (OUP 1965), the second edition of which (1974) included a new chapter covering the works composed between 1965 and 1972.

But there are two special debts that must be acknowledged. Stewart Craggs, in both his *William Walton: A Catalogue* (OUP, second edition 1990) and its companion *William Walton: a source book* (Scolar Press 1993), has surely done the groundwork for all future commentators on the composer. This is a debt that one cannot stress too highly, and it was rightly acknowledged in the Introduction to the second edition of Craggs' *Catalogue* by another researcher and writer to whom one is endlessly grateful: the late Christopher Palmer. Not only did he provide an illuminating introduction to the *Catalogue*, but in his own inimitable style he wrote perceptive notes for the complete series of recordings by Chandos Records Ltd. He went further. He saved a number of works from neglect by preparing performing editions and suites: for example, of many of the film scores, and the music for the epic 1942 radio play *Christopher Columbus*. These all form part of the Chandos complete recorded edition. Had he lived longer he would no doubt have written an absorbing book on Walton.

In climbing on the back of these experts, I am not attempting to displace any existing study of Walton. One may even ask whether yet another is necessary – a question thrown at me by the veteran radio and film producer, the late Dallas Bower. The centenary, in 2002, of Walton's birth provides sufficient justification: centenaries and similar anniversaries are often times for reassessment and re-evaluation, and a composer of Walton's stature deserves examination from a variety of perspectives. But a further compelling reason is that in recent years new biographies of a number of people close to Walton – among them Sir Osbert Sitwell, Lord Berners, Hubert Foss, Stephen Tennant, Siegfried Sassoon and Edith Olivier – have thrown fresh light on the composer, and these I have shamelessly plundered. Further personal research, into the first public performance of *Façade* (which was far from being the riot that the Sitwells – and Walton – would have us believe), into the circumstances of the commissioning of *Belshazzar's Feast* and *Christopher Columbus* (both BBC initiatives, as was *Troilus and Cressida*), and into the background to the fourteen films for which he provided music, will hopefully broaden our knowledge of the man.

I hope, then, that this book can be read as a parallel commentary on the composer. I have attempted to present the facts as much as possible using the words of Walton and others involved, through letters, through contemporary reviews, and with the help of numerous broadcast interviews in addition to those I have conducted myself. Tony Palmer's revealing 1981 television documentary of Walton, *At the Haunted End of the Day*,[1] has been one such valuable source that I readily acknowledge.

For certain illustrations appearing between pages 146–147, acknowledgement is made to Oxford University Press (No. 1), the Raymond Mander and Joe Mitchenson Theatre Collection (No. 3), Viscount Wimborne (No. 7), Roger Wood (No. 8), Sotheby's (No. 14), Mrs Diana Sparkes (No. 15), Sidonie Goossens and Kyla Greenbaum (No. 16), Lionel Carley (No. 21) and Douglas Glass (No. 22).

Quotations from letters from Sir William Walton appear by courtesy of the William Walton Trust, and I am most grateful to Lady Susana Walton and the William Walton Trust (Artistic Director Stephannie Williams) for granting me permission. I would like to thank Simon Wright, Music Copyright & Hire Library Manager, Oxford University Press, for allowing me access to OUP's Music Department Archives, quotation from which is made by kind permission of the Secretary to the Delegates of the Oxford University Press. Quotations from the writings of Dame Edith Sitwell and Sir Osbert Sitwell appear by permission of David Higham Associates, with additional thanks to Mr Frank Magro, Sir Osbert's literary executor. I am extremely grateful to Mrs Diane Sparkes, daughter of Hubert and Dora Foss, for not only generously making available to me her mother's unpublished Memoirs of Walton (part of the Hubert Foss Archives) but also allowing me permission to quote from them.

There are many others I would like to thank: the Boston Public Library for supplying a copy of Constant Lambert's important 1926 article on Walton that is here re-printed for the first time as Appendix 1; Neil Somerville, senior assistant at the BBC Written Archive Centre, Caversham, Reading, for guiding me through the BBC's Walton files and for allowing me permission to quote from material in its keeping; Paul Collen and Oliver Davies at the Department of Portraits, Royal College of Music, for providing me with copies of certain programmes, including the recently discovered one for the first public performance of *Façade*; Roy Douglas, Kyla Greenbaum and Sidonie Goossens for kindly sparing the time to talk to me about Walton, and similarly the late (and sadly much under-rated) Dallas Bower for several

---

[1] This television documentary can be seen at *La Mortella*, Walton's home at Ischia.

hours of reminiscence, and the late Carole Rosen for introducing him to me; Robert Tucker, Senior Librarian at the Barbican Centre, London; The Executive Director of Planning & Conservation for the Royal Borough of Kensington and Chelsea; Tony Benson, Paul Guinery, John Hely-Hutchinson and Maureen Murray, all of whom have been very helpful in a number of ways. I thank also the staff at the British Library for making available the correspondence to Lady Aberconway (Mrs McLaren), Edward Clark, Sir Adrian Boult and Harriet Cohen, the latter only recently coming into the public domain. It is with much regret that, for reasons of distance, I was not able to see the Sitwell-Sassoon correspondence and additional Sitwell papers at the Washington State University Libraries.

I would like to express my gratitude to my editors Caroline Palmer and Cathy Harrison and all at Boydell & Brewer for bringing to completion a seven-year project.

Three people deserve special thanks: I am particularly grateful to Stewart Craggs for his generous assistance at many stages during my research; to Lewis Foreman for his continued help and encouragement throughout the writing of this book and, by reading early draft chapters, eliminating many errors and not a few howlers – any that remain are mine; and to Bruce Phillips without whose support this book would not be appearing in print.

Last, but by no means least, I would like to thank my wife Pauline to whom I dedicate this book, for patiently sharing with me journeys of research to Ischia, Amalfi, Ravello, Pallanza and Ascona, and – even more patiently – enduring the lonely 'computer hours'.

Stephen Lloyd
January 2001

1

Oldham and Oxford

William Walton had two façades. One was the brilliant, witty Entertainment of that name, composed in collaboration with Edith Sitwell, that brought him a degree of notoriety and ultimately lasting fame. The other was the cool exterior that masked a cauldron of emotions which gave birth to music as vital and exciting as any of his generation, with a verve and energy that few composers could match. Laurence Olivier, his friend for nearly forty years, remarked on this paradox:

> His exterior – and his personality – is remote, removed, distant, rather chill; and his look is the same: rather cold. His look is very very pale, very very pale sort of hair, very pale sort of eyes, and what comes out of him is the most gutsy bash and crash and bang you ever heard in your life, and it doesn't go with his face. It doesn't go with his personality at all when you meet him. . . .[1]

> You expect a genius to act and behave like a genius, and to look like a genius, but . . . he looks, as he always has, the most normal person on earth, with the shortest cut hair you ever saw – 'choir-boy cut' I call it – in the thirties, and it's remained like that ever since. . . . What's so unusual is what is so unexpected about him, because he's always had the appearance, when he was young, of being rather a delicate flower without being in the least bit willowy . . . when here's this music, that's got more guts and more spunk and more attack and almost more *venom* than one could possibly imagine would be hidden within that form of person and personality. . . .[2]

---

[1] In Tony Palmer's film profile of Walton, *At the Haunted End of the Day*, London ITV *The South Bank Show*, 19 April 1981.

[2] Interview with John Amis, in a BBC Transcription Services programme *Portrait of Walton* presented by John Amis and broadcast on Radio 3 on 4 June 1977. Repeated in Radio 4's memorial *Kaleidoscope* tribute, also presented by John Amis, and broadcast on 8 March 1983 with a repeat on 20 July 1983. BBC Sound Archives T083853; National Sound Archives NP6825W.

To another friend who knew him in the late 1920s, he was 'an Enigma, a Sphinx'.[3] Often uncomfortable and evasive in interview, Walton was a very shy man. With an output that is the smallest of any major British composer, composition was for him a slow and difficult process – he even described himself as lazy, but this denies the thoroughness with which he approached the task. His works may be comparatively few in number but half a dozen remain as landmarks in British music. *Façade* and *Belshazzar's Feast* have been matched by no-one, while the violin and viola concertos, his first symphony and the film score for *Henry V* stand among the finest of their kind.

Like Elgar and Delius, Walton was mainly self-taught. When someone referred to him in a letter as having been an *enfant terrible* of the Royal College of Music, he responded sharply: 'I wasn't at the RCM – *or anywhere else*.'[4] Like Elgar and Delius, Walton gained an early reputation on the Continent, and like Delius in time he abandoned his home roots, choosing to live abroad. But, unlike both of those composers, he did not entirely make his own way. 'Looking back, I can trace a distinct element of luck that has been a major asset in my career – that, and some very staunch friends, not to mention a certain amount of musical talent and a great deal of persistent hard work,' he observed as he approached his sixtieth birthday.[5] Luck certainly played a significant hand in a life that was, to a large extent, dependent upon the help, friendship and generosity of others.

William's parents were both singers. His mother, née Louisa Maria Turner from whom he took his second name, was a contralto from Stretford, close to Manchester. She came from a family of upholsterers and furniture makers, and her father was an excise man in Hull. She had met her husband while singing at a recital at Chorlton-cum-Hardy. After they were married in 1898, they lived in Oldham. Charles Walton, a bass-baritone from Hale in Cheshire, had been one of the first students at the Royal Manchester College of Music when it opened in 1893. His teacher of singing there was Andrew Black, who at that time was just establishing his name in the round of the provincial festivals. He was to sing the title-role in Elgar's *Caractacus* at the Leeds première in 1898, Judas at the Birmingham première of *The Apostles* in 1904, and he was the first to sing substantial extracts from the opera *Koanga* in Delius's privately financed London concert in 1899. Charles's part in college concert performances included 'Wotan's Farewell', leading rôles in *The Magic Flute* and *The Marriage of Figaro*, and Mephistopheles in Gounod's *Faust*. He left in 1897, but returned in 1902 to take part in a concert performance of *Don Giovanni*. Exactly a week later, on 29 March, the Waltons' second child,

---

3   Stephen Tennant, in a letter to Dr Stewart Craggs from Wilsford Manor, 10 June 1975.
4   1 October 1936, replying to a letter from Kenneth Wright, 12 August.
5   *Sunday Telegraph*, 25 March 1962.

William Turner, was born at 93 Werneth Hall Road. A brother, Noel, had preceded him in 1899, to be followed by a sister, Nora, in 1908 and another brother, Alexander, in 1910. Their father was by then both a teacher of singing and choirmaster at the local church of St John's in the Parish of Werneth. A strict disciplinarian, he made young William, from about the age of five, and Noel sing in the choir, and if either sang a wrong note he would rap him on the knuckles with his ring. It was perhaps for this reason that much later Walton could confess: 'I'm not too fond of church music.'[6] One incident that stuck in his memory was a scene that ended in tears because he was not allowed to sing a solo in the church choir when about six.

William's upbringing, strictly Church of England, was simple and unpretentious. The Waltons lived in a typical terrace house with an outside toilet. School was a nightmare for William. While his brother Noel went to the grammar school, their father could not afford to send both, so William was sent instead round the corner to the rough school that stood next to a stable for tram horses. The boys were separated from the girls by iron railings – 'What a pity!' he wryly remarked in old age. Women were to play a strong part in both his personal and his creative life.

By the time he had gained some recognition as a composer, Walton spoke with gratitude in a newspaper interview about his parental upbringing:

> I expect I have been singularly fortunate for home influences have been the greatest possible aid in a career such as mine. My father, the late Mr C. A. Walton, was a well-known local musician, and my mother, Mrs Louisa Walton, who now lives at Werneth Hall Road, still teaches singing. In some households it is dangerous to dabble with art, and to sit down and write music often meets with a good deal of ragging and bullying. In fact, most people, I think, will agree that an artistic career is a very difficult one, but my parents never raised any objections and from both I have had every possible encouragement in my work.[7]

The next stage in William's career, in 1912 when he was only ten, was when luck first intervened.

> It was luck that my father, a singing teacher in Oldham, happened to notice an advertisement for Probationers in the choir of Christ Church, Oxford. Luck, that, in spite of missing the train connection, my mother and I managed to arrive just in time for me to do my piece, do a few rudimentary ear-tests and be chosen for the vacancy.[8]

Having spotted the advertisement in the newspaper, his father decided to let him have a go. But it was his mother who took him to Oxford, although

6 Interview with Alan Blyth, *Radio Times*, 23 March 1972, 15.
7 *Oldham Chronicle*, 1 May 1926.
8 *Sunday Telegraph*, 25 March 1962.

in fact we almost didn't go at all. When the moment of departure arrived, the ticket money had disappeared. My father had been to the pub the night before and had somehow lost the fare. We had to borrow the money from the local greengrocer. I'd never been on a train before, at least not for such a long train journey, and you can't imagine the excitement. I remember I was very sick. My mother really had to beg Dr Strong, the Dean of Christ Church, to let me have a go. I cried, I think. Eventually I had to do a few tests which was all new to me. Then I sang what I had prepared, a thing by Marcello: *O Lord our Governor.* Luckily for me they took me on, and I joined up as a probationer. . . . It was horrid. The problem was I had a broad Lancashire accent and the other boys used to sit on my head until I spoke the same as they did, properly, as they thought.[9]

And so the ten-year-old from Oldham found himself at Oxford, with a scholarship to Christ Church Cathedral School[10] where he was to stay for the next six years. For most of that period, war would be raging across Europe. In contrast with the rough local school at Oldham, Oxford provided Walton with his first 'cushion' from the hardships of the outside world. But his future after Oxford seemed very uncertain. Although he was good at sport, he had shown no aptitude for musical instruments. Earlier attempts at home to learn the violin had come to nothing. What path should he follow? 'So I thought, . . . I must make myself interesting somehow, otherwise when my voice breaks I'll be sent back to Oldham. What can I do to make myself interesting? Write music! So I did.'[11]

His earliest signs of composition had been *Variations for Violin and Pianoforte on a chorale by J. S. B.* that progressed no more than a dozen bars. 'Not very interesting and wisely decided to stop,' he much later recalled.[12] For a while no further attempts were made. But at Oxford he tried his hand at writing something for the choir. 'I had begun some tentative compositions – settings of Shakespeare from the plays we happened to be studying, some organ pieces and a march for a wedding. Two pieces from this time were eventually published.' The first of these, dated Easter 1916 (the year in which he was confirmed in Christ Church Cathedral), was *A Litany* (*Drop, Drop Slow Tears*), a motet for unaccompanied mixed chorus, with words by Phineas Fletcher, that is remarkably adventurous both harmonically and structurally for a boy only just fourteen, and then two years later *The Winds*, a song to a text by Swinburne, with a rapid restless semi-quaver accompani-

9 Tony Palmer, *At the Haunted End of the Day*, ITV.
10 In 1994 the Sir William Walton Centre was added, incorporating a large assembly hall for concerts, recitals and drama.
11 Tony Palmer, *ibid.*
12 Letter to Hubert Foss in 1932; Dora Foss, 'Memoirs of Walton' (unpublished), part of the Hubert Foss Archives in the private possession of Mrs Diana Sparkes, née Foss. He gave no date to this first effort, adding only 'However broke loose again about 13'.

ment. Swinburne seems to have been a favourite poet of his at that time as in July 1918 he set three more of his verses – *Child's Song, Love Laid his Sleepless Head* and *A Lyke-wake Song* – for voice and piano.[13] Of the Shakespeare settings, *Tell Me Where is Fancy Bred* from *The Merchant of Venice*, dated 2 July 1916, is among his earliest surviving compositions. It was arranged for soprano and tenor voices, three violins and piano – 'all far too high . . . full of high B flats', he recalled. His most ambitious score from that year was a cantata for soprano and tenor soloists, double female chorus and orchestra, setting Matthew Arnold's *The Forsaken Merman*. It was 425 bars in length, and he completed it in short score that summer. It has not been performed. Fourteen years were to elapse before he was to write for mixed voices again, and then spectacularly, in *Belshazzar's Feast*. Another Shakespeare setting, of *Where the Bee Sucks*, seems not to have survived, along with many other works of that period. As he admitted, 'After that [I] fairly went in for it and produced about 30 very bad works of various species, songs, motets, Magnificats, etc.'[14] He may have had the excitement of two or three of his songs being performed at a private function early in July 1919, as he wrote home that some of them were to be given at the home of Lady Glenconner, the mother of his future friend Stephen Tennant.

Walton's great fortune at Oxford was that the music staff with whom he came into contact were open-minded and did not discourage individuality. There was no beating him into conformity. One of his first teachers at Christ Church was the assistant organist Basil Allchin who gave him piano lessons. (He was never to become an accomplished pianist – Alan Frank, of Oxford University Press, went so far as saying that he played 'excruciatingly badly', and he was to write very little for that instrument – but an early surviving manuscript is of an 89-bar *Valse in C minor* dated 2 February 1917.) Walton would sometimes show Allchin reams of manuscript paper covered with notes, mostly cast in the form of elaborate motets for double choir with unorthodox part writing. Beyond pointing out the unorthodoxy of these youthful efforts, Allchin to his credit was not discouraging.[15]

Walton's musical instruction came mainly from Dr Henry Ley, organist of Christ Church and one of the most brilliant of his day (later professor of organ at the Royal College of Music), and Hugh Allen (organist of New College and Professor of Music at Oxford, and soon, in 1918, to succeed Parry as Director of the Royal College of Music). When Allchin's military commitments became too demanding, Ley took over Walton's piano and

---

13 Unpublished. The manuscripts of these three songs were auctioned at Sotheby's in 1989.

14 Brief biographical notes in a letter to Hubert Foss, 1932; Dora Foss, 'Memoirs of Walton'.

15 Frank Howes, *Oxford Mail*, 2 April 1962, and Frank Howes, *The Music of William Walton* Vol. 1, 'The Musical Pilgrim' series, OUP 1942, 7.

organ tuition. But his guardian was Dr Thomas Banks Strong, a double doctor, of music as well as divinity, Dean of Christ Church and later Bishop of Ripon and of Oxford. It was Dr Strong more than anyone else who prepared Walton's future path as a composer. 'I am to go to him for money when I am without,' William wrote home in October 1918. The war had drastically affected his father's income through the decrease in the number of his singing pupils so that he was not in a position to meet the full costs of his son's education. Even at an early stage Walton's financial concerns were to be handled by others.

Strong, Ley and Allen were quick to recognise Walton's very considerable musical gifts, as did Sir Hubert Parry who, staying with Strong at Oxford, happened to notice some manuscripts of Walton's. 'There's a lot in this chap, you must keep your eye on him!' was Parry's perceptive comment.[16] 'An awfully jolly old person' was the young chorister's description of England's senior composer when they met in June 1917. Walton's introduction to contemporary music came not only through the fine collection of scores he avidly studied in the Ellis Library of Music in Oxford – new works of Stravinsky, Debussy and Ravel as they came out – but also through Dr Strong. 'Do you like your T. Strong?' was a standing joke of the time.

> [He] used to have a group of us to the Deanery after Sunday morning service for religious instruction. Occasionally, perhaps as a recompense, he would play what seemed to us very odd music indeed – pieces such as the Schoenberg op. 11 and op. 15. I also remember him once playing some music by [Leo] Ornstein [who] was notorious around 1914 as a sort of John Cage of his day.[17]

The young William by now was determined not to go back to Oldham, 'home of cotton mills, brass bands and other things . . . not my favourite part of the world'.[18] He remained at the choir school from 1912 until 1918, staying on, through the intervention of the Dean, after 1916 when his voice broke. There was even talk of him furthering his musical education in London. He wrote home rather grandly on 8 October 1916: 'The Dean has been saying something to me about the Royal College of Music. He says it is unpatriotic of England to let slip such a musical brain.'[19] When he had reached the end of his time in the choir school, Dr Strong suggested to Walton's father that his son, although only sixteen, should join Christ Church as an undergraduate, continue his musical studies there and obtain his

---

[16] Letter from Thomas Strong to Hubert Foss, 8 January 1938; Hubert Foss Archives.
[17] Murray Schafer, *British Composers in Interview*, Faber & Faber 1963, 74. Schoenberg's op. 11 was *3 Klavierstücke*, op. 15 the song cycle *Der Buch der hängenden Gärten* to verses by Stefan George.
[18] Tony Palmer, *At the Haunted End of the Day*, ITV.
[19] Michael Kennedy, *Portrait of Walton*, 9. In his letters home he signed himself as Billy.

MusBac and BA degrees. Again through the Dean's intervention, the fees would be paid by a fund that existed to support needy undergraduates. This arrangement met with Mr Walton's approval, especially in view of the increasing financial problems he was having to face in Oldham since the outbreak of war.

This arrangement also suited his son only too well. As a result of the war Oxford was not overflowing with undergraduates. 'There was nobody there, that's why they took me in,' he admitted much later. 'I didn't work at all. I couldn't be bothered when I suddenly had masses of scores there to be read.'[20] Having successfully passed the first half of his Bachelor of Music examination in June 1918, he was awarded an in-College Exhibition for two years.

Greek was one of the requirements for his degree course, and having the same Greek tutor as Walton was the South African-born Roy Campbell whom Edith Sitwell generously regarded as 'one of the very few great poets of our time'. Walton was a year younger than Campbell, but the two became good friends, 'my great pal', as he recalled many years later. '[Roy] wasn't quite so . . . well, he was a bit quieter in those days. We neither of us did any work, and both failed Responsions.'[21] In the second of his two autobiographical volumes, *Light on a Dark Road*, Campbell remembered Walton in glowing terms:

> The first person I met in Oxford was one of the greatest men who have been there this century, a real genius, and, at the same time, one of the very finest fellows I ever met in my life . . . We walked out with two young ladies, who were also good friends, and who were employed as waitresses. Of course, needless to say, Willie's one eventually became a countess. Something magical seems to happen to everything he touches.[22]

> During the year I was at Oxford . . . William introduced me to the people who have influenced and helped me most in my subsequent literary career, Edith, Osbert, and Sacheverell Sitwell, Eliot, Wyndham Lewis, Thomas Earp, Philip Heseltine, Cecil Gray, and others.[23]

But, as Roy Campbell added, 'it was soon apparent both to William and myself and to our excellent tutor [of Greek] Mr Young that we were not cut out for scholars of the routine sort'.[24] In December 1919 Walton failed at his third attempt to pass Responsions. 'Some time I'd pass in Algebra and fail in

---

20 *Sunday Times*, 25 March 1962.
21 *Ibid.*
22 Roy Campbell, *Light on a Dark Horse: An autobiography (1901–1935)*, Hollis & Carter 1951, 181.
23 *Ibid.*, 183.
24 *Ibid.*, 183.

Greek; otherwise I'd pass in Greek and fail in Algebra. I could never do them all at the same time. So I was sent down finally'[25] – for two terms.

At this juncture a former Christ Church undergraduate, the up-and-coming conductor Adrian Boult (who had himself experienced Dr Strong's kindness and understanding – 'that great man' he described him[26]), was approached by Henry Ley to see if any musical job in London could be found for 'this wonderful Lancashire boy who had been kept at Ch. Ch. by the Dean and was now to come to London and MUST find a job'. Boult obliged by arranging an interview with the publishers Goodwin & Tabb for a proof-reading job, only within a few days to receive from Walton a letter in which he wrote that he had 'decided to starve in a garret and compose all day rather than enjoy a nice job'.[27]

In June 1920 he passed the second part of his BMus, but near the end of the year his grant was terminated. Fortunately for Walton a garret was already being prepared for him, one in which there would be no question of starving. In fact, board and lodging and a small income would be provided. His meeting with the Sitwells was another stroke of fortune that would alter the course of his career.

25 Interview with John Pearson in his radio portrait of the Sitwells, *Façades*, broadcast on BBC Radio 3, 13 November 1978. NSA T38610.
26 Adrian Cedric Boult, *My own Trumpet*, Hamish Hamilton 1973, 25.
27 Michael Kennedy, *Adrian Boult*, Hamish Hamilton 1987, Papermac 1989, 76.

2

Sitwellian Patronage

In January 1919, after completing his time in the army, the twenty-one-year-old Sacheverell Sitwell went up to Balliol College, Oxford. To his great disappointment he found life at Oxford in the immediate post-war years dull and depressing. Most of his fellow undergraduates were ex-servicemen whose only intent was to obtain a degree. Not only was the climate unbearable but the food was poor, and he left after two terms. One pleasure amongst such gloom, however, was that his friend, the poet Siegfried Sassoon (1886–1967), had rooms in Oxford for a short while that winter. Sassoon, who received the Military Cross 'for conspicuous gallantry' while serving in France, had tried to convey the harsh realities of the conflict in such anti-war poems as the collection *Counter-Attack* published in 1918. In 1917 he had sent to his senior officer 'A Soldier's Declaration' in which he criticised what he saw as the deliberate prolonging of the war. Copies were sent to certain influential personalities and one even found its way into the columns of *The Times*. Friends, managing to convince the military authorities that Sassoon was suffering from shell-shock, saved him from a court martial. He eventually returned to active service in France, only to receive a head wound that put him on indefinite sick leave for the remainder of the war. Sassoon lived on a private income that was to become a frequent source of financial assistance to Walton.

Through another poet, the Canadian Frank Prewitt, Sassoon had met the young Walton at a meeting of the Oxford Musical Club in February, and it was through Sassoon that Sacheverell Sitwell met Walton, as his brother Osbert remembered:

> One day, when [Sacheverell] came up to visit me, he mentioned, I remember, the sole redeeming point of Oxford for him: that he had met in a – as it seemed to him – leaden city, the only English musical genius it had ever been his lot so far to encounter, a boy of sixteen, called W. T. Walton – and that was the first time I heard the name. I did not pay much attention, since we already possessed among our friends an undoubted and more

mature musical genius, Bernard van Dieren. [. . .] We must, Sacheverell continued, find some way of being of use to him, and of advancing his chances and genius. . . . But what could we do?[1]

The Sitwells, a sister and two brothers, were the remarkable offspring of an extraordinary family. Their father, the remote and eccentric Sir George Sitwell, had married the beautiful Honourable Ida Denison when she was seventeen. It proved in every way an ill-matched union. Edith, their eldest child, born at Scarborough in 1887, had a very unhappy childhood. She recognised that from birth, because of her sex and her looks, she was a great disappointment to her parents. They were 'strangers to me from the moment of my birth', she wrote in her autobiography. 'I was in disgrace for being a female, and worse, as I grew older, it was obvious that I was not going to conform to my father's standard of feminine beauty'. As a child the only companions with whom she could share her love were her nurse and – a typically Sitwellian touch – a peacock in the grounds of the family home of Renishaw Hall in Derbyshire. Fortunately, all her life she enjoyed a very close relationship with her brothers, Osbert, born in 1892, and Sacheverell, born in 1897. A family scandal broke in 1915 when their mother, Lady Ida, was sentenced to three months in Holloway Prison in consequence of debts that Sir George refused to honour. But by the summer of 1914 Edith had found her freedom in London, sharing a shabby, small, fourth-floor Bayswater flat with her former governess, now her companion, Helen Rootham, who had similar interests in poetry and music. Soon her brothers, whose feelings for their tyrannical father amounted almost to hatred, also escaped the stifling confines of Renishaw for life in London. There they tried to manage on what they regarded as a meagre allowance from their father, setting themselves up as supporters of all that was new in art, literature and music, and declaring themselves the enemies of the Philistine. But their extravagant life-style, especially Osbert's, frequently put them in debt, and token visits home in the summer were made in the vain hope of persuading their tight-fisted father to increase their allowance. What additional income they had came from their writing, but that was insufficient to redress the balance.

The Sitwell trio were determined, as Sacheverell put it, 'to tie the three of us together . . . and leave a mark of some sort of kind'[2] and so live down the disgrace of the family name. Their contribution to the artistic world was to discover any new 'genius' and take him under their wing. The first of these discoveries had been the author Ronald Firbank (1886–1926), probably

1 Osbert Sitwell, *Laughter in the Next Room*, Macmillan 1949, 169–70, St Martin's Library (paperback) edition 1958, 181–2. In subsequent footnotes page references in brackets refer to the St Martin's Library 1958 paperback edition.
2 John Pearson, *Façades: Edith, Osbert and Sacheverell Sitwell*, Macmillan 1978, Fontana Paperbacks 1980, 97.

known best for the novel *Valmouth*. As Sacheverell's biographer Sarah Bradford points out, this was more truthfully a *re*discovery because Firbank was
then living a reclusive life in Oxford. (While in his autobiographical *Siegfried's Journey*[3] Sassoon describes in detail his and the Sitwell brothers' first
meeting with Firbank in Oxford, he makes no mention at all of their meeting
with Walton.) Walton remembered going to see Firbank: 'He was so shy he
couldn't speak, simply put a bowl of peaches in front of me. I was so shy I
simply sat and ate the lot.'[4]

As Sacheverell later admitted, geniuses were then rather thin on the
ground, but the next recipient of Sitwellian patronage was Walton. It would
be fair to point out that he too was not actually a Sitwell discovery as his
talents had already been spotted by Henry Ley and Dr Strong, and in making
enquiries at Oxford about any undergraduate of interest Sacheverell had been
told about this young musical 'genius'. However that may be, the Sitwells
'adopted' Walton – or 'Willie' as his friends often called him – and set the
path for his future.

That February Walton invited Sassoon and the Sitwell brothers to his
rooms in Oxford. As Osbert described it:

> We arrived at Christ Church in the early afternoon. The room was very
> dark, blue-papered, with a piano opposite the window, and in the middle a
> table laid for tea, with, in the centre of it, thrown in for the sake of the
> almost ostentatious sense of luxury it would inevitably evoke, an enormous
> plate of bananas. Our host, not quite seventeen years of age, we found to be
> a rather tall, slight figure, of typically northern colouring, with pale skin,
> straight fair hair, like that of a young Dane or Norwegian. The refinement
> of his rather long, narrow, delicately shaped head, and of his bird-like
> profile showing so plainly above the brow the so-called bar or mound of
> Michelangelo that phrenologists claim to be the distinguishing mark of the
> artist – and especially of the musician –, even his prominent, well-cut nose,
> scarcely gave a true impression either of his robust mental qualities or of
> the strength of his physique. Sensitiveness rather than toughness was the
> quality at first most apparent in him. He appeared to be excessively shy,
> and on this occasion spoke but little, for I think he was rather in awe of us,
> as being his elders. Talk was desultory, though there were sudden deter-
> mined bursts of amiably-intentioned conversation from his guests. The
> atmosphere was not, however, easy; music showed a way out of the
> constraint, and after tea we pressed him to play some of his compositions
> to us. Accordingly, he got up from the table and then sat down at the piano,

---

3 Siegfried Sassoon, *Siegfried's Journey, 1916–1920*, Faber & Faber 1945, 135–7.
4 *Sunday Times*, 25 March 1962. Frederick and Jelka Delius experienced Walton's
   shyness when he visited them c. 1921 while they were in London. Much later, a friend
   of Jelka's wrote: 'William Walton came to see them, & he sat for 2½ hours & never
   said a word in spite of all her efforts – he was so shy!' In Lionel Carley, *Delius: A Life
   in Letters II 1909–1934*, Scolar Press 1988, 244.

the few steps between clearly indicating the burden of his hospitality, a feeling of strain, almost of hopelessness, combined with that of a need for intense concentration. As he began to play, he revealed a lack of mastery of the instrument that was altogether unusual, and as a result it was more difficult than ever to form an opinion of the music at first hearing. He played the slow movement from his Piano Quartet, later published by the Carnegie Trust, and other compositions which have no doubt disappeared. ... It was, indeed, as impossible that afternoon to estimate his character or talents as it was to foresee that for the next seventeen years he would constitute an inseparable companion and friend, and an adopted, or elected, brother to Edith, Sacheverell and myself.[5]

On looking back, Sacheverell recalled how it had been Walton's profile – almost that of a family likeness – that had particularly caught his attention on that first auspicious meeting. That likeness was indeed remarkable, as Edith Sitwell – whose own nose Lytton Strachey once described as 'longer than an ant-eater's' – commented near the end of her life:

> His profile[6] and mine (he probably will not thank me saying this) were so much alike in character and bone structure that many people who did not know us thought my two brothers, William and I were brothers and sister.[7]

At the time of the Sitwells' introduction to Walton, Edith was hoping to make her name as a major poet as well as giving what support she could to young deserving poets through her anthology *Wheels*, six issues of which appeared between 1916 and 1921. Osbert and Sacheverell were fast establishing themselves as patrons of Modern Art. Both had been devoted followers of Serge Diaghilev's *Ballets Russes* since its first London season in 1911. The company triumphantly returned to London in September 1918 after an absence during the war years and Diaghilev himself had dined with Osbert at his Chelsea house on Armistice night, to be joined later for the celebrations by Sacheverell who became a good friend of the impresario. The range of Sacheverell's musical interests at that time can be judged from a letter he wrote to an acquaintance about a concert of European music he was hoping to arrange to coincide with an exhibition he was organising in Paris of works by the Vorticist artist (Percy) Wyndham Lewis and his circle:

> I believe the Philharmonic Quartette could be produced, and ... perform a quartet by van Dieren, of whom it is time people heard – songs by Delius – van Dieren – Stravinsky – Schoenberg – and piano solos by Béla Bartók –

---

5 Osbert Sitwell, *Laughter in the Next Room*, 172 (183–4).
6 In her 1959 *Face to Face* television interview with John Freeman, Edith characteristically pronounced the word as '*pro*feel'.
7 *Sunday Times*, 18 March 1962.

Laszlo – Kodály (the young Hungarian musicians) and Prokofiev or Stravinsky etc. . . .'[8]

This was the artistic world into which the young Walton was soon to move.

In May 1919 Sachie (as Sacheverell was familiarly known) wrote to
Osbert from Oxford: 'Little Walton is coming up for a day or two to hear
Opera etc.: he has never been to London before.'[9] Sachie left Oxford for good
on 21 June at the end of the Trinity Term, and eight days later Walton wrote
to his mother: 'I'm going to London on Wednesday to stay with the Sitwells. I
shall be staying probably until the end of the month as there will be a great
deal to be seen at Covent Garden and the ballet.' And on 17 November he
wrote of being invited by the flamboyant patroness of the arts, Lady Ottoline
Morrell,[10] who lived near Oxford at Garsington: '[She] asked me over to her
house last Sunday. It was very entertaining.' In that same letter he told his
mother: 'I went to London yesterday for the afternoon and saw the new ballet
Parade [Satie]. It was very marvellous, especially the scenery. I'm going to
meet Stravinsky next month or perhaps before so that will be too exciting for
words.' Up till then his musical experiences had been largely confined to
choral music sung in the chapel, although he had vivid memories of Beecham
conducting Rimsky-Korsakov's *Le Coq d'Or* at Manchester.[11] His introduction to the moderns had been, besides Dr Strong's Sunday gatherings,
through Hugh Allen bringing orchestral scores vividly to life on the organ
and his playing of *Petroushka* on the piano. Sachie Sitwell considered
Petroushka to be in many ways the supreme Russian ballet, adding that 'no
artist in any of the arts who saw it could have been unaffected by it'.[12] It left
its mark on a number of composers at that time – Gustav Holst, Constant
Lambert and Arthur Bliss among others – and its impact was to be heard in
Walton's overture *Portsmouth Point* and his *Sinfonia Concertante*.

The Sitwell brothers' next move was to convince Walton's father of the
advantages of their patronage, such as it was. In his autobiography, Osbert
wrote that, because of their attitude, they 'incurred a certain amount of
odium, both from those who did not believe in [Walton] and from those who

---

8 27 March 1919; Sarah Bradford, *Splendours and Miseries: A Life of Sacheverell
   Sitwell*, Farrar Straus Giroux 1993, 92. The concert scheme never materialised, but the
   exhibition opened in August after many delays.
9 Sarah Bradford, *Splendours and Miseries*, 93.
10 An acquaintance of Siegfried Sassoon, rather than the Sitwells who tended to avoid
   her.
11 Beecham's only staged performance of *Le Coq d'Or* of that period at Manchester was
   on 7 January 1920, but he conducted excerpts at a Hallé concert on 11 January 1917.
   At one point in *Le Coq d'Or* the singing was accompanied by dancing, perhaps making
   the performance more memorable for the young Walton.
12 In his Prologue to *Gala Performance: A Record of The Sadler's Wells Ballet over
   Twenty-Five Years*, edited by Arnold Haskell, Mark Bonham Carter and Michael
   Wood, Collins 1955, 15.

did. Especially were we blamed . . . for being responsible for his not attending in London one of the two or three [music] colleges'. When this odious talk reached Charles Walton's ears he set out for London to seek out the truth for himself. But instead of finding either Osbert or Sacheverell at home, he met their aunt who was almost eighty years old. He went home apparently reassured, uttering the words, 'Let William have his own way: he knows what he is doing. . . .'[13]

And so this adopted 'brother' came to live with Osbert and Sacheverell, first in their small house in Swan Walk, Chelsea, near to the Thames. Osbert continued:

Instead, then, of sending William to Kensington or Bloomsbury, we were able to keep him in touch with the vital works of the age, with the music, for example, of Stravinsky, and to obtain for him, through the kindness of our old family friend E. J. Dent, an introduction to Busoni, a modern master of counterpoint, who looked at some of William's compositions and wrote him a kindly polite letter about them. He also at times had the benefit of consulting Ernest Ansermet on various problems of composition.[14]

After seeing one of Walton's early compositions, Busoni had commented in a note of mild encouragement, dated 5 July 1920: 'The music has interested me. You have a happy inclination to polyphonic lines; this will lead you safely through the waters and fires which stand between you and Parnassus.'[15] Walton's introduction through the Sitwells to Edward Dent brought a further bonus. Dent (1876–1957) was President of the International Society for Contemporary Music, and it was quite likely through his influence that Walton's early string quartet was selected for performance at the first festival under the Society's aegis, at Salzburg in 1923, and *Portsmouth Point* at Zürich in 1926.

Walton was set up with an annual sum of £250, paid by the Sitwell brothers with generous contributions from such friends as Siegfried Sassoon, the composer Lord Berners, Dr Strong, and the society hostess Christabel McLaren whose husband was in charge of the trust. With no other source of income Walton admitted in later life that he felt like a scrounger. Nevertheless, as he acknowledged: 'If it hadn't been for them, I'd either have ended up

---

13 Osbert Sitwell, *Laughter in the Next Room*, 170 (182).
14 *Ibid.*, 170 (182).
15 Quoted in 'Collecting key signatures', Christopher Lambton's article on Ronald Stevenson's correspondence with other composers, *Daily Telegraph*, 2 January 1999, A6. Busoni's comments to Walton contrast sharply with his observations in writing to his wife on the same day: 'The young man Walton . . . sent me some manuscript music. He has a little gift for counterpoint. In other respects, they all write according to a formula: notes, notes, notes, all "hither and yon", without imagination and feeling.' Kennedy, *Portrait of Walton*, 19.

like [Sir Charles] Stanford, or would have been a clerk in some Midlands bank[16] with an interest in music. Life would have been a very great deal duller.'[17] Despite its elegance and gaiety, living with the Sitwells was not for him a life of luxury, as Dora Foss later observed on his first staying visit: 'He was rather shy and diffident, and at that time desperately hard up. He had borrowed Osbert Sitwell's pyjamas, a most striking orange and black pair, to come to us with, but his hairbrushes and other dressing table accoutrements appeared to date from his choirboy's days. However, he always appeared to be immaculate and extremely elegant in what he informed me sometime later were Moss Bros. misfits.'[18]

Christabel McLaren[19] (who became Lady Aberconway in 1934 on her husband's accession to the title) was one of several important women in Walton's life. She was a social beauty, a generous patroness of the arts and a great friend of Osbert's to whom she was devoted. Her relationship with Sachie and Edith was nothing like so warm; in their eyes she was inclined to be bossy, and at times they regarded her as a troublemaker. Walton confided in Christabel, as their correspondence shows, and his feelings for her were deep, as the simple dedication of the Viola Concerto – 'to Christabel' – suggests ('dedicated to whom I was in love at the time', he later admitted[20]), although, as she good-humouredly commented twenty years later to Susana Walton on their first meeting: 'Of all the women you will meet tonight, I will probably be the only one that William has not been to bed with.'[21] In her autobiography she named her husband, Osbert and Sam Courtauld as her three greatest friends. Married in 1910, she wrote that 'we lived happily ever afterwards, except for a few fierce tiffs and many arguments, good for both of us, but with shared, continuous and varied interests and pleasures.'[22] George Bernard Shaw, H. G. Wells, Virginia Woolf, Somerset Maugham (another 'Willie') and even Royalty were among Christabel McLaren's other friends and acquaintances.

One cannot help registering some surprise that this quiet, thin young lad,

---

16 His younger brother, Alec, worked in the bank while his older brother, Noel, followed their father as an organist and music teacher.

17 John Pearson, *Façades*, 134.

18 Dora Foss, 'Memoirs of Walton'. Dora was the wife of Hubert Foss, music editor for Oxford University Press. Both became close friends of Walton.

19 Christabel Aberconway (1890–1974) lived at 38 South Street, Mayfair, London. Born Christabel Macnaghten, she had five children, one of whom, Anne McLaren, appeared as a child in the closing scenes of the 1936 film *Things to Come*. In 1910 she married Henry McLaren (1879–1953), private secretary to Lloyd George.

20 Interview with John Amis in *Portrait of Walton*, BBC Radio 3, broadcast 4 June 1977. Yet Walton is hardly mentioned in her 'book of memories', *A Wiser Woman?*, Hutchinson 1966.

21 Susana Walton, *Behind the Façade*, OUP 1988, 35

22 *A Wiser Woman?*, 81–2.

not out of a public school and with a Lancashire accent, should have fitted so well into the Sitwell household and with them moved at ease in London's fashionable circles. Both Osbert and Sachie had been at Eton and both had served in the Grenadier Guards. How a Royal College education would have changed Walton is something one can only guess at, but living under the Sitwell patronage brought several indisputable advantages. With them he attended productions of the *Ballets Russes* that had an undeniable influence on his work. Through them he mixed with artists, poets and musicians and was introduced into society with its continual round of parties, visits to the opera and ballet. Through them he met rich and titled women, encounters that left a trail of affairs, the emotional results of which lie at the heart of three of his major works. Through the Sitwells he received an education in art that opened up a world that had been for him until then unknown, and with them he had the great experience and enjoyment of travelling across Europe during those years when foreign travel was the luxury of the rich. They took him regularly to Italy with the result that not only did his music in places take on an Italianate feeling but he was eventually to settle there for the rest of his life. But just as important, when living with the Sitwells he was largely left on his own, with no pressure of a composition being expected in return for the financial support and free lodging he was receiving. Of the two brothers it was probably Sachie (over four-and-a-half years his senior) with whom he got along the easier, while Osbert he descibed as 'half an elder brother, half a father. I wouldn't go against his wishes'.[23] The Sitwells' – especially Osbert's – childish capacity for picking private quarrels with anyone who offended them could have seriously isolated Walton from a number of useful friends and acquaintances. It was as the result of one of Osbert's private animosities that he and the Sitwells became the subject of *The Strange and Striking Adventures of Four Authors in Search of a Character*, a pamphlet written in 1926 by C. K. Scott-Moncrieff,[24] a long-standing enemy of Osbert's who was a translator, chiefly of Proust and Pirandello. Although this was not to be the only instance of Walton being satirised in print by one of the Sitwells' acquaintances, he fortunately remained largely unaffected by these disputes and Scott-Moncrieff's effort proved a rather damp squib. 'Had I been a writer, things might have been uncomfortable, but as a musician I just had my room at the top of the house, and I was left in peace to get on with my work. . . . For a raw young composer who knew nothing about anything it was an extraordinary education simply to be with them, and especially to meet their friends.'[25] Nor did Osbert's homosexuality pose a real threat. After one

---

23 Walton in conversation with John Pearson, quoted in Philip Ziegler, *Osbert Sitwell*, Chatto & Windus 1998, 107.
24 P. G. Lear and L. O. Cayme Press Pamphlets No. 2, 1926 (see Philip Ziegler, *Osbert Sitwell*, 140–1).
25 John Pearson, *Façades*, 181.

advance had been gently rebuffed, there were no recurrences.[26] It was more Walton's fondness for women that was to upset his patron. When, according to Susana Walton, he started to flirt with Edith, Osbert was quick to give him a stern warning that were such behaviour to continue he would be ejected.[27] It was other more serious relationships – and one in particular – that were to annoy Osbert.

Musically Walton was essentially self-educated, avidly studying scores in the days when gramophone recordings were few and music broadcasting had not yet begun. In this respect he shares a background with Elgar and Delius (notwithstanding the latter's unprofitable time at Leipzig). Like Delius, travel was to be an important factor in his development and, like Delius, he was eventually to make his home on the Continent. (Walton once made the interesting suggestion that, never being consciously stimulated by the Italian climate or geography, the nostalgia caused by his long periods away from England may have possibly made his music more English.[28])

After Oxford, life in Chelsea was comparatively peaceful. 'The young composer seemed still more shy and silent,' Osbert remembered. 'Most of the summer days he appeared to spend in his room at the top of the house, where he sat by the window for long periods, eating blackheart cherries from a paper bag, and throwing the stones out of the window, down on to the smooth brown-tiled pavement outside the door. Swan Walk was so quiet that there was only to be heard a distant booming of traffic, and nearer, this dry staccato rattle of cherry stones.'[29]

Soon Osbert hired a piano for him, as a result of which William seemed to stay in his room for even longer periods. Periodically, Osbert's housekeeper, Mrs Powell, would peer in cautiously through the door to see if he was all right.

> She had quickly become attached to him, and possessed great faith in his talent. For the next twelve years, until her death, she looked after him also with much imaginative tact and consideration. The piano, though he attacked it so often, was seldom, through some process of personal magic, heard downstairs. If it were, I would sometimes advise him to have a dumb-piano to practise upon, when he would grow very indignant. He had, it may be noted, always to be near a piano, though his playing of it, I apprehend, never very much improved.[30]

---

26 Susana Walton, *Behind the Façade*, 51.
27 *Ibid.*, 61.
28 Murray Schafer, *British Composers in Interview*, 78.
29 Osbert Sitwell, *Laughter in the Next Room*, 176 (188).
30 *Ibid.*, 176 (188).

Osbert and Sachie's house was regularly the home for literary and artistic gatherings. Arnold Bennett, who was a guest at 5 Swan Walk on 5 June 1919, described his visit in his journal:

> Dined at Osbert Sitwell's. Good dinner. Fish before soup. Present, W. H. Davies, Lytton Strachey, [Leonard] Woolf, [Robert] Nichols, S. Sassoon, Aldous Huxley, Atkin (a very young caricaturist), W. J. Turner, and Herbert Read. . . . A house with much better pictures and bric-à-brac than furniture. . . . But lots of very modern pictures, of which I liked a number. Bright walls and bright cloths and bright glass everywhere. A fine Rowlandson drawing. . . .[31]

Edith also held her own literary gatherings, Saturday afternoon tea parties, chiefly for poets, at her rather shabby flat in Bayswater. These Walton often attended. But his contact with those friends of Edith's and Osbert's in the literary world had little long-term impact on the young composer who had not the flair for detecting a possible musical text as, for example, Benjamin Britten was to have. As Sacheverell later remarked, he showed no inclination towards poetry. He set no Sassoon and little else beside Edith Sitwell. His literary tastes may be summed up by a discovery that Osbert made:

> On one occasion, when he was staying with me at Scarborough[32] in 1920 or '21, he was suddenly taken seriously ill and had to be removed to a nursing-home. There, . . . a tirelessly kind, middle-aged matron, of prim outlook and near-church pursuits, who without ever reading or thinking was nevertheless almost professionally cultivated within Church-Bazaar limits, offered to sit with him and read aloud. But she came only once. William's taste in all things was naturally good, and often unexpected, and the book he handed her, open at one of its most rollicking passages, was Urquart's translation of Rabelais! William saw no harm in it, and took pleasure in its exuberance.[33]

Nevertheless, Osbert records that the young Walton was a great admirer of George Moore and he once accompanied a friend of Moore's, Ada Leverson (Oscar Wilde's 'Sphinx'), on a visit to the Irish writer. 'Who is it?' a voice shouted down the stairs. 'It's Ada. I've brought a great admirer of yours to see you. William Walton the composer. He's only eighteen!' 'I don't care if he's eighteen or eighty,' came the sharp reply. 'I won't see him. Tell him to go away!'[34]

---

31 *The Journals of Arnold Bennett*, selected and edited by Frank Swinnerton, Penguin Books 1954, 330.
32 At that time the Sitwells spent Christmas at Wood End, Scarborough, the home of their grandmother, Lady Londesborough. The house is now a natural history museum.
33 Osbert Sitwell, *Laughter in the Next Room*, 177 (189–90).
34 Osbert Sitwell, *Great Morning*, Macmillan 1948, The Reprint Society 1949, 254–5.

More significant were the composers and musicians to whom Walton was introduced. Among them was Lord Berners (1883–1950), a friend of Stravinsky who once described him as 'an amateur, but in the best literal sense'. Walton remembered Berners 'inviting me to lunch to meet Stravinsky the day after he had conducted the *Symphony of Psalms* at Queen's Hall.'[35] An eccentric dilettante, Berners was also a writer, a painter and a diplomat. His five ballet scores, the major share of his musical oeuvre, exhibit a delightful mixture of whimsy, parody and irony, as well as period charm and elegance. Berners' music had more points of contact with Stravinsky and the Parisian 'Les Six' than with English music and, partly because of the quaint titles of some of his songs and piano pieces, he has not unreasonably been called the English Satie. Serge Lifar, in his biography of Diaghilev, writes that the impresario, who commissioned a ballet from Berners, had the 'highest admiration' for his work.[36] Walton was an occasional guest at Berners' Berkshire home, Faringdon House, and much later, in February 1932 at his London home, he made up, with Sachie and his wife, 'a frequent foursome at social events'.[37] As Sarah Bradford, Sacheverell's biographer, tells us, 'they were now very much a part of Emerald Cunard's circle and through her on the fringes of royalty'.

In his 1941 novel *Far from the Madding War*, Berners quite likely had Walton in mind in the character of Francis Paltry, a composer of a new symphony who is regarded as the white hope of English music and who has 'set out to get to know all the most influential musical authorities in the country' whom his wife Lady Caroline, taking his musical career in hand, asks to luncheon.[38] The allusions are much stronger in his other novel that same year, *Count Omega*.[39] Here the principal character is Emmanuel Smith, a penniless twenty-three-year-old composer, fair-haired, of slender build, living in a

---

35 *Sunday Telegraph*, 25 March 1962; in the 1931/2 season of Courtauld–Sargent concerts.

36 *Serge Diaghilev: His Life, his Work, his Legend. An Intimate Biography*, G P Putnam's Sons 1940, 210.

37 Sarah Bradford, *Splendours and Miseries*, 233.

38 *Far from the Madding War*, Constable & Co. 1941, 50–1. Berners was quite likely drawing a parallel with the way Walton's career was shaped through the influence and the social contacts of the Sitwells and Christabel Aberconway. In the novel the symphony is performed in a hall called the Pandemonian. Paltry and Lord FitzCricket (i.e. Berners himself) 'did not get on very well', partly because the former 'had once written rather rudely about Lord FitzCricket's compositions' in an unsigned article (p. 163). If there was an occasion when Walton had written over-critically about Berners' works, it has not come to light.

39 *Count Omega*, Constable & Co. 1941; re-issued in *Collected Tales and Fantasies of Lord Berners*, Turtle Point Press and Helen Marks Books 1999. At an early stage the novel's title had been *The Last Trump, the tale of a Symphony and its Composer*. The lavish supper party in the opening chapter may well have hinted at those given by Alice Wimborne for the Symphony's two premières.

third-floor bed-sitting room and in a state of agitation over the completion of his first symphony, the finale of which has for a while been hanging fire. He has amorous entanglements with two women, and at a fashionable party in the opening chapter a mysterious hand appears through a small door in the wall panelling – an obvious allusion to *Belshazzar's Feast* that was dedicated to Berners. At that same party the long single B flat played on the trombone is another clear reference to *Belshazzar's Feast* which begins with that very note intoned by trombones. (B flat is also the key of Walton's symphony). Good-humouredly, Berners gave Walton advance notice of the novel, first disclaiming any earlier similarities:

> If you read *Far from the Madding War* you may have imagined that the musician Francis Paltry was meant to be you. But it wasn't. I am reserving you for a forthcoming novel *Count Omega*, which I will send you as soon as it appears. I thought it only fair that the funniest English composer should be immortalised by my pen. I must inform you that, should you, in Sitwellian fashion, propose to take action for libel, the book has been gone through by a lawyer and that I have insured myself against possible damages for libel.[40]

Berners took the leg-pull further and wrote to Walton's solicitor: 'I am shortly bringing out a book, called "Ridiculous Composers I have known". If your client Mr. William Walton should consider it necessary to see a copy before publication, will you kindly tell him to apply.'[41]

Quite how seriously Walton took this is not clear, although he did consult his solicitor, if only to keep up his end of the joke. After he had read the book he replied rather oddly that he thought the composer 'too much like Edmund Rubbra for my liking'.[42] Using acquaintances as the basis of characters in his novels was just another aspect of Berners' humour. He had earlier transformed several friends, the photographer Cecil Beaton and the designer Oliver Messel among them, into *The Girls of Radcliff Hall*, privately published in 1937, with himself as the headmistress and the title making an obvious tilt at the lesbian writer Radclyffe Hall.

One of Walton's earliest composer acquaintances was Philip Heseltine (1894–1930) who introduced him to the works of Schoenberg, Bartók and Gesualdo, at a time when these composers were little known in England. Seven-and-a-half years older than Walton, Heseltine had also gone up to Christ Church, for a year only, in 1913, and he held a high opinion of Dean Strong whom he described as 'a charming man' if 'somewhat embarrassingly

---

40 Quoted, undated, in Mark Amory, *Lord Berners: The Last Eccentric*, Chatto & Windus 1998, 201.
41 *Ibid.*, 201–2.
42 *Ibid.*, 202.

gushing and affectionate'.[43] Heseltine was a great admirer – in effect a disciple – of Delius, but this was an enthusiasm not shared by Walton. Although Heseltine's often unhappy life was to end in suicide, he made his mark – under the pseudonym of Peter Warlock – as one of England's finest song writers.

Another to meet the young Walton at about this time was the critic and composer Cecil Gray (1895–1951) who was introduced to him by Philip Heseltine. In Gray's eyes Walton 'was a shy, diffident, awkward, inarticulate, rather devitalized young man, and I frankly admit that I was not greatly impressed either by his personality or by the work of his which I saw. But Philip thought otherwise. "You will see," he said to me one day, "that youth will go a long way", and he certainly has fulfilled the terms of that remarkable clairvoyant prediction.'[44]

Then there was the Dutch-born Bernard Van Dieren (1884–1936) whose personality encouraged a close circle of admirers (among them the Sitwells, Cecil Gray and Philip Heseltine) to make extravagant claims on his behalf and to bestow on him the epithet genius. Even Constant Lambert, who championed his music, once remarked enigmatically: 'I will never, never forget what I owe to Bernard,'[45] and classed him and Alban Berg as 'two of the greatest musicians of our day'.[46] Not all musicians shared this admiration. In 1935 the composer–conductor Eugene Goossens, who was rather jealous of Walton's success at that time, wrote: 'I don't know two notes of Van Dieren's music which have ever warranted the slightest attention and if he is the giant that we are asked to believe in, why doesn't someone let us hear some of this miraculous music? It is rather on a par with the exaggerated adulation that is being bestowed on Walton at the present moment.'[47] Van Dieren's music has never elicited any enthusiasm from the musical public at large, but Walton did not dismiss it. He first became aware of it when he was eagerly helping Sachie, within a few weeks of their acquaintance, to promote a concert that was to include some Van Dieren songs but which had eventually to be cancelled owing to the illness of Helen Rootham who was to sing. In 1936, despite his reluctance to appear publicly off the rostrum, Walton gave a talk at Oxford on Van Dieren's opera *The Tailor* of which the Oxford Opera Club was intending to give the first performance, Hyam Greenbaum conducting.[48]

---

43 Barry Smith, *Peter Warlock: The Life of Philip Heseltine*, OUP 1994, 50.
44 Cecil Gray, *Musical Chairs or Between Two Stools: An Autobiography*, Home & Van Thal 1948, 285.
45 Richard Shead, *Constant Lambert*, Simon Publications 1973, 46.
46 Preface to the second edition, *Music Ho! A Study of Music in Decline*, Faber & Faber 1936, 6.
47 Letter to his parents, 10 August 1934, in Carole Rosen, *The Goossens: A Musical Century*, André Deutsch 1993, 183.

Then, in 1947, when asked to suggest works for the BBC's new Third Programme, Walton put forward Van Dieren's name. 'Having thrown a crumb to Van Dieren by performing a few songs & piano pieces, might not half a loaf be added by the performance of one of his quartets. No 3 or 6 are I think the most accessible & the Zorian [Quartet] might like to tackle one if properly subsidised! It would I think be a 1st perf. & not before its time. The *Chinese Symphony* & the *Diaphony* might be revived too.'[49] The Symphony, which he had heard once, struck him 'as being very rich and profound.'[50]

Another composer with whom Walton had a slight acquaintance was Kaikhosru Shapurji Sorabji (1892–1988), who was a friend of Sachie's and Heseltine's. Of Parsi and Spanish–Sicilian parentage, he lived in London at Clarence Gate, Marylebone. An admirer of Busoni, at that time only a tiny handful of Sorabji's elaborate and extraordinarily virtuosic works, that included solo piano pieces and concertos and symphonies for piano and orchestra, had been performed, and the few that had were with the composer as pianist. (When, in March 1936, he heard that one of his works had been unduly laboured in performance, he slapped down a musical fatwah, forbidding any further performance of his works. This ban effectively lasted until 1976, making Sorabji, with his reputation for scores of great length and enormous difficulty, a cult figure.) In November 1921 Sorabji wrote to Heseltine: 'I had Willie Walton and Sachie Sitwell here the other afternoon and dosed them with Sonata II, which they *said* impressed them enormously.'[51] On 9 November 1925 Walton wrote to the recently married Sachie that he had just finished *Portsmouth Point* and that Sorabji, Constant Lambert and Philip Heseltine were coming to tea. Some while later, probably in May 1928, Walton wrote to Sorabji: 'I enjoyed so much hearing the movement from the Organ Symphony [the first performance of the Second Movement only, on 17 May 1928 by E. Emlyn Davies], and only wish that I could have heard it all. I was much struck to find it so clear, logical, and easy to follow (a fact, which you may admit, does not seem obvious when it is seen on paper), – and it makes the most beautiful patterns of sound, especially towards the end – and the climaxes are very exciting.'[52] Sorabji, who could be an acerbic critic, was

---

48 Although rehearsals had begun using the piano score, on the arrival of the full score the work was found to be written for a large chamber ensemble rather than a normal orchestra, with a number of very complicated passages that were beyond the scope of the amateur players, and the production was abandoned.

49 Letter to George Barnes, Head (later Controller) of Third Programme, 31 January 1947. BBC Written Archives, Caversham.

50 Murray Schafer, *British Composers in Interview*, 81. Walton probably heard the work at the Van Dieren Memorial Concert given as part of the BBC's concerts of contemporary music on 9 April 1937 when Lambert was the conductor. Lambert gave Van Dieren's *Serenata* and *Sonetto VII* in the Third Programme on 12 August 1950.

51 Paul Rapoport (ed.), *Sorabji – A Critical Celebration*, Scolar Press 1992, 238.

52 *Ibid.*, 280.

favourably disposed towards Walton's music – and Lambert's too, except where he could detect the influence of Stravinsky, Schoenberg or Bartók. In 1947 Sorabji's name was also on Walton's list of suggestions, with that of Van Dieren and Carl Nielsen, for the BBC: 'As the 3rd P[rogramme] seems intent on an orgy of atonalism & what not (very enjoyable & I hope an early repeat of the Berg [Chamber] Concerto Vl. & pfte. will be forthcoming) why not indulge in a few works of Kaikhosru Sorabji either played by him (he's a magnificent pianist) or another. Though he was supposed to be the last word in the days of my youth, it may sound as tame as Schönberg by now.'[53]

But the composer who was to play the most significant part in Walton's life was Constant Lambert (1905–51) who, at the time they first met, was a brilliant student at the Royal College of Music. Walton recalled: 'I used to see him in the King's Road when he was still in Christ's Hospital as a boy, [with] this striking costume of the yellow stockings and this blue gown, and this extraordinary head that he had even in those young days. And then I got to know him, I think, through the Sitwells, and he was then a student at the College. . . .'[54] Lambert was living in Glebe Place, Chelsea, close to the Sitwell brothers, and, as Osbert remembered, 'it must have been in the winter of 1920 or 1921 . . . that one day the front-door bell rang and on the doorstep stood a pleasant-looking young, very young, man, who said, handing me an envelope, "I have a letter of introduction." I looked at him again, and noticed that he had a courageous look. . . . I said, "Come in, won't you?" And soon we were talking like old friends.'[55] Among his earliest compositions while studying at the Royal College were two settings for soprano of poems by Sacheverell Sitwell, *Serenade* and *The White Nightingale*, not, as one might expect, with piano but the more interesting combination of flute and harp. In 1924 Lambert invited the Sitwells to a performance of his settings at the College.[56] Walton, who throughout his apprentice years had the happy knack of meeting people from whom he could benefit, went along as well, their friendship by that time having firmly taken root. As Osbert has written:

> William came to make friends with great facility: but at first he chose them principally among musicians. My brother, my sister and I already counted Van Dieren and Berrners among our friends, and a year or two later we

---

53 Letter to George Barnes, 31 January 1947.

54 BBC radio programme, *Remembering Constant Lambert*, broadcast on 23 August 1975. BBC Sound Archives NP7054BL, National Sound Archives T8495/02.

55 'Portrait of a Very Young Man', in Osbert Sitwell, *Queen Mary and Others*, Michael Joseph 1974, 77–80, reprinted in *Constant Lambert, 1905–1951*, South London Art Gallery exhibition souvenir, 1976, 28. Lambert was born on 23 August 1905, so he was fifteen or sixteen at the time he met Osbert. The dating of their meeting by some commentators as 1922 does not concur with the notion that if Walton had not set the *Façade* poems Lambert would have been asked instead.

56 6 March 1924.

added to them Constant Lambert, at the age of seventeen a prodigy of intelligence and learning, and gifted with that particularly individual outlook and sense of humour which, surely were born in him and are impossible to acquire. William had soon adopted these friends and had been adopted by them.[57]

Walton found Lambert 'a fascinating companion, a wonderful talker, and I learnt an enormous amount from him. He led me into the many highways and byways of music, which I probably should not have explored much by myself, such as the Russian composers, and he was one of the first people to start the Sibelius craze.'[58] Later in life Walton spoke of missing Constant Lambert more than anyone.[59]

Constant Lambert's family background made him far more widely versed in the Arts than Walton was ever to become. His father, born in St Petersburg, was a distinguished Australian painter, and Constant's brother Maurice was a sculptor whose somewhat futuristic head of Walton was exhibited at the Coupil Gallery, London in April 1925. Maurice was subsequently commissioned by Osbert Sitwell to create a head of Edith, which he did in aluminium. Constant was occasionally a guest at Renishaw where, Osbert remembered, he and Walton 'would devote their days to . . . the only pianos, a Bechstein, an enormous obsolete instrument, so old and unused as to count as an antique, and a younger one hired from Sheffield . . . and the sound of their musical skirmishes would reach me in various distant parts of the house.'[60]

The first substantial work to come from Walton's pen was a four-movement piano quartet in A minor, begun in 1918 but not completed until 1921, the same work that Osbert and Sachie had heard him play in his Oxford rooms. There had been a reason for choosing that combination of instruments. One of the most successful new English chamber works then had been a three-movement piano quartet – also in A minor – by Herbert Howells, himself only fairly recently out of the Royal College. It had been among the first batch of works to be selected for publication under the auspices of the Carnegie United Kingdom Trust. For Walton the success of another composer would occasionally act as a spur to composition, and the Howells quartet was one such instance. In an interview with the critic and musicologist John Warrack, he admitted the influence: 'I wrote it really to emulate

---

57 Osbert Sitwell, *Laughter in the Next Room*, 178 (190–1).
58 Walton's memoir of Lambert, sent to Hubert Foss. Duncan Hinnells, *An Extraordinary Performance: Hubert Foss, Music Publishing, and the Oxford University Press*, OUP 1998, 50. On 31 March 1925 Lambert conducted the slow movement of Sibelius's Fourth Symphony at the Royal College of Music.
59 Angus Morrison; talk given at the British Music Information Centre, London, 25 September 1982.
60 'Portrait of a Very Young Man', 28.

Herbert Howells, to be quite honest, because he'd had a great success with his Piano Quartet and I thought I'd have a go. It got the Carnegie Award like his did, so I was justified to a point.'[61] He finished the quartet (dedicated 'to the Right Rev. Thomas Banks Strong, Bishop of Ripon') in Amalfi, after which the manuscript was lost for a couple of years. 'For some reason I sent it back to England by post – I don't remember why – and of course it got lost.'[62] When it was eventually found some revisions were made. In the version heard today it is a very striking piece, with bold themes in the first movement (its opening theme strongly hints at one of Howells's) and a deft scherzo with Walton's first use of fugal textures. The slow movement, of melting beauty, is an essay in the English pastoral vein – and a fine one too. It is interesting to read in Howells's diary of 28 January 1919: '[I] found W T Walton in his rooms at the House [Christ Church, Oxford], busy with his highly-coloured chords. He showed me the first movement of a Piano Quartet. If he gets in the right hands, he'll be an interesting musical personage.'[63] Had Howells seen the opening to the slow movement he would surely have recognised the influence of his own quartet because the parallels are very close, especially their harmonic affinity. Howells's Piano Quartet in A minor (1916) was a work to which Allen had given much encouragement before its first performance, and Walton may well have come across it through him. Coincidentally, when Walton's Quartet also received a Carnegie Trust award, in 1924, Allen was one of the adjudicators. It was first performed on 19 September the same year, in Liverpool, by the McCullagh String Quartet. The angular rhythms and snatches of biting dissonance in the last movement give a hint of the Walton to come. The Trust's report described it as 'a work of real achievement . . . clear and transparent in texture, restrained in feeling, well-written throughout, and rising at moments of climax into a strain of great beauty and nobility'. When the work was performed at a Gordon Bryan concert at the Aeolian Hall on 30 October 1929, together with some other youthful works, the *Times* critic held a rather different opinion, dismissing it as a 'finicking and unbalanced work whose slow movement pitilessly exposed the weakness that is not so evident in the swifter movements'. Walton shared the concert with Constant Lambert and Patrick Hadley whom the reviewer collectively identified as 'three young English composers who are fast establishing reputations for themselves'. Walton's song *The Winds*, also performed,[64] was

---

61 BBC 2 'Workshop' interview with John Warrack, 26 May 1968, printed in the *Listener*, 8 August 1968, 177.
62 *Sunday Times*, 25 March 1962.
63 Christopher Palmer, *Herbert Howells – A Celebration*, Thames Publishing 1996, 349 (revised edition of *Herbert Howells – A Centenary Celebration*, Thames Publishing 1992).
64 A private performance of *The Winds* quite likely took place in December 1921 when Osbert Sitwell arranged for it to be sung at the London home of Lady Grey, Stephen Tennant's mother.

better received: 'real feeling, and as a juvenile composition . . . really remarkable'. More harmonically daring was the song *Tritons*, dating from 1920, which, together with *The Winds*, had been accepted by J. Curwen & Sons for publication in 1921 before Walton was twenty.

Walton's only other substantial work written before he was twenty could not be in sharper contrast, and shows how he was at that time very much in search of a style. This was his first string quartet, written in 1919, initially in two movements. It was essentially a technical exercise. When it was performed in 1921, the *British Music Bulletin* noted 'the freedom of its harmonic scheme'. In the absence of the manuscript one cannot compare it with the revised version completed over a year later, but the 'harmonic freedom' probably owed much to his dabbling in Schoenberg and his introduction by Philip Heseltine to the quartets of Bartók. His own quartet, he confessed, was 'largely undigested Bartók and Schoenberg. I was particularly interested in the two Bartók quartets and when I came to write a string quartet, it was much influenced by both these composers.'[65] To those two names should be added that of Beethoven, whose *Grosse Fuge* Op. 133 hovers over the last movement. But the quartet, with its exploration of atonalism, turned out to be a compositional cul-de-sac. 'I never got very far with it, though. The style was too impersonal. It didn't come naturally.'[66] Fortunately at this juncture the lost piano quartet turned up: 'I decided that this was much more my style than the other. And so I went back to composing the way I do now, more or less.'[67]

In November 1919 Osbert and Sachie, feeling the need for larger premises in which to hold court to literary and artistic London, moved from Swan Walk to a more spacious four-storeyed house at 2 Carlyle Square, Chelsea. Their housekeeper Mrs Powell, who had kept such a motherly eye on Walton, went with them, and also, it is fair to assume, the print by the English caricaturist Thomas Rowlandson (1756–1827) that Arnold Bennett had noted with pleasure at Swan Walk. Was it the one to inspire either the unpublished and unperformed 'pedagogic' overture of that period, called *Dr Syntax* (1920–21), or the post-*Façade* overture *Portsmouth Point* (1924–25), Walton's first work to establish itself in the orchestral repertoire? Of *Dr Syntax*, only a page of the score has survived, although it was included among his list of works in the third edition (1928) of *Grove's Dictionary of Music and Musicians* and other music dictionaries of that period. Written for a large orchestra, with triple woodwind, it was sent in 1921 to the young Eugene Goossens, probably in the hope that it might be included in the series of concerts of modern orchestral works he was giving that year. In June, with

[65] *Sunday Telegraph*, 25 March 1962. Only the first two of Bartók's six quartets had then been written.
[66] *Oldham Chronicle*, 1959.
[67] *Sunday Times*, 25 March 1962.

a hand-picked orchestra of 105, Goossens had conducted the first concert performance in England of *The Rite of Spring*, as well as Lord Berners' *Fantasie Espagnole*, John Ireland's *The Forgotten Rite* and Ravel's *La Valse*. This concert was such a critical success that not only did he repeat *The Rite of Spring* a fortnight later (this time with a work of his own) but in the autumn he presented four more equally adventurous programmes of contemporary music, including British works by Arnold Bax, Arthur Bliss, John Ireland, Gustav Holst, John Heath, Josef Holbrooke and Cyril Scott. The last concert concluded with yet another performance of *The Rite of Spring*. But Walton's work did not find a place in this series and the score has not survived. Another lost work of that period, never to reach performance, is a setting of Marlowe's *The Passionate Shepherd*, for tenor and ten instruments (1920).

Walton rapidly developed a taste for London life and enjoyed frequent visits to the ballet and theatre, visits for which he had to 'scrounge' money from friends for a night out on the town. A favourite venue was the old Lyceum Theatre. Some of the revues at the Lyceum may have provided a seed for the dance measures that were an important element of his next work, one that was to bring his name before the public at large, the Entertainment *Façade*.

3

Poetry through a Megaphone

At the age of eighty, Sacheverell Sitwell reflected on the days of the Entertainment's creation in a poem called *Octogenarian* – a title borrowed from one of Edith's poems used in the earliest version of *Façade*. Referring to Walton, he wrote:

> No lover of poetry in particular,
> But he worked instinctively I remember,
>   as if blindfolded or under a spell,
> And as though led or guided –
> The poems themselves,
>   that is the wonder of his partnership with my sister,
> Being, as has been said, like nothing else before or since. . . .[1]

Elsewhere Sachie wrote that Walton was not 'a fervent lover of poetry [but] he was attuned to them and had, when directed to them, an instinctive understanding. This can be the only explanation of the extraordinary conveyancing into another medium of the ideas and images expressed in the [*Façade*] poems.'[2] A number of these poems had already been written and even published a year or two earlier. The others were newly conceived.

Façade was originally intended as a private recitation of Edith's poems, with musical accompaniment, before an invited audience. Recitations with music were a commonplace in late Victorian and early Edwardian drawing-rooms and concert halls. The genre, much encouraged at the Royal Academy of Music, where Stanley Hawley was a celebrated exponent and composer, usually involved declaiming texts to a piano accompaniment. Academy Principal Sir Alexander Mackenzie and Academy students like Bax and Bantock all contributed to this tradition. Richard Strauss's *Enoch Arden* (1897), to the

---

1 Quoted in Victoria Glendinning, *Edith Sitwell – A Unicorn among Lions*, Weidenfeld & Nicolson 1981, Phoenix Paperback 1993, 73.
2 OUP *Façade* de luxe edition, 1972, xiv.

poem by Tennyson, is another example. Some were recited with orchestra, as in the larger cases of Grieg's *Bergliot* (1888), Delius's *Paa Vidderne*[3] (1888) and Elgar's dramatic war-time *Carillon* (1914), and Stravinsky was to contribute some notable examples. But *Façade* was no unfolding of a romantic text, and two striking features of the original presentation that made it stand apart from other recitations – and now generally dispensed with in modern performances – were the elaborate curtain with its painted masks that concealed the performers, and the megaphone (or sengerphone), a papier-mâché affair that fitted over the speaker's face and through which the verses were projected.

Osbert claimed that the idea of using a curtain was his. The question of who would be the most suitable person to design it was something that the Sitwells discussed among themselves in October 1921 at Scarborough, from where Sachie sounded out Wyndham Lewis's opinion: 'We are debating in our minds about Dobson, or [Jaques] Lipchitz. I think in many ways Dobson. . . .'[4] Frank Dobson, a London-born artist whose interests in primitive art had led him to sculpture, agreed to design a suitable curtain[5] while Osbert was one day having his head modelled in clay.

If the curtain was Osbert's idea, it was Sachie who suggested the use of a megaphone; he and Walton went by bus to Hampstead to speak to Mr Senger, who had devised the instrument named after him. The name *Façade* itself is variously attributed to Sachie (who was then writing on European architecture), to Edith's charlady at Pembridge Mansions ('All this carry-on is just one big façade'[6]), and to the remark of a critic who had reputedly said of Edith: 'Very clever, no doubt – but what is she but a façade!'[7]

Walton at first regarded the whole thing as a joke:

> They had great difficulty in persuading me to write the music.[8] . . . Osbert and Sachie were both very much excited and involved with it all once I had started, and they were the ones who were really keen on making me continue with the music. I remember thinking it was not a very good idea, but when I said so, they simply told me that they'd get Constant [Lambert] to do it if I wouldn't – and of course I couldn't possibly let that occur.[9]

---

3 Not actually performed until 1981, when it was recorded for Norwegian Television.
4 Letter dated 7 October 1921. Sarah Bradford, *Splendours and Miseries*, 112.
5 Dobson's curtain was used for all *Façade* performances until the Siena Festival in 1928 when the designer was Gino Severini. For the 1942 performance in the Aeolian Hall it was John Piper.
6 John Pearson, *Façades*, 182.
7 Osbert Sitwell, *Laughter in the Next Room*, 186 (198).
8 *The Façade Affair*, BBC Radio 3, 12 June 1973. Sir William Walton, Angus Morrison, Peter Quennell and Ambrose Gauntlett talking with Bernard Keeffe. BBC Sound Archives MT41111, NSA M4959YBD1.
9 John Pearson, *Façades*, 180.

In the early years the contents of the Entertainment were to change with each successive performance, and as it evolved, the more its numbers related to dance and popular music forms. One of the first poems they tackled was the Hornpipe, which Sachie suggested would be more effective if accompanied by music. Osbert recalled 'the rather long sessions, lasting for two or three hours, which my sister and the composer used to have, when together they read the words, she going over them again and again, while he marked and accented them for his own guidance, to show where the precise stress and emphasis fell, the exact inflection or deflection'.[10]

Edith regarded her *Façade* verses as nothing more than

> *abstract* poems – that is, they are patterns in sound: they are, too, in many cases, virtuoso exercises in poetry (of an extreme difficulty) – in the same sense as certain studies of Liszt are studies in transcendental technique in music. My experiments in *Façade* are in the nature of enquiries into the effect on rhythm, and on speed, of the use of rhythms, assonances and dissonances, placed outwardly and inwardly (at different places in the line) and in most elaborate patterns. They experimented, too, in the effect upon speed of the use of equivalent syllables. . . . There are experiments, also, in texture, in the subtle variations of thickness and thinness brought about in assonances, by the changing of a consonant or labial, from word to word. . . .[11]

The virtuosity is to be found in such lines as 'Thetis wrote a treatise noting wheat is silver like the sea;/ the lovely cheat is sweet as foam; Erotis notices that she/ will/ steal/ the/ wheat-king's luggage . . . ,' while the interplay of rhyme and assonance is heard in 'Old Sir Faulk,/ Tall as a stork,/ Before the honeyed fruits of dawn were ripe, would walk,/ And stalk with a gun/ The reynard-coloured sun. . . .'

Façade was in many ways a literary parallel to Wyndham Lewis's Vorticist movement in art, Lewis's short-lived periodical *Blast* (1914–15) finding a counterpart and successor in Edith's *Wheels* anthologies (1916–21). Georgian anthologies were then the standard fare of conservative literary London, and Edith's poems were a conscious reaction against them. As she has written: 'At the time I began to write, a change in the direction, imagery, and rhythms in poetry had become necessary, owing to the rhythmical flaccidity, the verbal deadness, the dead and expected patterns, of some of the poetry immediately preceding us.'[12] Any overtones of Rimbaud in her verses would

---

10 Osbert Sitwell, *Laughter in the Next Room*, 186 (198–9).
11 Decca sleeve-note, LXT2977 and ECS560.
12 Edith Sitwell, *Taken Care of – An Autobiography*, Hutchinson 1965, 123. She had discussed the *Façade* poems and their origins at greater length in 'Some Notes on my own Poetry', included as a preface to her *The Penguin Poets – Edith Sitwell: Selected Poems*, Penguin Books 1952, ix–xxxix, and revised in *Collected Poems*, Macmillan 1954, xv–xlvi.

have derived from Edith's friend and companion, Helen Rootham, who had a wide knowledge of French symbolist poetry (and whose translation of *Les Illuminations* was recommended by Benjamin Britten to be printed in programmes when his song-cycle was performed). Edith's was not a lone literary reactionary voice: the year in which *Façade* was first performed also saw the publication of T. S. Eliot's *The Wasteland* and James Joyce's *Ulysses*.

There can be little doubt that in the *Façade* poems Edith revisited episodes and personages from her deeply unhappy childhood. 'I often wonder what my poetry would have been like if I had had a normal childhood,' she much later confided to a friend.[13] Her long poem *The Sleeping Beauty* (1924) and the anthologies *Bucolic Comedies* (1923) and *Troy Park* (1925) are full of autobiographical allusions. Among the profusion of images in *Façade* are many references to the sea that probably recall happier times on the Scarborough sea-front. But in *Black Mrs Behemoth* was she remembering her mother's occasional rages? While 'Jane, Jane, tall as a crane' in *Aubade* is, in her words, 'about a country girl, a servant on a farm, plain, neglected and unhappy, with a bucolic stupidity, coming down in the dawn to light the fire', on her own admission she herself was that crane-tall Jane (all the Sitwells were over six feet in height). A variant *Aubade* in *The Sleeping Beauty* begins with the words 'Jane, Jane, forget the pain in your heart.' Old Sir Faulk, she has told us, was based on Colonel Hume, the father of two of her few childhood friends. He was 'a tall stork-like personage who resembled a character in *Strewelpeter* . . . or like a character in Mr Stravinsky's *Chansons Plaisantes*'.[14] She mentions both these works as having greatly influenced her early poetry. *Strewelpeter*, an illustrated collection of rather frightening moralistic verses showing children what happens to those who misbehave, could, in part at least, mirror Edith's unhappy childhood. The Black-a-moor is one *Strewelpeter* character that appears in *Façade* (such a character also appears in *Petroushka*). But more important still was the influence of Stravinsky's *Pribaoutki* or *Chansons Plaisantes*, song games for voice, flute, cor anglais, clarinet, bassoon, violin, viola, cello and double-bass, based on Russian popular texts, composed in 1914 and first performed in Paris in May 1919. In these songs Stravinsky made use of a form of very old Russian popular poetry, consisting of a succession of words which have almost no sense, but which are connected by association of images and sounds. He liked to 'make sudden contrasts in music between the portrayal of one subject and another completely different and unexpected subject'.[15] Certainly Edith's *Façade* poems abound in such sudden and often startling contrasts of images.

---

13 Letter to John Lehmann, 25 May 1951, quoted in John Pearson, *Façades*, 422.
14 *Taken Care of*, 33.
15 Romain Rolland, *Journal des Années des Guerres, 1914–1919*, Albin Michel, Paris 1952, quoted in Vera Stravinsky and Robert Craft, *Stravinsky in Pictures and Documents*, Simon & Schuster, 1978, 131. In *Expositions and Developments*, Faber 1962,

It is quite likely that Edith – and perhaps Walton too – attended the Wigmore Hall lecture–recital in August 1920 when Ernest Ansermet spoke about Stravinsky and, among other things, the *Pribaoutki* and *The Soldier's Tale* were both performed. Sacheverell also cites as an influence the ballet *Parade* (which Walton had seen in November 1919), with its music by Satie and the fairground curtain by Picasso, and with one of the circus managers, concealed within a three-dimensional Cubist structure, declaiming through a megaphone, an idea that had probably come to Cocteau from music-hall. Even Edith, discussing her verbal experimentation in *Facade*, wrote: 'At other moments, as Jean Cocteau said of another work of more or less the same kind, the ballet *Parade*, in which he, Picasso, and Satie collaborated, the work is "the poetry of childhood overtaken by a technician".'[16]

The nearest English counterpart at this time was Arthur Bliss whose experiments in voice and music could surely not have gone unnoticed by the Sitwells with their ears ever attuned to the avant-garde. Bliss's *Rout*, a seven-minute work for nine players to which a soprano sings 'a medley of made-up words', was originally written for and in December 1920 performed at one of those fashionable musical parties given by wealthy patrons and patronesses. Its first public performance followed in May 1921 at the Steinway Hall. Two days later it was heard again, this time at Diaghilev's request in orchestral dress, and in this form it was given as an interlude during Diaghilev's season that year. In an earlier Rhapsody for soprano, tenor and small chamber ensemble, given in October 1920, Bliss had his singers vocalise to 'ah', treating the voices as instruments within the ensemble. He experimented further with the voice in his Concerto for Piano, Tenor Voice, Strings and Percussion. In this he chose English words 'for their sound and rhythm, but of so abstract a character as not to interpose a logical meaning'. The work was actually encored at its Wigmore Hall first performance in June 1921, but Bliss felt that 'the experimental idea had failed'[17] and rewrote the work for two pianos and orchestra.

Stravinsky's *The Soldier's Tale* was quite likely another influence on *Façade*, with its narrator and small ensemble of violin, double bass, clarinet, bassoon, trumpet, trombone and percussion (reflecting the influence of jazz on Stravinsky at that time), and its use of such popular music forms as the tango, ragtime, pasodoble, waltz and march. Neither can Schoenberg's

---

121, in conversation with Robert Craft, Stravinsky offered a further explanation: 'The word *pribaoutki* denotes a form of popular Russian verse, to which the nearest English parallel is the limerick. They are always short – not more than four lines usually. According to popular tradition they derive from a type of game in which someone says a word, which someone else then adds to, and which third and fourth persons develop, and so on, with utmost speed. . . . One important characteristic of Russian popular verse is that the accents of the spoken verse are ignored when the verse is sung. . . .'

[16] 'Some Notes on my own Poetry', Penguin Books, xi.

[17] Arthur Bliss, *As I Remember*, Faber & Faber 1970, 66.

Pierrot Lunaire, first performed in 1912 in Berlin, be overlooked as a possible model. It was not heard in London until December 1923 when Darius Milhaud conducted three performances. When asked about its influence, Walton somewhat ambiguously replied: 'Schoenberg wasn't actually a very great help because, though one had the music, I'd never heard it and nobody I knew could play it and I couldn't read it, and so I was completely in the dark about it. But I pretended that I was an expert on Schoenberg.'[18] *Pierrot* uses flute and piccolo, violin and viola, clarinet and bass clarinet, cello and piano, while *Façade* (in its final version) requires flute doubling piccolo, clarinet doubling bass clarinet, alto saxophone, trumpet, percussion and cello. *Pierrot* was originally performed with the instrumentalists hidden from the audience's view (as was *Façade*), with the speaker in costume alone on the stage. Just as the speaker in *Pierrot* is required to employ *Sprechgesang*, or speech-song, so *Façade* calls for its own special, spoken delivery of the poems that makes it stand apart from any conventional song-cycle.

It was also the arrangement of the *Façade* poems into seven groups of three for the 1942 Aeolian Hall performance, when *Pierrot* was also given, conducted by Erwin Stein, that further invited the comparison with Schoenberg's three groups of seven. Walton later confessed to the intended similarity (which had been suggested by Lambert): 'In the end we decided as Schoenberg had done three times seven poems in *Pierrot Lunaire* we should do a trick and have seven times three, a sort of typically Schoenbergian inversion. . . .'[19] There the similarities cease. The pianist Angus Morrison,[20] who was a close friend of Lambert and Walton, suggested that *Façade* had probably started under the influence of *Pierrot*, but as it evolved and the more Schoenbergian numbers were discarded, its comic, burlesque side came more to the fore.[21] Morrison also recalled that 'in his bedroom at Carlyle Square Willie had a number of modern scores of which *Pierrot Lunaire* was certainly one – scores which he pored over and studied very intensively during those early years'.[22] Yet none of this detracts from the brilliant originality of *Façade*. As for the instrumentation, Walton remarked laconically that it was chosen for 'economy in the first place. Clarinet was the most useful instrument, and the cello. . . . You had to have a bass of some kind. . . . Percussion covers a multitude of sins – and still does.'[23]

[18] Interview with Bernard Keeffe, *The Façade Affair*, BBC Radio 3, 12 June 1973.
[19] *Ibid.*
[20] Angus Morrison studied at the Royal College of Music and was soloist in the first (broadcast) performance of Lambert's *The Rio Grande* on 27 February 1928.
[21] Interviewed by Michael Oliver for *Music Weekly* programme on Walton, BBC Radio 3, 28 March 1982. BBC Sound Archives T4862BW.
[22] 'Willie: The Young Walton and his Four Masterpieces', a talk given by Angus Morrison at the National Sound Archive on 31 January 1984, printed in the *Royal College of Music Magazine* 1984, 121. NSA recording T8850C1.
[23] *The Façade Affair.*

It was through the instrumental rehearsals for *Façade* that Walton felt he really learned how to write the music,[24] often by a process of trial and error. For the players' part, the clarinettist, Paul Draper, is reported to have enquired: 'Excuse me, Mr Walton, has a clarinet player ever done you an injury?' The story, attributed to Lambert, is that Walton had noticed a passage for clarinet in *Pierrot Lunaire* that he thought unplayable, and so to find out whether this was true he incorporated it into one of the early numbers of *Façade*.[25] The cellist, Ambrose Gauntlett, remembered it all as 'very difficult, really. He set us some problems, which we overcame.' In retrospect he regarded the rehearsals as 'really great fun'.[26] This was Walton's first experience of conducting, and Osbert, with a novelist's eye and from a distance of some twenty-seven years, described those rehearsals:

> The drawing-room is of the usual L-shaped London type. Three windows look out on the square, and one, at the back, on to a tall sycamore, the branches of which in this peculiarly bitter February [sic][27] weather looked black as night. . . . The instruments formed a sextet: flute, clarinet, saxophone, trumpet, 'cello and percussion.[28] The players sat at the wide end of the room, near the three windows. . . . As the strange new sounds shaped themselves under the hands of the rather angry players, the evening outside began to envelop the world in a grape-bloom blue, the lights had to be turned on, and the pictures glowed from the white walls. . . . I say the players were rather angry, and so at first they were: irate with the young conductor who seemed to know his way about in this new and difficult world he had evolved. He stood there, holding his baton, with something of the air of an elegant and handsome snipe . . . But William possessed persistence as well as genius, and led his players safely through.[29]

---

24 In his interview with Murray Schafer, *British Composers in Interview*, 76, Walton claimed that the music for *Façade* was written in three weeks.
25 'Willie: The Young Walton and his Four Masterpieces', 122.
26 *The Façade Affair.*
27 In 'Moving House', in *Queen Mary and Others*, 171, Osbert remembers it as a winter's evening in November. 'In spite of two large coal fires, the players had to be brought to by copious draughts of sloe gin.'
28 In Tony Palmer, *At the Haunted End of the Day*, Walton referred to four players for the first private performance. In Murray Schafer, *British Composers in Interview*, 76, he specified clarinet, trumpet, cello and percussion. Yet in a letter to Mrs. Louisa Grace Hughes on 4 April 1922, Edith Sitwell listed an accompaniment of trumpet, clarinet, flute, drum and cello. The programme for the Aeolian Hall performance lists six players: flute R. Murchie, clarionet P. Draper, saxophone F. Moss, trumpet H. Barr, cello A. Gauntlett, percussion C. Bender. For the first of the two Chenil Galleries performance there were two changes, the line-up being: flute and piccolo B. Macrae, clarinet and bass clarinet Paul Draper, saxophone A. Cox, trumpet Herbert Barr, percussion Charles Bender, and cello Ambrose Gauntlett.
29 Osbert Sitwell, *Laughter in the Next Room*, 187–8 (200–201).

The first, private performance took place at 9.30 p.m. at 2 Carlyle Square on Tuesday[30] 24 January 1922. The typewritten programme announced: '*Façade* – Miss Edith Sitwell on her Sengerphone with accompaniments, overture and interlude by W T Walton'. Sacheverell recalled that the 'haunting and sinister' fanfare 'was adapted from an itinerant fortune-teller's trumpet-call which we heard in Syracuse or Catania [in Sicily] a year or two before';[31] Osbert said that it had been 'inspired by a travelling showman with a devil in a bottle at Palermo'.[32]

Near the end of her life, Edith wrote that the first performance of *Façade* 'took place privately and peacefully'. Osbert remembered that in the comparatively small drawing-room 'the sheer volume of sound was overwhelming . . . that many of the more orthodox friends whom we had invited to be present were so perturbed by a performance unlike any other they had seen or heard . . . that they did not know what to say, or where to look'. Nevertheless, the 'painters, musicians and poets, of whom a large proportion of the audience consisted, were naturally enthusiastic in their reception'. Afterwards a general air of well-being was restored by an ample supply of a hot rum punch – 'an unusual but efficacious restorative'. Among the guests was Mrs Robert Mathias, a patroness of the *Ballets Russes* and, in Francis Toye's words, 'a high-priestess of modern art',[33] who was 'so pleased and stimulated by it that, in spite of the no doubt numerous remonstrances of her less enterprising friends and relations'[34] she asked Osbert to arrange another performance at her house in Montagu Square. That took place a fortnight later on the evening of 7 February. Edith described this second performance in a letter to Brian Howard:

> It was not songs which were done at Mrs. Matthias', but I recited a great many of these and other of my own poems down a sort of megaphone, to the accompaniment of music by W. T. Walton (who will probably be the best composer we've ever had in England). Flute, trumpet, clarinet, cello, and drum. All done behind a huge curtain painted for me by Frank Dobson. The audience was stunned.[35]

Meanwhile word soon got round in fashionable circles, and within a fortnight after the second performance Virginia Woolf was writing to her sister

---

30 Not Sunday, as has often been stated.

31 OUP *Façade* de-luxe edition, 1972, xiii.

32 Frank Howes, *The Music of William Walton*, OUP 1965, second edition 1974, 18.

33 Francis Toye, *For What We have Received: An Autobiography*, Heinemann 1950, 164. Toye incorrectly writes that 'it was at her house that the Sitwell–Walton *Façade*, Edith trumpeting through a megaphone, was first revealed to a sniggering London'.

34 Osbert Sitwell, *Laughter in the Next Room*, 190 (203).

35 Edith Sitwell to Charles Orange [i.e. Brian Howard], n.d., *Selected Letters of Edith Sitwell*, edited by Richard Greene, Virago Press 1997, revised 1998, 38. Brian Howard was the model for Anthony Blanche in Evelyn Waugh's *Brideshead Revisited*.

that she had heard from a friend that 'the Sitwells have been reciting what seem to her sheer nonsense through megaphones'.[36] Virginia Woolf was present herself at the first public performance, but, she wrote to a friend, 'Though I paid 3/6 to hear Edith vociferate her poems accompanied by a small and nimble orchestra, through a megaphone, I understood so little that I could not judge.'[37]

After the private presentations,[38] that first public performance of *Façade*, considerably revised and much extended, took place at 3.15 p.m. in the Aeolian Hall on Tuesday 12 June 1923. *The Times* advertisement ran:

Osbert Sitwell presents
Miss Edith Sitwell and W T Walton
in *Façade*
A New and Original Musical Entertainment

The cover of the sixpenny programme gave Edith and Walton equal billing. The afternoon opened with a fanfare, followed by a 'Preface' from Osbert, after which came the Overture and then twenty-eight poems[39] arranged in eight groups of varying sizes. But the occasion could not be accounted a success. The attendance was rather poor, with the hall only about half full, the audience largely made up of men and women of the arts. Among those present were Ada Leverson, Evelyn Waugh, Lytton Strachey, Desmond Harmsworth, Francis Palmer, Clive Bell, St John Hutchinson and Eugene Goossens. The legend has since come down that this was one of those premières that caused an uproar if not a riot. The chief authors of this legend have been Edith and Osbert Sitwell. According to Edith, the performance

> caused alarm and raised an uproar among such custodians of the purity of our language, such upholders of tradition in Aesthetics, as writers of Review, firemen on duty in the hall, and passing postmen [an invention of Edith's], who, on being lassoed and consulted by journalists, expressed the opinion that we were mad. And that in no uncertain terms. I hope it will not be thought that I am imputing lack of education to firemen or postmen – I

---

36 Victoria Glendinning, *Edith Sitwell*, 77.

37 30 July 1923, *Collected Letters III*, Hogarth Press 1994.

38 It is possible that Marie Adelaide Belloc Lowndes, novelist and sister of the poet Hilaire Belloc, offered to play hostess to a further private performance, because Edith wrote to her at that time: 'It is a great pleasure to me to think that you are going to have *Façade*. I enclose the two copies in different covers, as I have not an envelope large enough to contain the two.' Undated letter in Richard Greene (ed.), *Selected Letters of Edith Sitwell*, 39. However, it is not certain from this letter that Edith is referring to a performance, and if so, that the performance took place.

39 *Serenade* and *The Octogenarian* were grouped as one. See Appendix 4.

Frank Dobson's curtain design for *Façade* that was used for all the early performances up to 1928.

mean, only, that on this occasion they were precipitate in giving their opinion.[40]

In her autobiography *Taken Care of*, completed just before her death in December 1964, she wrote that it 'was anything but peaceful. Never, I should think, was a larger and more imposing shower of brickbats hurled at any new work. . . . Indeed, the attitude of certain of the audience was so threatening that I was warned to stay on the platform, hidden by the curtain, until they got tired of waiting for me and went home.'[41]

Osbert, in his autobiography *Laughter in the Next Room* published in 1949, wrote of the press as having been

engaged for days past in trying to whip up the public to pretend to feel rage and resort to insult. Many hours before the curtain rose – or, more precisely in this case, was lowered – the air had grown so tense that I recollect how it rendered my brother and me ill at ease to the extent of being unable to eat any luncheon. . . . A large audience had already assembled when we arrived to join my sister in the Artists' Room, I proceeded on to the platform first, walking in front of the curtain to make a speech describing the novel elements in the performance, and attempting to explain its aims. After acknowledging the applause, I went behind the curtain to announce the various items of the entertainment through the mouth of the mask, smaller than the principal head in the middle. Then the fanfare which heralds

40 Decca sleeve-note, LXT2977 and ECS560.
41 Edith Sitwell, *Taken Care of*, 122.

Façade sounded, and the fun began. . . .

The front rows, especially, manifested their contempt and rage, and, albeit a good deal of applause countered the hissing and indicated interest and enthusiasm in certain quarters, nevertheless the atmosphere was so greatly and so evidently hostile that at the end of the performance several members of the audience came behind the curtain to warn my sister not to leave the platform until the crowd had dispersed. For several weeks subsequently, we were obliged to go about London feeling as if we had committed a murder. . . . In fact, we had created a first-class scandal in literature and music.[42]

Such has the legend grown that even Walton, when asked in an interview broadcast in 1977[43] whether there had been a rumpus, replied that 'everyone was standing on their chairs and screaming with temper – more against the Sitwells than me'. It has been easy for others who were not present to add a little colour of their own as, for example, did Spike Hughes: 'It caused a first-rate literary and musical *scandale*. There were shouting and whistling and indignant patriotic demonstrations against such "ultramodern" – and therefore un-English – goings on.'[44] It is not unusual to read today, for example, that the Aeolian Hall 'achieved notoriety . . . as the scene of the first-night riot during William Walton's *Façade*',[45] suggesting perhaps a scandal to be compared with that at the première of *The Rite of Spring*. What indeed were 'the scandals created by the earliest productions of *Façade*'?[46] None of this is evident in any of the reviews. In fact, nothing of the sort took place at all, and Walton himself, concealed behind the curtain and concentrating on the music, was hardly in the best position to judge. Even Osbert's own accounts of that afternoon differ according to the perspective of time. In 1927 he merely remarked that 'the performance was not then a marked success, for it did not run smoothly enough. Rudimentary though it was, though, it was yet a sufficiently stimulating development to interest the intelligent.'[47] It seems that Edith and Osbert, who would react strongly against the

---

[42] Osbert Sitwell, *Laughter in the Next Room*, 191–2 (204–5).

[43] Interview with John Amis in *Portrait of Walton*, BBC Radio 3 broadcast on 4 June 1977.

[44] Patrick Cairn Hughes ('Spike' Hughes) in 'Nobody Calls Him Willie Now', for *High Fidelity*, September 1960, Vol. 10, No. 9, 43.

[45] Piers Burton-Page, *Philharmonic Concerto: The Life and Music of Sir Malcolm Arnold*, Methuen 1994, 32

[46] Edward Johnson's note for the CD release of the première recording of Walton's Violin Concerto, Biddulph WHL016.

[47] 'Façade and the Fireman', Chapter 6 in 'A Few Days in an Author's Life', a preface by Osbert Sitwell to Osbert and Sacheverell Sitwell, *All at Sea: A Social Tragedy in Three Acts for First Class Passengers Only*, Duckworth 1927. Ernest Newman's *Sunday Times* 2 May 1926 review of the Chenil Galleries performance of *Façade* was included, slightly censored, as an appendix.

ÆOLIAN HALL
NEW BOND STREET, W.

Tuesday Afternoon, June 12th, 1923, at 3.15.

Poems by

EDITH SITWELL

Music by

W. T. WALTON

Curtain by FRANK DOBSON

Sengerphone	-	EDITH SITWELL
Flute	-	R. MURCHIE
Clarionet	-	P. DRAPER
Saxophone	-	F. MOSS
Trumpet	-	H. BARR
'Cello	-	A. GAUNTLETT
Percussion	-	C. BENDER

Conductor :

W. T. WALTON

Programme
Sixpence

slightest unsympathetic reception or review, could only imagine what, short of an artistic triumph, the Sitwell trio had failed to achieve: 'a first-class scandal in literature and music'.

It is important to read exactly what the reviewers and others who attended did say. They, after all, would have been only too ready to report any hint of an uproar had one taken place. All they do convey in many cases is either boredom, surprise or a total lack of comprehension. Most of the critics were nonplussed, perplexed, and under the circumstances this was hardly surprising. They missed the key point that *Façade* was designed quite simply as an entertainment.

One of the clearest accounts comes from Harold Acton. 'Oh, I'm working so hard for Façade. Is there any chance of your being in London for it?' Edith had written to him in May. In his *Memoirs of an Aesthete* he recalled:

> The stage was hung with a black-cloth painted by Frank Dobson the sculptor: this consisted of two masks, the large one in the centre half pink and half white, and the small one on the right a blackamoor, with senger-phones protruding through their open mouths. Osbert Sitwell announced each poem through the blackamoor's mouth and Edith recited through the lips of the pink and white mask. Osbert had explained that the purpose of reciting behind a back-cloth through a sengerphone was to stop the reader's personality from invading the poems.[48]
>
> Very distinctly, stressing the rhythms in a dispassionate voice, Edith read to the accompaniment of a sextet by William Walton, a series of tunes which have since been orchestrated for ballet and popularised by frequent broadcasts. No dance can serve as a proxy for such flashing poems, and I preferred their first performance. Willie Walton interpreted Edith's colour-schemes with extra-ordinary precision. . . . Some people in the audience tittered and made inopportune remarks, but the poems moved so buoyantly that it did not matter. The performance ended with 'Sir Beelzebub at the Hotel', lines that seemed to shower confetti on the audience and slam a door behind them. . . . In the evening there was a party at Osbert's house in Carlyle Square . . . Charades were played . . . and the most amusing represented the demise of a Teutonic Princess, impersonated by St. John Hutchinson, with Eugene Goossens as the doctor, Lytton Strachey and Clive Bell as attendant royalties.'[49]

Angus Morrison, who was also present, had memories that differ significantly from Edith's and Osbert's:

> Everyone was perfectly good-mannered and no one objected violently at all. There were certainly no boos or cat calls. On the other hand there

---

[48] The sengerphone had the additional purely practical function of making Edith's voice heard above the instrumentalists.

[49] Harold Acton, *Memoirs of an Aesthete*, Methuen 1948, 128–30.

wasn't much enthusiasm, either. As a performance, the Aeolian Hall *Façade* simply wasn't very good, and then a hot summer afternoon in a stuffy London hall isn't the place to listen to a new production like *Façade*. The hall wasn't very full, and the whole thing fell distinctly flat.[50]

He summed it up as making 'a mild sensation'. Even Walton admitted: 'The performance at the Aeolian Hall was a shambles. It was badly performed and the music wasn't right. By the time of the next performance at the Chenil Galleries, we got it right, and it was all a great success, but at the Aeolian Hall it was disastrous.'[51]

One obstacle to a clearer understanding was commented on by the *Daily Telegraph* critic. For copyright reasons, unlike at the first private performance, the poems were not printed in the programme – which asterisked nineteen of the twenty-seven titles as being 'found in Miss Sitwell's recent book *Bucolic Comedies* (Duckworth, 3/6)' that had been published that April.[52] But that was no help to the listener who could not hear clearly – let alone understand – the poems as they emerged through the sengerphone from the disembodied voice behind the curtain. Many were understandably baffled. The *Telegraph* critic continued:

> [Miss Sitwell's] main object seemed to be to hammer out the rhythm of the poems, and opting for that purpose an unvarying monotone, and leaving it to her hearers to catch as best they could the words and their meanings, the result was often better imagined than described.
>
> But, unfortunately, the composer's methods, however appropriate they might appear to anyone acquainted with the text of Miss Sitwell's 'Bucolic Comedies' and the rest, served only to increase the bewilderment of the uninitiated. Here and there, as in 'The man from a far countrie', for instance, the music seemed to be talking sense, and one is quite willing to believe that Mr Walton's unbroken dissonances provided the right sort of commentary on the poems themselves. But at least in one of them – a 'Trio for two cats and a trombone' – one's ears failed to detect any sounds bearing analogy to the title. The easy recognition, in the accompaniment to 'Hornpipe', of a familiar tune – ornamented with squeaks and grunts in the woodwind – so greatly delighted the audience that they called for a repetition of the number.[53]

One of the reviews seized upon by Edith and Osbert was that by 'Mr London' in the *Daily Graphic*, on his 'Wonderful London Yesterday' page:

[50] John Pearson, *Façades*, 183–4.

[51] *Ibid.*, 184.

[52] The programme for the first private performance of *Façade* had announced that 'All these poems, and some additional ones, will appear in a book called 'Façade' which Miss Edith Sitwell is publishing privately in a limited edition with a special frontispiece in colour by Gino Severini – at the Favil Press, Kensington.'

[53] 13 June 1923.

Drivel They Paid to Hear

If Beerbohm wanted to do a really funny drawing of the Sitwells, instead of the stupid one of them now on view at the Leicester Galleries, he should have gone to the ridiculous recital at the Aeolian Hall, which I am surprised to see was taken seriously by some newspapers.

A friend of mine who was there tells me that, when he laughed, as Edith Sitwell recited drivel through a megaphone, a woman turned round and said, 'How can I study a new art if you laugh?'

That sums up the whole performance. If three had laughed, the Sitwells wouldn't dare do it again.

Fireman Tells the Truth

Edwin Evans sat through a series of meaningless, rhythmless, childish words called 'Ass Face', but Noël Coward was strong enough to walk out, while the fireman, asked his opinion at the end, said that, never in twenty years' experience of recitals at that hall, had he known anything like it.

Surely it is time this sort of thing were stopped. If people want to make fools of themselves, they might do it in their own homes. After all, one of the many millions of people who have never heard of the Sitwells might have been induced by the announcement to pay to go in.

Grant Richards wore a white carnation specially for the occasion, his son wore another carnation. But otherwise it was all dreary and hopeless.[54]

The much-quoted fireman's statement is as unrevealing as it was truthful. *Façade* being the novelty it was, nothing like it *had* been seen at the Aeolian Hall before. This did not stop Edith much later from distorting the truth when she wrote in her autobiography:

Certain newspaper critics, engaged and alarmed by the performance, rushed from the hall and, lassoing a passing postman, asked him what he thought. Dashing back to the hall they waylaid a fireman and anxiously asked his opinion. These modern substitutes for the Delphic Oracle replied promptly, and in no uncertain terms. They opined that we were mad.[55]

'The Dilettante', in the *Sunday Express*, wasted few words on such an arty occasion:

Latest Gossip of the London Season
Were you there?
Poetry Through a Megaphone

Miss Edith Sitwell monotones her own lines with musical accompaniment. Foghorn effect. Usual audience. Long-haired men, short-haired women. Megaphone in great form.

---

[54] 'Mr London', *Daily Graphic*, 14 June 1923, 5.
[55] *Taken Care of*, 122.

Bas – kets – of – ripe – fruit – in – air.
The – bird – songs – seem – suspended – where

Very depressing, but raises the status of the megaphone.[56]

K. K. in the *Evening Standard* (see Appendix 5 for the full review), who could not resist tilting at Edith in verse –

> In the afternoon, at the Aeolian Hall,
> Through a megaphone we heard Edith bawl,

– noticed, besides puzzlement at the title and initial coldness, some enthusiasm:

> The audience seemed a little cold at first; the first sign of real emotion was when three members of the audience went out hurriedly. . . . Gradually, under the influence of Miss Sitwell's fervent chanting of her exotic lines, the audience became attuned to the spirit of the Sengerphonist, as was shown by the enthusiasm that followed the sonorous rendering of a 'Trio for Two Cats and a Trombone.'[57]

The *Daily Express* critic was rather more baffled:

> If Miss Edith Sitwell considers that the best way to recite her poems is through a megaphone in a tragic voice, that is her affair. She wrote them, and ought to know best.
>
> The Aeolian Hall was half filled yesterday to hear her do it.
>
> Across the platform was stretched a curtain representing, chiefly, a piebald face, one half red, the other white. Mr Osbert Sitwell introduced this as 'Venus'. Where the mouth should have been a gaping megaphone protruded. Miss Sitwell called it a sengerphone.
>
> There were twenty-eight items on the programme, but only one note came through the sengerphone except once, when Miss Sitwell seemed to forget herself and spoke two or three words quite naturally.
>
> The music did wasps and caterpillars and earwigs all over the basket, with the birds snapping at them [in *Gardener Janus catches a Naiad*].
>
> At the first interval, a woman looking round at the audience, exclaimed tragically, 'Where are the intelligentsia? Where are the intelligentsia?'
>
> Oh, but they were there. In the semi-darkness, groups of pale young women and men, both with bobbed hair, could be seen hugging themselves in ecstasy.
>
> Much delayed applause followed the story of Herodia's flea in F, and a hornpipe – also in F, but with a quicker rumty-tum, rumty tum-tum in the measure.

---

[56] 'The Dilettante', *Sunday Express*, 17 June 1923, 6.
[57] K. K., *Evening Standard*, 13 June 1923, 3.

It will be difficult to put the sound of the Sitwell Sengerphone out of one's brain. Doh-dah, doh-doh-doh-dah, doh-dah.[58]

Percy Scholes, in the *Observer*, was not impressed:

I am personally thankful that Dame Ethel [Smyth] made her opera[59] out of Maurice Baring's 'Fête Galante' and not out of Ethel [sic] Sitwell's poem of the same name. For how could I, as a critic, have grumbled at tongueless, toothless articulation if it had been exercised upon such lines as:

> But the Marquise in the bocage
> Laughs like the sharp rockage
> Of her gallant grottoes, cold as water-wells,
> And shakes her curls, as pearly as their shells!

Nay, an had they mumbled such lines as these, I might have been constrained to unaccustomed praise. Even Mr W. T. Walton, whose string quartet, a couple of years ago, convinced me he was the boldest of the bold amongst the youngest of the young, would, I believe, hesitate at setting a Sitwell opera, but he has actually gone so far as to set 28 Sitwell lyrics, or rather write music for simultaneous performance. If this was kindly meant to distract our minds, let me say regretfully that it failed. 'If this was a new form of art,' said Mr Osbert Sitwell, 'it would not be nice for others to copy and spoil it.' Let him set his mind at rest.

Walton's music . . . in itself . . . is harmless.[60]

Some critics were wary of having their leg pulled, uncertain of a joke at their expense. The *Morning Post* critic was one of them:

There are few things more depressing than a joke – especially if it be an elaborate, pretentious joke – which falls dead flat, as did the attempt made at Aeolian Hall yesterday afternoon 'to introduce a more abstract quality into recitation.'

On a crudely-painted curtain (by Mr Frank Dobson) leered a monstrous face, half-white, half-pink, with closed eyelids and an aperture for mouth, from which protruded at intervals a 'Senger phone'. Behind this apparatus was Miss Edith Sitwell, who, in a sing-song monotone, delivered a large number of her 'poems', crude as the setting itself, and with 'music' no less crude by Mr W T Walton by way of accompaniment.

Truth to tell, this latest device – 'Façade' it is called – made to *épater le bourgeois*, proved to be rather tiresome and not a few of the audience had had more than enough long before the last of the eight groups was reached. If the 'joke' was intended as a satire at the expense of that noxious thing the

---

58 13 June 1923.

59 Ethel Smyth's one-act opera *Fête Galante*, after a story by Maurice Baring, had only just received its first London production the day before, on 11 June 1923.

60 P. A. S., *Observer*, 17 June 1923.

average 'recitation', one can only express one's preference for the original evil.[61]

Edwin Evans, in the *Pall Mall Gazette*, was more discerning:

> There have been several [probably two] performances of 'Façade' in private houses, but yesterday, for the first time, it was performed at the Aeolian Hall. It is a novel way of presenting a selection of poems by Miss Edith Sitwell.
> Behind the curtain is Miss Sitwell, reciting in a severely metrical chant and accompanied by half a dozen instrumentalists, whom Mr W T Walton has provided with a clever but somewhat self-conscious score.
> The effect is hard to describe of course, the easiest thing is to poke fun at it, but it is scarcely more difficult to deal with in solemn earnest.
> Both accounts would, however, be misleading.
> 'Façade' is neither a practical joke nor a philosophy, but something between the two and a little more stimulating than either, for it contains, provokingly expressed, some elements of aesthetic truth.[62]

The *Manchester Guardian* critic found Edith's verses 'blinding with colour, bulging with imagery and deafening with relentless cacophony' and thought Osbert's 'experiment in avoiding the usual bugbear of ordinary recitation . . . hardly successful'.

The Times critic seemed to understand more than most what the Sitwells were trying to achieve:

> Miss Edith Sitwell and her brothers have always been apostles of what has been called *épatism* and on Tuesday afternoon at the Aeolian Hall they carried their assault on the accepted things a step farther. Their entertainment, called *Façade*, consisted of a recitation of her poems by Miss Sitwell to an accompaniment of four wind instruments, violoncello and percussion, devised by Mr W T Walton. The poems were read in monotone with great rhythmic emphasis through what was called in the programme a 'Sengerphone', which protruded through the mouth of the monstrous head painted on the curtain by Mr Frank Dobson. The object was, as Mr Osbert Sitwell explained, to prevent the personality of the reciter from getting between the poem and the audience. That much was achieved; but it was almost impossible to make words clearly audible through a megaphone unless they are spoken slowly and distinctly. Mr Walton's accompaniments obviously owe a great deal to Stravinsky and are for the most part too spasmodic. Here and there he succeeded in throwing a gleam of light on the words; and when he had definite dance-rhythms to build up he produced clever results.[63]

---

61 13 June 1923.
62 E. E. *Pall Mall Gazette*, 13 June 1923.
63 14 June 1923.

And the *Daily Mail* critic had an ear more clearly attuned to the music than most:

[Miss Sitwell's] sharply defined and clearly accentuated rhythm . . . might have been monotonous without the extraordinarily stimulative running commentary of Mr Walton's music.

His musical invention is as original and witty as Miss Sitwell's poetry and fits the rhythm of the spoken line as though words and music were cast in one mould. He manages to get a pleasing variety of colour out of the six instruments used: flute, clarionet, saxophone, trumpet, 'cello and percussion; and this variety forms a valuable contrast to the deliberately monotonous chant of the recitation.

Façade received a very warm reception.

But the fullest and sanest account appeared in *Vogue* (see Appendix 5 for the full review). It sufficiently pleased Edith for her to write a letter of thanks to its author Gerald Cumberland[64] who thought that an ill-prepared audience, for the most part unfamiliar with Edith's work, had done its best. After commenting on the 'clever' music that was 'played with airy delicacy and occasional pomp', he summed up the occasion:

Miss Sitwell, then, has discovered and tried a new method of interpretation. The experiment was well worth making; but I am inclined to think that her success was in no small measure due to the strangeness and beauty of her poetry. Her bizarre work demands a bizarre setting, a bizarre delivery. No other poetry known to me would survive this particular kind of presentation. But the brittle loveliness of Miss Sitwell's work, its kaleidoscopic colour, its ellipses so full of imagination, and its darting cleverness are all enhanced by this deliberately sought artificiality.[65]

If the listeners had doubts and uncertainties, Edith and William had theirs too. *Façade* was now subjected to a continuous process of revision and refinement. Of the sixteen numbers that had been performed at the private première (not including the instrumental Overture and Interlude), thirteen had been kept for the first public performance and another fifteen were added, and only six of the original poems were to survive for the final published version in 1951. For the next public performance in April 1926, nine were taken out and a further seven added, with the order of the items being constantly changed from performance to performance. When *Façade* was performed again in June, four were removed and three added. (These changes can be seen in Appendix 4.)

There was an amusing sequel to the public première of *Façade*. That young man seen walking out of the entertainment was Noël Coward who was

[64] His real name was Charles Kenyon.
[65] July 1923, Vol. 62, No. 13, 36 and 70.

soon to provide an entertainment of his own. Ironically, his presence had been at Osbert's suggestion. Out dining at a restaurant one day, Osbert had apparently stopped at Noël's table and informed him of the coming perform-ance of *Façade*, suggesting that he might pick up some ideas. He most certainly did, though not quite in the way Osbert had intended. In his first review, called *London Calling!* which opened at the Duke of York Theatre on 4 September 1923, Coward included a sketch entitled 'The Swiss Family Whittlebot' (a variant on Aldous Huxley's name for the Sitwells – the Shuf-flebottoms). On paper this 'short exposition of Modern Art' seems innocent enough.[66] In it Hernia Whittlebot (played by Maisie Gay), assisted by her brothers Gob and Sago, presents a recital of four poems, including one by Gob 'to which special music has been set by my brother Gob on the Cophuti-can' that ends with the line 'Thank God for the Coldstream Guards' (a clear reference to Osbert and Sacheverell having served in the Guards). Hernia is dressed in undraped dyed sacking; 'her face is white and weary, with a long chin and nose, and bags under her eyes'. Gob is wearing 'cycling-breeches and a bottle-green velvet coat with a big floppy bow, cloth-topped boots and a tweed shooting hat', while Sago is 'faultlessly dressed in a slightly Victorian morning suit'. At first Hernia expounds on Life and Art: 'To me life is essen-tially a curve, and Art an oblong within that curve.' As she recites she is ac-companied by her brothers on musical instruments 'rather queer in shape'. When she launches into 'a very long and intensely primitive poem entitled *The Lower Classes*', the Stage Manager tries unsuccessfully to signal to her that their time is up and resorts to getting the orchestra to strike up the next number. At this Hernia produces a megaphone until she and her brothers are pushed off stage as the Manager begins to set the next scene.

The similarity to the Sitwells was unmistakable. Sir John Gielgud remem-bered 'laughing uproariously' at the sketch. The *Daily Telegraph* critic[67] found 'diverting moments' in the 'skit on the new-fangled poetry of the Sitwell type'. Reports of the sketch reached the ears of the trio who could not bring themselves to see it and laugh it off. Such an offence was, in their eyes, unforgivable. Noël Coward wrote in his autobiography:

> During the first two weeks of the run, I received to my intense surprise, a cross letter from Osbert Sitwell; in fact, so angry was it, that I first of all imagined it to be a joke. However, it was far from being a joke, and shortly afterwards another letter arrived, even crosser than the first. To this day I am still a little puzzled as to why that light-hearted burlesque should have aroused him, his brother and his sister to such paroxysms of fury.[68]

Matters did not stop there. According to Coward's biographer,

---

66 *Collected Sketches and Lyrics by Noël Coward*, Hutchinson 1931, 87–9.
67 5 September 1923.
68 *Noël Coward: Autobiography*, eventually issued in one volume, Mandarin 1992, 117.

the fictional Hernia Whittlebot became so widely known that Noël was invited to speak her verse from the brand new 2LO Wireless Station; he made his first ever broadcast in a fifteen-minute reading of Miss Whittlebot's poems. . . . Later Miss Whittlebot herself began to make regular appearances in the gossip columns, to which Noël would feed such information as 'Hernia is busy preparing for publication her new books, *Gilded Sluts* and *Garbage*. She breakfasts on onions and Vichy water.'[69]

Hernia Whittlebot's verses even appeared in print, as a collection of *Chelsea Buns*, 'edited by Noël Coward'.[70]

A feud was started between the Sitwells and Coward that continued for years. The artist Christopher Nevinson, who painted Edith, recorded in his autobiography that 'at dinner with Osbert one night we were talking about Noël Coward, and another guest happened to say he wished someone would exterminate the little patiche. Osbert at once turned, and said: "I wish you would. Edith would be so obliged." '[71] An interim truce was reached when Coward met Osbert in New York: 'He was extremely nice about the whole affair and persuaded his sister by cable to forgive me.'[72] There must have been a brief exhange of words for in December 1926 Edith wrote a curt note: 'Dear Mr Coward, I accept your apology. Yours sincerely, Edith Sitwell.'[73] But it was not until September 1962 that the hatchet was finally buried and Coward could write in his diary:

> I have made up my lifelong feud with Edith Sitwell. I wrote her a fan letter about her book [*The Queen and the Hive*] which . . . is wonderfully readable and, at moments, brilliant. Anyhow, she sent me a sweet and friendly telegram back and I shall go and see her when I'm in London.[74]

Noël Coward's antics in *London Calling!* had quite unsettled Edith. When there was talk of performing *Façade* at Oxford later in 1923, she had written to Harold Acton:

> . . . I am feeling miserably disappointed. I've seen Osbert, who tells me it is impossible for me to do *Façade* at Oxford. He says in the first place, they have decided to go abroad, which will mean Willie Walton will not be here, – and I cannot manage the music side of it, – also he says that after *London*

69 Sheridan Morley, *A Talent to Amuse: A Biography of Noël Coward*, Heinemann 1969, Penguin Books 1974, revised 1975, 85.
70 Hutchinson & Co., 1924, with a cubist portrait of Miss Whittlebot as frontispiece.
71 C. R. W. Nevinson, *Paint and Prejudice – The Life on an Artist*, Harcourt, Brace & Co. 1938, 234.
72 'Explanatory Preface' to *Collected Sketches and Lyrics by Noël Coward*, 12.
73 *Edith Sitwell: Selected Letters*, edited by John Lehmann and Derek Parker, Macmillan 1970, 31.
74 25 September 1962, *The Noël Coward Diaries* ed. Graham Payne and Sheridan Morley, Weidenfeld & Nicolson 1982, 513–14.

Calling I cannot risk it, as probably little Coward's supporters (being far in excess of intelligent people in number) would flock to the performance to insult me, and that it would be too undignified to expose oneself to it.[75]

There was a sequel to *Façade* of a different kind in the summer of 1927 when the future Labour politician Tom Driberg, in his last term at Oxford, put on a concert misleadingly called 'Homage to Beethoven'. Over an ensemble of four-handed piano, a few strings, some wind instruments and typewriters, to music by Archie Browne he declaimed through a megaphone verses of his own that became increasingly nonsensical as the performance progressed. Oddly enough, that same year the megaphone was to make another stage appearance. The Sitwell brothers rather unwisely tried their hands in Coward territory by writing and performing in a play called *First Class Passengers* for five nights at the Arts Theatre Club in November 1927 when *Façade* was also performed. With designs by Cecil Beaton, it was set aboard a transatlantic liner with, in Act 2, the three Sitwells, appearing on stage as guests at a cabaret party, declaiming poems through a megaphone.[76] Were they at last able to laugh at themselves?

The next performance of *Façade* did not take place until 27 April 1926 (a week before the start of the General Strike) when it was given at the New Chenil Galleries in Chelsea, in a further revised form and at the much later time of 8.45 p.m. Again there were eight groups but this time twenty-five poems and with a short interval, the second half beginning with a repeat of the Fanfare and an 'Introduction'. Edith did not always find it easy to keep in time with the music, and on this occasion, according to Osbert, she decided 'only to recite a few of the slower poems' while an Old Vic actor, Neil Porter, declaimed the remainder of the verses.[77] Yet Osbert's memory may have been unreliable and changes could have been made between rehearsal and performance because Constant Lambert wrote to his mother: 'Façade was great fun. I ended up by doing about half the programme. The house was very crowded and most enthusiastic.'[78] The re-numbering for this performance on

---

75 John Lehmann and Derek Parker (eds), *Selected Letters*, 29–30.
76 Sarah Bradford, *Splendours and Miseries*, 173. Though the trio were alluded to in the text, their appearance was omitted when the play was printed as *All at Sea* in *All at Sea: A Social Tragedy in Three Acts for First Class Passengers Only*, Duckworth 1927.
77 *Laughter in the Next Room*, 200 (214).
78 Lambert arrived in Monte Carlo two or three days before the première of his ballet *Romeo and Juliet* on 4 May 1926. The letter to his mother, quoted in Shead's *Constant Lambert*, 48, is dated there as May 1926. This would seem to suggest that, contrary to Osbert's statement, Lambert was co-reciter at that April performance. Yet photographs (most likely taken on a rehearsal day) show the Sitwells, Walton and Porter (with Sengerphone) outside the Chenil Galleries. Newman's *Sunday Times* review does not identify the reciter(s), only stating that 'someone (was it Osbert?) declaimed Miss Sitwell's poems'. *The Times* review of 29 April is not revealing. It is possible that either Edith or Porter withdrew at the last moment and Lambert stepped in. Andrew Motion,

some of the surviving manuscripts of the poems in Lambert's familiar red pencil would seem to confirm his participation.[79] He was also involved in another way. According to the published score, one of the seven new numbers, 'Four in the Morning', had been written 'In collaboration with C[onstant] L[ambert]' who is said to have been responsible for the first eleven bars. Whoever it was on this occasion that actually recited the verses, the *Musical Opinion* critic sneered at what was 'like a cavalry-galloping exercise over cobblestones, a purely physical thrill to an accompaniment of broken and perverted rhythms' which 'served as an excuse for drawing into one hall most of the men who look like women and the women who dress and crop like men in Chelsea!' That number included Augustus John, Arnold Bennett, the painter Nina Hamnett with the writer Jack Lindsay, and the wealthy young Allanah Harper with a new adherent to the Sitwell circle, Cecil Beaton, who wrote in his diary:

> The Chenil Galleries were crowded with arty people and not a seat to be had in the place. There were masses of people standing and we had to stand. Everyone seemed very thrilled and expectant: the artiness of the place was terrific. Half the audience seemed nicely arty and the other half merely revoltingly arty. The poems started. They were recited through a megaphone put through a hole in a painted scene representing a face, and they were accompanied by modern music by Walton. I rather liked the music. I rather liked the poems but I felt too restless to settle down properly to understand them. There were too many distractions – arty people moving about and arty people in the outer room talking too loud. I found the programme much too long and monotonous and didn't bother or couldn't concentrate to listen to the poems towards the end. The reception was extremely friendly and enthusiastic and the Sitwells were only too delighted to give repeated encores.[80]

Arnold Bennett, in his diary, wrote: 'Crowds of people, snobs, high-brows, low-brows, critics and artists and decent folk. I enjoyed this show greatly. The verses are distinguished; the music (Walton) equally so. The "scene" (flat) by Frank Dobson was admirable.'[81]

One of the most enthusiastic members of the audience was Dora Stevens, the future wife of Hubert Foss, music editor for Oxford University Press –

---

in *The Lamberts: George, Constant and Kit*, Chatto & Windus 1986, Hogarth Press 1987, 147, confirms that 'he shared with Edith the narration at the first official performance [sic] at the Chenil Galleries'.

[79] See Stewart Craggs, *William Walton: A Source Book*, Scolar Press 1993.

[80] Beaton's original diary entry, in Hugo Vickers, *Cecil Beaton: The Authorized Biography*, Weidenfeld & Nicolson 1985, 70, which differs slightly from the published version in *Cecil Beaton's Diaries: 1922–1939 The Wandering Years*, Weidenfeld & Nicolson 1961, 89–90.

[81] Quoted in Osbert Sitwell, *Laughter in the Next Room*, 200–201 (214).

soon to become Walton's publishers. On the strength of the reviews of the first public performance, she had bought tickets for five of the best seats for her family. She was aware that it was a 'portentous occasion . . . the scintillating music, spiky and brittle, combined with the enchanting poems, with their wit and coloured words seemed to me completely fascinating and I was entirely captivated. William came on to receive the wild applause. Pale, willowy and shy apparently, but rather appealing and charming withal, he made his bows.'[82] A strong friendship soon developed between Walton and the Fosses.

This time there was no need for the Sitwells to hide away from the public. Instead, they were off to a party afterwards at the Eiffel Tower restaurant. But most important of all, the Entertainment received a public blessing in the *Sunday Times* from the doyen of critics, Ernest Newman, who – in spite of the uncomfortable chairs – clearly enjoyed himself thoroughly:

> A jolly good entertainment it was in many ways. . . . How much I enjoyed the fun may be estimated from the fact that I – a critic – actually not only stayed to the end but added my voice and my umbrella to the clamour for encores of the best items long after the official proceedings were finished. . . . The entertainment owed a great deal also to Mr Walton's music. All I knew of this young man's before Tuesday was a horrible quartet of his that was given at the Royal College three or four years ago. On the strength of this, I take leave to dislike intensely Mr Walton's serious music – if, indeed, that quartet *was* serious and *was* music, both of which I doubt. But as a musical joker he is a jewel of the first water. . . . Here is obviously a humorous musical talent of the first order. . . . Mr Walton ought to seek out a librettist after his own heart and give us a little musical comedy in the jazz style.[83]

For the next *Façade* performance a month later, at the same time on 29 June, also given at the New Chenil Galleries, there were further revisions, with twenty-five poems arranged in seven groups. This time Lambert, as well as helping as copyist, was the sole reciter, with Walton conducting as before. In a radio broadcast, Walton remembered Constant coming round after one of the early performances of *Façade* and saying: ' "Of course you made a great mistake. You ought to have had me reciting it." . . . And the next time we did, in 1925 or 6, *he* did it and of course it was a roaring success and he recited marvellously.'[84] Lambert came into his own as the reciter for *Façade*. Walton,

---

82 From Dora Foss, 'Memoirs of Walton'. Dora Foss's 'Memoirs' do not, unfortunately, solve the question as to who recited the poems. Dora's daughter, Diana Sparkes, reads extracts from the memoirs on a CD of songs and readings, *Hubert Foss and his Friends*, HJF001CD (1998).

83 2 May 1926, reprinted in *Essays from the World of Music* selected by Felix Aprahamian, Volume One, John Calder 1956, 101–4.

84 BBC Sound Archives recording used in the documentary *An Extraordinary Relation-*

who admired his 'clear, rapid, incisive, tireless' voice with its 'extraordinary range of inflection', said that Constant 'always adored doing *Façade* and he maintained that he was by far the best interpreter – in which I agree with him. . . . He would build in imitations of friends, common acquaintances and so on, and you never quite knew who he was going to be imitating . . . though one remembers, in the last number . . . he used this curious, rather sinister hissing voice that Professor Edward Dent, the Cambridge Professor of Music, used.'[85] Richard Shead, Lambert's first biographer, has written that 'by the 1940s Lambert's interpretation and his voice had deepened, and he had also acquired the habit of introducing at what he conceived to be appropriate points imitations of such persons as Winston Churchill, John Ireland and the late Professor Dent – "moving in classical metres" in "When Sir Beelzebub" was recited in Lambert's "Dent" voice.'[86]

Present at the third public performance of *Façade* was Serge Diaghilev who, only the previous evening, had inserted *Portsmouth Point* as an interlude into his season of ballets. He apparently told Sachie that, good as it was, Walton's music had shades of Elgar in it.[87]

Constant Lambert was the reciter when *Façade* received its first European performance at the ISCM Festival in Siena in September 1928. Osbert wrote of him that 'in Paris, The Hague, London and Siena, Constant Lambert, possessed of so many rare gifts, has proved himself to have yet one more: to be the perfect instrument of this performance, a speaker *sans pareil* of the verse, clear, rapid, incisive, tireless, and commanding vocally an extraordinary range of inflection, from menace and the threat of doom to the most debonair and jaunty inconsequence.'[88] His unique interpretation was fortunately preserved when, on 28 November 1929,[89] he and Edith made the celebrated recording of eleven numbers for the Decca Record Company in the New Chenil Galleries,[90] with Walton conducting. Certainly no subsequent recording – and one may dare suggest performance – has quite matched these performers, and no-one has equalled Lambert's faultless delivery of the fast section of the *Tango–Pasodoble*. Walton himself considered it 'the best

---

ship broadcast by BBC Radio 3 on 31 May 1990 and repeated on 29 August 1991. NSA B5928/07.

85 Andrew Motion, *The Lamberts: George, Constant and Kit*, 147–8.
86 Richard Shead, *Constant Lambert*, 142.
87 Sarah Bradford, *Splendours and Miseries*, 158.
88 Osbert Sitwell, *Laughter in the Next Room*, 197 (210–11).
89 There were two earlier recording sessions, on 12 July and 13 August, but the 'takes' from the third session were those issued. For each occasion Walton received 10 guineas, and Lambert and Edith Sitwell (who was not present on 13 August) 5 guineas. See Alan Poulton, *The Recorded Works of Sir William Walton: A Discography*, Bravura 1980, 22–5.
90 The New Chenil Galleries were used by Decca in its early years as a recording studio.

recording there is; [Lambert's] performance is the best I've ever had or ever shall have.'[91]

The first complete broadcast (eighteen poems in six groups) took place on 3 March 1930 at Central Hall, Westminster. The reciters on that occasion were Edith and Constant. Walton wrote beforehand to Edward Clark: 'Each group should be announced by a separate voice and Constant will tell you anything you want to know about the conduct of the performance. It should last about 25 to 30 minutes. The balance between the voices and the music should be about equal, if anything with the music slightly dominating.'[92] For conductor Walton recommended Leslie Heward who had been present at the Decca recording sessions.

Edith recorded *Façade* twice again, complete for Decca in 1954 with Peter Pears as co-reciter and Anthony Collins conducting, and in America on 21 January 1949 with Frederick Prausnitz conducting. This last recording followed a public performance at the Museum of Modern Art, New York, during Edith and Osbert's triumphant American lecture tour when they were fêted by the national press. She found, however, that at the age of 61 she could no longer manage that rapid staccato in the *Tango–Pasodoble* without stumbling, and so Osbert's close friend and companion, David Horner, stepped in for that one number for the performance and the subsequent recording.[93] Walton himself made only one other commercial recording of *Façade*, in May 1969,[94] when the speakers were Peggy Ashcroft and Paul Schofield, dubbing their parts onto the pre-recorded track. But it is Edith's first two recordings, especially the one with Lambert, that are unmatched and which surely represent *Façade* in the spirit in which it was initially performed. In more recent performances and recordings the reciters (who are sometimes singers rather than actors) try to characterise their readings too much and do not present the verses for what they were intended: exercises in sound and rhythm.

In January 1947 Lambert recited *Façade* on the Third Programme after conducting his own Piano Concerto (which he had originally designed as a companion piece to *Façade*).[95] Drink and overwork were taking their toll of

---

91 *Remembering Constant Lambert*, BBC, 23 August 1975.

92 1 January 1930, from Amalfi. Letters to Edward Clark, BL Add. 52257 fols 139–148b.

93 There are other divergences: the recording omits *Tarantella*, and the order of the movements is nearer to the 'definitive version' of 1942 than the published score of 1951.

94 Archive recordings exist of Walton conducting public performances of *Façade* in 1965 and 1973.

95 Humphrey Searle, who produced the broadcast, wrote in his memoirs: 'One of the BBC programmes which I asked Constant to do involved his conducting his Concerto for Piano and 7 instruments, a rather neglected work which is one of his best, though it is not easy to perform, and also doing the speaking part in the Sitwell–Walton "Façade" entertainment, of which he did several performances about that time. As all programmes still went out live, I asked Edith Sitwell to give a talk about the *Façade*

Lambert, causing Walton to request the BBC that, if another performance were to be given, 'could it be put on by itself & with no concerto or speech beforehand? Either the Concerto or Façade, but not both, as C. L. was obviously so exhausted by his exertions on the former, as to be at times almost incoherent. And he can do it so well especially if he has been on a diet of bread & water, at any rate on the latter if not the former.'[96] When on 10 December 1948 Lambert recited *Façade* again, it was given on its own (with a recorded repeat in January 1949, Leighton Lucas conducting in both broadcasts). This may have encouraged Desmond Orland of the BBC to write to Walton on 25 July 1950 that the Third Programme was 'anxious to make a [final[97]] authoritative recording with Constant Lambert as speaker and yourself as conductor of *Façade*', adding a distinguished list of suggested players: Edward Walker (flute), Bernard Walton (clarinet), Wilfred Hambleton (bass clarinet), Walter Lear (alto saxophone), Harold Jackson (trumpet), James Blades (percussion) and Raymond Clark (cello). On 1 August Walton, then very busy with his opera *Troilus and Cressida*, replied: 'I should be delighted. . . . At the moment I'm preparing the work for publication and as soon as a new set of parts is out we could begin to consider about dates. I'll let you know about this later on.' But it was not to be; Lambert died on 21 August 1951. When the score was eventually published, in the year of Lambert's death, it was fittingly dedicated to him.

Soon after the first public performance of *Façade* in 1923, Walton planned to extract five of the numbers, group them under the title *Bucolic Comedies* and provide orchestral accompaniments. It is not known how far he progressed with them, but in 1932 three songs – *Daphne* (a new setting of the poem that had been part of the Entertainment from the first public performance up to a 1930 broadcast), *Through Gilded Trellises* and *Old Sir Faulk* – were published with piano accompaniment and first performed by the dedicatees, Dora and Hubert Foss, who recorded them in 1940. The original Entertainment meanwhile went through a process of constant revision, with both the poems and their grouping changing from performance to performance (see Appendix 4), as did the overall shape and character, before reaching a definitive version for the 1942 Aeolian Hall presentation. This became the published edition in 1951 (but with the numbers in a different order), lasting about forty minutes. In 1936 Lambert, describing the changes that *Façade* was then still going through, wrote of the original Entertainment as dating from what he called Walton's Central European period (in which he included the early String Quartet). In keeping with what Angus Morrison called the

poems in the interval while Constant took a short but necessary rest.' *Quadrille with a Raven*, Internet.

96 Letter to George Barnes, Head of Third Programme, 31 January 1947. BBC Written Archives, Caversham.

97 The word 'final' was ominously added in an internal memo.

more Schoenbergian numbers, 'the instruments were mainly occupied by complicated arabesques and the melodic interest was slight.' The then current version, however, was 'one good tune after another and each number a gem of stylisation or parody.' He went on to add: 'What distinguishes Walton's parodies from the comic polkas and waltzes of Stravinsky or Milhaud is that he can "guy" a type of music and yet write good music at the same time. The waltz in *Façade* is an excellent waltz, the tarantella is an excellent tarantella. Theirs is not the obvious humour of a lampoon but the far more subtle humour of a Beerbohm parody. They are not only like the originals but ridiculously like.'[98]

At the time of his seventy-fifth birthday Walton was persuaded to return to the original version and assemble eight of the unpublished numbers, with the original Fanfare, into a group called *Façade Revived* which was performed at a special birthday concert in London on 25 March 1977.[99] Charles Mackerras conducted and Richard Baker was the reciter. This highlighted the more astringent nature of some of the early settings. After a second performance (that was broadcast), conducted by Colin Davis in the Queen Elizabeth Hall on 3 June the same year with Cathy Berberian and Richard Baker the reciters, Walton revised and reshaped the group, renaming it *Façade 2: A Further Entertainment*. He rejected three numbers, replacing them with new ones, and inserting a brief Flourish instead of the Fanfare. This had its first performance at The Maltings, Snape on 19 June 1979 with Steuart Bedford conducting and Peter Pears reciting.[100] Subsequently, Cathy Berberian and Robert Tear recorded both *Façade 2* and *Façade* with Steuart Bedford at Snape, the LP being issued by Oxford University Press together with a facsimile of the autograph score of *Façade 2* (dedicated 'To Cathy Be[r]berian') and a booklet containing the texts for *Façade*.

Façade can now be appreciated for its extraordinary range of wit, ingenuity and skill, a work that grew as rapidly as Walton developed as a composer. It spawned numerous versions, from its original form for recitation by one speaker (later two), to ballet scores, two suites for orchestra, and versions for solo piano, piano duet and two pianos. A ballet based on the First Orchestral Suite was given in September 1929 in Hagen to choreography by Günter Hess, conducted by Georg Lippert. Frederick Ashton's version was first performed in London on 26 April 1931 by the Camargo Society that had

---

98 Constant Lambert, 'Some Angles of the Compleat Walton', *Radio Times*, 7 August 1936, 13. Printed in full as Appendix 1.

99 One of them, *Herodiade's Flea*, had already been revived in the BBC 2 *Counterpoint* Walton seventieth-birthday programme on 29 March 1972, with John Amis reciting and Marcus Dods conducting the Nash Ensemble. Much revised, it was re-named *Came the Great Popinjay* for use in *Façade 2*.

100 A recording of this performance, broadcast on 9 October 1979, exists in the BBC Sound Archives, MT40230.

been created to fill the vacuum left by Diaghilev's death in 1929. Ashton had heard a performance of the Entertainment and would have choreographed his ballet to the original version had not Edith refused to have anything to do with it. So he used instead the First Orchestral Suite, only to find out later while staying at Renishaw that Edith regretted her refusal and wished after all to be associated with the ballet. The wit implicit in the music was made explicit on stage with some humorous invention, and Ashton's version was an instant success. 'It's successful in what I set out to do – which was a parody of dances at the time,' he commented many years later.[101] It had a distinguished cast that included Lydia Lopokova, Alicia Markova, Anthony Tudor and Ashton himself. Constant Lambert conducted. The Camargo Society's successor, the Vic–Wells Ballet, staged *Façade* in October 1935 with Margot Fonteyn, Robert Helpmann and Frederick Ashton, and Lambert once again conducting. It has since rarely been out of the repertoire for any length of time. It was first seen through the new medium of television on 8 December 1936, with Fonteyn and Helpmann dancing and Walton conducting the BBC TV Orchestra. It was repeated two days later. In July 1972 at the Aldeburgh Festival, the Royal Ballet New Group performed *Façade* as Ashton had first intended, using the original version, and with Peter Pears as reciter. Another notable ballet version was that choreographed by John Cranko for the Würtenberg State Theatre in March 1961.

The First Orchestral Suite of five numbers was premièred, with Walton conducting, during a season of the *Ballets Russes* in December 1926. For this brilliant transcription, in addition to several small changes, the *Tarantella-Sevillana* was considerably lengthened. The Second Suite, of six numbers, with the *Noche Espagnole* (originally *Long Steel Grass*) and the aptly named *Popular Song*[102] similarly extended, had its première in New York on 30 March 1938, with Barbirolli conducting the New York Philharmonic-Society Orchestra. It was given in London at the Proms on 10 September 1938 with Sir Henry Wood conducting. Lambert's close association with *Façade* in so many different ways made him the ideal consultant in the assembling of the second suite. As Hubert Foss wrote to him in November 1936:

> Willie and I were talking about Facade Second Suite today. I am keen to go on with it but I am not quite sure what numbers to publish in it. It appears that the only numbers that you use at Sadler's Wells which are not in the First Suite are Fanfare, which Willie does not want, I gather, to perpetuate, 'Scotch Rhapsody', a popular song and 'Country Dance'. Is this so? If so, I

---

101 In conversation with Clement Crisp, BBC Third Programme, 21 March 1963.
102 This became widely known through its use as the signature tune for BBC TV's *Face the Music*, a light-hearted quiz programme on which Walton appeared as a guest in March 1972.

think we must find at least two other numbers to make a reasonable suite. So far Willie can only think of 'The Man from the Far Countree'. Let us meet and discuss this soon. I much want your advice.[103]

Both Walton and Lambert recorded the two suites for the gramophone: Lambert with the Philharmonia in 1950, and Walton twice, with the London Philharmonic Orchestra in 1936 and 1938, and with the Philharmonia in 1955 and 1957. Of his two recordings the earlier is marginally the finer. The Orchestre Raymonde conducted by 'G. Walter' (Walter Goehr) recorded four movements as arranged by Goehr. Walton himself made one arrangement from *Façade* for piano, of the *Valse*. All other piano arrangements were made by others, including Roy Douglas, Matyas Seiber, Herbert Murrill and Lambert. In one version or another, *Façade* has ensured that Walton's name would remain before the musical public.

In August 1939 *Façade* drew some unwanted attention when it was discovered that the well-known song 'I do Like to Be Beside the Seaside'[104] quoted in *Tango–Pasodoble* was still in copyright. Glover-Kind's tune had been published in 1909 and its unauthorised treatment came to the attention of its publisher. A few weeks later Walton wrote to Foss:

> I saw Mr. Feldman on Tuesday and managed to calm him down somewhat. In fact, barring a certain animosity against OUP generally he couldn't have been sweeter and we got on like a house on fire. He was perfectly willing to discuss sharing the proceeds on the one piece only & in fact doesn't want to take any royalty or anything that doesn't strictly belong to him. What had got his goat was that three months had elapsed without him yet having seen the figures we promised to send him. . . . I think that not receiving the figures made him a bit suspicious we are concealing something for he produced his own royalty sheet for what 'I do like to be etc.' produced in the last three months, a large sum of about £125 & I vaguely think he thinks we are getting the same. How I wish we were![105]

Things did not go quite so sweetly as Walton was hoping. In an OUP memo Foss reported a telephone call in which Walton had said he was anxious to avoid the publicity. 'I told him that any payment must be made by him, not by us. The conservation was cut off. . . .' In May 1940 it was finally settled by recourse to arbitration, with Feldman receiving ⅓ of ⅕ of all Walton's payments under his royalty agreement on *Façade Suite No. 1* from the date of its publication and the same amount on all future royalties, with the sum of £25 in acknowledgement of the infringement. This last figure was met by OUP and Sir Humphrey Milford, head of the firm, was furious. 'Confound

---

103 Hubert Foss to Constant Lambert, 14 November 1936; OUP files.
104 In the score the title of the song is printed as the sub-title to that movement.
105 Walton to Hubert Foss, 5 September 1939: OUP files.

(and any stronger word you can find to use) the Walton case,' he wrote to Foss. 'Why should I be blackmailed into paying £25 just because Walton had been stupid and obstinate throughout about the whole affair?'[106] This was not to be Walton's only unintentional copyright infringement.

[106] Humphrey Milford to Hubert Foss, 6 June 1940: OUP files.

4

The White Hope of British Music

In the spring of 1920 the Sitwell brothers took Walton by train to Italy for the first time. The previous year he had been sent down from Oxford, having failed Responsions after three attempts. Perhaps the benevolent Sitwells felt that travel would do him good. Dr Strong was quite likely of the same opinion, as he gave the errant undergraduate some financial assistance for the journey. It was in fact Walton's first time abroad. It rained all the way through France, but emerging through the Alpine tunnels they found Italy bathed in sunlight. 'There was suddenly a blinding flash and one was in Italy and there was sun everywhere. It has remained with me always, that first sight of Italy.'[1] He could hardly have realised then that Italy would in due course become his home. Having turned his back on Oldham, as he was soon to turn his back on Oxford, eventually he would leave England and settle there permanently. On this, his first encounter with the country he was to grow to love, he stayed with the Sitwells in Amalfi. They took rooms – or cells – in the white-walled Hotel Cappuccini Convento that clung about half-way up to the town's cliff edge with splendid views from its terraces across the Gulf of Salerno. Once a monastery, dating back to the thirteenth century, in 1821 it was converted to a hotel approached by a steep pathway, although visitors today have the easier access of an external lift that was installed for Mussolini's visits. There Walton learned to settle into the routine of what would be their working holidays, with the three of them meeting for lunch and for dinner, but otherwise retiring to their individual cells during the day; Osbert and Sachie would be writing and William composing. On this first holiday he was finishing his Piano Quartet,[2] which he dedicated to Dr Strong. Osbert remembered that William

---

[1] BBC 2 interview with John Warrack, printed in the *Listener*, 8 August 1968, 177.
[2] As the original version of the quartet is said to have been completed in Oxford, work at Amalfi may have concerned revisions rather than completion. When the score later resurfaced, it was further revised.

spent most of the time by himself in a room containing a typical South Italian piano. . . . Here he would sit composing and copying out at a large table facing a window on the cloister, the whiteness of which in the sun filled the smoky air with a redoubled and spectral light; he would hardly move except to go to the window-ledge from time to time, where he would cut a Toscana cigar in two with a safety-razor blade he kept for that purpose. He smoked these half-cigars almost always as he wrote.[3]

In June he was back at Oxford to sit the second part of his BMus – successfully as it turned out. The Michaelmas Term, starting in October, was his last. Then, not long after taking up residence with the Sitwells, he had his first London performance. On 4 March 1921 the two movements that origi-nally comprised his first String Quartet were played at the first concert of the London Contemporary Music Centre. The violist was Bernard Shore, who was later to give Walton some advice on the Viola Concerto. Shore remem-bered how Hugh Allen brought 'a pale and thin young man' to the Royal College of Music and requested a play-through of his quartet. After they had left, the work came in for some biting remarks: 'After all, it's only like a Beethoven quartet with all the instruments playing in different keys!' 'And played backwards!'[4]

That spring Walton went south again with the Sitwells, staying this time at Rapallo where they met Max Beerbohm, before going on to Florence, where they called on Aldous Huxley and his wife. (Huxley was soon to be out of favour when he unflatteringly portrayed Osbert under the thin disguise of Lord Badgery, 'patron of men of letters, of painters, and musicians', in his short story *The Tillotson Banquet*. In the autumn of 1922 Osbert retaliated in the short story *The Machine Breaks Down*, his first attempt at prose writing, by casting Huxley in the character of the writer Erasmus. It may well have been a private joke to give Erasmus, who is travelling with the narrator on his first visit to Italy, the first name of William.) Towards the end of the year there were busy preparations for *Façade* that was to have its first two private performances the following January and February.

In September 1922 the Sitwell brothers[5] and Walton were together in Germany, and in Munich they came across Berners and Sassoon, who was travelling with his lover, Prince Philipp of Hesse (to whom he refers in his diaries merely as 'P'). Sassoon, who had been a guest at Renishaw the pre-vious summer, was now in the middle of a feud with the Sitwells that lasted until July 1924, and when they happened to dine at the same restaurant, Osbert and Sachie made a point of speaking to Berners but ignoring Siegfried.

---

3   Osbert Sitwell, *Laughter in the Next Room*, 141 (153).
4   Bernard Shore, *Sixteen Symphonies*, Longmans 1949, 366.
5   Sassoon wrote of seeing 'the three Sitwells and Willie Walton' in Germany, but Edith almost certainly was not there. *Siegfried Sassoon Diaries, 1920–22* edited Rupert Hart-Davis, Faber & Faber 1981, 254.

Sassoon had already incurred Edith's displeasure in 1920 by seeing into print a collection of his friend Wilfred Owen's poems, when she felt that Owen was her own discovery after producing the 1919 memorial edition of *Wheels* that contained seven of his poems. Now it was Sassoon's turn to feel piqued. Osbert had ridiculed two of his friends in 'a silly and badly-written satire' printed in the 1921 issue of *Wheels*, and as a result he had not 'seen or spoken to any Sitwells since November 7th [1921]. . . . What a brilliant, disintegrating family they are! And why can't they just be a little different, just a little more tolerant and human and free from their perennial spirit of mockery?' he recorded in his diary.[6] 'O.S. seems incapable of any generous appreciation of anyone except his own family and intimates. Everything he writes leaves an impression of *spite* against everyone who doesn't flatter him.'[7] In October Sassoon 'caught sight of' them again in Venice where they were staying for a fortnight on the Grand Canal before going on to Naples and Sicily. In Venice they also met Wyndham Lewis who was with Nancy Cunard, and Walton inadvertently became the subject of an artists' challenge, as Lewis recalled:

> Osbert and Sacheverell Sitwell were both there, the pleasant corpulence of the former vibrating to the impact of his own and Hugo [Rumbold]'s[8] pleasantries; Sacheverell with the look of sedate alarm which at that period was characteristic of him. We would meet in the café every day. . . . An impromptu combat was arranged in the café one night, when an Italian painter challenged me to a match of draughtsmanship. Egged on by the Sitwells, I took him on. William Walton – now the premier composer of Britain – was the object chosen for the exercise of our skill. Walton sat with his head on the plush back of the seat and we drew him. I won this match hands down.[9]

At about that time Wyndham Lewis was involved in a projected one-act ballet, *Dr Syntax*, devised by him and Sachie, for which Lewis was to provide the scenario and Walton the music. Whether or not this was related to the similarly named 'pedagogic overture' of 1920–21, nothing came of either. Only the title page exists in holograph and there is no evidence of any music having been composed. The score was intended for Diaghilev, but its chances of success in that direction were slim because Diaghilev showed no liking for Lewis's work when it was brought to his attention by Sachie. The project may

---

6   *Ibid*, 103 and 255.
7   2 June 1923, *Siegfried Sassoon Diaries, 1923–25*, ed. Rupert Hart-Davis, Faber & Faber 1985, 33.
8   Hugo Rumbold was a stage-designer.
9   Wyndham Lewis, *Blasting and Bombardiering: An Autobiography (1914–1926)*, Eyre & Spottiswoode 1937, revised edition Calder 1982, 234. Wyndham Lewis's drawing of Osbert and Sacheverell is reproduced in the National Portrait Gallery's catalogue *The Sitwells*, 1994, reprinted 1996, 103.

have got no further than the 'wonderful satiric mask in the style of Dr Syntax' that Sachie remembered Wyndham Lewis painting on a wall in his London studio.[10]

After Venice it was back to work as usual, and at Amalfi, on 23 November 1922, Walton finished revising his [First] String Quartet, adding a middle scherzo movement. On 5 July the following year it received its first performance at another London Contemporary Music Centre concert, this time at the Royal College of Music, when it was played by the young all-female McCullagh String Quartet, who took it a month later to the International Society for Contemporary Music Festival in Salzburg (and who were also to première the Piano Quartet in 1924). Walton and the Sitwell brothers travelled there to attend the concert, and Lord Berners, whose *Valses Bourgeoises* were also to be performed at the Festival, was much in evidence. The quartet, lasting about thirty-five minutes, was placed at the end of an already long programme and, the *Times* critic wrote, 'the lengthy treatment in the scherzo of an apparently meaningless figure of two notes lost the attention of the hall and this was never regained'. Earlier, a moment of humour had been injected into the concert when the cellist's prong became embroiled in the mechanism that worked the platform's trapdoor. To the audience's amusement the players started to descend from view.

Walton later withdrew the quartet, dismissing it as an unsuccessful venture into atonal music. He was, as he owned up in a radio interview with the broadcaster John Amis, 'no good at counting – I can't add up – can't get my mathematics right'. But he did single out the scherzo as 'one rather good movement'.[11] It was not until after his death that the work was performed again, in October 1990 at Swansea, by the Gabrieli Quartet who recorded it soon afterwards.[12]

Even if the quartet made little impact, having his name on the programme of a prestigious Continental festival was an important step for Walton. It was at this Festival that he met Hindemith for the first time. And there was also the opportunity for rarer meetings: with Alban Berg and Arnold Schoenberg. Osbert recalled:

> Berg greeted Walton as the leader of English atonal music, and took him, with Berners [who acted as interpreter], to see Schoenberg, living near one of the neighbouring lakes. They found the austere master composing at a piano, but were quickly hurried out of the room, and when they returned all signs of work had been hidden. . . .[13]

10 Prologue to *Gala Performance*, 31.
11 Interview with John Amis, recorded in Ischia, 18 February 1972, BBC Radio 3 broadcast, 17 March 1972. BBC Sound Archives LP34276.
12 Chandos CHAN8944, a recording made with the assistance of the William Walton Trust.
13 Osbert Sitwell, *Laughter in the Next Room*, 182 (194–5).

Walton's only other chamber work of this period was a Toccata for Violin and Piano which followed soon after the String Quartet, both belonging to what might be called Walton's 'experimental' phase. Constant Lambert, describing it as a rhapsodical work, found in it traces of Bartók and Sorabji and suggested that it had 'greater and more genuine vitality than the String Quartet'.[14] Although it was heard at another London Contemporary Music Centre concert in May 1925 (with Walton's friend Angus Morrison as the pianist), it was later withdrawn. Looking at the work again over sixty years later Morrison wrote: 'I have always remembered it as being very compli-cated – but it seems to me even more so now than it did at the time.'[15] It is a substantial work, lasting nearly a quarter-of-an-hour. The solo violin's exoti-cism suggests Szymanowski, but the piano's virtuosity in places certainly recalls Sorabji, whether as a result of hearing the composer himself privately play through his Sonata No. 2 or because of a possible acquaintance with Sorabji's own *Toccata*, for solo piano published in 1920.[16]

Plans for a visit to Spain in the autumn of 1924 had to be put aside because Osbert went down with gastric 'flu, and Walton's father was dangerously ill; he died that November. But another incident that year had threatened to break up the Sitwell trio and even pose a question over Walton's future with them. Sacheverell had fallen in love with a beautiful eighteen-year-old Canadian girl, Georgia Doble, whom he was soon to marry. In September Walton, the poet Arthur Waley[17] and Gerald Berners were guests at Weston Hall, the Sitwell house in Northamptonshire that became Sachie's in 1927. Georgia was invited, and Sachie and 'Dear Willie' would meet her at the station. She stayed for three days in her future home. In December William, Osbert and Sachie were back at Rapallo, though the brothers were trying desperately to keep their presence there a secret from their parents, more particularly from Sir George in case he should suddenly turn up. 'For Heaven's sake don't say where we are,' Sachie wrote to his future wife, 'they think we are at Cap d'Ail. Also don't talk about Weston too much; or about poor little Willie, whom they hate.'[18] Within twenty-four hours of arriving, they met Beerbohm and Ezra Pound, and several days later they were being driven at breakneck

14 *Boston Evening Transcript*, 27 November 1926 (see Appendix One).
15 Letter, 29 October 1987, to Bruce Phillips of OUP, in Stewart R. Craggs, *William Walton: A Catalogue*, second edition OUP 1990, 38.
16 The *Toccata* was revived at the 1998 Walton Festival in Oldham by Paul Barritt and Catherine Edwards who gave the work's first broadcast on 8 May the same year. The Chandos recording made in 1992 by Kenneth Sillito and Hamish Milne lacks the first page of the manuscript that was only subsequently discovered in OUP's archive. It starts instead with the piano trill that seems almost to anticipate the clarinet opening of Gershwin's *Rhapsody in Blue* without its run-up.
17 Arthur Waley is chiefly known for his English translations of Chinese poetry and Japanese Noh plays.
18 Sarah Bradford, *Splendours and Miseries*, 139.

speed across Italy by Sachie's close friend, the artist Richard Wyndham, in his Hispano Suiza, 'with Osbert, Sachie and Walton clinging on for dear life'.[19] They went on to Parma and Bologna, returning to Rapallo on Christmas Eve.

In March 1925, still abroad, they were off to Spain, to Madrid via Genoa, Sachie enigmatically reporting that 'the last few days at beastly Rapallo were enlivened by Willie's conduct with the daughter of an English colonel. . . .'[20] They toured Cordoba, Cadiz and Seville, and then went on to Granada where they were joined not only by Dick Wyndham and Constant Lambert but also by Edith, who was recovering from a recent operation for back trouble. A young Cyril Connolly saw them in the Washington Irving Hotel: 'They were really quite alarming – alarming rather than forbidding. All of them were wearing black capes and black Andalusian hats and looked magnificent. Dick Wyndham was with them and Constant Lambert and Willie Walton. I'd never met them before, but they *seemed* like Sitwells.'[21] Walton was jokingly referred to as Osbert's fag because of the way he was often being asked such things as, 'Oh, Willie, do fetch that book for me.'[22] But this joke led to a coldness between Osbert and Cyril Connolly, who wrote:

> I was in Paris that autumn [1926] and one evening happened to meet William Walton, Constant Lambert and Philip Heseltine. We all got very drunk, and one of them started to insult me, saying I was Desmond MacCarthy's bum-boy. I shouted back that I was no more Desmond's bum-boy than he [i.e. Walton] was Osbert Sitwell's. As I say, it was all very drunken and extremely silly and that, I thought, was that. But word of what happened was duly reported back to Osbert, as always seemed to happen with the Sitwells. They had their hatchet-men who loved to stir up trouble, and shortly afterwards, when I was staying with Harold Nicholson in Berlin, I received a letter from Osbert's solicitor saying that I must instantly withdraw the slanderous accusation I had made or he would sue. Harold advised me how to deal with it, but the affair produced a total coldness between us that lasted for a long, long time.[23]

The writer Peter Quennell treated the incident with the cynicism it deserved: 'I must say Cyril dear it was scarcely tactful to attack the Sitwells so, little Willie of all people. . . . It must have been a diverting evening.'[24]

Osbert's quick rise to Walton's defence (he almost certainly regarded the remark more as a personal slight on himself) does not disguise the fact that for him 'Willie' was often the object of fun and even ridicule. 'I have no

---

[19] *Ibid.*, 139.
[20] *Ibid.*, 142.
[21] John Pearson, *Façades*, 189.
[22] *Ibid.*, 181.
[23] *Ibid.*, 211–12.
[24] Clive Fisher, *Cyril Connolly: A Nostalgic Life*, Macmillan 1985, 100.

news, except a new Willie story, better told, alas, than written,' he wrote to Christabel, with whom he regularly corresponded. And on another occasion: 'Willie is rather excited, because in an effort to give him something to think about, I told him that I'd two grown-up illegitimate sons. He quite believes me. I said they were in the navy.'[25]

In October 1928 Walton's feelings for Christabel were at their most intense, with the Viola Concerto that he was dedicating to her in the throes of composition. She had been staying with the Sitwells at Montegufoni, Sir George's castle near Florence, and while she returned to England, Osbert and William had gone on to Amalfi. Osbert wrote to her soon after their arrival that while he was lying down after luncheon he had heard 'the most pitiful bull-calf bellowings from the next room. I entered it to find the poor imp standing with his head against the wall, howling it – and my head as well – quite off. This I gathered was not unconnected with you but whether it was in the nature of a display of remorse, or whether merely of affection I am unable to decide. It was though, in its way, rather pathetic.' Osbert clearly enjoyed playing the fairy godmother rôle and shrouding in secrecy some of the money gifts that regularly came Walton's way. 'How wonderful and marvellous!' he wrote from Renishaw to Christabel that same year. 'I shall write to Willie and say that there has been an anonymous "donation" of £50', adding a few days later: 'Willie is revelling in his anonymous wealth, bless him, and has quite lost the use of his pen from excitement.'[26]

Walton would quite often accompany the Sitwells on their habitual August stay at Renishaw, their ancestral home in Derbyshire, where Sir George 'appeared to have become more or less detached from the other members of his family, and lived a solitary, self-sufficient life',[27] and Lady Ida spent much time in bed. On his visit in 1925 he experienced the Renishaw ghosts. 'The ghosts are being very active – after Willie at the moment – they played a harp in his bedroom and a number of other tricks last night,' Sachie reported.[28] Of greater moment, however, was Sachie and Georgia's wedding in Paris on 12 October. In the absence of Sir George and Lady Ida, the Sitwell side was represented by Osbert, Edith, Christabel and Walton.

With Sachie married and living at Weston, Walton was without his immediate provider of funds. To his alarm he was met one day with bailiffs from both the Army & Navy Stores and Chappell's demanding the settlement of bills for groceries, gramophone records and the piano hire. 'I know you'll be furious,' he wrote to Sachie. 'Wire brass. I am so contrite about it.'[29]

25 31 October 1928, Amalfi. Letters to Lady C. Aberconway, c. 1924–1961, BL Add. 70831–8.
26 Letters to Lady C. Aberconway, c. 1924–1961, BL Add. 70831–8.
27 Peter Quennell, *The Marble Foot: An Autobiography, 1915–1938*, Collins 1976, 131.
28 21 August 1925; Sarah Bradford, *Splendours and Miseries*, 151.
29 18 October 1925; *ibid.*, 155.

In November he was back in Amalfi where, besides Osbert, Sachie and Georgia, the company included the art historian Adrian Stokes and Peter Quennell who described the working arrangement:

We were each engaged, apart from Georgia, on some arduous creative project and, the hotel having been built as a Capuchin monastery, each of us occupied a separate cell, and only emerged just before luncheon and dinner, when we met in Osbert's sitting-room for conversation and one or two of the anodyne cocktails that were then called White Ladies. Osbert was writing a novel [*Before the Bombardment*, his first novel]; Sachie, weaving the rich autobiographical tapestry of *All Summer in a Day*; Adrian, launching an imaginative expedition into modern art-criticism; William Walton, at work on his latest score, or hammering away at a decrepit upright piano.[30]

If Sachie was now a rarer companion in London, Constant Lambert had become an important figure in Walton's life. He made his mark in 1926 when he took on the rôle of reciter in *Façade*. He was more than three years younger than Walton, but even while still at the RCM the younger composer's output was impressive. By the time Walton was completing his first orchestral score, *Portsmouth Point* in 1925, Lambert had turned out three ballet scores, *Prize-Fight*, *Mr Bear Squash-you-all Flat* and *Adam and Eve*, as well as an early piano concerto. *Mr Bear Squash-you-all Flat*, a one-act ballet based on a Russian children's tale, owes a debt to Stravinsky's *The Soldier's Tale*, while Lambert called his nine-minute satirical *Prize-Fight* a 'realistic ballet' with obvious acknowledgement to Satie's ballet réaliste, *Parade*. Lambert's ballets showed an extraordinary absorption of the new directions being taken by Diaghilev's *Ballets Russes* with which Lambert and Walton were both to try their luck.

Diaghilev, meanwhile, had incurred debts of about £11,000 with his lavish 1921–22 London production of Tchaikovsky's *The Sleeping Princess* that had not been a critical success. Nevertheless, four years later he was pinning his hopes on England for the future success of his company, and hoping to recoup his losses by finding financial backing from wealthy men like the press barons Lord Beaverbrook and Lord Rothermere.[31] To encourage this much-needed support, he was looking for an English ballet subject and to employ English musicians and painters, although he held out little hope that an English composer would provide him with a suitable score. He discussed his scheme with Sacheverell Sitwell who suggested Walton as the most suitable among contemporary British composers. Walton had long wanted to write a ballet for Diaghilev. In the summer of 1925 he had met Diaghilev's protégé, the Russian exile and composer Vladimir Dukelsky, when dining

---

30 *The Marbled Foot*, 142.
31 It was Lord Rothermere who became Diaghilev's financial saviour in England.

with Eugene Goossens, who frequently conducted for the *Ballets Russes* seasons in London. That autumn it was arranged through Dukelsky that he should play his new and as yet unperformed overture *Portsmouth Point* to the impresario at the Savoy Hotel. Walton wanted Lambert to accompany him – whether out of moral support or in the selfless hope that the meeting might also benefit Constant. But Diaghilev had taken an initial dislike to Lambert who had already approached him, boldly inviting him to attend a concert performance of a suite he had arranged from Glinka's *Ruslan and Ludmilla* that he was to conduct at the RCM.[32] Had Lambert's combination of orange shirt and black tie[33] offended Diaghilev's sartorial tastes? Lambert was nevertheless 'smuggled in' to the Savoy audition. As Walton was no pianist, it is no surprise that his playing did nothing to impress Diaghilev with the score. (Diaghilev's dislike of jazz may have been one reason. All the same, Walton wrote to Sachie on 26 November that Diaghilev had praised it as 'a most brilliant, fresh & exhilarating work'.[34]) Lambert then took the opportunity of playing Diaghilev part of his *Adam and Eve* ballet music which produced a more favourable response. 'Are you English?' Diaghilev is reported to have enquired, and when the reply was in the affirmative, he explained: 'That's most surprising. I don't like English music, yet I like your ballet. I'm going to produce it, but not with that silly title.' And he substituted 'Romeo and Juliet' in his big red pencil.[35] Thus *Adam and Eve*, with omissions and additions, became *Romeo and Juliet*, first produced at Monte Carlo on 4 May 1926 while Lambert was still a student at the RCM. It went to Paris a fortnight later, and its London première followed in June.

Angus Morrison remembered another occasion when, undaunted by the failure of Walton's first attempt, efforts were made to woo Diaghilev:

A wonderful luncheon party was given at Carlyle Square – Osbert had a wonderful cook. I lived in Oakley Street which was only a stone's throw away – with two pianos! The idea was they should have a wonderful lunch, a lot of wine, and listen to the music Willy had written the previous autumn, which he later turned into a *Sinfonia Concertante* – not one of his best works – but the three movements were written ostensibly in short score for two pianos, which were samples of what he could have done for the ballet if invited.

So the party took over and Diaghilev always travelled with an entourage,

32 14 July 1925. He repeated the work, also at the Royal College of Music, on 4 December 1925.

33 Richard Buckle, *Diaghilev*, Weidenfeld & Nicolson 1979, 460. In Christopher Wood's splendid 1926 portrait of Lambert, he is wearing a dark blue shirt with red tie.

34 Sarah Bradford, *Splendours and Miseries*, 156. Richard Buckle (in *Diaghilev*, 460) writes that Walton's 'rendering of *Portsmouth Point* left Diaghilev cold'. However, it must have made sufficient an impression for Diaghilev to include it as an entr'acte.

35 Richard Buckle, *Diaghilev*, 460.

Maurice [Cocteau], one or two composers who were in London for the season, and they all went over to my house and Willy and I played these pieces. It was all very carefully arranged. But Diaghilev didn't bite. . . . He made some very charming remarks. I think he said, 'You'll write better things later.' . . . The only person who was politeness and charm itself was Diaghilev, thanking us for letting him come over to hear it. He was wonderfully courteous. All the rest sat around and couldn't have been more bored.[36]

The ballet score intended for Diaghilev that eventually became the *Sinfonia Concertante* was more than likely written in response to Lambert's success with *Adam and Eve*. As Walton remarked much later, he considered that he and Constant were the only two important British composers of his generation, and he would often respond to the challenge posed by the success of another composer. Just as his Piano Quartet was written in response to Howells' Quartet, so in a few years' time he would match the tremendous success of Lambert's choral *The Rio Grande* with *Belshazzar's Feast*. Lambert's Diaghilev commission could not be allowed to pass by unchallenged. But to Walton's great disappointment, Diaghilev's next (and only other) English ballet commission was from Lord Berners, *The Triumph of Neptune* – for which Sacheverell Sitwell provided the scenario. Salt was further rubbed into the wound when Walton was then asked to help with the orchestration of both the Lambert and the Berners ballets. Berners did not have enough time to score *The Triumph of Neptune* himself before its première in London in December 1926, so Walton was called in at the last minute to orchestrate 'four large numbers'.[37] The ballet was a great success with nightly performances, and when it went to Monte Carlo the following year Berners revised it and re-orchestrated it himself.[38] Parody was an essential part of his style, and *The Triumph of Neptune*, with its use of waltz, hornpipe, Schottische and popular song, has much in common with *Façade*. It is also worth pointing out that about six years before Walton began his overture *Portsmouth Point*, Berners had been working on an orchestral score of the same name, possibly intending it as a ballet. While this did not develop very far, a boisterous, dissonant piano sketch lasting about three minutes has survived.[39]

36 Talk to the London University Music Diploma Society at the British Music Information Centre, London, on 25 September 1982. Text printed in the Journal of the British Music Society, *British Music* 15 (1993), 27.
37 Mark Amory, *Lord Berners*, 101. Stewart R. Craggs, in his *William Walton: A Catalogue*, 44, identifies seven numbers as being wholly or partly orchestrated by Walton.
38 Beecham's first recording of a *Triumph of Neptune* suite (seven numbers) made in December 1937 almost certainly used Berners' and not Walton's orchestrations.
39 This was reworked as the last movement of Berners' *L'uomo dai baffi* (*The Man with the Moustache*), music to accompany a marionette show given in Rome in April 1918.

Walton's part with the Lambert score was probably more substantial.[40] Once again Walton was helping out a friend, although how much of the orchestration is actually Lambert's and how much is Walton's is open to question.

For all this disappointment there was some compensation. Diaghilev had had the novel idea of inserting into his programme of ballets what he termed 'symphonic interludes' that consisted of new or unfamiliar orchestral scores.[41] The difficulty at first was to persuade the audience to listen to them instead of talking in their seats or flocking to the bar. The idea was gradually accepted, and in this way, in June 1926, *Portsmouth Point* received its first English performance when Eugene Goossens conducted it as an entr'acte during the London première of Stravinsky's *Les Noces* at His Majesty's Theatre. And when *The Triumph of Neptune* was first staged on 3 December 1926 at the Lyceum Theatre, four of the numbers from the first *Façade* suite similarly provided entr'acte music, this time with Walton himself conducting.

As for the ballet score that he had hoped Diaghilev would accept, in 1927 he rewrote it as a three-movement *Sinfonia Concertante* for piano and orchestra, each movement dedicated, in the published full score, to – and in essence a portrait of – one of his benefactors: 'To Osbert', 'To Edith', and 'To Sachie'. (The dedications were removed when the score was revised in 1943, probably because his relationship with the Sitwells had by then broken off – after some disagreement, according to Angus Morrison.) As if by a family likeness, the three movements are linked thematically. Behind the slightly pompous *maestoso* opening to the first, one may sense Osbert's slight restlessness and occasional outbursts, punctuated here and there with his brilliant conversational chatter. (Was this what the *Musical Times* critic meant by describing the work as 'gossiping music'?) The middle movement is the gem of the piece, its great lyricism offering as fine and warm a portrait of Edith as any of those by Wyndham Lewis, Feliks Topolski, Pavel Tchelitchew or Rex Whistler, while the Stravinskyian sparkle of the finale alludes perhaps to Sachie's fondness for the *Ballets Russes*. The quiet reflective moments are the most impressive of the whole work, and its pervading quality is one of elegance that owes much to its ballet origins. The 1943 revisions consist mainly of thinning out much of the counterpoint, re-scoring several passages, and allowing the solo piano to merge more within the orchestral texture.

---

40 According to Christopher Palmer, in his 'Introduction' to Stewart R. Craggs, *William Walton: A Catalogue*, 3, the orchestral score of Lambert's *Romeo and Juliet* is entirely in the hand of Walton.

41 They were introduced for the first time during the 1919 season and Sacheverell Sitwell occasionally assisted in the selection of the works. See his Prologue in *Gala Performance*, 31. In addition to Walton, the British music represented from 1919 until 1929 included works by Bax, Berners, Bliss, Elgar, Gibson, Goossens, Howells, Lambert and Quilter.

Contemporary with the *Sinfonia Concertante* is the Australian composer and pianist Arthur Benjamin's Concertino for Piano and Orchestra, also of 1927, which owes as much to Gershwin as to Stravinsky (with pre-echoes of the Ravel concertos). But a more interesting comparison can be made between the *Sinfonia Concertante* and Lambert's *Music for Orchestra*, dating from the same year (and dedicated to Berners).[42] Both are neo-classical in form, and the opening of the Lambert work is very close in mood to the *Sinfonia Concertante*. The Walton opens and the Lambert closes with a similar grand rhetorical statement, and *Music for Orchestra* contains a rocking figure very much like the one Walton was to use much later at the start of his Cello Concerto.

Walton avoided the concerto tag by first describing the *Sinfonia Concertante* as being 'for orchestra with piano continuo', changing this to 'with piano obbligato' in the revised version. But its substantial solo element did not stop it from being treated as one, and because of this it was quite frequently performed. For an all-Walton Prom on 11 August 1936 the composer had hoped that the programme would consist of *Portsmouth Point*, the Viola Concerto, the *Façade* Suite (only the first suite then existed) and the (First) Symphony. But because piano concertos were big crowd pullers, Kenneth Wright of the BBC wrote to Walton:

> Our intention . . . was to pack the house for you, which makes for a good concert, great enthusiasm and the general impression to the listeners outside of 'a successful evening'. The Viola Concerto is the least attractive from the point of view of the Promenade public and in view of this I do hope you can agree to forgo purely aesthetic considerations and agree to the programme comprising the Façade Suite, the Sinfonia Concertante with Solomon, some songs and the Symphony.[43]

But Walton got his way and the Viola Concerto prevailed.[44] However the *Sinfonia Concertante* was of sufficient interest and merit for the young Benjamin Britten to buy a copy of the piano score with school prize money in September 1930, and when he had joined the Royal College of Music his piano teacher, Arthur Benjamin, gave it to him to work at in June 1932.

Lambert's famous row with Diaghilev at Monte Carlo over the production of his *Romeo and Juliet*[45] closed the door as far as Lambert was concerned

---

[42] *Music for Orchestra* was first heard in a broadcast on 14 June 1929, conducted by Leslie Heward. Its first public concert performance was at the Proms on 29 August 1929 with Lambert conducting. It was also heard that year during the Diaghilev season.

[43] In Lewis Foreman (ed.), *From Parry to Britten: British Music in Letters, 1900–1945*, Batsford 1987, 190–1.

[44] Walton conducted the first and last works in the programme, *Portsmouth Point* and the Symphony. Henry Wood conducted the Viola Concerto (with William Primrose) and the *Façade* Suite (No. 1). See Lambert's *Radio Times* article in Appendix One.

[45] This was chiefly over Diaghilev's rejection of Christopher Wood's designs. See Richard Shead *Constant Lambert*, 54–8, for the full story.

for further commissions for the *Ballets Russes*. Yet while the Sitwells were creating an imaginary riot instead of the indifference that had greeted *Façade*, when *Romeo and Juliet* went on to Paris it provoked the real thing: a riot directed at the décor, however, rather than the music. Lambert was to have some success elsewhere with another ballet. While Walton was working on his *Sinfonia Concertante*, Lambert had written a pastoral movement, *Champêtre*, which Guy Warrack conducted on 27 October 1926 at one of his Aeolian Hall concerts. With admirable economy, this movement was then incorporated in a seven-movement *Divertimento*, partly written while at Renishaw, that Antony Bernard conducted on 16 November at the Chelsea Music Club. This work, with the addition of a movement from his *Adam and Eve* score, became the ballet *Pomona* which was staged on 9 September 1927 in Buenos Aires. Its first and much praised British performance was on 19 October 1930 as part of the newly formed Camargo Society's first programme. Its neo-classical lines and its clean, economical scoring – post-*Petroushka* Stravinsky – signalled both a considerable advance on *Romeo and Juliet* and a clear divergence from the course that Walton was following.

In the 1920s Lambert and Walton were considered the white hopes of British music. Yet despite – or even because of – Lambert's extraordinarily diverse skills, as a perceptive writer and critic, as a scholar and arranger of other composers' works, as a conductor and a driving force behind British ballet post-Diaghilev, as well as a composer, an occasional broadcaster, and of course as an unsurpassed speaker in *Façade*, his music just lacked the edge that lent distinction to Walton's. In spite of such fine scores as the popular *The Rio Grande* (1927), the choral *Summer's Last Will and Testament* (1935) which Walton rated his masterpiece, and the ballet score *Horoscope* (1937), Lambert wrote nothing to approach either the Viola Concerto or *Belshazzar's Feast*. Heseltine touched on this difference in a letter written in 1930 to fellow composer E. J. Moeran:[46]

> Walton's work improves at every hearing. He is the best musician this country has produced for a long while. Lambert is perhaps more talented, but I do not feel that music is his ultimate mode of expression. His keen observation, sensibility, wit and critical intellect seem rather to point to literature as his medium, whereas Walton is specifically musical or nothing.[47]

Whatever rivalry there may have been between the two, Walton had much to thank Lambert for. Lambert lost no opportunity in promoting Walton's

---

[46] As Moeran's friend Lionel Hill recalled, 'He had a great admiration for Walton, especially his Violin Concerto'; Lionel Hill, *Lonely Waters: The Diary of a Friendship with E. J. Moeran*, Thames Publishing 1985, 61.

[47] Heseltine to Moeran, 6 October 1930, in Lewis Foreman, *From Parry to Britten*, 139.

music, not just merely by reciting *Façade* but also by staging the ballets, making one or two arrangements[48] and conducting many performances. Walton did his share of promotion also. In 1926, when Lambert's Royal College student days were barely over, he wrote to the conductor Edward Clark, who was shortly to conduct *Portsmouth Point*: 'May I take the liberty of recommending to your attention the works of Constant Lambert, particularly a suite, which he's made from "Ruslan".'[49]

There were other bonds. At one time the two composers shared a deep interest in jazz. Lambert became especially fascinated by Negro singing, and Walton recalled 'going night after night with him to hear Florence Mills, that great coloured singer, and to hear Will Vodery's band in Mr Cochran's revue *Dover Street to Dixie*, all of which left its mark when he came to write *The Rio Grande*, the Piano Sonata, the Concerto for piano and seven instruments and the *Elegiac Blues* in memory of Florence Mills.'[50] In 1926, in an article in the *Boston Evening Transcript*, Lambert revealed that 'for more than a year [Walton] did nothing but study jazz, writing and scoring foxtrots for the Savoy Orpheans Band and working at a monumentally planned concerto for two pianofortes, jazz band and orchestra. Although the concerto was finished and about to be performed, Walton suddenly abandoned the jazz style in a fit of disgust.'[51] This *Fantasia Concertante* was work in progress during 1923–24,[52] before, it is worth pointing out, Gershwin's *Rhapsody in Blue* had been heard in England.[53]

Walton came to know Gershwin through the composer Vladimir Dukelsky,

---

48 Lambert arranged the *Façade* Suite No. 1 for piano duet and *Portsmouth Point* for small orchestra, and he selected the music of Bach for Walton to orchestrate as *The Wise Virgins*.

49 5 October [1926]. Letters to Edward Clark, BL Add. 52257 fols 139–148b. The suite was the one already mentioned that Lambert arranged from Glinka's *Ruslan and Ludmilla* and had conducted at the Royal College of Music.

50 *Constant Lambert: In memoriam*, 7 October 1951, BBC Radio *Music Magazine* 1951, repeated in *Constant Lambert (1905–1951): a portrait* 11 June 1966 and in *Remembering Constant Lambert*, BBC, 23 August 1975. Printed in *Selections from the BBC Programme Music Magazine*, Rockliff 1953, 114–17. See Appendix Two, 273–5. Cochran's show opened in May 1923 but only ran for about three months. The troupe of coloured artists known as The Blackbirds, with Florence Mills as the star, returned in September 1926 for a season at the London Pavilion. It was after hearing The Blackbirds show that Walton's friend Spike Hughes, fascinated by the band, absorbed himself in jazz and soon formed his own orchestra. He gave up jazz in 1933. Lambert was particularly taken by the trumpeter and the fanfare that introduced the show.

51 *Boston Evening Transcript*, 27 November 1926. The complete article is reprinted as Appendix 1, 267–70.

52 While Walton was at work on his *Fantasia Concertante*, Lambert was completing a seventeen-minute concerto for piano, two trumpets, timpani and strings that was not performed until 1988.

53 *Rhapsody in Blue* was premièred in New York on 12 February 1924 and first heard in England on 15 June 1925 in a broadcast relayed from the Savoy Hotel with Debroy

who was wavering between serious music (he wrote the ballet *Zephyr et Flore* for Diaghilev) and popular music (he became better known under the name of Vernon Duke for *April in Paris*): 'He took me one day to see George Gershwin,' Walton recalled, 'who at the time was living in a flat in Pall Mall. I had long been an admirer of his brilliant and captivating tunes. He was in the middle of writing his Piano Concerto in F,[54] and I was hypnotised by his fabulous piano playing and his melodic gift.'[55] George's brother, Ira, recorded in his diary another meeting, in Paris in March 1928. Walton arrived just after Gershwin had had a rather heated hour's discussion with Dukelsky who 'had argued with George about parts of *American in Paris*, saying that George was 1928 in his musical comedies and in most of his concert music, but that in *A.I.P.* he allowed himself to become somewhat saccharine in spots.' Gershwin told Walton that Dukelsky had also been criticising him for the musical company he was keeping while in Paris, to which Walton advised him to 'disregard Dukelsky's advice as Duke was influenced by Prokofiev and thought anyone who wrote in another style old-fashioned; also, that nothing of Duke's had become popular, etc.'[56] When Walton played to them, Ira was unimpressed, as Diaghilev had also been. 'He played us a parody, a tune [probably from *Façade*] and a part of his symphony [in fact *Portsmouth Point*] which had been played recently by Koussevitzky – all pretty bad.' Osbert Sitwell also knew George Gershwin, of whom he wrote: 'I knew and liked him, and he would usually come to have luncheon with us when he visited London.'[57] Walton may have also met him on such occasions.

According to Lambert, the influence of Gershwin was detectable in Walton's first commission for the stage: 'So great, indeed, was his obsession with ragtime that even when writing incidental music for Lytton Strachey's Chinese melodrama, *The Son of Heaven*, he was unable to prevent some unmistakable touches of Gershwin from entering the score!'[58] This play received two fund-raising performances at the Scala Theatre, London, opening on Sunday 12 July 1925 with a matinée the following day. Walton conducted the theatre orchestra, with Lambert exercising his talents as timpanist. *The Stage* critic wrote that the music, 'ambitious and decidedly heavy, [was] composed by W T Walton who conducted a proficient small orchestra'. Strachey disowned this early 'tragic melodrama' to the extent that he purposefully missed the production by going abroad.

Somers conducting the Savoy Orpheans and the Savoy Havana Band, with Gershwin as soloist [*Radio Times*].
54 The Concerto was first performed in December 1925. Gershwin had been in London that May and June. A printed copy of Walton's Piano Quartet, inscribed to Gershwin and dated 28 May 1925, pin-points the meeting.
55 *Sunday Times*, 25 March 1962.
56 Edward Jablonski, *Gershwin: A Biography*, Simon & Schuster 1988, 161.
57 Osbert Sitwell, *Laughter in the Next Room*, 179 (191).
58 *Boston Evening Transcript*, 27 November 1926.

Another useful contact, through Osbert, was Richmond Temple, a director of the Savoy Hotel, who in turn introduced Walton to Debroy Somers who led the popular eleven-piece dance band, the Savoy Orpheans, which started up in 1923.[59] Walton attempted some arrangements for Somers but, as he later admitted, he 'wasn't slick enough, somehow . . . to write those sort of tunes.' (Heseltine made at least one arrangement for Somers, his send-up of César Franck's Symphony in *The Old Codger.*) But if none of Walton's arrangements came to performance, it was an experience he was later able to put to good use when it came to the fox-trots in the film score *Next of Kin*.

The importance in Walton's development of his encounter with jazz and popular music cannot be over-stressed. Although he never completed a work as jazz-inspired as Lambert's *The Rio Grande*, nevertheless what one might loosely call jazz rhythms (cross-fertilised with Stravinsky) were to form a fundamental element in his musical language. For several years he was much exposed to jazz and its derivatives, whether through his visits to places like the Savoy or through contact with friends like the composer and jazz musician Spike Hughes (1908–87) whose Ellington-inspired *A Harlem Symphony* was first tried out on Walton's piano in Carlyle Square and noted down in pencil sketches on the back of the orchestral parts of *Belshazzar's Feast* (a work that could not have been written without exposure to jazz-influenced music) that Walton was copying for the work's first London performance.[60] He expressed a liking for swing music from such exponents as Duke Ellington, Spike Hughes and Benny Goodman.[61]

If, as Lambert tells us, Walton suddenly abandoned the jazz style in a fit of disgust, it left its mark on his first surviving orchestral score, *Portsmouth Point*, first performed in Zürich at the fourth ISCM Festival on 22 June 1926 with Volkmar Andreae conducting, six days before London heard it during the Diaghilev season. Edward Dent wrote from Zürich to the pianist Harriet Cohen that Dr Andreae 'is very much pleased with . . . *Portsmouth Point* which we are doing – and it is so full of force that you feel as if the orchestra ought to play it in their shirtsleeves!'[62] In anticipation of the première, Osbert Sitwell had written to Christabel McLaren: 'We heard yesterday that Willie (Walton's) new overture is the only piece of English music chosen for the International Festival at Zürich which is very pleasing, for all the great names

---

59 In his *Journals*, 356, Arnold Bennett recounts how he and Siegfried Sassoon were invited to dinner at the Savoy on 29 September 1923 when the Savoy Orpheans were introduced. This band followed – and often complemented – the Savoy Havana Band.
60 *Second Movement – Continuing the Autobiography of Spike Hughes*, Museum Press 1951, 140.
61 Interview with Charles Stuart for the *Yorkshire Observer*, 21 December 1942, 2.
62 N.d., in *A Bundle of Time: The Memoirs of Harriet Cohen*, Faber & Faber 1969, 106.

(such as Bliss and Bax) were competing. . . . It is for a huge orchestra and ought to be thrilling.'[63]

In this exhilarating six-minute work all the bustle and activity in the Rowlandson print that inspired it is conveyed in the sharp rhythmic bite of its themes and their cross-accents which tumble over one another, an almost obligatory sailor's hornpipe among them. Stravinsky can be felt to be looking over Walton's shoulder in places – 'No young composer could escape that great man's influence and I certainly showed it in the rhythmical complexities of *Portsmouth Point*', he later acknowledged[64] – and attending Goossens' performance of *The Rite of Spring* in 1921 had been for him one of the major musical experiences of his life-time.[65] But if the freshness of the orchestration owed much to Stravinsky, the true Walton voice was emerging. The idea for the opening had come to him on top of a number 22 bus, and he nearly had to get off the bus to write it down.[66] After some lessons on conducting from Eugene Goossens, Walton conducted *Portsmouth Point* himself at the 1927 Proms, and afterwards he wrote about it from Carlyle Square to 'Dearest Christabel':

> The performance went off quite grandly and went down very well (I was recalled three times). Though I say it myself I conducted quite magnificently, really excelling myself, the score, being enormous slipped off the tiny desk in the middle of the work, but quite unperturbed I conducted the rest by heart – in fact a really well stage managed effect, though it might have been disastrous. My shares went up with the orchestra accordingly. My only wish is that you had been there.[67]

The rhythmic complexity of *Portsmouth Point* and its large orchestral demands (triple woodwind and three percussion players) caused Lambert to re-score it for smaller orchestra, making it more accessible to orchestral societies not only by reducing the instrumentation to the minimum required but also simplifying the tricky time-signatures by adapting frequent changes of 5/8 2/4 3/8 2/4 etc. to the more familiar 4/4 3/4 etc. with the cross-rhythms indicated by marks of phrasing and accentuation. Lambert himself conducted the first performance of this version in June 1932 during the season of the Camargo Ballet Society.

Portsmouth Point was dedicated to Siegfried Sassoon, by sixteen years

---

63 25 January (1926). Letters to Lady C. Aberconway, c. 1924–1961, BL Add. 70831.
64 *Sunday Telegraph*, 25 March 1962.
65 Even in a small detail *The Rite of Spring* left its mark in *Façade*: on the flute and clarinet beginning to *Gardiner Janus Catches a Naiad* and the ominous processional accompaniment in *Aubade*.
66 Interview with John Amis in *Portrait of Walton*, BBC Radio 3, broadcast 4 June 1977. Buses seem to have stimulated other British composers as Bax and Ireland also spoke of getting ideas when travelling on one.
67 13 September 1927. Letters of Lady Aberconway, 1927–1940, BL 70776 fols 77–99v.

Walton's senior, who gave him considerable financial assistance over a period of time. And yet, despite Sassoon's invaluable support and the evidence of much correspondence – on Walton's part often begging letters – their friendship is not something that could be deduced from Sassoon's published diaries: two brief entries in the 1920–22 diaries and nothing from 1923 to 1925. But Walton's alliance with the Sitwells would have made any close friendship rather difficult for Sassoon when from November 1921 until July 1924 he was engaged in a long-standing feud with Osbert – which is probably why he was not at the première of *Façade* and why on the afternoon of its first public performance he chose to go to the theatre instead.[68] It was later, through mutual friends such as Edith Olivier and Stephen Tennant, that their meetings were more frequent. Despite his deep love of music, especially Elgar's, Sassoon would at first sight appear an unlikely patron. Before he became acquainted with the Sitwells, in 1915 he had met Edward Dent with whom he formed a close friendship, and Dent could possibly have played some part in Sassoon assuming the rôle of Walton's friendly banker. When Sassoon attended the first performance of *Belshazzar's Feast* at Leeds in 1931 he felt that his patronage had been well placed: 'My heart swelled with pride when my protégé bowed (with immense ease and suavity) his acknowledgements to the audience (including Princess Mary!), the choir and the orchestra,' he wrote to a friend.[69]

It was Sassoon who had suggested that *Portsmouth Point* be offered to Oxford University Press, thereafter the publisher of all Walton's works. Its music department, founded in 1923, was fast becoming an important force in British music, largely due to the efforts of its enthusiastic music editor Hubert Foss (1899–1953), a respected friend of many of the up-and-coming young composers. To its rapidly expanding catalogue that included the major works of Vaughan Williams were soon added new scores by Walton, Lambert, Van Dieren, Moeran and others. By the end of the 1930s Vaughan Williams and Walton were its chief composers. An influential figure at OUP was Thomas Strong who, as a Delegate of the Press, was one of a small committee that decided policy. If the name of Walton had needed any recommendation, Strong would surely have supplied it. *Portsmouth Point* was published first in Walton's own piano duet arrangement (completed 'London: November 1925') in 1927. The orchestral score, revised, followed the next year.

Walton's next work, in 1926, was the first to reflect his love of Italy.

---

68 Nevertheless, in May 1922 Sassoon, who thought Edith's poetry 'original, and beautiful in its modes of fantastic plumage', wrote a short review of her published collection *Façade* for the *Herald* in which he was 'over-generous . . . and praised her poetry more than it deserves' (*Diaries, 1920–1922*, 155–6).

69 18 October 1931, to the neurologist Dr Henry Head, quoted in Niel Tierney, *William Walton: His Life and Music*, Robert Hale 1984, 67.

Siesta, for small orchestra, is a delicate mood picture somewhere between Bax's *Mediterranean* and Delius's *Summer Night on the River*. Although it was first heard with the composer conducting on 24 November 1926 at one of Guy Warrack's Aeolian Hall chamber orchestra concerts, it seems then to have been forgotten, for when Anthony Bernard put it into one of his New English Music Society concerts[70] in November 1929 it was advertised as 'a new work by William Walton'. It was well summed up on that occasion by the *Times* critic: 'Quiet in mood, as its title suggests, it has a fresh lyrical quality. The contrapuntal treatment of the themes and the skilful handling of the orchestra give real interest to what might otherwise have been a triviality.' As Christopher Palmer has pointed out,[71] the siciliana-like 6/8 rhythm of *Siesta* was also much favoured by Lambert and Heseltine (Warlock), both of whom in turn quite likely inherited it from Delius. However, there is no evidence to suggest that Walton had any interest in Delius's music, despite the 'bitter--sweet' parallels that Palmer draws.[72]

Siesta was dedicated to the effeminate artist Stephen Tennant, the eccentric and flamboyant youngest son of Lady Grey (formerly Lady Glenconner) whose eldest son, Edward, had been killed on the Somme. It was with Stephen Tennant that Siegfried Sassoon was to have an intense but ill-fated relationship in the late 1920s, and it was among Tennant's circle of 'bright young things' that Walton found himself at that time. He was occasionally present at their free-and-easy week-ends at the Tennant family home, Wilsford Manor, in Wiltshire. Cecil Beaton described Stephen as a 'remarkably poetic-looking apparition . . . a golden-haired young man who resembled the youthful Shelley'.[73] To David Herbert, second son of the Earl of Pembroke, he was 'intensely feminine . . . a painter, aesthetic and willowy, talented and golden-haired, beautiful, heavily made-up and flamboyantly dressed'.[74] In a letter written much later in life, Tennant had this to say of Walton:

> He, with Siegfried Sassoon, Rex Whistler, & Beryl de Zoete[75] [Arthur Waley's mistress] came often to stay with me. . . . I first met Willie, dining with Osbert Sitwell, in his London house (1925?)[76] Constant Lambert was

---

70 Anthony Bernard made the first orchestral Walton record, *Portsmouth Point*, with the New English Symphony Orchestra. It was amongst the earliest Decca releases, in January 1930, on a 10-inch 78 rpm, M94.

71 Christopher Palmer, *Delius: Portrait of a Cosmopolitan*, Duckworth 1976, 162–3.

72 He cites in particular the scoring of the Auvergne folk-song, after Jean Canteloube, in the film-score of *Henry V*, ibid. 164–5.

73 Cecil Beaton, *The Wandering Years*, 152.

74 David Herbert, *Second Son – An Autobiography*, Peter Owen 1972, 47.

75 Beryl de Zoete contributed a substantial article on Walton to the *Monthly Musical Record* in 1929. A pupil of Emile Dalcroze, she had a particular interest in Eastern dance and ballet.

76 Philip Hoare, in *Serious Pleasures: The Life of Stephen Tennant*, Hamish Hamilton

often there. . . . Almost always Willie was at Osbert's parties. . . . I was very jealous of his genius. Like all men of true Genius, he was a remote, mysterious young man, very fair, flaxen yellow hair – very quiet & very enigmatic – Courteous & wise, very serene. . . . Christabel Aberconway (Lady) adored Willie; he had Heavenly friends. I often met him at her house. – All his friends deeply loved & admired him always. But nobody understood him, really. I often went to the Russian Ballet with him & Edith. Lady Wimborne liked him. I heard Turandot with Willie in Munich & other operas. . . . But, on the whole he was not very easy to talk to and had no conversational virtuosity; he was an Enigma, a Sphinx. He was devoted to me; & I to him.[77]

Stephen Tennant thought that Walton's shyness was due to the Sitwells who, being 'so conceited and exhibitionistic', swamped his personality. He felt that Sachie teased him too much and 'reproached Willie for his Oldham background, as being too "low" & vulgar, (half in fun! of course)'. Stephen was an after-dinner guest at Osbert's one evening in the summer of 1927 (together with Walton and Lambert) when he first met Sassoon. That October at Wilsford, with Stephen then twenty-one, his circle of friends amused themselves with a sequence of elaborate fancy dress escapades. On their first evening some of them had dressed up as nuns and then, following a short black-out, appeared in pyjamas and danced to the gramophone. 'It was very amusing, and they were painted up to the eyes, but I didn't quite like it,' Sassoon wrote in his diary.[78] The next day they paraded as baroque, rococo shepherds and shepherdesses for a series of eighteenth-century tableaux to be filmed by Cecil Beaton. Osbert, Sachie and Siegfried refused to take part, but Osbert nevertheless 'was wandering delightedly in and out of the rooms, urging Stephen to longer lashes, Cecil to a healthier complexion, and Willie to madness'.[79] Rex Whistler, Cecil, Georgia, William, Stephen and the Jungman sisters, all in costume, posed for the camera as they sat on or leaned against a wooden rail on a bridge spanning the nearby Avon. Behind this play-acting, the true sexual sub-plot was unfolding. As Sarah Bradford has put it: 'while Sachie cherished his romantic dream of Zita [Jungman], she was attracted to Osbert, but had a powerful rival in the form of Christabel. Walton pursued Baby [Teresa Jungman] in his customary lustful, uncomplicated way and

---

1990, 60, suggests that they first met in 1921 at the Tennants' house in Queen Anne's Gate when Osbert had arranged for Walton to be invited to perform one of his songs at a private concert. They met again at the opening night in London of Stravinsky's *Les Noces* on 14 June 1926 when *Portsmouth Point* was receiving its English première as one of the musical entr'actes.

[77] Letter to Dr Stewart Craggs from Wilsford Manor, 10 June 1975.

[78] Quoted in Laurence Whistler, *The Laughter and the Urn: The Life of Rex Whistler*, Weidenfeld & Nicolson 1985, 113.

[79] Diary entry of Zita James (née Jungman), 19 October 1927, in Bradford, *Splendours and Miseries*, 170.

Sassoon was falling passionately in love with Stephen.'[80] Passions were further stirred when Walton informed Zita that Osbert had confided in him that he intended to marry her. This unlikely story only made Christabel the more protective of Osbert. Siegfried later confided to Christabel: 'I was present at the first showing of the Wilsford film, & thought that you, & perhaps me also – provided a much needed note of austerity!'[81]

Dressing up, whether for fancy-dress balls or home parties, was a popular activity in the 1920s. That same week-end Osbert, Siegfried, Christabel and Stephen descended upon a surprised Lytton Strachey who wrote of their invasion: 'In the evening they were all going to dress up as – God knows what – but they begged and implored me to return with them and share their raptures. When dressed up they are all filmed – and the next week-end, I suppose, the film is exhibited. . . . Strange creatures – with just a few feathers where brains should be.'[82] Back at Wilsford there was a fancy dress dinner, after which they played hide-and-seek.

On 3 January 1928 Walton wrote from Carlyle Square to Christabel of further activities in which she had not been involved:

> Sachie and Georgia gave the most lovely Xmas party consisting of Stephen and Cecil, Dick Wyndham, Siegfried, and alas! Elizabeth Ponsonby – Baby, bless her had to go to Ireland. Stephen and Cecil were in fantastic form, especially the latter. We were dressed up the whole time, and did a lovely new film which we see on Thursday. I took the part of a boot boy, Sam Snigger by name, and had a lovely scene seducing Stephen, one of the girls at the school! It was all the more fun as, when everyone should have left noone wanting to a bit, it was found to be impossible, owing to the snow, and we were unable to get away till Friday.[83]

Six days later came a cautious post-script: 'The film is too lovely, not much approved of by Lady Grey, and I think Stephen's & my big scene had better be cut. It is too genuine – think of the great-grand children.'

Ten days later another of that circle noted in her diary: 'Watched silly films of ourselves at Wilsford. Stephen always looks beautiful. . . . Osbert and Sachie v. good at character parts and so – to my surprise is Willie Walton

---

80 Bradford, *Splendours and Miseries*, 170. Zita and Teresa 'Baby' Jungman were daughters of the society hostess Beatrice Guinness by her first marriage. Cecil Beaton, who described Zita as 'quite beautiful . . . a perfect young lady', had had his photographs of the sisters and Edith Sitwell accepted for *Tatler*.

81 Letter dated November 1 [1927]. Sassoon, Siegfried Loraine. Letters to Mrs C. M. M. McLaren, 1927–1933. BL Add. 70775 fols 102–110v.

82 Letter to Roger Fry, 27 October 1927, in Michael Holroyd, *Lytton Strachey – The New Biography*, Chatto & Windus, 1994, 589.

83 Letters of Lady Aberconway, 1927–1940, BL 70776 fols 77–99v.

– who is really a comic lead.'[84] This was the author Edith Olivier,[85] one of several society ladies whose hospitality Walton cultivated with care and, doubtless, even cunning. They after all could effect the right contacts and offer him tastes of the artistic and society life so typical of the period, with long week-ends at large country homes, mixing with both up-and-coming and well-established artists and other personalities. Edith Olivier was a true intellectual. The Daye House (formerly a dairy) in Wilton Park, near Salisbury was, as Cecil Beaton has recorded, a spiritual home for many young artists at the beginning of their careers. David Herbert described her appearance, if accurately yet rather unkindly, 'as ratlike. A fidgety, dynamic rodent with mulberry-coloured hair and sharp black eyes that darted here and there unceasingly. Her nose was long and slanted slightly to the left.'[86] Her greatest friend was the painter, Rex Whistler, who not only illustrated many of her books but filled her house with his paintings. She liked to lie on her chaise-longue, reading aloud to guests. Walton was a frequent visitor to the Daye House and she was to provide a sympathetic and understanding ear to his amorous affairs.

Walton stayed the first week-end of November 1929 at Stephen Tennant's, joined on this occasion by Arthur Waley, Rex Whistler, E. M. Forster and Lytton Strachey. The latter recorded in his diary:

> We had lunch on the lawn, in such blazing sun that out host was given an excuse for sending for a yellow parasol for himself and a series of gigantic straw hats for his guests. We were filmed almost the whole time by a footman. . . . Finally, we went indoors, and in a darkened chamber were shown various films of the past. . . . Stephen was extremely amiable, though his lips were rather too magenta for my taste; Arthur Waley was positively gay; Morgan shone as required; W. W. said absolutely nothing. . . .[87]

Walton learned to tread carefully among the influential artistic company with whom he came in contact, particularly when there were helping and even financial hands to be grasped. At other times there could be a show of ingratitude. In 1932 Stephen Tennant abruptly terminated his affair with Siegfried Sassoon, and when seven years later he confided to Walton that he wanted to make a rapprochement, the reply was unequivocal: 'But why? It was he who behaved badly, not you, he was so stupid & dense: he behaved abominably.'[88] It seems that once he was more financially independent,

84 Penelope Middleboe (ed.), *Edith Olivier: From her Journals (1924–48)*, Weidenfeld & Nicolson 1989, 70.
85 Edith Olivier (1872–1948) was first cousin of Laurence Olivier's father.
86 David Herbert, *Second Son*, 156.
87 Michael Holroyd, *Lytton Strachey*, 646.
88 Stephen Tennant's journal, 17 September 1939, in Hoare, *Serious Pleasures*, 178.

Walton could afford to disown one of his chief benefactors. And for what reason, when he revised *Siesta* in 1962, making only a few minor changes, did he erase its dedication to Stephen Tennant? There had been little, if any, contact between the two since the war, yet it seems as if this was an earlier part of his life that he wanted to forget.

Walton was wary of the directions certain relationships might lead him. From 1925 to 1928 Philip Heseltine was sharing a cottage in Eynsford, Kent with E. J. Moeran. Week-ends were usually occasions for visitors, often with much drinking. It was the drinking that was the undoing of a number who were drawn into the Heseltine circle, most prominently Moeran and Lambert. Osbert wrote that Walton held Heseltine in high regard and greatly enjoyed his conversation, and that, 'together with Constant, would go down to spend convivial evenings with him in Kent, where Heseltine was living: whence the two young composers would return very late, with footsteps faltering through the now uncertain immensity of night. . . .'[89] Walton wisely steered a clear course away from such influences. 'I knew [Heseltine] well but well enough to avoid his somewhat baleful influence. I couldn't keep up with his drinking luckily, whereas Moeran could, with, I feel, deleterious effects on him.'[90]

1928 got off to a promising start with the first performance on 5 January of the *Sinfonia Concertante*, at a Royal Philharmonic Society concert at Queen's Hall, with pianist–composer York Bowen as soloist and Ernest Ansermet conducting. There was a luncheon party at the Café Royal, from which Stephen Tennant, Cecil Beaton, Dick Wyndham and Rex Whistler went on to Queen's Hall, and afterwards to the Savoy Grill for supper and then on to the Chelsea Arts Ball.[91]

Four days later Walton wrote an account of the première to Christabel, using one phrase that is a prophetic anticipation of *Belshazzar's Feast*, still three years ahead:

> I hope you didn't listen in on Thursday, the performance was bloody though the applause tumultuous. The work was terribly underrehearsed, in fact the players just about knew the notes, and that was all. There were only two rehearsals for such an enormous programme and I doubt if more than one hour and a half was given to my work which needed very careful playing.
>
> However it went down well, though the press has been not too good . . . but the 'Times' etc stupid and unsympathetic, attacking especially the orchestration which I prophesied would happen owing to the lack of rehearsal. But all that hasn't bothered me, as so many intelligent people seemed to like it, particularly Oscar [sic] Fried, the conductor of the Berlin

---

[89] Osbert Sitwell, *Laughter in the Next Room*, 179 (191).

[90] Letter to Rhoderick McNeill quoted in the latter's thesis, 'A Critical Study of the Life and Works of E. J. Moeran', University of Melbourne, December 1982.

[91] Sarah Bradford, *Splendours and Miseries*, 176.

Philharmonic, who was so impressed that he is going to give it in Berlin probably with Schnabel playing the piano part.

The supper after [the] concert was very 'hair raising'. People made such complimentary speeches about me that I didn't know where to look and what was more awful, was that I had to get up and speak myself, which I did very badly, but I was perhaps rather effective, from being so nervous & blushing, and my tongue cleaving to the roof of my mouth.

After that I had a riotous time at the Albert Hall Ball & got home at 5.30 since when I've been feeling rather exhausted.[92]

Walton's name was now becoming established, and performances of the *Sinfonia Concertante* were planned for Bournemouth, the Three Choirs Festival, New York, Paris, for Koussevitzky in Boston, and Sir Thomas Beecham in Leeds. Not all of these materialised, but at Bournemouth Gordon Bryan was the soloist with Walton conducting. One critic prophesied: 'This young man will some day do something worth while, but he will have to make up his mind what he wants to say.' Another interpreter was Harriet Cohen who played it with Lambert conducting the Frankfurt Symphony Orchestra at a Festival of British Music in Bad Homburg in July 1930. 'My rehearsals of the Concertante with Willie and Constant were often hilarious and brought great joy to me,' she recalled in her autobiography.[93] The following year she introduced it to America, in Cincinnati with Eugene Goossens conducting.

Walton first met Harriet Cohen in 1923 at one of Arnold Bennett's parties to which he had gone with the Sitwells. She and her circle of friends were regular attenders at the Promenade Concerts where they 'were often joined by the young composers such as Berkeley, Lambert and Walton'. In 1929 she had approached Walton about performing his *Sinfonia Concertante*. 'I shall be delighted if you play the piano part . . . ,' he replied. 'I know it will be in safe hands.'[94] An early exponent of the *Sinfonia Concertante* had been the South African-born composer and pianist Victor Hely-Hutchinson. Harriet's interest in the work brought another even more positive response from Walton: 'I have been longing for you, in fact anyone besides V. H. H. to play it, & feel very much like Henry IInd & Thomas à Beckett. "Will no-one rid me of this turbulent V. H. H." and I hope you will come forward & do so, for which I shall be eternally grateful, as it is absurd to make out that it is his spiritual property. You may shower all the blame on to me, that is if it really entails that.'[95]

Susana Walton, in her book on her husband, has suggested that it was

---

[92] 9 January 1928. Letters of Lady Aberconway, 1927–1940, BL 70776 fols 77–99v.
[93] *A Bundle of Time*, 161.
[94] Letter, n.d., quoted in full in *A Bundle of Time*, 155.
[95] N.d., Harriet Cohen Papers, BL Deposit 1999/10.

Harriet who was keen on Walton rather than the other way round, and relates a story of his that is quite likely spiced with his own humour:

> It amused William to tell that she had once played the *Sinfonia Concertante*, and then invited him back to her home for a drink. While William was sipping a glass of whisky, she had changed into a chiffon garment and asked William to hold on to a corner of the material. She then glided away, turning while walking until the chiffon had unwound and she stood stark naked. William couldn't stop laughing; la Cohen was very cross.[96]

Harriet has written of their 'stormy yet delightful friendship'. She added: 'The irritation we often felt for each other did not lessen the underlying affection.'[97] Walton for his part carried on a flirtatious relationship with her, in correspondence at least, addressing her with such endearments as 'Harriet, my sweet', and often signing himself as 'Willow'. In May 1930 he was thanking her for sending a ' "sex appealing" photograph' of herself. Lambert was also a good friend of Harriet's, causing Walton to write teasingly: 'Constant . . . by the way, is continually asking after you – why from me I don't know. I think he's got it badly and is writing a Piano Concerto for you in 13/8 time.'[98] She in turn enjoyed their company: 'I did manage to dance a few times with Willie and Constant,' she wrote in her memoirs.[99]

In 1932 Walton wrote to Hubert Foss: 'I just had a wire from Harriet Cohen saying that as a token of [and here he inserted a blank] she is playing the Sinfonia in Montreal and paying for it herself, which, all things considered, is extremely nice of her.'[100] Later that year he was asking Dora Foss for a 'pen-picture-postcard of Harriet's goings-on'. The stormier aspect of their relationship would arise when there was rivalry with other composers' works, bringing forth the less charitable side of Walton's nature. 'Don't be a lump,' he once wrote. 'Why this sudden break-down? If you don't want to play the S. C. obviously you won't, so you should play V. W.'s work [Vaughan Williams' Piano Concerto which was written for her] instead – but it will only give you pain & no pleasure.'[101] It is quite likely that Walton agreed on

96 *Behind the Façade*, 149.
97 *A Bundle of Time*, 137. Harriet Cohen (1895–1967), who charmed and flattered many leading figures from G. B. Shaw to Elgar, was the mistress of Arnold Bax whose works she championed.
98 26 November 1930, Harriet Cohen Papers, BL Deposit 1999/10. The Concerto in question was the Concerto for Piano and Nine Instruments, first performed in December 1931 and dedicated to the memory of Philip Heseltine who had died the previous December. In 1938 Lambert dedicated his *Elegy* for piano to her.
99 *A Bundle of Time*, 161.
100 12 January 1932, from Faringdon House. Dora Foss, 'Memoirs of Walton'.
101 N.d., Harriet Cohen Papers, BL Deposit 1999/10. Harriet Cohen, in *A Bundle of Time*, 198, remembers Walton's opinion of Vaughan Williams' Piano Concerto as being far more favourable: 'Willie Walton, Paddy Hadley and Arnold [Bax] . . . came back for

some minor changes to the solo part to suit Cohen's technique. She was not to record the work, however. After a more thorough revision in 1943, he recorded it with Phyllis Sellick and the City of Birmingham Orchestra in August 1945. Much later, in 1970, he recorded it once again, with Peter Katin and the LSO.

In February 1928, Walton was invited by Stephen Tennant to stay with him at a *pension* near Garmisch in Bavaria where he was undergoing treatment for tuberculosis. Walton provided much needed companionship because Sassoon, with whom Stephen was then going through an intense relationship, was unable to go. As usual Sassoon responded to the request to 'forward the brass for the ticket'. Walton, for his part, provided Stephen with London news that he was eager to hear, 'indiscreet secrets about our London friends . . . private scandals . . . his details are hair-raising'.[102] Both ended up with what Tennant described as a 'chic sunburn'. The two also enjoyed a three-day visit to Munich where they were able to take in the opera.

In July, Walton, Sachie and Georgia, Zita Jungman, Stephen Tennant, Cecil Beaton and Dick Wyndham were among the regular guests of Oswald and Cynthia Mosley[103] at their Elizabethan farmhouse near Denham in Buckinghamshire. Much of the week-end was taken up by making a film to a script by Stephen that involved car chases, seduction and abduction. Cynthia, or 'Cimmie' as she as known, was very beautiful and, as one might expect, Walton was a little in love with her. He was very upset to receive news in 1933 of her sudden death at the age of thirty-four from appendicitis. He wrote to Christabel:

> I can hardly believe it is true about dear Cimmie. It is unthinkable that I shall never see her again. She really meant a very great deal to me, & I shall always regret that, owing to my stupidity, youth and 'gaucheness', I never really appreciated her when I knew her best. But thank heaven, we made it up & I tried to explain to her why I was so stupid & I think she understood, in fact I'm sure she did. But I must say I should rather anything have happened than this.[104]

While by 1928 the name of Walton was beginning to be taken seriously, his relations with Osbert had started to become strained. Sachie's marriage

---

supper. Tired as I was I made them run-through the *Romance* from V. W.'s concerto from the orchestral score (two pianos) and even from that we all agreed it sounded marvellous. Willie thought the work far finer than the *Sea Symphony*: as for me I was truly ravished.'

102 Undated letter from Stephen Tennant to Cecil Beaton; Philip Hoare, *Serious Pleasures,* 101.

103 In the 1930s (Sir) Oswald Mosley was leader of the British Union of Fascists.

104 1 June 1933. Letters of Lady Aberconway, 1927–1940, BL 70776 fols 77–99v. After Cimmie's death, in 1936 Mosley married Diana Guinness (née Mitford) with whom he had for some while been having an affair of which Cimmie had been aware.

had already driven a wedge into the cosy ménage, and now Walton was beginning to become a shade too independent for Osbert's taste, and flirtations with young ladies within his own circle were upsetting him.[105] A separation seemed inevitable and before long Walton's visits abroad would not be in the company of the Sitwells but instead with a woman with whom he was to have an intense relationship.

However, he and the Sitwells were together at Siena for the two presentations of *Façade* on 14 September at the 1928 ISCM Festival. Hubert Foss, Walton's publisher at Oxford University Press, reviewed it for the *Musical Times*:

> *Façade* was given twice, and after some opposition (mostly Italian) met with the success it deserves. As a form of entertainment it cannot be repeated. It suits Miss Edith Sitwell's poems uniquely, and one was, therefore, surprised (and pleased) that so many of those who could not have understood one word enjoyed it. That speaks well for the music, which, quite apart from its vigour and gaiety, its satire and its high spirits, succeeds largely by its skill.[106]

(The Italians may have taken offence to the treatment in the *Jodelling Song* of the well-known *Allegro vivace* tune from Rossini's *William Tell* Overture, but Spike Hughes writes that it was the irreverent parodying in the *Tarantella* of a national dance that caused shouts and calls, with hats and shoes being thrown at the stage. Nevertheless, the *Popular Song* was repeated three times.[107] Much later Walton drily suggested that the uproar may have arisen because 'we were very English and started the performance on time – fatal!'[108])

Lambert was the reciter and Walton conducted, and they both stayed with Osbert, Edith, Sachie and his wife Georgia, and many guests at Sir George Sitwell's castle of Montegufoni near Florence. It was when the rest of the house party had gone to bed, Osbert has written, that every night 'William and Constant would carouse with Henry Moat [Sir George's faithful butler].'[109] Osbert had by now begun his long-term relationship with David Horner to whom he wrote, rather sarcastically, on 24 September: 'Siena was great fun, and Willie a success beyond his merits (as a person). He was referred to as "Il world-famous Wanton" in one paper. *Façade* went

---

105 John Pearson, *Façades*, 248.
106 *Musical Times*, October 1928, 937.
107 *Opening Bars – Beginning an Autobiography by Spike Hughes*, Pilot Press 1946, 363. However, Hughes later wrote, in 'Nobody Calls Him Willie Now' for *High Fidelity* September 1960, Vol. 10, No. 9, 43–6, 116–17, that it was the *Tango–Pasodoble* that was 'cheered so wildly that the number had to be played three times'.
108 In conversation with Spike Hughes in *Appointment with Music*, BBC Home Service, 24 April 1958, with Walton conducting the BBC Concert Orchestra in an hour-long programme of his own music.
109 'Portrait of a Very Young Man', 30.

extremely well, and was really a lovely performance. Christabel [McLaren] is here and Siegfried and Willie and Constant. Edith left yesterday.'[110] Sassoon had been staying in Bavaria with Stephen Tennant. The two had driven from there to Siena but, to their – and especially Edith's – annoyance, they arrived too late for *Façade*. For this display of bad manners Edith would not speak to Siegfried for three days.

There had also been a mild panic before the Festival performance. Walton had forgotten the address of the scene painter to whom he had entrusted the job of reproducing Severini's new curtain design. Osbert's mother, Lady Ida, and Christabel McLaren saved the day by tracking him down in the bar in Florence in which he had been commissioned for the task, their only clue being that all Walton could remember was that his name was Barone. Even then Christabel had to convince an obstinate Sir George that it was possible for the rolled backcloth to be carried in the car by laying it across the inside with one end projecting through a window.[111]

After *Façade* the guests stayed on for over a week. One evening they found themselves dining in the kitchen while Walton entertained them on the piano with jazz and popular songs.[112] (In August at Renishaw, Walton's piano playing had been put to another use: each evening after dinner he and Berners would strike up violent impromptu duets in order to drive Sir George to bed.[113]) One day three carloads of guests went to Viareggio, near to where Shelley had drowned in 1822, and a day or two later Tennant, Sassoon, Lambert and Walton left, driving first to Florence, and from there to Venice. That winter Walton spent with Osbert at the Hotel Cappuccini in Amalfi, he working on the Viola Concerto – with the aid of a cloister piano – while Osbert was starting a new novel. This rather solitary existence was broken by the arrival of the young writer Godfrey Winn who found that Osbert and Walton had monopolised the only private sitting-room in the hotel. 'There were many days when we were all three equally stuck with our work – glum and silent in the evening: at such moments, neither the oil of inspiration nor of conversation would flow: at such moments, with aching heads and burning eyes, we would long to drown our sorrows in wine, women and song.'[114]

In the spring of 1929 Walton was again invited by Stephen Tennant to Bavaria. This time other friends, including Edith Olivier, Rex Whistler and Siegfried Sassoon, came as well. For Walton the only cloud over the general air of happiness was the unfriendliness shown towards him by the owner of the *pension*, Walter Hirth who, as Rex Whistler's biographer put it so succinctly, 'had recognised that he was not of gentle birth with the acuity of

---

110 John Pearson, *Façades*, 248.
111 Christabel Aberconway, *A Wiser Women?*, 90–2.
112 Philip Hoare, *Serious Pleasures*, 120.
113 *Edith Olivier: From her Journals*, 80.
114 Godfrey Winn, *The Bend of the River*, London 1949, 30–1.

one who was not himself'.[115] This difference of class and upbringing was something of which Walton must have been constantly aware while enjoying such company. In Bavaria there were celebrations for Tennant's twenty-third birthday, but it was not all holiday for Walton. While Whistler sketched him,[116] he was putting the finishing touches to a score that was to be his first recognised masterpiece, the Viola Concerto.

---

[115] Laurence Whistler, *The Laughter and the Urn*, 137.
[116] On Whistler's death in 1944, that drawing was given to Osbert who used it as plate VII in his autobiographical *Laughter in the Next Room*, first published in 1949.

5

'Throw in a couple of brass bands'

If *Façade* had brought Walton's name before the public with a hint of notoriety, it was the Viola Concerto that made the critics sit up and take him seriously. It might seem surprising that he should choose the viola for his first string concerto. The higher, brighter registers of the violin would surely have suited his orchestral palette far better than the darker hues of the viola. But the idea of writing for that particular instrument had not initially been Walton's. That great champion of the viola, Lionel Tertis, had made it his life's crusade to beg viola compositions from the younger British composers of the day to enrich what was then a very limited orchestral repertoire for his instrument. There was Berlioz's *Harold in Italy* (written for Paganini, who, after seeing the first movement, rejected it on the grounds that there was too little to play), and Mozart's *Sinfonia Concertante* for violin and viola. But even the Mozart was much less performed in the early part of the century than it is today. Soloists had to turn to now forgotten composers such as Arends, Heynberg, Hubay and Sitt for concertos for their instrument. As Tertis has written: 'It was pure generosity in those days at the beginning of the century to write for the solo viola. Publishers would not consider anything of the sort, to them it was a distinctly bad commercial proposition. However, my composer friends continued to write a number of works for me.'[1] None of the older generation of British composers, Mackenzie, Cowen, Parry and Stanford, had written for viola and orchestra. One of the earliest was J. B. McEwen whose concerto Tertis introduced in 1901. In time similar works followed: York Bowen's Concerto (1908), Benjamin Dale's Suite (1911), W. H. Bell's *Rosa Mystica* (1917), Arnold Bax's *Phantasy* for Viola and Orchestra (1920), Vaughan Williams's *Flos Campi* (1925) and W. H. Reed's Rhapsody (1927), nearly all of which Tertis premièred. All the composers of these works – with the exception of Vaughan Williams – had studied at the Royal Academy of Music where Tertis was a professor.

---

[1] Lionel Tertis, *My Viola and I: A Complete Autobiography*, Paul Elek 1974, 33.

It had been Beecham (in whose orchestra Tertis had been principal viola) who suggested that Walton should write a concerto for him, a shrewd judgement, as Beecham then had not conducted a note of Walton's music.[2] It was extremely ironic, then, that this one work, which was in time to prove more durable than any of those British scores already mentioned, should suffer a fate similar to Berlioz's *Harold in Italy* and be initially rejected by its intended soloist. As Tertis himself explained:

> One work of which I did not give the first performance was Walton's masterly concerto. With shame and contrition I admit that when the composer offered me the first performance I declined it. I was unwell at the time; but what is also true is that I had not learnt to appreciate Walton's style. The innovations in his musical language, which now seem so logical and so truly in the main-stream of music, then struck me as far-fetched. It took me time to realise what a tower of strength in the literature of the viola is this concerto, and how deep the gratitude that we who play the viola should feel towards the composer – the gratitude, too, to Beecham for having suggested to Walton the composition of a viola concerto for me. I remember that, when Walton came to me with it and I refused the honour, he was generous enough not to seem to take it too much amiss but asked me to suggest someone else to undertake the performance. I immediately thought of Paul Hindemith. . . . So it was that Hindemith played the work for the first time at Queen's Hall. I was a member of the audience, and felt great disappointment with his playing. The notes, certainly, were all there, but the tone was cold and unpleasing and the instrument he played did not deserve to be called a viola, it was far too small.[3]

Walton had in fact been so disappointed by Tertis's refusal that he 'threatened to make it over for the violin', but, *pace* Tertis, it was Edward Clark, then a programme planner for the BBC and a strong advocate for contemporary music, who suggested sending it to Hindemith.[4] As Walton himself remembered:

> I sent it to Tertis, who turned it down sharply by return of post, which depressed me a good deal as virtuoso violists were scarce. However, Edward Clark, who at that time was in charge of the music section of the

---

2 The first Walton work to be conducted by Beecham was probably the first *Façade* Suite, as a Symphonic Interlude on 28 July 1928 during the season of Russian Ballets. He repeated the work on 6 October at the Leeds Triennial Festival and on 23 November at Hastings.

3 Lionel Tertis, *My Viola and I*, 36–7.

4 Meirion and Susie Harries, *A Pilgrim Soul: The Life and Work of Elisabeth Lutyens*, Michael Joseph 1989, Faber & Faber n.d., 80, and confirmed by Walton himself in an interview with John Amis in BBC Radio *Portrait of Walton* broadcast 4 June 1977.

BBC and was rather the William Glock of his day, suggested we should go to Hindemith.[5]

Edward Clark's invaluable help was not forgotten and in 1953 Walton was instrumental in obtaining for him a Civil List pension.[6]

The Concerto's progress can be charted in Walton's correspondence with Siegfried Sassoon (which also follows the ups and downs of Walton's financial state). On 5 December 1928 he wrote from Amalfi:

> I am so sorry to have been so long in writing to you but there's been no news of much interest to tell anyone. Consequently I am much in arrears with my correspondence and therefore in disgrace with not a few people. I have been working hard at a viola concerto suggested by Beecham and designed for Lionel Tertis. It may be finished by Xmas and is, I think, by far my best effort up till now. Hoping to be here until April, I imagine I may get two other works finished as well. . . . Facade entertainment is being done [in Paris] some time in January by the Pro Musica Society, and the Sinfonia is being done on February 22nd by Ansermet with the new Société Symphonique de Paris. Portsmouth Point has just been given by Glasgow and Edinburgh so on the whole things are not going too badly. . . .[7]

Further news came on 2 February 1929:

> Both Osbert and myself have been ill with a nasty attack of 'flu caught from the American tourists who descend on this place in their thousands. It's the only drawback of being here but it's probably worse elsewhere. It's been a great nuisance as it has robbed us both of about three weeks valuable working time. Nevertheless, I finished yesterday the second movement of my Viola Concerto. At the moment I think it will be my best work, better than the Sinfonia, if only the third and last movement works out well. At present I am in the painful position of starting it, which is always full of trials and disappointments. However, I hope to be well away with it in a day or two. . . . I have really got into a mess with the bank through the fault of the O[xford] P[ress] as they hadn't informed me that they didn't pay out royalties till the work was in print and I was expecting £20 or £30 last October from the many performances here and in America. Now I find I can't get paid until next October and I had overdrawn on that expectancy so if you can wait till then I shall be in the position, I hope, to pay you back. I hope that you are working at your next book[8] and that it's going well. I'm

---

5   *Sunday Telegraph*, 25 March 1962, quoted in Frank Howes, *The Music of William Walton*, OUP 1965, 80.
6   Meirion and Susie Harries, *A Pilgrim Soul*, 175.
7   In *Keeping one's head above water*, a BBC Radio 3 interval talk compiled from unpublished correspondence by Carole Rosen with script adviser Dr Stewart Craggs. BBC Radio 3 Prom interval feature, 8 September 1987.
8   Sassoon's *Memoirs of a Fox-hunting Man* was published in 1928, and *Memoirs of an Infantry Officer* followed in 1930.

so sorry to trouble you but there is this bill also for my piano, but I can hold it over until the next quarter as they are amicably inclined but I don't want it to accumulate into being an ungovernable amount. It will be most kind of you if you can do anything about all this and I shall be eternally grateful.[9]

Sassoon as ever obliged and Walton responded from Amalfi on 12 February: 'Thank you so much for your letter, and a thousand thanks for the glad news – it is really most generous of you. . . . Otherwise I've no news, except that *I have started on the 3rd movement* & hope to complete it soon.'

At some stage during the composition of the concerto Walton wrote to his friend, the pianist Angus Morrison, saying that his style was changing and becoming more melodious and mature. Morrison remembered:

When very soon after he returned to London the following Spring he came and played it to me, I realised the true significance of the remark. In this work he had in fact reached complete maturity of style and given full rein for the first time to his entirely personal lyrical gift. To my astonished ears, it seemed to me, in spite of his woefully inadequate piano playing, a masterpiece in the real sense of the word.[10]

Another to hear the work before it had reached performance was the critic Basil Maine, who recalled:

When I was living in Chelsea, I had a telephone call early one evening from William Walton, who lived near. He said he had just completed a concerto for viola and would like to come round and play some of it from the manuscript. He arrived soon after, and, in the indescribable idiom of his pianoforte-playing, gave some idea of the orchestral score, and occasionally a sketchy vocalise of the viola part.[11]

Maine detected passages he felt to be reminiscent 'by implication rather than by statement' of the Elgarian voice, while rather more interestingly the critic Peter Pirie has suggested that the figuration of the Concerto is very close to that in the music of Van Dieren.[12]

The Concerto had been completed, and rejected by Tertis, by the time Walton wrote to Sassoon on 3 July from Carlyle Square:

Your letter and cheque arrived at a most opportune moment as I was just beginning to despair about my piano. Cash is not exactly plentiful anywhere round here at the moment. Scandal have I none, though lately I have been more abroad in the great world. I went to the new ballet, The

9 *Keeping One's Head above Water.*
10 'Walton in the 20s': a talk in BBC *Music Magazine* 'Sir William Walton: A 70th Birthday Tribute', 26 March 1972. NSA MT34453.
11 Basil Maine, *Twang with our Music*, Epworth Press 1957, 112.
12 'Scapino: The Development of William Walton', *Musical Times*, April 1964, 258–9.

Prodigal Son. Scenery by Rouault, music by Prokofiev. Lovely the former and mediocre the latter, except for the end which is I think better than anything he has done. . . . There's very good news about my concerto. Hindemith is playing it on Oct. 3rd., myself with the baton. On the 12th I make grandiose records of Façade, two double-sided ones for the new Decca company. Unfortunately I get precious little for it. However, it will be a good advertisement. I have more or less got to go to Germany to see Hindemith about the V. C., but how I'm going to go I can't think. He's going to be at the Baden-Baden Festival on the 25th and I hope to meet him there as it will be better than going to Berlin.[13]

Walton had already met Hindemith, at Salzburg in 1923 at the ISCM Festival when his early String Quartet had been performed. Hindemith was at Baden-Baden in July 1929 for the first performance at the Festival of his own oratorio *Lehrstück*, and, thanks to Sassoon's generosity, Walton was able to go over to Germany and meet him again. On 28 July he sent a post-card: 'Arrived here safely last night. Thank you so much for enabling me to get here. I see Hindemith in half an hour's time. The Festival is interesting.' He discussed the concerto with Hindemith who agreed to play it, and the première could now go ahead.

But the scheduled Prom performance nearly did not take place. It was to be Hindemith's first engagement in England as soloist, but his friend and publisher, Willy Strecker, had hoped that Hindemith's London début would be at a Courtauld–Sargent concert for which, as he wrote to Hindemith, each work was allowed 'as many rehearsals as necessary – something hitherto unknown in England'. He wrote to Hindemith's wife:

> The London affair is very regrettable. I want your husband, appearing there for the first time before the larger public, to do it in a worthy setting, and as a composer, not just as a soloist. An appearance with Wood to play a concerto by a moderately gifted English composer – and that is what Walton is – is not as I see it a début. Wood's Promenade Concerts are, like their conductor himself, a worthy institution, at which the playing is so-so, 30 to 40 soloists appear, and never a sensation of the sort I am hoping for. . . . Your husband should make himself harder to get.[14]

Fortunately, Hindemith did not share Strecker's views. He liked the work and, as it turned out, Walton conducted the première himself on 3 October 1929[15] at Queen's Hall. But with limited rehearsal time things did not augur

---

13 *Keeping One's Head above Water.*

14 Geoffrey Skelton, *Paul Hindemith: The Man behind the Music. A Biography*, Victor Gollancz 1977, 97.

15 Originally planned for 29 August, the date of performance was changed to 3 October at Walton's request. According to BBC documentation rehearsals were arranged for 1 and 3 October at 10 p.m. and 2 October at 4 p.m. Walton also conducted the *Sinfonia Concertante* at that season's Proms, on 14 September.

well and the previous evening Hindemith had written rather scornfully to his wife:

> I have just come from the rehearsal (evening around 7); it should have been early this morning but wasn't because other things were being rehearsed. . . . It won't be up to much. So far Walton has only had one rehearsal in which he managed to play the first movement just once. The orchestra is bad, consisting mainly of women and English ones at that.[16]

Nevertheless, the day after the première he was able to write that 'it went well and was a good success'.[17] Of Hindemith's performance, Walton commented: 'His technique was marvellous, but he was rough – no nonsense about it. He just stood up and played.' Violist Bernard Shore, who had studied with Tertis (and to whom Walton had turned for some advice in the writing of the concerto), played in the première and remembered the feverish activity that went on behind the scenes beforehand to get the orchestral parts ready:

> Up till seven o'clock on the night, the artists' room was full of copyists, while an anxious Walton and an irritated Hindemith (who wanted more rehearsal) paced up and down, debating over the score and agreeing upon various vital code-signs. Wood, very indignant, was meanwhile heard to mutter: 'These young composers! I can't even get into my artists' room! What next?'[18]

New works by Bax, Howells and Goossens were also in the programme, and *The Times* critic wrote that, after Bax's colourful *Three Orchestral Pieces*,

> the low scale of tone, partly conditioned, no doubt, by the nature of the solo instrument, made its colour sound a little drab. Once the ear had adjusted itself to the new values, its subtlety, its rhythmic vitality and its lyrical charm were evident enough. The mastery in the handling of the material chosen, and the restraint which had been imposed upon his facility consti- tute a real and astonishing advance in the composer's development. The solo part was played excellently by Mr Paul Hindemith.

According to Hindemith's biographer, Walton admitted to being influenced by Hindemith's viola concerto, *Kammermusik No. 5* (1927), while writing his own: 'I am surprised he played it. One or two bars are almost identical.'[19] Apart from the brooding slow movement of the Hindemith, any similarities would almost certainly be between the third movement of *Kammermusik No.*

---

16 *Selected Letters of Paul Hindemith*, edited and translated from the German by Geoffrey Skelton, Yale 1995, 54.
17 *Ibid.*, 55.
18 Bernard Shore, *Sixteen Symphonies*, 367.
19 Geoffrey Skelton, *Paul Hindemith*, 98.

5 and the finale of the Walton. Hindemith's springy theme would not be out of place in the Walton. There is another important influence. The contour of the work's opening theme is rather Prokofian, and with a slow first movement followed by a scherzo Walton was not only setting the pattern for his two later string concertos but also following the example of Prokofiev's First Violin Concerto in which, like the Walton, the opening theme makes a memorable return in the coda of the last movement. When asked if he had consciously taken a work as a model, he admitted that the Prokofiev had been – up to a point.[20] But for an explanation for the work's new-found lyricism one should look elsewhere, to the dedication of the concerto, 'To Christabel', Christabel McLaren, with whom Walton was in love. Yet, despite the closeness implied in the dedication, it was not an intimate relationship and the concerto, as Walton much later admitted, was inspired by love that was frustrated.[21]

Hindemith did not, it seems, play the work again. When he came to England a year later to play his own viola concerto at a Courtauld–Sargent concert, it received some scathing reviews in the British press. Walton wrote to Harriet Cohen that 'the only bright spot in [a] dirty, dreary & desultory world, was the arrival of Hindemith to play his new Concerto which was quite lovely but noone else except Sir Henry & myself seems to think so. I saw him a great deal while he was over & it was nice to meet an intelligent composer besides Arnold [Bax] and Constant [Lambert]. . . .'[22] Walton was deeply grateful to Hindemith for taking over from Tertis, and he was to repay this act of friendship much later in the dedication to Hindemith and his wife of the *Variations on a Theme by Hindemith*. There was further irony when Tertis was invited – but refused to play – Hindemith's concerto with the Berlin Philharmonic Orchestra. 'I perused the score and found that most of it was crammed with fiendishly difficult passage-work – a technique that was peculiarly his own and which he himself played marvellously. It was not music to me, and I reluctantly had to refuse the offer.'[23]

To his credit, Tertis, who was present at the first performance of the Walton concerto, realised his mistake in rejecting that work and very soon took it up, taking it to the ISCM Festival at Liège on 4 September 1930 with Walton again conducting. He played it with Ansermet conducting at a Queen's Hall Royal Philharmonic Society concert on 26 March 1931 (Walton scathingly wrote that 'though the V.C. had a slight success last night, the orchestral playing & accompanying was abominable'[24]) and with the composer at the Proms the same year, and with the Zürich Tonhalle with

---

20 Interview with John Amis, 17 March 1972.
21 *Ibid.*
22 26 November 1930, Harriet Cohen Papers, BL Deposit 1999/10.
23 Lionel Tertis, *My Viola and I*, 37.
24 Letter to Harriet Cohen, 27 March 1931, Harriet Cohen Papers, BL Deposit 1999/10.

Volkmar Andreae conducting in November 1931. He gave its first Hallé performance under Harty on 14 January 1932, and its first Scottish performance in Edinburgh on 1 December 1932 with Adrian Boult conducting the Reid Orchestra. On that occasion, the concerto was so well received that Boult suggested playing it again in the second half of the programme. Tertis wrote afterwards: 'I am still amazed at the courage of Dr Boult in suggesting to the audience a second performance. I SHALL NEVER FORGET IT!'[25] Sir Donald Tovey wrote an extensive essay with sixteen music examples that concluded with the strongest recommendation: 'There are so few concertos for viola that (even if I happened to know any others) it would be a poor compliment to say this was the finest. Any concerto for viola must be a *tour de force*; but this seems to me to be one of the most important modern concertos for any instrument, and I can see no limits to what may be expected of the tone-poet who could create it.'[26] Tertis played it on 21 April 1936 in Zürich with Boult and the BBC SO, and he included the concerto and *Harold in Italy* in his 'retirement' 60th birthday concert, also with the BBC SO, at Queen's Hall on 24 February 1937, alongside Hindemith's *Mathis der Maler*, with Ansermet conducting. He also played it at the Proms that year on 2 September. That he was not to record the work is particularly regrettable since Walton held such a high opinion of his playing, as he wrote after a performance he conducted in Germany in 1930 to 'My sweet, sweet Harriet' [Cohen]:

> The orchestra was bloody, the rehearsals ditto – in fact everything seemed, with the exception of Mr Tertis, who was a saint & angel throughout – to be all wrong, till at the performance, I found myself at the top of my form, & behaved like Toscanini & it all went perfectly. If the orchestra had been good, the performance couldn't have been better. It consisted of the professors & students of the Conservatoire the average age of the former being about 90 & the latter about 15. However, they did try & in fact rose a certain distance for the occasion & the concerto made the hit of the Festival – at any rate so far. The applause – tears – & cheers, couldn't have been better, & Tertis & I were more tired by walking on & off than by playing.
>
> My arm is fatigued by autograph signing & I was touched by the number of orchestral players who asked if I had written concertos for their several instruments.
>
> You have no conception what Tertis has made out of the work – if you liked it before, you will just pass out when you hear him play it. I nearly did myself.[27]

---

[25] Letter to Mary Grierson quoted in her biography, *Donald Francis Tovey: A Biography Based on Letters*, OUP 1952, 273–4.

[26] *Essays in Musical Analysis, Vol. iii: Concertos*, OUP 1936, 226; reprinted in *Some English Symphonists: A Selection from 'Essays in Musical Analysis'*, OUP 1941, 73.

[27] Harriet Cohen Papers, BL Deposit 1999/10.

Benjamin Britten, in his second year at the Royal College of Music, listened in to the broadcast of a British Night at the Proms on 10 September 1931 when Tertis played the Concerto with the composer conducting. 'Walton's wonderful Vla Concerto (beautifully played by Tertis) stood out as a work of genius,' he wrote in his diary. He had bought a copy of the score the day before – 'a fine work but difficult' – and was soon playing through the work, himself on viola with an accompanist. After listening to another broadcast Prom that included Ireland's Piano Concerto and Holst's *The Planets*, he commented: 'I feel no music of that generation can be compared to works like Walton's Viola Concerto.'[28] Britten's piano teacher at the RCM, Arthur Benjamin, was equally impressed by the Viola Concerto and dedicated his own Violin Concerto of 1931 to Walton 'with great admiration'.

The Concerto had many admirers among composers. Edmund Rubbra, in a seventieth-birthday tribute, remembered the impact that it had, not just on him alone:

> I first became acquainted with Walton's work when, in the late Twenties, I visited Constant Lambert, taking with me a score I had dedicated to him. On Lambert's piano was the score of Walton's Viola Concerto, which had not then been performed, and I remember how we both went through it with enormous enthusiasm. It seems to me now, as it did then, to be a work of phenomenal maturity in its assured musical progress, and in the certainty of the orchestral presentation of the ideas.[29]

Yet another admirer was Arnold Bax who, according to Harriet Cohen, especially adored the last movement 'and was ambitious for Willie always to keep up to that splendid standard'.[30] They had met in June 1930 when Toscanini conducted Elgar's *Enigma Variations* at Queen's Hall[31] and afterwards Walton asked Arnold Bennett if he could join his party, that included Harriet Cohen and Arnold Bax, at the Savoy Grill. When Walton expressed a wish to become better acquainted with the older composer, Hubert Foss arranged a dinner so that they could meet informally. Bax readily accepted the invitation: 'I like the idea of the party you suggest . . . and I am ever glad to meet William Walton,' he had written to Foss.[32] Although the two were not subsequently to become close acquaintances, the party was nevertheless a success. As Dora remembered: 'Hubert initially pushed the conversational wheels with a few interpolations, but by the time we returned to the drawing-room, the two composers were more or less oblivious of us and we just sat back and

28 Donald Mitchell and Philip Reed (eds), *Letters from a Life*, 204, 201 and 207.
29 Edmund Rubbra, 'William Walton's 70th Birthday', *Listener*, 23 March 1972, 394.
30 *A Bundle of Time*, 199.
31 Toscanini's first visit to England, conducting two concerts with the New York Philharmonic.
32 Letter dated 20.8.31 quoted in Dora Foss, 'Memoirs of Walton'.

enjoyed ourselves. Part of the discussion and general talk was about other composers, both past and contemporary, and the contemporary ones were wholeheartedly and jovially pulled to pieces.'[33]

Although the concerto was soon recognised as a masterpiece ('one of the most remarkable of recent compositions, British or otherwise', Eric Blom wrote in the *Musical Times*), there was one person who did not share that opinion. Basil Maine remembered a Three Choirs' Festival performance at Worcester in 1932 when 'Elgar was seen pacing up and down behind the orchestra gallery and deploring that such music should be thought fit for a stringed instrument.'[34] This had been Walton's entrée into the hallowed grounds of the Three Choirs, conducting both *Portsmouth Point* and the Concerto, with Tertis as soloist. (Had the Worcester authorities known what had inspired the Concerto, Walton joked with friends, they would not have considered it suitable for Cathedral performance.) He had been extremely nervous before the concert and Hubert Foss had taken him on to the terrace outside the cathedral and given him a swig of brandy to build up his courage. It was at that festival that he met Elgar, in a lavatory of all places. It was hardly a fruitful meeting, as he told Dora Foss: Elgar would not have any form of musical conversation with him, but would only discuss horses and racing.[35]

Walton greatly admired the music of Elgar. One wet Sunday in June 1927 he had been present, with Osbert (who found Elgar's music obnoxious) and Sachie, Arnold Bennett, Siegfried Sassoon and 'a great crowd of cars and fashionable persons',[36] at a seventieth-birthday 'Homage to Elgar' organised by his wealthy patron and friend Frank Schuster at Bray near Maidenhead. Sitting in the open air just outside the open doors of the crowded music-room, they had listened to the three chamber works. Only a year before his Three Choirs encounter with Elgar, Walton had been one of many signatories in protest at a chapter on British Music that E. J. Dent had written in a German publication, Adler's *Handbuch der Musikgeschichte*. In the protestors' eyes Dent had belittled Elgar by giving him far too little space and by castigating his music as being 'for English ears . . . too emotional and not quite free from vulgarity . . . pompous in style and of too deliberate nobility of expression' and describing his chamber music as 'dry and academic'. Despite the debt that Walton owed Dent, his signature joined those of George Bernard Shaw, Hamilton Harty, John Ireland, E. J. Moeran, Augustus John and many others on a letter organised by Philip Heseltine and widely distributed to the principal newspapers in England and Germany. Walton's admiration of Elgar did

33 Dora Foss, 'Memoirs of Walton'.
34 Basil Maine, *Twang with our Music*, 113–14.
35 Dora Foss, 'Memoirs of Walton'.
36 *The Journals of Arnold Bennett*, 429–30. Osbert Sitwell recalled the occasion in greater detail in *Laughter in the Next Room*, 195–7 (208–10).

not waver. During a war-time visit to Huddersfield to record *Belshazzar's Feast* for the gramophone, he was interviewed by a reporter for the *Yorkshire Observer* who quoted him as saying: 'There's no other English composer to touch Elgar. He's bigger than Delius, bigger than Vaughan Williams. He's becoming bigger all the time. Consider his *Falstaff*. A superb work . . . a much finer tone poem than [Richard Strauss's] *Don Quixote*.'[37] Asked if he saw any affinity between his own later work and that of Elgar's, he replied that he could see very little.

The Viola Concerto quickly established itself and was not short of interpreters. When it appeared in the 1930 Prom season, the soloist was Bernard Shore who had recently been appointed principal viola of the new BBC Symphony Orchestra. Frederick Riddle was the first to record the concerto, with the composer conducting the London Symphony Orchestra, in the Kingsway Hall in December 1937. Another interpreter was violinist-turned-violist William Primrose who, as well as premièring the work in America, was twice to record the work, in July 1946 with the composer conducting the Philharmonia Orchestra in EMI's Abbey Road Studios, and with Sargent conducting the Royal Philharmonic Orchestra, a record released in 1955. He made his début with the work at a Royal Philharmonic Society concert on 27 February 1936 conducted by Sir Thomas Beecham who was making a rare excursion into Walton.[38] It proved to be an uncomfortable experience for Primrose. As one account[39] has it, while there were adequate rehearsals Beecham had only attended the last one and during the actual performance things came adrift in the scherzo. Beecham's only comment was, 'Well, at least we finished together, dear boy!' For this performance, with the apparent approval of the composer, Primrose rewrote some passages in all three movements. These included playing 'rapid, virtuosic passages an octave higher than was the composer's intention, in order to avoid that unseemly scrubbing that so often resulted from placement on the lower two strings'. He continued

---

37 Interview with Charles Stuart, *Yorkshire Observer*, 21 December 1942, 2. Jürgen Schaarwächter has pointed out the similarity between the trio in the *Battle of Britain* March and Elgar's *Falstaff* (presumably the broad Prince Hal theme at figure 4) in 'On Walton's Late Music', *British Music* (The Journal of the British Music Society), Vol. 20 (1998), 54.

38 Beecham returned to the concerto at Eastbourne on 1 April 1939, with Frederick Riddle and the LPO, but only as a late replacement for a Handel oboe concerto owing to the indisposition of Leon Goossens. When Riddle and Beecham repeated the work at a Royal Philharmonic Society concert at the Royal Albert Hall on 19 November 1947, Vaughan Williams presented Walton with the Society's Gold Medal. Another occasion when Beecham conducted Walton was in the *Sinfonia Concertante* at Queen's Hall on 11 March 1934 with the LPO and soloist Harriet Cohen who has memorably written of the rehearsals and performance in her autobiography *A Bundle of Time*, 235–7. The only Walton work that Beecham conducted with any frequency was the first *Façade* Suite which he introduced to America with the New York Philharmonic Orchestra in January 1936.

to use these slight revisions in public performances and in his two recordings for the gramophone. When, in 1964, a revised version of the concerto was published, Primrose was surprised to find that none of his revisions had been incorporated in the score and wrote to Walton. 'His reply was less than enlightening, and I continued in my ignorance! Time passed, and much later I learned from an obscure source . . . that in a local performance of the work when Walton was present, the soloist had enquired in his own behalf the right or wrong of the matter and elicited the authoritative word that the composer indeed preferred his original conceptions to the emendations I had presumed to insert.' Primrose's suggestions have since been published in David Dalton's *Playing the Viola: Conversations with William Primrose* (OUP 1988).

Primrose, it seems, was not alone in taking liberties with the score. In October 1935 Tovey wrote to Foss: 'Please tell Mr. Walton that the reason why I cannot come to hear his symphony is that I am producing his viola concerto here with a local player [John Fairbairn]. . . . Incidentally, he is following the printed text, as he shares my feeling that Tertis is a little too anxious to turn the viola into a violin.' He added: 'I am very glad that Walton likes my notes on the concerto.'[40]

Walton revised the concerto in 1961, thinning the orchestration to double instead of triple woodwind, omitting one trumpet and the tuba, and adding a harp. The revised version was first performed at the Royal Festival Hall on 18 January 1962, with John Coulling and the London Philharmonic Orchestra conducted by Sargent,[41] and it was this version that Walton recorded in October 1968 with Yehudi Menuhin and the New Philharmonia Orchestra in the Abbey Road Studios.

If Edward Clark had been instrumental in getting the Viola Concerto performed, he was also in at the birth of Walton's next large-scale work, *Belshazzar's Feast*. On 21 August 1929, six weeks before the première of the Concerto, in his capacity as one of the BBC's programme planners, Clark wrote to Walton: 'With reference to the suggestion we discussed recently concerning the writing of special music for broadcasting, I should be much obliged if you would let me know at the earliest possible moment the results of your cogitations, as the matter has now to be dealt with officially.' The idea of specially commissioning works for broadcasting had arisen from Clark who had recently been impressed by some successful German scores, Kurt Weill and Paul Hindemith's collaboration, the 1929 radio cantata *Lindberg's Flight* among them. He was looking for other new works on similar lines, written for a small choir, soloist, and a small orchestra not exceeding fifteen, that would be suitable for broadcasting with all its then inherent limitations.

---

[39] Bryan Crimp's sleeve-note to the LP release on Imprimatur IMP6 (1982) of Primrose's 1946 recording with the composer.

[40] Mary Grierson, *Donald Francis Tovey*, 290.

[41] BBC Transcription Service recording 109928–9.

This whole question was discussed internally at the BBC when Clark was able to report on 12 January 1930 that three composers had been approached and had informally agreed with the following subjects: Constant Lambert, with *Black Majesty (The Emperor of Haiti)* to a text of his own from the book of the same name; Victor Hely-Hutchinson,[42] with *The Town* to a text by C. Day Lewis; and Walton, with *Nebuchadnezzar, or the Writing on the Wall*. In an internal memo on 13 March fees were set at 50 guineas each for Walton and Lambert and 20 guineas for Hely-Hutchinson who, as a member of the Music Department, rather felt that he should receive no fee at all but hoped instead to be allowed time off to compose. Unfortunately, no sooner had Clark discussed the matter than Walton 'spilled the beans to the Press', saying that he had been definitely commissioned.

On 13 January 1930 Osbert Sitwell wrote from Amalfi to Christabel: 'I have finished a biblical libretto for Willie,' and a letter that Walton wrote on 2 March 1930 to Siegfried Sassoon, also from Amalfi, confirms that *Belshazzar's Feast* was now work-in-progress. It also gives a further picture of his precarious financial state and his need to turn to Sassoon from time to time to be bailed out:

> It must seem that whenever I write to you that my letters consist of either acknowledgements for favours granted or for favours which I hope to be able to acknowledge. I need hardly add that this letter belongs to the latter category. The enclosed bill will show you what straits I am in, as regards my piano, but that's not my only trouble. The question is how am I to exist between April 17th when I leave here for Berlin, and April 24th when I get paid (Mks 500) for my concert, and incidentally how to get there even. . . . You are enough in touch with Osbert's state of finance to know that to expect help from him is not easy or possible: so I am more or less forced to come to you again for help. Except for my concert in Berlin next month, I don't see that I shall be having anything coming in till my royalties are due in October, unless as I believe is possible the BBC repeat my concert in London. But anyhow that won't be till June. My hopes however for the autumn are comparatively high. I had a letter from C. B. Cochran hinting that he would like my help in his next revue, both in a ballet and as a jazz merchant,[43] but I suppose one shouldn't be too sanguine about it. My royalties also ought to be higher this year as I have been having many performances, that hardy annual *Portsmouth Point* having been toured by the Chicago Symphony and played in New York by Koussevitzky, in Paris on

---

42 The South African-born composer and administrator Victor Hely-Hutchinson (1901–47) joined the BBC in 1926 and was eventually to become its Director of Music from 1944 to 1947. Today he is probably best known for his *Carol Symphony*.

43 Berners' ballet *Luna Park* formed part of Cochran's 1930 Revue that opened on 27 March. Walton's friend Spike Hughes was involved as an orchestrator for the 1931 Revue and, on Walton's recommendation, 'Bumps' Greenbaum was the conductor of some Cochran shows in 1932 and 1933.

the radio, in Birmingham by Boult, and even it has penetrated the forbidding portals of the Royal College. The *Sinfonia Concertante* has done less well, but that's to be expected, only having been played in Paris, Geneva and London. It was a great pity that Beecham was ill for the latter performance. The Viola Concerto is not yet out so it can't really start its career until the autumn. A deluxe signed by author and the composer edition of *Façade* is going to appear in the autumn, 300 copies at 3 guineas which I hope will do as well as it ought to bring me in about £70. Incidentally, the records are out this month and it's being broadcast tomorrow by Edith and Constant Lambert. Work goes tolerably well on *Belshazzar* but I always am uncertain of its merit anyway at this comparatively early stage of its creation.[44]

Siegfried had enjoyed an idyllic holiday in Sicily with his lover Stephen Tennant, about whom Walton added: 'Stephen may well blame me for my insipid letters, but I have no equivalent of the exciting Siracusan life to describe so he can hardly expect anything else. It is good news to hear that he is so well – so pink & chubby & I hope you are the same.' His pleas were answered: Siegfried paid for his fare and Stephen provided him with enough to purchase a new piano.

The subject of the new work had now focused on one aspect of the story of Nebuchadnezzar:[45] King Belshazzar's orgiastic feast that is interrupted with the writing on the wall. Osbert skilfully pared down chapter 5 of the Book of Daniel into a workable text, prefacing this with the prophesy of Isaiah and paraphrasing Psalm 137 for the lament of the Israelites and Psalm 81 for the hymn of praise that brings the work to a jubilant close.[46] Osbert had wanted to end with the nursery verses 'How far to Babylon?' but Walton rightly would not agree.[47]

On 3 May, when asked about progress, Walton replied to 'Harriet, my sweet' from Ascona: 'Your enquiry about "Belshazzar" can be answered faithfully & briefly in two words of the lowest parlance, "bloody awful". Anyhow that is what I think about it, though Sir Thos. B. & Sir [sic] Hubert Foss think otherwise, but they haven't seen the last part yet, which contains two or three minutes of boredom unsurpassed by any of the A. B.'s (this is not

---

[44] *Keeping One's Head above Water*, and Michael Kennedy, *Portrait of Walton*, 56.

[45] George Dyson later composed a *Nebuchadnezzar*, written very much in the shadow of *Belshazzar's Feast* and first performed at the 1935 Three Choirs Festival.

[46] In 1942 Osbert managed to convince OUP that he was entitled to royalties. Broadcasting fees were afterwards shared equally between Osbert, Walton and OUP whereas previously Walton had received two-thirds and OUP one-third. Philip Ziegler, in *Osbert Sitwell*, 185, notes that 'in 1996 by far the largest single royalty earned by Osbert's literary estate came from the libretto he wrote for *Belshazzar's Feast*'.

[47] Angus Morrison, talk given at the British Music Information Centre, London, 25 September 1982.

to be repeated) or anybody, & it is all quite unsingable. I shall remain here for ever, and I can't face anybody after this.'[48]

While the BBC was remarkably slow in sending any official letter of commission, a report from Clark dated 30 May 1930 suggested not only amazing speed on Walton's part but – inaccurately as it turned out – that the work was by then finished.

> I saw Willie Walton on Wednesday, who has just returned from abroad where he has completed the composition of 'Belshazzar' which is the work discussed between us and him in connection with the above mentioned project [Music for Broadcasting].
>
> It is for two soloists, small choir and small orchestra. Whilst abroad he has shown this work to various people whom it has evidently much impressed, and has been told by Berlin that they wish to broadcast the performance of this work, and also by Volkmar Andreae that he proposes to give it a public performance during the course of next season at Zürich.
>
> Part of the arrangement being that the first performance should, of course, be given by the BBC, Walton is asking us to let him know when he may expect this to take place in order that he may make arrangements for subsequent performances abroad.

News of this progress spurred the BBC to send a formal letter of notification of the commission on 6 June 1930. But Walton was not satisfied with its terms and asked his publisher, Hubert Foss, to negotiate on his behalf. On 14 June 1930 Foss wrote to Richard Howgill, one of the BBC staff of administrators, about the 'choral work which he is now working on', stating that 'as it stands I feel the offer is not a satisfactory one, but no doubt a short conversation will adjust the whole affair.'

In his next letter to Howgill, on 25 June, Foss quoted from one that he had just received from Walton which gives a clear outline of the form the work was originally taking:

> The BBC seem to have misunderstood about the length and nature of the work they commissioned me to do for them. Though I am only about half-way through, I can foresee more or less exactly how long it will last. Its duration will be a little over the half hour – certainly not more than 40 minutes. The material required for its performance is a chorus (not less than 16 and preferably about 24 or 32), two soloists (baritone and mezzo-soprano), speaker and small orchestra – its title being Belshazzar's Feast.
>
> It is in four sections, connected by a speaker:
>
> Speaker foreshadows the captivity of Israel.
> 7 minutes. I The Hebrews in captivity

---

48 Harriet Cohen Papers, BL Deposit 1999/10. The A. B.s referred to would be Arnold Bax and Arthur Bliss (but presumably not the third eminent A. B. of the period well known to Harriet, the writer Arnold Bennett).

Speaker, describes Babylon. (chorus with baritone solo)
II The description of the Feast. (Chorus with baritone solo) including the
(18 mins) worship of the various gods (orchestral variations)
                                    leading to
III A song of the Hebrews (duet for baritone and mezzo-soprano with
     chorus in the background for the entertainment of the King)
Speaker narrates (with orchestral background) about the 'writing on the
     wall' and the destruction of Belshazzar and the capture of Babylon
IV Song of Thanksgiving (chorus)

Walton was asking a fee of £25 for each of the four parts, but the BBC's response on 30 July was that there could be no increase on the £50, suggesting instead that Walton should write something else as his commissioned work. The BBC, blowing cold over *Belshazzar's Feast*, then looked in Lambert's direction, and on 1 October Foss (who was his publisher as well) wrote that Lambert was 'very delighted and interested and would like to hear more'. But by 5 November Lambert found that the idea of a choral work held little attraction for him. He was, however, completing 'a new work of quite novel character'. This was his Concerto for Piano and Nine Instruments, 'planned originally to act as a prelude to William Walton's *Façade*'. Would this be acceptable in place of the original commission? The BBC's reply was that it would rather stick to a choral work. But when it was discovered that no letter of commission had been sent to Hely-Hutchinson, the plan for commissioned works fizzled out.

Walton nevertheless continued with *Belshazzar's Feast* but, as ever, progress was slow. Later in 1930 he installed himself at Sachie's home in Northamptonshire. From there on 26 November he wrote to 'My dear, sweet, neglected Harriet [Cohen], . . . "Belshazzar" has hardly moved at all, in fact it is going damn badly & I shall probably meet the fate of that American friend of yours, Mr. Arthur Bliss, except, however I try, I can't work as badly as he does – but it is a pretty near thing. That is why I've come down here, to really try & get a move on. I have found London quite impossible, & my life has been altogether too low & hectic – in fact I need your chastening influence. . . .'[49] Three years later he described his difficulty to Hubert and Dora Foss: 'I got landed on the word "gold" – I was there from May to December, (1930) perched, unable to move either to right or left or up or down.'[50] It was not until the early months of the following year that he had broken the back of the work and the end was in sight.

Once *Belshazzar's Feast* had outgrown the scope of its BBC commission, news of a new large-scale choral work from Walton was fairly common knowledge in musical circles and it was only a matter of time before it was

---

[49] *Ibid.*
[50] Letter, early February? 1933, Casa Giachetti, Ascona to Hubert and Dora Foss, in Dora Foss, 'Memoirs of Walton'.

snapped up for one of the big English provincial festivals, such as the triennial festivals held in Leeds, Sheffield, Norwich, Gloucester, Hereford and Worcester. Of these perhaps the grandest was the Leeds Festival that had first been placed on a triennial footing in 1874 and had given the premières of numerous choral works by such composers as Sterndale Bennett, Macfarren, Sullivan, Mackenzie, Stanford and Parry. Dvorak's oratorio *St Ludmilla* had been quite a coup in 1886, while Elgar's *Caractacus* had been produced there in 1898, and Vaughan Williams's *A Sea Symphony* in 1910. Oratorios and cantatas had been the regular fare of these festivals. Sir Thomas Beecham put Walton in touch with the Leeds authorities, and *Belshazzar's Feast*, dedicated to Lord Berners (who had given him the £50 that the BBC offered) and now written for much larger forces that included a double choir and a single soloist, was announced for the 1931 Festival when it was to create a considerable stir and shatter the mould.

Beecham had been in charge of the Leeds Festival since 1928, and was to remain so until the war. The concerts were planned on a grand scale. The 1931 Festival opened on 7 October with Handel's *Solomon* and Beethoven's *Eroica* Symphony occupying the morning and afternoon. In the evening, Cherubini's Mass was followed by Elgar's Cello Concerto and Strauss's *Don Quixote*. The morning of the second day opened with Delius's *A Mass of Life*, followed after an hour-and-a-half interval by the première of Frederic Austin's *Pervigilium Veneris*, and Brahms's Symphony No. 3. The evening concert, which Beecham handed over to Sargent, began with Vaughan Williams' *Towards the Unknown Region*, followed by Bach's Double Concerto and Eric Fogg's *Poems of the Four Seasons* (another première). Then, after a fifteen-minute interval, came *Belshazzar's Feast*, and, to conclude, Rimsky Korsakov's *Antar* Symphony. It was Fogg's misfortune to have his work placed in the same concert as the Walton. As *The Times* critic concluded his review:

> Both the new works of the evening were received with acclamation, but the earlier events paled before the uncompromising directness of *Belshazzar's Feast*. The unaccompanied recitatives for baritone solo, boldly declaimed by Mr Dennis Noble, contributed to the powerful impression produced by the work, an impression cemented by a choral performance of unflagging energy and amazing volume of tone under Dr Malcolm Sargent.

The *Yorkshire Observer* critic was in no doubt as to the importance of the occasion:

> An electrifying result was achieved, and Dr Sargent was an infallible and inspiring leader throughout. Mr Dennis Noble declaimed the solo passage powerfully and with conviction. This was a great performance of a work which bears the indubitable stamp of greatness, and if for nothing else the Leeds Festival of 1931 would be remembered for having provided its first

public hearing. An ovation was given to the composer, who stepped on to the platform.

Frank Howes, in the *Musical Times*, hinting at rehearsal difficulties, similarly wrote that

> Dr Sargent secured a brilliant performance: the deadly effectiveness of the orchestral touches (the sickening taps of a wooden rattle, for example, at the description of the writing on the wall) was matched by the certainty and power of the singing of a choir which at first mistakenly thought that displaced accents and dissonant harmonies were too difficult for it.

If the choir faced difficulties, so did the orchestra, and Beecham paid for extra rehearsals for *Belshazzar's Feast*.[51]

Since the première, a legend has surrounded *Belshazzar's Feast* to the effect that the work was considered unsingable, thereby adding considerably to Sargent's skills in bringing off a successful performance. The *Daily Telegraph* review of 10 October certainly supports this view. 'It is credibly reported that when William Walton's *Belshazzar's Feast* was first tried by the festival choir something like mutiny broke out in the ranks, for its difficulties appalled even singers who were not new to modern technical exigencies. With the first full rehearsal under Dr Malcolm Sargent came a change of heart, and as the work of preparation proceeded difficulties and suspicion gave way to appreciation and enthusiasm.' Walton's story is that 'the chorus was sent the work in sections, and began to rebel against the difficulties of the choral writing. Sir Thomas sent down Malcolm Sargent to quell the incipient insurrection, which he did with that hypnotic power he possesses over choral masses.'[52] Sargent's biographer, Charles Reid, played down this element of revolt. He sought out some Leeds veterans who had sung in that performance and they denied finding it impossible. Yet difficulties there were. The rhythm was one thing. No work they had sung before, certainly no work in that festival, made such demands in a jazzy style that was alien to them at that time, with time signatures that changed rapidly from 3/4 to 2/4 and 4/4 with insertions of 3/8 bars. Pitching the notes was another matter. One solution to the work's difficulties for the choir may have been, as was Sargent's habit with northern choirs, to use Tonic Sol-fa notation, of which an edition was published in 1933.

The Times reviewer suggested that Festival novelties 'fall into two categories, those remembered because they got a hearing at the Festival, and those which make the Festival memorable'. He went on, 'We shall be surprised if *Belshazzar's Feast* does not create another landmark in the history of the Leeds Festival.' Just as at Birmingham in 1900 Elgar's *The*

---

[51] Maurice Pearton, *The LSO at 70: A History of the Orchestra*, Victor Gollancz 1974, 86.
[52] *Sunday Telegraph*, 25 March 1962.

Dream of Gerontius had effectively marked the end of the oratorio, so *Belshazzar's Feast* – rather nearer cantata than oratorio by virtue of its length – was to shake up the former form. Everything else by comparison seemed very staid. Not even Walton himself was to match it in any later work, and its closest counterpart is probably Peter Racine Fricker's *Vision of Judgement*, first heard at the Leeds Centenary Festival in 1958.

The first London performance of *Belshazzar's Feast*, at Queen's Hall on 25 November 1931 under Boult, did not have quite the same impact as it had at Leeds. (Such was the importance of the occasion, however, that Boult suggested relaxing the BBC rule of not inviting the press to rehearsals, and indeed they were admitted to the final one.) 'It was inevitable that those who heard *Belshazzar's Feast* at Leeds should miss the stalwart quality of the Yorkshire voices which had such overwhelming effect there,' wrote *The Times* critic. 'There were a good many places where a pardonable nervousness made their singing indecisive. . . . There were some faults of intonation, and some failures to sustain the impulse of such episodes as the clamorous description of the feast and the exultant triumph song of the final.'[53] Nevertheless Walton 'had a wild ovation, called six times and looking as white as a sheet, and very thin, as he bowed stiffly in all direction'.[54] A month later he described the performance and his reception to Harriet Cohen: ' "Belshazzar" in spite of a very indifferent & uninspired performance was a "riot" – in fact I've never witnessed such a scene in Queen's Hall before, if I may immodestly say so.'[55]

Benjamin Britten was among the audience at that first London performance, having bought a copy of the vocal score in anticipation of the concert. 'Very moving & brilliant (especially Ist half) – but over long – & to[o] continuously loud – I felt,' he noted in his diary. Of the National Chorus: 'mod.[erately] good'.[56] When he heard it again at a BBC concert on 2 November 1932, with Dennis Noble soloist and Boult conducting – 'a by no means perfect performance' – he thought it 'amazingly clever & effective music, with some great moments, I feel'.[57]

While the work is tackled today with comparative ease by professional and amateur choirs alike, one should not forget the problems it posed singers (and the broadcasting engineers) in those days. Boult was somewhat happier with that second performance as he wrote to the composer:

> I certainly think that we gave a better show of 'Belshazzar' than last time, in particular I think we solved the problem of 'The Kings of the Earth' [the

---

53 *The Times*, 26 November 1931.
54 *Edith Olivier: From her Journals, 1924–48*, 129.
55 29 December 1931, Harriet Cohen Papers, BL Deposit 1999/10.
56 Donald Mitchell and Philip Reed (eds), *Letters from a Life*, 217.
57 *Ibid.*, 283.

semi-chorus at figure 62], expensive though the solution is, for as you know the Wireless Chorus is entirely professional. I expect you were able to hear the rather slow tempo and determine whether you found it too slow. Personally I thought it worked out just right though we reduced the Double Basses to two and had a good deal of trouble with the bass line altogether, Bass Clarinet and Bassoons and so on had to be very much damped down. This with rather an exaggeration of the portamento between the high crotchet and quaver of the accompanying figure I think gave the passage its right value and meaning, and the unaccompanied passage finished dead in tune.[58]

The strengths of the work's première and the problems it posed for other early interpreters were emphasised in Neville Cardus's review of its first Manchester performance, on 17 November 1932, under Harty:

> To those of us who heard the work at Leeds last year this performance lacked savagery and the bite of drastic, reckless, yet masterful attack in choir and orchestra. Sir Hamilton Harty achieved driving tempi and by sheer rhythmical impetus he covered up much tentative vocalism and instrumentation. The pace during the climaxes swept everybody over one or two sinister chasms. . . . The Hallé Choir does not readily forget its respectable upbringing.[59]

Belshazzar's Feast never fails to make its impact in performance, right from its arresting opening which is a stroke of genius – the repeated-note trombone call that precedes the male voices' *a cappella* entry announcing the prophesy of Isaiah. Walton cleverly holds back his massive forces, through the expressive setting of Psalm 137 ('By the waters of Babylon'), with the poignant wailing of alto saxophone, and – another masterstroke – the solo baritone's 'shopping list' of the wealth of Babylon, until the feast itself when everything is unleashed at the praising of the false gods. The writing on the wall is eerily depicted, and Belshazzar's death is triumphantly proclaimed with a great shout of 'slain!'. If there is any truth in the statement that 'throughout his boyhood the music of Handel exercised a strange charm' upon Walton,[60] one might see the final Alleluia section as a grand Handelian chorus. The thrilling entry of full organ during the last held chord was a late addition that came about at a performance abroad.

The composition of *Belshazzar's Feast* had been spurred on by friendly rivalry. Lambert's *The Rio Grande* had proved a considerable success after its first performance at the BBC Savoy Hill studios on 27 February 1928.[61] The

---

58 11 November 1932, in Lewis Foreman (ed.), *From Parry to Britten*, 158.
59 Quoted in Michael Kennedy, *The Hallé Tradition: A Century of Music*, Manchester University Press 1960, 262–3.
60 Donald Brook, *Composers' Gallery*, Rockliff 1946, 106.
61 Lambert conducted, and the soloist was Angus Morrison.

first concert performance was given at Manchester on 12 December 1929, with Lambert conducting the Hallé Orchestra and Sir Hamilton Harty the piano soloist, and when the same artists repeated the work the following day in Queen's Hall, the *Daily Express* critic reported: 'There are only two composers who have anything to say just now. One of them is Constant Lambert, whose *Rio Grande* is as fine a piece of work as this syncopated age has heard. . . . Just before the music began, the other young-man-who-has-something-to-say came up and said: "Don't miss a second of this. It's great. Much better than I have ever written." That man was Mr William Walton.'

There is no doubting Walton's admiration for Lambert, even if their rivalry brought the occasional fragile moment. The following January Osbert wrote to Sassoon: 'Constant Lambert's success with his *Rio Grande* has, I am sorry to say, tinged a little their carefree friendship with a certain acerbity. In fact, I thought the other day that I distinctly heard him referred to as "that little beast".'[62] (This slightly malicious comment has to be weighed against the fact that by then the Walton–Sitwell relationship was beginning to fracture.) One striking feature of *The Rio Grande*, apart from the obvious influence of jazz and the elaborate cadenzas for the solo piano, was its battery of percussion (employed with much subtlety). This Walton was to emulate in rather grander fashion. To Lambert's bass drum, tenor drum, side drum, tambourine, castanets, triangle, cymbals, xylophone, glockenspiel, gong and block he added an anvil[63] and slapsticks, omitting only the cow-bell. The piano would have a percussive and not a showy part, *ad lib.*[64] And if a poem by Sacheverell Sitwell had been the basis of *The Rio Grande*, why should Osbert not do something similar for *Belshazzar's Feast*? The addition of two brass bands is famously attributed to Beecham who is reported to have said to Walton that as he was unlikely to hear the work again he might as well throw them in as well. What he was probably more seriously suggesting was that as extra brass were required for the performance two days later of Berlioz' Requiem, they would be at hand if required. Walton seized the opportunity.

In 1948 he made considerable revisions to the score, the most noticeable of which were re-scoring the last twelve bars with the top notes of those repeated chords sounding a couple of octaves higher, and extending the final chord to four bars. Roy Douglas, who worked on the revised version, particularly regretted the thinning out of much percussion. Walton recorded the

62 Letter from Osbert Sitwell to Siegfried Sassoon, 17 January 1930, in Michael Kennedy, *Portrait of Walton*, 55.

63 The anvil had been used to dramatic effect by Bax in his Third Symphony, premièred by Henry Wood in March 1930, and performed quite regularly at the Proms in the 1930s.

64 The piano is heard to advantage in Boult's 1953 recording of *Belshazzar's Feast* for Pye, with Dennis Noble and the London Philharmonic Choir and Orchestra, re-issued on CD PVCD8394.

work twice, in 1943 under the auspices of the British Council with Dennis Noble, the soloist at the première, and in 1959 with Donald Bell, the Philharmonia Choir and Orchestra. While the later version is technically the finer, the earlier has the edge in tension and excitement, and also illustrates clearly the work's original ending.

Just as there had been Anglican objections to the performance of so essentially Catholic a work as *The Dream of Gerontius* at the Three Choirs Festival because of its invocations to the Blessed Virgin Mary and the saints, it was the mention of eunuchs and concubines that delayed the appearance of *Belshazzar's Feast* at that festival until 1975 at Worcester. Thereafter it has made fairly frequent appearances. It became a firm favourite at the Proms where it was championed by Sargent. Walter Legge remembered a performance in Vienna in June 1948 under Herbert von Karajan – a conductor one least associates with British music – that 'moved William Walton to tears and privately to say that he could not believe he had ever been capable of writing such marvellous music'.[65] Karajan even conducted the First Symphony in Rome in December 1953 but these were rare occasions indeed for him, even though before his only performance of *Belshazzar's Feast* he had described the work to the chorus master Wilhelm Pitz as 'the best choral music that's been written in the past 50 years. I strongly recommend it to you'.[66] In 1934 there had been talk of the Vic–Wells Company presenting *Belshazzar's Feast* as a ballet[67] but this was probably ruled out because of the large costs involved. On 23 March that same year Walton wrote to Edward Clark, thanking him 'for getting Prokofiev interested in "Belshazzar", I hope with fruitful results'. The result of this fascinating contact is not known, but Leopold Stokowski conducted two performances of *Belshazzar's Feast* that January with the Philadelphia Orchestra.

Like *Façade*, *Belshazzar's Feast* was unrepeatable. It was to remain Walton's finest choral achievement. Only twenty-nine years old, he was at a creative high. His next orchestral work was to scale similar heights as he now turned his thoughts to a symphony.

65 Elisabeth Schwarzkopf, *On and Off the Record: A Memoir of Walter Legge*, Faber & Faber, 1982, 230.
66 In a letter quoted in Richard Osborne, *Herbert Von Karajan*, Chatto & Windus 1998, 225.
67 David Vaughan, *Frederick Ashton and his Ballets*, A. & C. Black 1977, 110 and 133.

6

Unfinished – con malizia

For sheer power and drama, the twin peaks of Walton's success before the war were *Belshazzar's Feast* and the new symphony. The latter achieved considerable publicity and attention – even before a note had been heard – from the fact that it was first performed incomplete, without its last movement. Although Walton was ever a slow-working composer, the symphony's gestation was particularly laborious. But this went hand-in-hand with a fastidious craftsmanship that shows through every bar of the finished score. Cecil Gray especially admired one aspect of Walton's approach:

> The quality I chiefly admire in William Walton, apart from the dogged tenacity with which he realised both his latent artistic potentialities and his ardent desire for worldly success, lies in his infinite capacity for accepting criticism, and learning from it – a very rare quality indeed.[1]

In Gray's eyes, Walton

> positively invites adverse criticism – that is what he wants. . . . I am thinking particularly of an occasion when he brought to me his symphony, which was in the throes of parturition, in order to play it over to me, stipulating in advance that I would give an absolute honest opinion without any regard for his personal feelings or *amour propre*. . . . On this occasion I am glad to say that I was able to praise the work unreservedly without a guilty conscience, except for one section in the slow movement, which I condemned equally unreservedly. So far from being annoyed, the composer was genuinely grateful, and in the sequel I was glad to see that the offending section was ruthlessly expunged from the final version. I do not suppose that he underwent this painful operation solely on my advice; indeed, I do not doubt that he consulted several other critical practitioners for their opinions before coming to the decision, and rightly so.[2]

---

[1] Cecil Gray, *Musical Chairs*, 286.
[2] *Ibid.*, 286–7.

Angus Morrison felt that Walton's willingness to accept criticism and advice was because of his growing awareness of what he had missed by not having a formal musical education. Lambert on the other hand, who had trained at the RCM, was inclined to be touchy about criticism. Morrison was one of those 'other critical practitioners' to whom Walton showed the unfinished symphony. As he remembered:

> Unlike somebody who is very cagey about his works until they reach a certain stage and they are more or less finished or in short score, he would show them to me and Constant and his other friends.

Morrison heard the early version of the slow movement ('incredibly beautiful – the best single movement he ever wrote') and may have criticised the same passage as Gray had done:

> He came and played it to me and it was much longer than it is now. There was a large middle section which became quick, rather jaggy, like the Scherzo in mood and in feeling, and then came back to the wonderful ending. He had his doubts and he played it to one or two friends. 'Do you think it's too long?' he said to me. And I said, 'Of course it's too long. You've said all that, you know, that sort of mood is in the Scherzo.' He said, 'You're right', tore out the page and left it on the piano.[3]

Hubert Foss was another to offer advice. In June 1933 he wrote to his wife: 'I think I have persuaded him to use for the slow movement that ravishing idea he played to us ages ago when he was starting the work.'[4] Angus Morrison also remembered Walton playing him that same tune, uncertain of where it should go. Eventually it became the languorous flute solo with which the slow movement begins. Morrison remembered that the first and second movements were completed first, but it was the slow movement that held Walton up. Even when the incomplete symphony was performed, the beginning and the coda of the finale had already been sketched. But meanwhile personal, rather than musical, problems had intervened.

Yet another person to whom Walton turned for advice and help was the composer and conductor Hyam 'Bumps' Greenbaum (1901–42), formerly a violinist in the Queen's Hall Orchestra and now married to Sidonie Goossens. Walton was a frequent visitor to their London flat in Wetherby Gardens that became a popular rendezvous for such people as Constant Lambert, Alan Rawsthorne, Patrick Hadley, Philip Heseltine, Spike Hughes and Cecil Gray. As Gray wrote in an obituary, several of that company, including Walton,

---

3   *British Music* 15, 30. Two discarded pages from the short score of that movement, once the possession of Angus Morrison, were reproduced as endpapers for Susana Walton's *William Walton: Behind the Façade*.
4   Hubert to Dora Foss, 11 June 1933, from Amsterdam; Dora Foss, 'Memoirs of Walton'.

would turn to 'Bumps' for help with their scores 'not merely for advice on technical matters but also for constructive aesthetic criticism in the process of composition. He had a deep understanding of, and insight into, all the problems of artistic creation.'[5] Having earlier given some assistance with the Viola Concerto, Hyam Greenbaum went down to Sachie's home in Northamptonshire when Walton was working there on the symphony.

The origins of the work date back to 14 January 1932 when Walton attended a Hallé concert in Manchester at which Harty conducted the Viola Concerto, with Tertis as soloist. He wrote to Siegfried Sassoon that month: 'Last week, I was in Manchester & heard a marvellous (the first good orchestral part) performance of the Viola Concerto. Harty has asked me to write a Symphony for him.[6] So I shall start on that when I come to Edith [Olivier]. A rather portentous undertaking, but the Hallé is such a good orchestra & Harty such a magnificent conductor besides being very encouraging, that I may be able to knock Bax of[f] the map.[7] Anyway it is a good thing to have something definite suggested & a date to work for.'

Work was begun the following month, first at Edith Olivier's home at Quidhampton, near Salisbury, and then at Sachie's at Weston. There he was given a room in the stables where, without interrupting the household, he could work at the symphony on the piano. In her memoirs of Walton, Dora Foss described the piano as 'a senile and disintegrating upright which Willie kept together and attempted to keep in tune with the aid of a spanner. I have never seen a more decepit instrument. On this pathetic wreck Willie was composing his great symphony.'[8] A date for its first performance was fixed, but by 10 August he confessed: 'I've been doing a good deal more ruminating than actual work.'[9] Things were looking up in October when he wrote to Dora Foss that 'the symphony shows 'definite signs of being on the move, a little spasmodic perhaps, but I've managed to get down about 40 bars which for me is really saying something.'[10] Yet to Sassoon on 20 December he reported: 'Though the symphony begins to progress a little, I've no hopes of finishing

---

5 'Hyam Greenbaum (1901–42), *Music Review*, August 1942. This view is supported by Spike Hughes in *Opening Bars*, 355, who also states that 'a great deal of Willie Walton's film music was scored at great speed and with typical expertness by Bumps Greenbaum when the composer was pressed for time'. It was Bumps who drew Spike Hughes to the music of Sibelius and he may also have intensified Walton's interest.

6 It was also at Harty's suggestion c. 1927 that E. J. Moeran wrote his symphony, not completed and performed until 1938.

7 28 January 1932. At that time Bax's first three symphonies had all been produced, the second having received its first London performance and the third its première, both in 1930. The fourth, which like the second was first heard in America, was to receive its first London performace in December 1932.

8 Dora Foss, 'Memoirs of Walton'.

9 Michael Kennedy, *Portrait of Walton*, 68.

10 From Ascona, n.d.; Hubert Foss Archives.

it for the April performance so I've written to Harty cancelling the date.'[11] And a few weeks later he told Foss that the symphony was 'not getting on in the way I feel it should do', especially when, as with *Belshazzar's Feast*, he had become stuck on a chord – 'in fact it[']s only an octave on A'.

Work was rather more advanced when he wrote to Harty from Ascona, Switzerland:

> I'm sorry that I've been so slow in producing my symphony, but actually I don't think it is any the worse for it, in fact, I hope & think, that it promises to be better than any work I've written hitherto, but that may be only an optimistic reaction to the months of despair I've been through, when I thought I should never be able to write another note. However the 1st movement is finished & the 2nd ought to be in another 10 days or so. But having disappointed you once, I feel chary about fixing any date to its ultimate completion, but it ought to be ready sometime next season.
>
> I must say, I think it almost hopeless for anyone to produce in any of the arts in these days. It is practically impossible to get away from the general feeling of hopelessness & chaos which exists everywhere, however one may try – so you mustn't think I'm an exception, & one capable of encompassing all difficulties – producing a masterpiece. But I'm trying my best.
>
> I am very grateful to you for taking so much interest in the work, & I really hope to produce something worthy of your genius as a conductor.[12]

In June 1933 Hubert Foss, writing from Amsterdam where *Belshazzar's Feast* had been a huge success at the ISCM Festival, provided some foretaste of the work in manuscript, as far as it had progressed: 'Willie's symphony is most exciting – really on the big scale and in the purest symphony manner: just like Beethoven and Sibelius and yet very personal. Rather tragic, and the second movement Scherzo really sinister. . . . It will I really think be a great work and of importance in re-establishing a symphonic ideal other than Brahms's.'[13] Amsterdam offered a temporary respite from the work, especially with Lambert as company. Foss described how, at an exhibition of old instruments, 'Willie behaved abominably of course: beating all the drums in ecstasy and turning a plaque of Richard Strauss to the wall!'[14] But the symphony's completion was causing problems, for its composer and others.

The unfinished symphony was now in demand by two orchestras. Not only was Harty announcing it in the 1933/4 prospectus of the London Symphony Orchestra, of which he was for a short time its principal conductor after the Hallé, but the BBC's preliminary leaflet for the 1933/4 season was offering

---

11 To Sassoon. Kennedy, *Portrait of Walton*, 69.
12 David Greer (ed.), *Hamilton Harty: His Life and Music*, Blackstaff Press 1978, 81, where it is undated. Susana Walton, *Behind the Façade*, 76, dates it as September 1933, but it almost certainly would be January or February 1933.
13 11 June 1933, letter from Hubert to Dora Foss; Dora Foss, 'Memoirs of Walton'.
14 Hubert Foss to Dora Foss, 10 June 1933. Dora Foss, 'Memoirs of Walton'.

two new works: Elgar's Third Symphony (a BBC commission) and Walton's 'new symphony'. The BBC's plan had been to build its second London Musical Festival[15] around these two important British premières. But it was not to be. The death of Elgar in February 1934 left only sketches of an unfinished work, while Walton's symphony, after postponements, was eventually performed near the end of the year incomplete – without its finale. (The year 1934 turned out to be one of unfinished British symphonies. Holst's death in May left only a single movement – a scherzo – from an otherwise uncompleted work.)

Walton now found himself in an awkward situation. He wrote in January 1934 to Kenneth Wright of the BBC Music Department:

> Having been ill, I wrote to Sir Hamilton Harty telling him that it had put me so much behind with my Symphony that it would be best not to announce it for performance on March 19th. In his reply [he] says amongst other things, 'As for me, I must look forward to the first performance of this work whenever it is finished, and I take it for granted that you will reserve this for me. If not ready in time for this season, it could be produced early in the next' etc.
>
> So you will see that the May Festival performance hangs on whether I can finish in time for March 19th. I'm not in complete despair about doing so, but I just want to warn you in time, in case I don't.
>
> I'm extremely sorry to cause you so much trouble by my indefiniteness, but I didn't quite realise in my talk with [Aylmer] Buesst [BBC Assistant Director of Music] how keen Harty was on the actual first performance. . . .[16]

But by 16 February 1934 he was informing Boult, BBC Director of Music:

> There is, I am ashamed and disappointed to tell you, quite definitely no hope of my finishing this symphony in time for its intended performance on March 19th – consequently as I've promised the first performance to Harty it will be necessary to abandon the idea of performing it at the May Festival. I am extremely sorry if this causes you much inconvenience, and I am sure you will realise that it is a rather painful situation for me to live down.[17]

The work had been advertised in the London Symphony Orchestra's 1933/4 season of concerts as a 'new symphony' by William Walton, placed second in an all-British concert under Harty for Monday 19 March. The delays caused a re-scheduling, and the 1934/5 prospectus now announced its first performance for Monday 3 December. Then, under pressure from both Foss and the

---

15 At the first London Music Festival in May 1933, Koussevitsky conducted *Portsmouth Point* and Bax's Second Symphony.
16 BBC Written Archives, Caversham.
17 *Ibid.*

self-governing LSO, and much against his will,[18] Walton was persuaded to allow the symphony to be performed in an unfinished state – without its finale. There was further embarrassment when the BBC hoped to lay claim to the second performance. Walton telegrammed: 'So sorry second perform-ance of Symphony reserved for Courta[u]lds.' On 19 November 1934 Foss tried to clarify the situation to Aylmer Buesst: 'I am afraid his first perform-ance of the complete symphony has, for a very long time, been promised to Sir Hamilton Harty, and the second performance, to the Courtauld–Sargent concerts. As the arrangement now stands, Harty will give three movements only on December 3rd, and the complete work, if it is completed by then, on March 18th. The Courtauld–Sargent performance is April 14th. I very much hope that this will not prevent you from including the work in your May Festival. . . .' Kenneth Wright wrote in pencil at the bottom of the letter: 'Let's wait and see. This arrives from a muddle betwixt composer & publish-er.' A much displeased Boult replied to Foss on 23 November: 'I fear we must leave it at this and wait until the work is quite finished before doing anything more about it; but the matter will certainly not be forgotten.'

The first – incomplete – performance did indeed take place on 3 December 1934, at Queen's Hall, with Harty conducting the London Symphony Orchestra.[19] The Symphony was placed before the interval, after a Bach Suite for flute and strings; the second half consisted of Glazunov's *The Kremlin* and three pieces by Berlioz whose music Harty particularly championed. The following day Harty wrote to Hubert Foss: 'I was satisfied that what powers I possess were all given to the Symphony the other night,' adding perceptively and somewhat ominously: 'Someday I should like to talk to you about the young man. Enormously gifted – something further has to happen to his soul. Did you ever notice that nothing great in art has lived that does not contain a certain goodness of soul and large compassionate kind-ness? Perhaps he has not noticed it either!'[20]

Almost a month before the concert, Walton had written to Patrick Hadley about the difficult decision he had been faced with, at the same time acknowledging the latter's advice:

[18] Interview with Eric Roseberry, BBC broadcast, 3 October 1965. BBC Sound Archives LP34332. NSA M454R.

[19] Rather surprisingly, according to Hubert Foss and Noël Goodwin, *London Symphony – Portrait of an Orchestra*, Naldrett Press 1954, 146, of the four rehearsals arranged for this new work because of its difficulty, only two were found necessary. Even so, *The Times* critic hoped that 'further rehearsal might smooth away some of the asperities of this hearing'.

[20] 4 December 1934; Dora Foss, 'Memoirs of Walton'. 'I am a terrific admirer of his,' Harty had written to Foss on 5 December 1932 after conducting *Belshazzar's Feast* in Nottingham and Manchester.

NINTH SYMPHONY CONCERT

MONDAY, MARCH 19

At 8.15

Norfolk Rhapsody .. .. *Vaughan Williams*

New Symphony .. .. *William Walton*

Poem: " Ulalume" .. .. .. *Holbrooke*

In a Summer Garden .. .. .. *Delius*

Overture: " Cockaigne" .. .. .. *Elgar*

CONDUCTOR

SIR HAMILTON HARTY

From the BBC Symphony Orchestra's 1933–34 Prospectus: the announcement of première that never took place.

LONDON SYMPHONY ORCHESTRA

FOURTH SYMPHONY CONCERT

Programme for

MONDAY, DECEMBER 3rd, 1934

Suite in B minor for flute and strings ... *Bach*
Solo Flute—GORDON WALKER.

New Symphony ... ... *William Walton*
(First Performance.)

" The Kremlin " ... ... *Glazounoff*
(For Orchestra and Brass Orchestra)
(First Performance in London.)

(*a*) Scherzo : " Queen Mab " ... *Berlioz*
(" Romeo and Juliet ")

(*b*) Chasse Royale et Orage (Les Troyens)
Berlioz

(*c*) Rakoczy March (Faust) .... *Berlioz*

CONDUCTOR

Sir HAMILTON HARTY

From the London Symphony Orchestra's 1934–35 Prospectus: the announcement
of the première of the incomplete symphony.

117

There is little doubt I could have pumped out, tolerably easily, a brilliant, out-of-the-place pointless & vacuous finale in time for this performance, or I might have got Arthur Benjamin to 'ghost' for me! (of course, please pass this tit-bit on!). But that is where you, or rather your letter, stepped in. Instead of doing that, egged on by you, I persisted in finding something which I felt to be right & tolerably up to the standard of the previous movements. This involved me in endless trouble & I've burnt about 3 finales, when I saw that they weren't really leading anywhere or saying anything. And it is only comparatively lately that I've managed to get going on what I hope is the last attempt. At the moment I need hardly add that I'm held up. . . . Whether it is a wise decision to have arrived at, I hardly dare to think. Harty, who has behaved like a lamb, was more or less willing to wait till March, but the LSO committee said that another postponement would be fatal, & that if I agreed they would do it without the finale. . . . Luckily, however, in this work, it is not a case of it being 'made' by the finale. The three existing movements, though I say it who shouldn't, are about as good as they could be & if I can bring 'off' a finale as good as them, the whole symphony will be a 'bit of orlright' which is, for me, saying a hell of a lot.[21]

He was soon to confess to Hadley 'of no longer being able to look at a piece of MS paper without acute nausea'.[22]

The symphony, incomplete as it was, created a great impression, and *The Times* critic probably expressed the general feeling when he wrote that Walton's

seriousness is beyond question. If anything, it is rather too much forced on the attention. That 'symphonic ideal', which Sibelius more than any other composer seems to have re-created for the rising generation, is consciously and strenuously pursued throughout the three movements. . . . The slow movement, including some passages of quite entrancing melodic arabesques, is the most interesting of them all, but does not afford mental relaxation. Is that what the finale is to do?

After the première there was a lavish party at the palatial London home of Lady Wimborne who, as will be seen, was now the most important woman in Walton's life. Two further performances of the three-movement symphony followed in the Courtauld–Sargent series on 1 and 2 April with Sargent conducting. After the first of these William McNaught, as critic of the *Evening News*, neatly put his finger on the symphony's standing:

---

[21] 9 November 1934, in Christopher Palmer's sleeve-note for Chandos CHAN8862 and Eric Wetherell, *'Paddy' – The Life and Music of Patrick Hadley*, Thames Publishing 1997, 37.

[22] Letter (1935), Wetherell, *op. cit.*, 157.

The symphony is full of effects that have to be classed as modernisms. Yet it is quite different from the modern type. In the first place it is romantic, and makes no concealment of its leanings in this direction. Over and over again it dwells upon the kind of effect against which the modern anti-romantic rule has been drawn. By the rule it is old-fashioned; but by reaching backward in its thought and forward in its expression it unites two worlds in a manner far more progressive than the ideal of being up to date and nothing more. . . . Walton's fourth movement is awaited with a certain confidence.

Walton was now under considerable pressure to complete the work. After the unrelenting tension of the first three movements, he had written the opening two or three minutes and the coda of the finale in ceremonial guise and then come to a stop, uncertain how to continue. In July 1934 he had written to Dora Foss: 'In spite of my having progressed a little with this last movement, I feel at the end of my tether. . . . As a matter of fact I'm not at all sure that I shan't have to begin this movement all over again. . . .'[23] The solution apparently came from Lambert – a fugue. And when Walton claimed not to know how to write one (although he had already written *two* in the last movement of his first string quartet) Lambert suggested consulting *Grove's Dictionary of Music and Musicians*. The article there on Fugue was written by none other than Vaughan Williams who had used one in his Fourth Symphony, which was first heard on 10 April 1935 in between the two premières of Walton's Symphony. (Before the première of Vaughan Williams' new symphony, Arthur Benjamin is reported as saying, 'I met Willy Walton on my way to the Hall and he said – having been to rehearsals – that we were going to hear the greatest symphony since Beethoven.'[24]) At first he 'jibbed about the fugue'. There was, he felt, a 'slight prejudice about fugues in symphonies',[25] carrying with it the suspicion that the composer could find no other way out. Yet there was an honourable precedent – the fugato section in the last movement of Elgar's Second Symphony.

Nevertheless, a fugue provided the solution to his problem. On 9 July 1935 he wrote from Sachie's to Hubert Foss: 'I've been here some ten days or so & have produced this for the 3rd subject, but am shivering on the brink about it I need hardly say.' And beneath he sketched out the fugal subject. 'There are still one or two things in the 3rd [movement] I've not yet made up my mind about,' he added, 'but will let you have it soon for engraving.'[26] The last movement was finished by the end of August – with *two* fugato sections – and approved by Harty in the first week of September.

[23] 21 July 1934 at Weston; Dora Foss, 'Memoirs of Walton'.
[24] Ursula Vaughan Williams, *R. V. W. – A Biography of Ralph Vaughan Williams*, OUP 1964, 205.
[25] Interview with Eric Roseberry, BBC, 3 October 1965.
[26] Hubert Foss Archives.

The completed work was first heard on 6 November 1935 at the end of what Richard Capell, in the *Daily Telegraph*, called 'an enormously long concert'. The programme this time opened with Strauss's *Don Juan*, followed by Chopin's Piano Concerto No. 1 (with Josef Hofmann as soloist), part of a Mozart Divertimento K334, and the Symphony. Once again the venue was Queen's Hall and once again the conductor was Sir Hamilton Harty, this time conducting the BBC Symphony Orchestra.

'The applause at the close was overwhelming, and when Mr Walton, a slim, shy, young man, came on to the platform he was cheered continuously for five minutes,' wrote the *News Chronicle* critic.[27] *The Times* critic found the Scherzo 'much clearer than at first hearing' and wondered whether the composer had revised the orchestration. 'The Adagio grows on one, the elegiac mood is a relief,' he continued, and he summed the work up with these words: 'This symphony, full of invention and containing passages of great beauty, especially in the Adagio, has a remarkable eloquence from first to last.' After describing the first three movements as 'acts of a vast heroic drama, Richard Capell summed the whole work as 'music of energy – straining, battering energy'. A deeply impressed Henry Wood wrote to Foss after the performance: 'What a work, *truly marvellous*; it was like the world coming to an end, its dramatic power was superb, what orchestration, what vitality and rhythmic invention – no orchestral work has ever carried me away so much.'[28] Even Harty went as far as declaring it to have been the finest work of which he had given the première.[29] Afterwards there was another lavish party at the Wimbornes' house.

When it was known that Walton had had difficulties in completing the work, a fact clearly advertised by its first partial performance, the floodgate was then opened for doubts and queries as to whether the finale provided a satisfactory solution. Vaughan Williams thought that the work ended beautifully with the slow movement and had suggested leaving the symphony as it stood.[30] After hearing the first incomplete performance, listeners may well have wondered how Walton would be able to maintain the intensity of the first three movements in the finale. The one question that no-one can answer is, if Walton had held the work back until it was completed, would such doubts have arisen at all? Ernest Newman doubted the wisdom in allowing the performance of the incomplete work.

---

27 7 November 1935.
28 11 November 1935. Dora Foss, 'Memoirs of Walton'.
29 Nicholas Kenyon, *The BBC Symphony Orchestra: The First Fifty Years, 1930–1980*, BBC 1981, 116.
30 Walton speaking in a BBC TV portrait presented by Gillian Widdicombe, 26 March 1983.

Queen's Hall

Sole Lessees: Messrs. Chappell and Co. Ltd.

Symphony Concert

Wednesday 6 November 1935 at 8.30 p.m.

SECOND CONCERT

Programme

Symphonic Poem, Don Juan (Op. 20)   **STRAUSS**
Born 1864

Concerto No. 1, in E minor,
   for Pianoforte and Orchestra (Op. 11)   **CHOPIN**
1810—1849

Variations and Finale
   (Divertimento No. 17, in D) (K.334)   **MOZART**
1756-1791

INTERVAL

Symphony No. 1   **WILLIAM WALTON**
(First performance of the complete work)   Born 1902

SOLO PIANOFORTE: Josef Hofmann

The B.B.C. Symphony Orchestra

Leader: Arthur Catterall   Organ: Berkeley Mason

CONDUCTOR: Sir Hamilton Harty

121

I am not at all sure that Walton was wise in letting the first three movements be produced in advance of the fourth. He got due credit, of course (and he deserves every credit), for saying frankly that the completion of the work in a way that would satisfy him was presenting unforeseen difficulties. . . . After the complete inner consistency of the other three movements, both with themselves and with each other, we cannot help feeling here and there in the finale that Walton has been up against difficulties which he has not quite been able to surmount. Something of the unity of idea and of the close welding of the earlier movements seems to have been lost here. On the whole, good as the music of the finale is in detail, and superb as the parting peroration is, I have the feeling that Walton is not yet ripe for the solution of the crowning problem of his great work. In this first symphony he has put so much into the earlier movements that only a man of much greater age, with three or four symphonies behind him, could have known how to go, so to speak, one better in the finale.[31]

And he went on to name Sibelius as an example. But he was in no doubt as to the quality of those first three movements:

For so young a man the weight and power of the thinking and the mastery of the technical means employed are truly astounding. . . . Walton clearly has a harmonic language of his own, of every turn and involution of which he is complete master. . . . I know of no other living composer, not even Sibelius, who could have made a better thing than Walton has done of the first three movements.

After the complete symphony had been performed, Constant Lambert wrote in the *Sunday Referee*:

Although thoroughly personal in style, the finale of Walton's No 1 recalls the eighteenth century in that it represents a facet of experience and not a final attitude. Because it is comparatively cheerful in mood it should not be looked upon as a 'silver lining' finale in the manner of Beethoven's No 5 or No 9. . . .
  Walton's symphony taken as a whole is still a sombre production, and the exuberant finale provides a physical rather than an intellectual answer to the questioning and agitated mood of the opening. Let it be said at once that the finale is a rattling good piece of music. The two fugato sections show a few stains of midnight oil, but the beginning is excellent, and the coda has an irresistible drive.
  The last three minutes, indeed, are as good as anything Walton has written, which is saying much. It cannot be said, however, that the finale is quite up to the intellectual and emotional level of the first three movements. It would be unreasonable to expect a composer at the age of thirty-three to conquer a problem which neither Beethoven nor Sibelius resolved

---

[31] *Sunday Times*, 10 November 1935.

until late in life, and it is a remarkable tribute to the work that it should drag Beethoven and Sibelius into the argument at all. This and Vaughan Williams's Fourth Symphony are, to my mind, the two most important novelties of recent years, whether in this country or in Europe.[32]

Over a month later, when reviewing the new recording of the symphony in the same journal, Lambert had this to add:

The performance has all the vitality one expects from this orchestra and this conductor in collaboration. The slow movement I consider unsurpassed in modern music. The scherzo, which at first seemed a little lacking in substance, is seen on closer acquaintance to be perfectly proportioned, both in length and texture.[33]

*

Edwin Evans, in his programme note for the work's first complete performance, had tried to explain the 'practically unprecedented' incident of a symphony being given a première 'with one movement short. . . . There is no previous record of any performance of an "unfinished" symphony by a living composer,' he wrote. 'Indiscreet as it may be to speculate as to the cause of this long hesitation, two alternative explanations suggest themselves as plausible. One is technical.' But he was nearer the mark when he continued: 'The other explanation is emotional. We have to deal with subjective expression, and the emotion which pervades the Adagio created special difficulties for the Finale.'

When work had started on the symphony in 1932, Harty was then chief conductor of the Hallé Orchestra. Asked in 1962 whether the première had originally been intended for the Hallé, Walton wrote: 'I can confirm that my first Symphony was composed for Sir Hamilton Harty personally & for no specific orchestra & that he was free to give the first performance with whatever orchestra he thought fit.'[34] One might therefore assume that the work was dedicated to Harty. But a glance at the score reveals that it was dedicated instead 'To the Baroness Imma Doernberg'. And therein lies the cause for the work's incompletion. A clue to the work's intensity may be gleaned from an interview[35] in which Walton described the symphony as being driven by 'jealousy and hatred'.

Mid-June 1929, Walton went to stay at Edith Olivier's, bringing with him two women. One was a very pretty golden-haired American girl, Alice Leone Moat, whom he had met while staying in Bavaria with Stephen Tennant who had then described her to Cecil Beaton as 'a crashing bore & exactly like a

32 10 November 1935.
33 22 December 1935.
34 David Greer, *Hamilton Harty*, 80.
35 With John Amis, BBC Radio 3, broadcast 17 March 1972.

million billion American girls, her conversation passes beyond belief!'[36] Edith Olivier recorded in her diary: 'Willy adores flirting with Alice tho', with some purpose, he told us the story of his life so that we should realise that he rose from the ranks and so far has made no money, so isn't marriageable. This made clear, he can let himself go and is having great fun.' Edith was amazed at Alice's 'obscenity. She has no other conversation. . . . Just to mention babies, bedrooms or waterclosets is funny in her eyes.' The kindest comment she could make of the American was: 'If she were dumb she would be charming.'[37]

Walton's other companion was the young Imma Doernberg, Princess of Erbach-Schonberg. Born in 1901 and first cousin to both Princess Alice, Countess of Athlone and Princess (later Queen) Juliana of the Netherlands,[38] she was the widow of Baron Hans-Karl von Doernberg who had died within a year of their marriage in 1923. Edith took an immediate liking to Imma who confided to her while they were out driving: 'Willy likes being the only man here – as if Rex [Whistler] had come, he would have been quite in the shade as Alice likes R. so much better and he would have had all her attention!' Full of sympathy for Imma in this situation, Edith wrote that 'Willy looks a piteable [sic] little cad – a diseased one too, rather like a maggot – but I believe he has more character than appears.' But when a few days later the three of them turned up again for tea, Edith observed 'Imma and Willy exchanging furtive glances while Alice holds the conversation and thinks she's holding her audience! . . . Willy enjoying a double flirtation – but Imma is the one he looks at.'[39] When on 20 July Imma and William came on their own for the week-end, Edith wrote: 'They are in love and she returns to Germany on Monday.'

In August he was at Sachie's. Edith Olivier was a guest and William's predicament was discussed: he wanted to marry Imma but did not have the income or a home to support her. Nevertheless, on 25 August he wrote from Sachie's to Osbert. Beginning with a few pleasantries, he continued: 'I am now fixed up with Imma for life. She is coming over in October for a short while. And we have more & less definitely fixed up to be abroad together in the winter (subject to your august approvals) at wherever we decide to go. Amalfi or perhaps you will find somewhere just as good & accommodating in Spain.' After boldly suggesting that they would as usual spend winter

36 Letter 15 February 1929, quoted in Philip Hoare, *Serious Pleasures*, 133.
37 16 June and 9 July 1929, *Edith Olivier: From her Journals*, 98–9.
38 When early in 1933 it was known that *Belshazzar's Feast* was to be performed in Amsterdam, Walton wrote to the Fosses: 'We would get the Queen (of Holland) there, but she hates noise so we shall have to put up with Princess Juliana (a violin virtuoso) instead, that is if Imma can persuade her to come, which I understand won't be very difficult.' Letter, n.d., from Casa Giachetti, Ascona. Hubert Foss Archives.
39 28 June 1929, *Edith Olivier: From her Journals*, 99.

abroad in Osbert's company, he continued: 'I don't see why it shouldn't all work well. I think you will get on with her & you know you have no need to taker any trouble about her, it will make a good deal of difference to my life & happiness, incidentally you won't find her a bore in spite of what little D.[i.e. David Horner] may say & anyhow we all have our bores & sometimes have to put up with them.' He concluded the letter by reminding Osbert of the première of the Viola Concerto on 3 October: 'I expect to see you there.'[40]

Now that David Horner, whom Osbert had known for several years, had become his lover, William's presence was an unwelcome intrusion into the relationship. With more than a touch of jealousy, David wrote to Christabel: 'Willie seems determined to give trouble – Can he expect to riot around Europe in open sin?'[41]

As it turned out, Walton spent the winter of 1929/30 at Amalfi with Osbert and David but without Imma. 'So far so good,' David informed Christabel in January. 'Only one little row between Willie and O., which I started by accident and hastily stopped.'[42] He also mentioned the arrival of an intruder, the loquacious twenty-year-old Godfrey Winn making a return working visit to the Hotel Cappuccini. His long stay was not welcome: 'O. & I found Willie very thick with a young person called Godfrey Winn – famous in theatrical & literary circles but until now unknown to me.' Nearly three weeks later, no doubt with malicious intent, he reported: 'Willie, I regret, now boasts to me openly of the passion he has inspired in Winn's breast.'[43] Godfrey Winn's own account of his stay makes no mention of this. In the first volume of his autobiography he described his companions: 'David Horner, with all the air and graces of a dilettante, and a young musician from Oldham, with palely fair, long hair, a pale face and eyes to match, who always looked half-starved though he had an excellent appetite . . . an incongruous figure besides the others, because he had clung to his Lancashire accent and possessed none of the courteous manners of Osbert.'

For most of the day, while the others stayed working in their rooms, Walton was composing with the use of a 'very dilapidated upright piano with several notes missing. . . . By the time the evening came, he would often look so white and exhausted that one felt rather concerned.' Some evening amusement was provided by a portable gramophone that Walton had brought along, together with a selection of his favourite records. 'On evenings when our morale was at its lowest ebb, he would cheer us up with a concert. Each of us would be allowed to choose a record in turn.' One record that Winn remem-

---

40 Walton to Osbert Sitwell from Weston Hall, 25 August [1929], in Letters to Lady C. Aberconway, c. 1924–1961, BL Add. 70831.
41 1 September 1929. Letters of Lady Aberconway, c. 1924–1961, BL Add. 70837A.
42 8 January 1930, *ibid.*
43 27 January 1930, *ibid.*

bered was Delius's *The Walk to the Paradise Garden*.[44] 'Peace reigns pretty steadily at the Convent,' David added, 'but occasionally I want to shake Willie when he puts on his drowned rat face.' Winn rather more sympathetically described Walton as a 'sad pierrot-faced drooping figure'. Relationships within the hotel's cloistered cells were understandably somewhat fragile. Walton may well have been looking exhausted and pale because he had just started composing *Belshazzar's Feast* – 'a new work for the BBC', David informed Christabel. 'Words (very biblical) by Osbert & music (very oratorio) by Willie. I had to censor the words as I found them too anti-Semite.' As a break from work Osbert and Walton would go for a swim, looking very blue when they emerged from the January Tyrrhenian Sea.

In May 1930, when the Sitwells were at their father's Italian castle at Montegufoni, Walton took Imma with him, as he did to Edith Olivier's for Christmas, neither having a home of his or her own. The rise of Nazism was making life increasingly precarious for Imma, as a result of which she had left Germany that December as a more or less penniless refugee. Nevertheless, to Edith they seemed 'radiantly happy'. She wrote in her journal: 'He is *sure* they will marry. She – not so, but resolved *not* to marry him if it is going to harm his career. She is however quite as much in love as he is and I never saw two people whose frustrated love made them more radiant.'[45] On Boxing Day they went with her to Wilsford to have lunch with Siegfried who was nursing a very ill Stephen Tennant. After Christmas they went to Sachie's for ten days where they were also joined by Siegfried.

In January 1931 Imma stayed with Edith while Walton worked on *Belshazzar's Feast* in the stables that Sachie made available to him at Weston. When he came over to Edith's mid-January she wrote in her diary: 'I think he is really getting on with *Belshazzar's Feast*, though he won't allow himself to think so. He and Imma gazed at each other with that peculiar, quiet, burning look of theirs!'[46] Work on *Belshazzar* continued in Switzerland at the Casa Angelo, a *pension* in Ascona, by Lake Maggiore, in which they lived together, Imma helping with the German translation. Walton was, he wrote to Sassoon, 'immensely happy' and 'doing a vast amount of work', but having to interrupt the completion of the work with a visit to England to hear Tertis play the Viola Concerto at a Royal Philharmonic Society concert on 26 March. In a later letter he explained to Sassoon the problems surrounding their relationship:

> Imma only just got out of Germany in time. You will have read the new decree about people leaving the country. She has £15 which has to last her

---

[44] Godfrey Winn, *The Infirm Glory – Vol. 1 of his Autobiography*, Michael Joseph 1967, 278–9.

[45] 29 December 1930, *Edith Olivier: From her Journals*, 120.

[46] 17 January 1931; *ibid.*, 122.

for two months; after that she is uncertain of what she gets. Consequently, she can't afford to stay here after I leave on September 6th. I'm afraid that this will be the last time for long ahead that Imma and I are together. It is too sad for me to dwell on.[47]

No money was coming from the Doernberg estate and the small allowance that Imma's father was providing her with was soon to terminate. In consequence she was having to find a job and was busy learning stenography. While with swimming and canoeing in the Swiss lake Walton felt 'the picture of health', the uncertain situation played on Imma's nerves which were 'in rather a bad state'. In the subsequent months her health became variable. Walton was soon writing that 'life has been very worrying, and such things as symphonies have fallen far into the background'. The state of the English pound was a further worry, but as usual Siegfried Sassoon was a saviour, guaranteeing overdrafts as Imma's financial situation became 'more and more precarious' and the likelihood of Walton having to support her completely drawing nearer and nearer. Sassoon, whose own relationship with Stephen Tennant was being severely tested, especially owing to the latter's alarming deterioration in health, spent April and May with them in Switzerland.

In August Osbert wrote to Christabel that, after some weeks of silence, he had received calls from Willie in Ascona 'three times a day whenever I sat down to a meal: to say either that he was, or wasn't, coming here to see me. I knew that meant lack of pounds.' When Walton rang finally to say that he wasn't coming, Osbert asked him bluntly if Siegfried had sent him a cheque. 'Willie, gasping at my perspicacity, admitted that he'd got one that morning from him! but not much, I think,' Osbert continued and asked Christabel for her help as an 'Unknown Donor; it would do well, at any rate, with a view to the future'.[48]

Edith Olivier and Rex Whistler were present at the first London performance of *Belshazzar's Feast* in November. Afterwards they went to a supper party hosted by Osbert Sitwell at the home of his society friend, Mrs Ronnie Greville. The company also included the Wimbornes, Siegfried Sassoon, Zita Jungman and Evelyn Waugh, but, as Edith noted in her diary, 'this party was *Hamlet* without Hamlet as Willy and Imma went to the Londonderrys.'[49]

In February 1932 Walton stayed at Edith Olivier's to make a start on the symphony. Only the previous December he had assisted her in the selection of a piano for her dining room. But although Edith encouraged him to lock

---

47 Susana Walton, *Behind the Façade*, 74.
48 Osbert Sitwell to Christabel Aberconway. Letters of Lady C. Aberconway, c. 1924–1961, BL Add. 70832.
49 25 November 1931; *Edith Olivier: From her Journals*, 129. Edith, Marchioness of Londonderry, lived in Park Lane.

himself away with the piano, he found every excuse to delay working, even to the extent of taking on household duties when one of the servants became ill. After a fortnight a start on the symphony still had not been made. 'The symphony is unspeakable, it has been christened the "Ichabod" or the "Unwritten", only time will decide which, if either are appropriate,' he wrote in some desperation to Dora Foss.[50] Edith much enjoyed his company in the winter evenings when, as was her habit, they would read aloud to each other or listen to the radio. 'If only I could ever write anything like that,' Walton would moan when something good was played.[51] His shows of desperation were well summed up by Edith's diary entry for Palm Sunday:

> Willy now is writing and varies between thinking he is getting going and feeling sure that all he has done must be torn up. This evening he says it is anaemic, sentimental, dull and worthless. Says he has never been inspired in his life – and can't think why he writes. Says that when he was at school, he wrote to impress the Dean and since then he has been pushed down the slope!![52]

These moods contrasted with what Edith saw as his often juvenile behaviour. Rex Whistler, while thanking her for a delightful Easter, wrote:

> We seem to have been laughing most of the time! but it was all that buffoon Willie's fault. How I revelled in the security of my bed on Wednesday morning with no Willie to come and pull all the clothes off the bed. I still grind my teeth with rage at the thought of his behaviour and still more at his cad[d]ishness in locking his door on the only morning I was up before him. . . .[53]

Apart from one or two breaks to London, Walton stayed at Wilton until April.

If making a start on the symphony was proving difficult, money was a continual problem. On 28 January he had written to 'dear Sieg' from Faringdon House, Berners' home in Berkshire:

> Being on the verge of financial embarrassment, perhaps you will be so kind as to sign the enclosed form guaranteeing me an overdraft, as you said you would. It is only as a safeguard as I am managing to keep my nose above water. As soon as the 'Daily Dispatch' pays me for the Xmas carol[54] I wrote for it [*Make We Joy Now in This Feast*] I shall be alright, as I shall

---

[50] Letter from Quidhampton to Dora Foss, n.d. (February or March 1932); Hubert Foss Archives.

[51] *Edith Olivier: From her Journals*, 130–1.

[52] 20 March 1932, *ibid.*, 132.

[53] 1 April 1932, *ibid.*, 132.

[54] It appeared in the Christmas Eve 1931 edition of that paper. Four years earlier Heseltine (Warlock) had composed a carol, *Bethlehem Down*, for publication in the *Daily Telegraph* on Christmas Eve. Christopher Palmer has suggested that Walton's

receive the magnificent sum of £10-10. Also I deposited my 120 Decca shares with the bank & the manager seems quite pleased with them! Incidentally they are now mine, as dear Lil Courtauld,[55] as I saw in her will, forgave all the paltry sums that she had lent to various 'down-and-outs'.[56]

No sooner had this been written than, like an answer to a prayer, there came a life-line. That wealthy patroness of music, Mrs Courtauld, had died the previous Christmas, and on 25 February Samuel Courtauld wrote to Siegfried Sassoon:

> I know that you are an old friend of William Walton and I am very pleased if you really think that my wife's bequest to him [of £500 per annum for life] will help him to produce the best that is in him. We both thought that what he has done already is far ahead of anything written in this country for a very long time and in the very front rank anywhere.[57]

Samuel Courtauld was a friend and great admirer of Christabel, and the bequest quite likely came at her suggestion. Walton had already been informed of the bequest and on 4 February he wrote from Carlyle Square to 'Darling angel Christabel':

> I am completely overcome, and can only cry & pray. I do so hope that I shan't let everybody down. I must write a work really worthy of Lil & Sam's wonderful & unbelievable trust and generosity. I hope I'm capable of it. Darling, I am so grateful, ever yours.[58]

In April he met up with Osbert in Venice. 'Willie is here for a few days and is fantastically himself,' Osbert wrote to Christabel and then, not able to resist a sneer, added: 'He said to me yesterday, which I thought very typical of his mental processes "They make soap here don't they? I know they have silk-worms." '[59]

In September 1932 he conducted the Viola Concerto at the Worcester Three Choirs Festival, staying with the Fosses at the Foley Arms in Malvern and enjoying with them a drive through the Wye valley. At the end of that week he stayed with Sassoon at Bath. The following month, news that Imma was ill made him travel to Ascona to be with her. 'I've had a rush of telegrams from the baroness asking me to join her at once,' he wrote to Dora

---

carols may have been modelled on those by Heseltine. *Make We Joy* may have been a homage to Heseltine whose death by suicide had occurred the previous Christmas.

55 Elizabeth Courtauld founded the Courtauld–Sargent Concerts (or The Concert Club as they were initially known), their first season being in 1929.

56 Siegfried Loraine Sassoon. Letters to Mrs. C. M. M. McLaren, 1927–1933, BL Add. 70775 fols 102–110v.

57 *Ibid.*

58 4 February 1932. Letters of Lady Aberconway, 1927–1940, BL 70776 fols 77–99v.

59 19 April 1932. Letters of Lady C. Aberconway, c. 1924–1961, BL Add 70832.

Foss. 'It is so difficult to know how bad she is, but I feel she must be otherwise I'm sure she wouldn't have wired for me.'[60] From Switzerland he kept the Fosses informed of Imma's condition: 'She is getting better slowly & I hope next week that she will be able to stay a[t] Pallanza further down the lake in Italy with some rich friends to recuperate,' he wrote later in October. On 21 December he wrote to Christabel to say that, after a fortnight in Rome, he was now 'installed in a commodious flat' as Casa Angelo was being pulled down and rebuilt.

> . . . Though the 1st performance of my symphony is announced for April 3rd the fact that there is not a hope of my finishing it by then, has made me write to Harty (who has been very nice about it, & may substitute your Viola Concerto[61] in its place) cancelling the date & having the performance next season. . . .
>
> Imma, though she is much better than she was, is still not very strong. She has prospects of getting a rather good job in the spring & there are hopes that the estate from which she derives her money will start paying again sometime in the coming year, so we shall accordingly I hope be in a very much better position financially speaking if all that materialises.
>
> What would be happening to us, except for that providential happening, heaven alone knows, & I'm full of gratitude & your slave for life (I was that before) for whatever part you may have had in it.
>
> Dear Christabel, what should I do without you? . . . Imma sends her love, as I do too, only more so.[62]

One of those 'rich friends' with whom Imma had been staying was a wealthy Scot, Captain Neil (Boyd Watson) McEacharn, who in 1931, in response to an advertisement in *The Times*, bought an Italian estate close to Pallanza on Lake Maggiore. With his experience of floriculture gained from the park surrounding his own home of Galloway Castle, he renamed the estate 'Villa Taranto' after an ancestor and set about transforming it into a grand English-styled garden. While Imma led 'a life of luxury' at Villa Taranto, Walton could at least get down to the symphony. Meanwhile Hamilton Harty, aware of the real reason for the symphony's delay, had wickedly suggested to Hubert Foss: 'Why don't you go over to Switzerland and wrest poor W.W.'s Baroness away from him, so that he can stop making overtures to her and do a symphony for me instead!'[63]

60 Letter 'In the train', n.d. Hubert Foss Archives.
61 Walton wrote with a similar intimacy to Elgar's writing of 'our concerto' and 'your symphony' to Alice Stuart Wortley who was the inspiration of both Elgar's Violin Concerto and the Second Symphony. Jerrold Northrop Moore, *Edward Elgar: The Windflower Letters – Correspondence with Alice Caroline Stuart Wortley and her Family*, Clarendon Press 1989, 54 and 82.
62 21 December 1932. Letters of Lady Aberconway, 1927–1940, BL 70776 fols 77–99v.
63 Hamilton Harty to Hubert Foss, 22 February 1933; Dora Foss, 'Memoirs of Walton'. 'Rather a good joke!' Harty added in brackets.

But it must have been only too clear to his friends that however much Walton loved or was infatuated by Imma, he was hardly in a position to support her in her accustomed style of living or able to pay for her doctors' bills. Imma's friendship with Neil McEacharn was eventually, by 1940, to lead to marriage, one largely of convenience in that it allowed her to escape internment during the war. They lived first in Canada and then Australia.[64]

Some idea of Walton's state of mind at that time – and the mental stresses under which the symphony was composed – can be gauged from a letter he wrote from Ascona to Harriet Cohen in the spring of 1933. On an earlier letter (perhaps since destroyed), with utter insensitivity and total disregard for Harriet's Jewish sensibilities, he had inscribed a swastika. While fumbling for an apology he tried to explain both the pressures he felt he was under with the expectation of his symphony and the turmoil in his personal life:

> I'm so sorry that I hurt you with my, what I thought, harmless if in somewhat bad taste, little joke & perhaps you will sometime both forgive & forget.
>
> It may or may not be evident that I've no sense of humour, but at the time when I got your letter I was considerably annoyed by it, rightly or wrongly, for at long last I had been going ahead, with what it may please you to call, my 'Sinfonetta', & the sense of being chivvied was & is, the thing that I'd been trying to get away from, & your letter, far from being a help, only gave me again that feeling that everyone is waiting for my next work only to turn on it & read & devour it, – of course, I may be quite wrong – but I'm sure that there are any amount of people waiting to say, 'of course, he may be able to write a choral work, but not a symphony,' & they're probably right.
>
> Again your prophesy of my coming 'bad luck' is not much of an encouragement either. If you feel those things, it might be as well to keep them to yourself & anyhow if it comes, I can't think that it will be due to a comparatively harmless joke of writing a swastika, but to other causes far more fundamental than that.
>
> On the other hand it may be that my 'bad luck' is past for I can't pretend that I've had much luck in the last year, nor has it been a particularly happy

---

[64] It was not to be a happy union because, as Imma soon discovered, McEacharn (1884–1964) was homosexual and his subsequent alcoholism led him to violent and sadistic moods. Imma returned to England in 1946 with a young Dutch officer whom she hoped to marry. Edith Olivier remained a close friend right up to Imma's rather sudden death in March 1947, from pernicious anaemia, within a few weeks of having heard from McEacharn that he would not oppose divorce. [*Edith Olivier: from her Journals*, 235, 305–8] In 1938 McEacharn presented the now famous villa and gardens to the Italian state. Until his death he travelled world-wide to gather plants for the gardens. He was buried in a chapel in Villa Taranto.

one for me, I admit largely owing to my own stupidity & foolishness. But these things are too difficult to explain in writing.

Anyhow about propitiation, I think if you saw the 'refugees' here, you even might be inclined to side with the Nazis, for they are mostly all sleek, fat & clean ones, living in luxury in the best hotels! Again, can one propitiate fate? Surely, fate is fate, like east is east & one can do nothing about it. Even when one does the stupidest things, with ones eyes wide open, the fact that one does them is surely fate, & one can't stop even knowing it to be wrong.

I must say, that in a time like this, when all the world is mad & suffering, I think it is next to impossible for anyone in any of the arts, to produce anything really permanently worth while, for however one may try to get away from it, it always forces its way between oneself & whatever one gets ones inspiration from. If it is not quite impossible, you must admit that it makes things considerably more difficult, not only in ones work but in ordinary every day life. But here I am again trying to explain to you something which is quite impossible to do with my limited literary talents.

I should like to see & talk to you very much, for though you may not think it, & though you may sometime, forgive my saying so, annoy & irritate me beyond words, I have a very deep & sincere regard for you. Why don't you come to Amsterdam to hear 'Belshazzar' on June 18th?

I don't know if you've heard it yet – perhaps you hated it, for you've never said a word to me about it. Otherwise, I shan't be in England till August I hope with the 'Sinfonetta' finished, if that awful fate you so kindly threaten me with doesn't break over my head. Since you've prophesied it, you might do something about stopping it! Anyhow I'm no fool & take you more or less seriously, & so I hope to be in some measure prepared for it. There is little doubt, to me, that I may deserve it, but for other reasons than the one you give. After all, one can hardly go through life having luck always on one's side – but perhaps one can, if one doesn't think about it too much.

Reading this again, I find it an impotently inexpressive letter, but I never could express myself in words, but with your instinct you will be able to fathom what I want to say.

Again please forgive any pain I caused you. Perhaps you will write to me soon.[65]

And he added the instruction 'Burn this.'

On 1 June 1933, just before going to Amsterdam to hear Constant Lambert conduct *Belshazzar's Feast* at the ISCM Festival[66] – 'my 5th work at these festivals!' – Walton wrote again to Christabel:

65 Harriet Cohen Papers, BL Deposit 1999/10.
66 On 30 March 1933 Boult wrote to Walton that 'the idea of sending the BBC Chorus over to sing "Belshazzar's Feast" has fallen through' as the expenditure of £600 was 'more than could be fairly undertaken in these hard times.' According to Foss, in a Prom programme note, 13 September 1951, 'Lambert had to conduct the choral

Between you and me, I've made a most idiotic mess of my life in the last year, but it is going better now. Imma came back from Berlin (she's been there since the middle of February) and we had a happy ten days staying with Neil McEacharn at Pallanza. She is now in Zürich & starts her job today. Of course, it is wonderful that she should have got one in these days & it will be a great financial help.

My symphony progresses, & I hope will be finished when I next see you which I hope will be at Renishaw in August.[67]

But the changes in his relationship with Imma were now seriously affecting both the composition of the symphony and his health. Hubert Foss, who was with him in Holland, had noticed how thin he was looking. Near the end of June Siegfried Sassoon wrote to Christabel that he had had 'no news of Willie for months'. At a Queen's Hall all-British concert in January 1934, that had included *Belshazzar's Feast*, Dora Foss thought he was 'not looking well – worry and malnutrition, I should think'. When asked in 1968 about Imma and the symphony, Walton commented slightly tongue-in-cheek: 'She was a very great friend of mine over several years, and this symphony is about a fearful quarrel we had in the middle of this idyllic . . . sort of business, and I wrote this rather awful tempestuous work – and it was really all her fault.'[68] In September 1933 Foss wrote to his wife: 'W. has been working on his last movement of the Symphony and is very depressed with its progress.' In December Edith Sitwell was looking forward to hearing him play through the slow movement. That winter he was going to stay again at Sachie's for a while, Edith's sister-in-law having written to her in anticipation: 'I hope to heaven he'll behave.'

And that is probably as far as the symphony went for a while, with the opening and closing material for the finale already sketched and Walton then orchestrating the three movements that were in short score.[69] In the summer of 1934 his mind was temporarily diverted from the symphony with the commission for his first film score, *Escape Me Never*, a title that might have been his plea to Imma.

But by mid-1934 the affair was virtually over. In August they both stayed at Edith Olivier's where Imma was able to convince William that it would be better for them both if they were not to marry but instead to remain just friends. Edith noticed how relaxed and happier they became once that decision had been made. On 3 December Imma, having first been picked up from

rehearsals, for want of space, in the Post Office at Rotterdam, he one side of the counter and grill, and the choir the other.'

67 Letters of Lady Aberconway, 1927–1940, BL 70776 fols 77–99v.

68 BBC TV, *The Lively Arts* programme, 'Walton at 75', introduced by Humphrey Burton.

69 Hugh Ottaway investigated the dating of the symphony's composition in 'Walton's First Symphony: The Composition of the Finale', *Musical Times*, 1972, 254–7, and 'Walton's First and its Composition', *Musical Times*, 1973, 998–9 and 1001.

Kensington Palace, joined Osbert and Sachie, Cecil Beaton and others at Queen's Hall for the final rehearsal of the incomplete symphony.

During the rehearsal Edith observed Walton 'pale and lean, smoking his interminable succession of bad thin cigarettes'. The difficult scherzo still seemed beyond the players' grasp but, she wrote with percipience, 'one has no doubt that this is an immortal work – a classic – something that will be a landmark in English music. . . . Incredible that this great, complex, rich creation should have sprung from him.' That evening at the concert everything went well. 'The orchestra played finely – quite another thing from the morning. It sounded glorious and was gloriously received – Willy being called 5 or 6 times. A stupendous occasion. It cries for the last movement. . . .'[70]

A few days after that première, William and Imma were staying at Weston, she confiding in Sachie's wife the problems of their relationship. Imma soon left Walton for a Hungarian, Dr Jacobus Tibor Csato, from whom she had been receiving treatment, who claimed that she had left Walton because he was impotent at the time. But in a life charmed with good fortune, Walton's affair with Imma was only to give way to another – happier – one. With Walton in such an emotional turmoil, it is hardly surprising that the symphony was still unfinished. He once identified the emotions that the symphony covered as 'frustration, in love actually, and it's why I stopped at the end of the slow movement and I couldn't go on until I got a new outlook on the whole thing which was created by another person.'[71]

That new person in his life was Alice Wimborne, the wife of one of the richest industrialists in England. As Walton's presence at Carlyle Square was less welcome now that Osbert's relationship with David Horner was well established, he stayed instead at Sachie's home at Weston. According to one story[72] this new romance blossomed when Malcolm Sargent arrived one day and suggested they visited the Wimbornes' country home at Ashby St Ledgers, near Rugby (famous as the manor used by the members of the Gunpowder Plot of 1605). But they had almost certainly met earlier. Alice had been a good friend of Osbert's, and Walton spoke of meeting her through the Sitwells.

Born Alice Katherine Sibell Grosvenor in 1880, the youngest daughter of Robert Wellesley Grosvenor, the second Lord Ebury, she had married Ivor Churchill Guest in 1902 (incidentally the year of Walton's birth). Viscount Wimborne, to give him his title, had a distinguished parliamentary career. A first cousin of Winston Churchill, he was Paymaster General from 1910 to

---

[70] *Edith Olivier: From her Journals*, 160.
[71] In an interview with Hans Keller, recorded 21 March 1972 and broadcast a week later on BBC Radio 3 during the interval of the Royal Festival Hall Walton Anniversary Concert. BBC Sound Archives LP34404, NSA M4390R.
[72] Sarah Bradford, *Splendours and Miseries*, 250.

1912 and Lord Lieutenant of Ireland from 1915 to 1918. It was because of his Labour sympathies that he helped settle the General Strike of 1926 – in his autobiography Osbert claims that he and Alice used much diplomacy to effect the negotiations that led to the settlement – and in 1931 he was elected the first president of the National Liberal Party. The family wealth came from steel works in South Wales. Described as a 'discriminating connoisseur of art', his main interests were hunting and polo, but Alice was extremely musical and Wimborne House in London became home to many musical soirées, including the private subscription concerts of the Quartet Society and even a chamber orchestra conducted by Hyam Greenbaum. ('A magic room for music, vaulted ceiling, rose red walls, great hanging candelabra . . .', wrote Edith Olivier.[73]) A painting by Sir John Lavery depicts a musical evening at Wimborne House in the late 1930s, with Ivor and Alice Wimborne and Walton in the foreground. Osbert drew this portrait in words of the woman to whom he too, in his own way, was devoted:

> Her great beauty, subtle and full of glamour though it was, and the fact that she was the wife of one of the richest men in England, were apt to blind people equally to her political intelligence, interest and experience. The attitude she presented to the world of a fashionable beauty who dressed with daring and loved admiration, the guise of an accomplished woman of the world, which was hers naturally, by birth, tradition and upbringing, hid from the crowd the clever woman who inhabited this exquisite shell.[74]

She and her husband, Lord Wimborne (who died in 1939), led independent lives, he being tolerant of her friendships with men much younger than herself, a fair return when his lecherous pursuit of Diana Manners some years earlier had led to rumours of divorce. Lord Wimborne was apparently a man 'who considered that his money entitled him to anything which the *droit de seigneur* would not anyway secure him'.[75] Walton spoke of fortunately getting 'on very well' with him.[76] More than any other woman, Alice was to have an extremely beneficial influence on the susceptible young Walton, to the extent of disciplining his composing and steering him away from the wrong social influences, especially the excessive drinking habits of friends like Lambert. Roy Douglas,[77] who began working with Walton during the war

---

[73] 30 June 1932, *Edith Olivier: From her Journals*, 138.

[74] Osbert Sitwell, *Laughter in the Next Room*, 212–13 (226–7).

[75] Philip Ziegler, *Diana Cooper: The Biography of Lady Diana Cooper*, Hamish Hamilton 1981, Penguin Books 1983, 102–5. Ziegler writes of Lord Wimborne that 'the various high offices of state that had been conferred on him – culminating in that of Viceroy of Ireland – had signally failed to curb his greed and lechery'. He adds that his redeeming feature was his generosity.

[76] Susana Walton, *Behind the Façade*, 79.

[77] Roy Douglas (b. 1907), a self-taught English composer and arranger, orchestrated many film scores by others, particularly all Richard Addinsell's from 1937 to 1943

on the film scores, remembered her as a 'fascinating, delightful woman'. He recalled how, on his visits to her home at Ashby St Ledgers, he and Alice would sit round a log fire after dinner and 'William would be up in the music room when after about an hour-and-a-half he'd come down with perhaps sixteen bars, having during the day plunged through chords on the piano and putting them down laboriously – a terribly slow worker. And of course she was very musical, and he'd play something to her, and she'd say, "Oh no, Willie, you can do better than that, that's not nearly good enough," and he'd meekly go away and do some more.'[78]

Despite the difference in their ages (Imma had been 28, less than a year older, when she and Walton met; Alice was 54 and Walton 32), her relationship with Walton blossomed, and in May 1935, to Osbert's great shock, the pair went off to Spain together. Edith Olivier wrote in her journal of 'much talk of Willy's liaison with Lady Wimborne who has wounded Osbert to the heart because they (being close friends) deceived him over it. Imma seems to have made him really happier about it. It has cured her of Willy I do think. She sees his vulgar, snobbish-*coarse* side.'[79] In November Imma and Princess Alice, Countess of Athlone were present at Lady Wimborne's party after the symphony's first complete performance, an even more lavish affair than the one she gave after the work's incomplete première. 'The Symphony seems to be *her* child,' Edith Olivier noted in her journal.[80]

Osbert took Walton's new relationship as a personal insult. In June 1936 he wrote spitefully to David Horner: 'Saw Willie and Alice walking down King's Road yesterday. She looked old and footsore and slummy.' In his four volumes of autobiography, *Left hand, Right Hand!*, he draws a discreet veil over the whole affair. As the Wimbornes were friends of Osbert's, he regarded Walton's behaviour as an act of betrayal and effectively severed their relationship from that time. Walton's fifteen years with the Sitwells had come to an abrupt close.

(including the popular *Warsaw Concerto* from *Dangerous Moonlight*). He also orchestrated Berners' last ballet, *Les Sirènes* (1946), the autograph score of which is entirely in Douglas's hand (in conversation with the author, Tunbridge Wells, 23 July 1996). From 1944 he was closely associated with Vaughan Williams by helping to prepare most of his later works for performance and publication, experiences he recalled in his *Working with Vaughan Williams* (British Library 1988). From 1940 until 1976 he performed similar services for Walton.

[78] In conversation with the author, Tunbridge Wells, 23 July 1996.
[79] 24 May 1935, *Edith Olivier: From her Journals*, 166.
[80] 6 November 1935, *ibid.*, 172.

*

It was Alice Wimborne who supplied the spark that enabled Walton to complete the symphony, and the turning point can be detected in that note of optimism that informs the last movement. She was also to be the inspiration behind the Violin Concerto and the A minor String Quartet.

The symphony was one of a number of English symphonic explosions during the 1930s, a decade that also witnessed the first performances of Bax's Fifth and Sixth Symphonies, Vaughan Williams's Fourth, and Moeran's G minor. If Stravinsky had been all the rage during the 1920s – and Walton's symphony certainly inherited some of that elemental savagery from *The Rite of Spring*[81] – then a potent influence on British music during the 1930s was that of Sibelius. By 1931 there was an excited air of expectancy as London awaited the appearance of Sibelius's promised Eighth Symphony.[82]

The last of Sibelius's five conducting visits to England had been as far back as 1921 but his popularity in the concert hall had not begun its rapid ascent until towards the end of that decade. His reputation had been advanced by such writers as Cecil Gray who devoted a whole chapter to him (and to Van Dieren) in *A Survey of Contemporary Music* (1924), and followed this with two books, *Sibelius* (1931) and *Sibelius: The Symphonies* (1934). Lambert, in his *Music Ho!* (1934), hailed him as 'the most important symphonic writer since Beethoven' and had himself conducted the slow movement only of the Fourth Symphony while still a student at the RCM in March 1925. In 1930 the Columbia Graphophone Company issued recordings of the first two symphonies under the baton of the composer's senior interpreter, Robert Kajanus, and these were followed by five volumes of Sibelius Society recordings between 1932 and 1935. There was the visit to London of the Finnish National Orchestra and George Schneevoigt in May and June 1934 with five of the seven symphonies, and the performances of Sibelius's symphonies in England continued to gain enormous momentum during that decade through the advocacy of conductors like Wood (who gave all the symphonies in the 1937 Proms) and Beecham (who mounted a Sibelius Festival of six concerts in 1938). Harty was another strong Sibelian, and it may be significant that when, on 24 October 1929, Walton conducted the Hallé Orchestra in the *Façade* suite (which Neville Cardus in the *Manchester Guardian* thought 'one of the wittiest things in music') Harty had included Sibelius's Fifth Symphony in the same concert.

---

81 David Cox, in his chapter on Walton in *The Symphony Volume Two: Elgar to the Present Day* edited by Robert Simpson, Penguin Books 1967, 192, suggests that the 'obsessive rhythmic pattern (nine bars before figure 68)' in the second movement 'must have been suggested by a similar passage in *Le Sacre de Printemps* (in the "Dance of the Chosen Virgin")'.

82 It had been announced for Basil Cameron's RPS Queen's Hall concert on 3 December 1932, and for some years the musical public were kept waiting – in vain.

Both Bax's and Vaughan Williams' Fifth Symphonies (first heard respectively in 1934 and 1943) were dedicated to Sibelius, the former in its opening bars making strong allusions to the slow movement of Sibelius's Fifth, and its finale concluding with a broad 'national hymn' that parallels *Finlandia*. (It is significant that in July 1937 Vaughan Williams asked the young Gerald Finzi to obtain for him all the available Sibelius recordings and Deryck Cooke went so far as to suggest that it was '[Sibelius's] example alone that enabled Vaughan Williams to compose his later symphonies and Walton to undertake his First.'[83]) Bax went on to quote from *Tapiola* in his Sixth Symphony (1935) and, Prospero-like, the *Tapiola* storm was to be conjured up again in the last movement of Moeran's Symphony (1938), a work that owes a heavy debt to Sibelius,[84] as do moments in Patrick Hadley's *The Hills* (1944). The popularity of the Finnish master at that time can be compared to the Mahler boom in the 1960s. After the second performance of Walton's Symphony at the beginning of April 1935, still then in its incomplete three-movement form, *The Times* critic observed that 'technically the symphony derives from Sibelius in method', and Richard Capell in the *Daily Telegraph* wrote that '[Sibelius's] influence is powerfully felt.' Certainly there are places where strong Sibelian parallels can be drawn.[85] As Walton, an avid concert-goer, later recalled: 'Musically the great figure of the time was of course Sibelius . . . and one couldn't help but know all his symphonies very well because every concert one went to one or the other of his symphonies was being played.'[86] On another occasion, he confessed somewhat defensively: 'He influenced me a lot in the symphony, although I was surprised, when I heard it the other day, how little there is actually of him – not how much.'[87] In 1979, after receiving an LP pressing of the Harty recording of the Symphony, he wrote to Christopher Morris of OUP: 'After 30 years or so it seems to me still rather a good specimen of its kind – and not at all, I find, like Sibelius! In fact I wish it was. Will you send me the min. score of S. Sinf. 6 & Tapiola neither of which I seem to possess, tho' I've got the marvellous Karajan recording of both works.'[88] He once admitted that the Fifth Symphony had had a great influence on him, and in 1982 he chose that work conducted by Karajan on the second of his two appearances on BBC Radio 4's *Desert*

---

83 Sleeve-note to Sargent's recording of the Symphony for EMI in 1966, ASD2299.

84 In 1934 Moeran was trying to convert Britten to Sibelius; from the diary of Henry Boys, quoted in Donald Mitchell and Philip Reed, *Letters from a Life*, 397.

85 Bernard Shore draws several such parallels in his *Sixteen Symphonies* which, besides providing an excellent analysis of the Symphony, also throws much light on Walton's own conducting of this work.

86 Interview with Eric Roseberry, BBC, 3 October 1965.

87 *Listener*, 8 August 1968, 177.

88 Walton to Christopher Morris, 3 March 1979: OUP files. The LP transfer of Harty's recording was not issued commercially until 1985 on Decca's London Enterprise label, 414659-1.

Island Discs. Although on another occasion he said that it was symphonies 4 to 7 that had particularly interested him, the influence of the Second cannot be overlooked. The repeated oboe note that opens the Walton is a strong characteristic of Sibelius's Second, and one feels a kinship of spirit between the broad sweeping passages for strings in both symphonies. But comparisons between the opening and closing bars of Sibelius's Fifth and the Walton show even closer similarities: the timpani roll with the open fifth on horns, and the slammed chords in conclusion (six for Sibelius, seven for Walton, something that Moeran was also to imitate but in a more bitter and disturbed manner). The bold, striding passage for horns in the last movement of the Sibelius finds its counterpart in the first movement of the Walton, and the use of pedal notes as a structural foundation and string ostinati further link the two composers. This caused Cecil Gray to comment that 'Willie Walton, in his symphony particularly, uses pedals so continuously that if it were a bicycle he would have crossed America from the Atlantic to the Pacific.'[89] Walton acknowledged that his symphony was built on tonal lines: 'basically it is more or less tonic and dominant'.

But despite the Sibelian influences, Walton's remarkable first symphony could have been written by nobody else. In performance, like *Belshazzar's Feast*, its effect is shattering. After the cumulative power of the first movement, and the nervous tension of the scherzo (marked, famously, *Presto, con malizia*), there is a slow – at time stormy – movement of great beauty, yet with an uneasy undercurrent of unrest, as suggested by its direction *Andante con malincolia*.[90] The jubilant, almost triumphant, finale was surely the only way to release the listener from the stern grip of what is arguably the finest post-Elgar English symphony. Arthur Hutchings was in no doubt about the work's importance when he wrote in his analysis of the work in the March 1937 *Musical Times*:

> There can be few more effective ways of realising the debt which English music owes to Walton than to imagine what it would be without him. . . .
> When all is allowed for insular prejudice, one can say for certain that we shall from now wait for every new work of Walton, as we once did of Sibelius, in the certainty of getting something of permanent value.[91]

---

89 Pauline Gray, *Cecil Gray – His Life and Notebooks*, Thames 1989, 135.
90 The programme for the first complete performance has *Adagio con melancolia*; the printed score has *Andante con malincolia*. In the 1936 printed full score, the words 'Andante' and 'con malincolia' are not set in the same type-face, suggesting that an alteration was made. Curiously enough, at the opening of his Fifth Symphony (first performed in January 1934), Bax had also used the expression *con malincolia*. The Italian word for melancholy is *malinconia*.
91 Page 215.

From a perspective of over thirty years, Deryck Cooke was later able to observe:

This tremendous work . . . had strong claims to be considered the greatest symphony of modern times, using the word 'symphony' in its traditional sense; the main challengers are Sibelius's Seventh, Nielsen's Fifth, and Vaughan Williams' Fourth. Certainly Walton's First is the most characteristic of our age, with its nervous rhythms, its piercing dissonances, and its hard sonorities. Its genuinely twentieth-century style is an entirely original creation: it owes little to the past, nor even to contemporaries, except rhythmically to Stravinsky, and even here Stravinskyan rhythms have been transformed out of recognition. Above all, the work is a true symphony, in that it says something fundamental in orchestral terms on a large scale.[92]

Such was the impact of the symphony that just over a month after its first complete performance Harty recorded the work with the LSO for the Decca Record Company, thus preserving his pioneering interpretation. Before the recording was made, approaches were made to Boult by Walter Yeomans of Decca to enquire whether 'this venture shall receive the unqualified support'[93] of the BBC by broadcasting the records. This met with a guarded reply from Kenneth Wright: 'Your suggestion once again raises the whole vexed question of broadcasting complete and lengthy works, and in fact, this would be a hefty example, as I imagine very few recorded works are fifty minutes or so in length.'[94] The recording, at an estimated cost of £650, was privately sponsored by E. G. Lewis who virtually owned Decca, and took place in Decca's Thames Street studio, on 10 and 11 December 1935. According to Constant Lambert, a few changes were made to the score immediately after the première: 'Since its first performance the finale has been slightly touched up. A judicious cut of a few bars has been made, and the coda has been rescored so that the fugato subject stands out clearly as an accompaniment to the main tune in between performance and recording.'[95] A brief cut was also made in the recording studio. Spike Hughes remembers[96] Walton remarking that a couple of bars in the finale sounded wrong. 'If you're not terribly devoted to them, why not cut them altogether?' He did just that.

Even speedier than the symphony going into the recording studio was its release on six double-sided 78s, price 30 shillings. It was in the shops before Christmas and it was reviewed in the January 1936 *Gramophone*. By the end of the year eighty-seven sets had been sold, that figure increasing to 400 by

---

92 Sleeve-note to EMI ASD2299, 1967.
93 13 November 1935.
94 15 November 1935.
95 *Sunday Referee*, 22 December 1935.
96 *Opening Bars*, 317.

February. Not long after the records' release, Harty received a letter of congratulations from John Ireland: 'It was the kind of performance any composer would envy, & Walton is very lucky to have such an interpreter of his work, which in your hands impresses me as the finest British work since Elgar.'[97] (Ireland much admired Walton. In a letter to Foss he had described him as 'a truly remarkable person . . . his versatility is astounding . . . the invention, imagination, & mastery of means are truly astonishing . . .'.[98])

Nearly twenty years later, while reviewing Walton's own recording of the work, Foss described the sessions:

> It was then thought rather a feat of recording, and in two senses it was; first, it was even more unusual then than now for a recording company to interest itself in a composition by a moderately new and not quite established musician; second, it was a difficult work to record, particularly under the conditions of the period. I happened to be present at all the sessions. We 'took' in the upper floor of a half-used warehouse near Cannon Street Station, in which there was an electric hoist that was liable to catch on the microphone, and make spoils, when in intermittent operation. The weather was cruelly cold, for instruments as well as players. My memory of the trials and tribulations of those grim hours is lightened by recalling the visits of distinguished guests who dropped in unheralded (especially for the last session) – Constant Lambert, Alan Rawsthorne, Spike Hughes and others. . . .[99]

The symphony's next performance was in Birmingham on 22 November 1935 when Leslie Heward conducted the City of Birmingham Orchestra. Hubert Foss was there and wrote to his wife: 'It really was a magnificent performance – the band is not really full of good players, but they went all out for this and pulled it off. The tears were rolling down my cheeks during the Epilogue, and so they were down many others! In some ways it was better than Hay's [Harty's], but not in breadth of experience. The thing that pleased me was the way it gripped the public: Willie had an ovation . . . took his bows splendidly and was noble all through.'[100]

Walton himself was soon in demand to conduct the symphony, at the 1936 Proms with the whole programme given to his music, and at the 1937 Bournemouth Easter Music Festival, on 26 February, with *Façade* and the

---

97 3 March 1936, David Greer, *Hamilton Harty*, 82. John Ireland made an almost identical comment in 1956 after hearing the first performance of William Alwyn's Third Symphony.

98 Duncan Hinnells, *An Extraordinary Performance*, 42.

99 *Gramophone*, February 1953, 228. Walton's own recording of the Symphony, made with the Philharmonia Orchestra on 17–18 October 1951, was issued by EMI in 1953 on ALP1027. It was re-issued in 1982 in a 3-LP boxed set 'Walton conducts Walton' SLS5246, and in a 4-CD set 'The Walton Edition' in 1994.

100 24 November 1935. Dora Foss, 'Memoirs of Walton'.

Sinfonia Concertante (with Angus Morrison as soloist) in the same programme. Just over a month earlier Constant Lambert had conducted its first
performance at a Royal Philharmonic Society concert in Queen's Hall, giving
it again soon afterwards at a BBC studio concert. (Sadly, in January 1936
Lambert's magnum opus *Summer's Last Will and Testament* had been
received with considerably less acclaim than the symphony, a disappointment
that not even one of Alice Wimborne's grand parties that was held after the
première could alleviate. But the omens were hardly favourable: nine days
earlier King George V had died and the capital was awaiting his funeral.)
Boult soon took up the symphony and, on 6 April 1938, Walton, 'now quite
recovered from my operation' (for a double hernia) wrote to Kenneth Wright:
'It really was a magnificent performance of the Symphony the other night [27
March] – Boult certainly did come up to scratch and I hope he will do it
again.'

For his next performance later that year Walton wrote to Boult with some
suggestions for strengthening the horns:

> There are a few places where the extra horns would be an addition. Namely
> at [40] 2 horns continuing for 13 bars. The 11th bar after [41] & from [44]
> to the end of the movement. The 8th bar after [70] 2 extra hns for 5 bars
> coming off the 1st crotchet of the 6th. At [78] all 4 hns for 13 bars. At [111]
> 4 hns starting on the 2nd beat & continuing till the end of the 3rd bar after
> [111].[101]

The symphony remained in Boult's repertoire and he recorded it in August
1956 with the LPO.[102] His last performance was for a BBC concert in
December 1975. A few weeks before the concert Walton, complaining of
sciatica, wrote to Boult who in recent years had fulfilled a personal wish to
record Elgar's *The Apostles* and *The Kingdom*:

> I can't tell you how delighted I am that you are conducting my 'first' for the
> B.B.C. I've been thro' the work with your Nixa record & tho' the record
> 'qua record' is abysmal, you've got it all right. The answer to three ques-
> tions are right & the metronome markings correct – perhaps the 'Maestoso'
> in the last movement might be a shade less so. . . . I've been having an
> interesting & enjoyable time with the 'Apostles' & the 'Kingdom' neither
> of which I had heard before. I like them both more than 'Gerontius' –
> perhaps your new recording will convert me! I hope so for I find Elgar's
> choral works rather inferior to the orchestral ones.[103]

---

101 24 October 1938. Letters to Sir A. Boult, 1938–1976, BL 60499. Walton wanted, if
     possible, eight horns to be used instead of four as demanded by the score. At Bourne-
     mouth in May 1949 Boult used six horns.
102 Pye/Nixa NCL16020, issued in November 1957, re-issued on Pye Golden Guinea
     GSGC14008 (LP) and on CD PVCD8377.
103 12 October 1975. Letters to Sir A. Boult, 1938–1976, BL 60499. Printed in full in

Walton was sent a tape of the broadcast (which has since been commercially released on CD[104]) and wrote afterwards from Ischia:

> The first & second movements are excellent. However I found the third movement too fast, but that is probably my fault – I must have given you the wrong metronome markings & as soon as I'm within distance of my metronome I will check these. Again at the end of the fourth movement I found it too fast, most likely for the same reasons, so I will go into it.[105]

Boult, then aged eighty-six, did not conduct the work again. The BBC tried to persuade him to repeat the performance at the 1976 Proms but he refused. 'Somehow I couldn't face all that malice a second time. . . .'[106]

The symphony has had many other fine interpreters: Malcolm Sargent, George Weldon, Basil Cameron, Constant Lambert, George Hurst, Colin Davis, André Previn, and not least the composer himself. The flautist Gerald Jackson had special memories of a war-time performance when Walton was conducting:

> Throughout, his face was marked by intense suffering, and I am certain it was not because of the orchestral players. It was a speciality of Sir Adrian's, and we knew it well. My impression was, and remains, that the composer must have endured a considerable amount of spiritual turmoil during its composition, and this he relived during what afterwards transpired to be an excellent performance.[107]

Once asked whom he would like to have conduct his symphony, he answered Wilhelm Furtwängler.[108] Possibly at the suggestion of Alan Frank (Hubert Foss's successor at OUP), Beecham was approached in January 1949 with a view to him conducting the work, but as Murrill wrote to Frank: 'He says he is not uninterested but could not contemplate the possibility of playing it in the immediate future.'[109] In fact he never did. When Beecham had programmed the work for a Royal Philharmonic Society concert in March

Music and Friends: Letters to Adrian Boult, edited by Jerrold Northrop Moore, Hamish Hamilton 1979, 192–3.

104 Carlton Classics 15656 91782, in their 'BBC Radio Classics' series.

105 *La Mortella*, 4 January 1976. Letters to Sir A. Boult, 1938–1976, BL 60499.

106 Michael Kennedy, *Portrait of Walton*, 281.

107 Gerald Jackson, *First Flute*, Dent 1968, 62.

108 On 27 January 1938, Walton wrote to Hubert Foss that 'Furtwangler wants the big score of the Symphony as there is an idea that he will do it at his concert of English music in June'. But as he was heavily involved in performances of Wagner's *The Ring* at Covent Garden the concert did not materialise. In the same letter Walton wrote that '[Walter] Legge writes me that Mengelberg wants scores of the Symphony & Viola Concerto'. The only occasion on which Furtwängler conducted Walton would seem to have been in November 1950 with *Scapino*.

109 Herbert Murrill to Alan Frank, 20 January 1949, BBC Written Archives, Caversham.

1939, Richard Capell wrote in his review that 'at short notice Mr Walton had been summoned to direct the performance of his symphony'. The recording manager and impresario Walter Legge once urged Herbert von Karajan, while visiting Ischia for a cure for back pain, to conduct the symphony – which eventually he did, having first suggested to Walton that he should revise the orchestration.[110] Unfortunately Walton was not informed of the performance, which took place in Rome, and so to his regret he missed it.

Walton's occasional uncertainty about his own music – that so often resulted in revisions being made – may have caused him to change the order of the inner movements when he conducted the work at a winter Prom in January 1948, with the result that the BBC Concert Manager enquired of him more than once if he would 'be playing the movements in the original order'. (Cameron followed this practice at the Proms later that year, as did Sargent on at least two occasions, in Amsterdam and Manchester in 1954.) When in 1944 the BBC seemed to be giving the wrong time allowance for the symphony in a programme, Walton wrote in with his own timings: Ist movement 12 minutes, 2nd movement 6 minutes, 3rd movement 9 minutes, 4th movement 12 minutes, making an overall time of 39 minutes.[111]

Sargent conducted the symphony at the Royal Festival Hall in April 1966 before recording it himself for EMI with the New Philharmonia in October that same year.[112] In the concert cymbal clashes were introduced at four places in the first movement,[113] making a very hollow sound in the context. Whether these tinkerings were Walton's or Sargent's (probably the latter's) they were removed when it came to the recording, two sessions of which Walton attended. When the recording was released in January 1967, the cover included a letter from Walton to Sargent, dated 2 November, in which he thanked Sargent, 'the orchestra and all concerned for a truly magnificent recording of my first Symphony.' Fine though Sargent's recording was, it was overshadowed by another which appeared the same month, from the London Symphony Orchestra and a new and ideal interpreter in their principal conductor-to-be, André Previn.[114] With his Hollywood training, Previn responded instinctively to the jazz inflections in the score, and it is by his

---

[110] Richard Osborne, *Herbert von Karajan*, 330.

[111] These compare interestingly with his own recording made with the Philharmonia in Kingsway Hall, London in October 1951 (13 minutes 51 seconds, 6 min. 10 sec., 10 min. 20 sec. and 12 min. 05 sec.) and a Henry Wood Prom performance on 18 August 1959 with the LSO (14 min. 15 sec., 6 min. 33 sec., 10 min. 29 sec. and 12 min. 54 sec.), National Sound Archives T350710.

[112] ASD2299, released in January 1967; CD release CDM763269-2 in 1990 and HMV 5 68026-2 in 1995.

[113] Between figures 25 and 26.

[114] Recorded 26–27 August 1966; issued January 1967 on RCA SB6691. CD release in 1989 on RCA GD87830. In December 1985 Previn recorded the symphony once more, with the RPO, for Telarc, on CD-80125.

recording, rather than the composer's own, that subsequent recordings have generally been judged.

The success of the symphony at the time of its appearance had stirred some strains of jealousy in another composer. Eugene Goossens, in America, wrote home to his parents in December 1934 after the first incomplete performance:

> Reading one of the criticisms of the Walton Symphony, one would think he were a second Beethoven. Why don't some of these critics maintain a sense of proportion instead of turning the heads of these youngsters? Here is the case of a boy with quite a facility of writing but with no real depth of senti-ment – at least he hasn't displayed it in any of his previous works. It is probably a hash of clichés and according to Mr R[ichard] C[apell] full of stark tragedy. Of all the untragic lives I know, his is conspicuous.[115]

When, on 16 October 1936, Eugene Ormandy introduced the work to Philadelphia, two hundred women are said to have walked out in keeping with that city's traditional stand against new music. Undaunted, Ormandy took the work on to Carnegie Hall, New York.

And the symphony brought forward some youthful derision from Britten who wrote in his diary for 28 July 1936:

> Lennox [Berkeley] has brought with him scores of the new Walton (Bb) & Vaughan Williams (F min) symphonies & we spend most hysterical evenings pulling them to pieces – the amateurishness & clumsiness of the Williams – the 'gitters' of the fate-ridden Walton – & the over pretentious-ness of both – & *abominable* scoring. The directions in the score too are most mirth conducive! It isn't that one is cruel about their works which are naturally better than a tremendous amount of British music – but it is only that so much is pretended of them, & they are compared to the great Beethoven, Mozart, Mahler symphonies.[116]

Britten had attended the first complete performance after which he wrote in his diary: 'A great tragedy for English music. Last hope of W. gone now – this is a conventional work, reactionary in the extreme & dull & depressing.'[117]

On 21 October 1935 Walton had written to Sassoon from a new London address, informing him of the symphony's performance. His letter also gives an idea of the range of other activities he was involved with at that time:

> It not only seems but is ages since I've seen you. However, I hope you'll be in London for the complete performance of my symphony at the BBC

---

[115] 18 December 1934, Carole Rosen, *The Goossens*, 155.

[116] *Letters from a Life*, 437.

[117] Humphrey Carpenter, *Benjamin Britten: A Biography*, Faber & Faber 1992, 70.

concert on November 6. Do come if you can. In some ways I think the last movement to be the best of the lot. At any rate it'll be the most popular, I think. There's been a slight chilliness between me and the Sitwells at Carlyle Square so I've settled down here and I must say I appreciate being on my own. You must come and see me here. I've several things, chiefly commercial, on foot. Firstly a ballet for Cochran with Osbert doing the libretto – in spite of the coldness, then music for the film of *As you like it* with Bergner, and lastly music for Sir J M Barrie's new play with Bergner, and Augustus John doing the scenery. So I shall be able financially to keep my head I hope well above water for the time being.[118]

Sassoon attended the concert and went afterwards to Alice's sumptuous party. 'This is Rome before the Fall,' he is reported to have said.[119]

The annuity from Mrs Courtauld and more substantial royalties had enabled Walton to move out of Carlyle Square and buy his own house at 56A South Eaton Square SW1. His musical horizons were also broadening in other directions. He was now entering the world of films.

[118] In *Keeping One's Head above Water*.
[119] Dora Foss, 'Memoirs of Walton'.

1. William Walton. A portrait taken in the 1920s.

3. 'The Swiss Family Whittlebot', in Noël Coward's satire of the Sitwells and *Façade*, in his first review *London Calling!* at the Duke of York Theatre in September 1923.

2. Walton's friend and fellow composer Constant Lambert, 'a speaker *sans pareil* of *Façade*, clear, rapid, incisive, tireless'.

4. Osbert, Edith and Sacheverell Sitwell, with Walton and Neil Porter (holding the Sengerphone) outside the New Chenil Galleries before the second public performance of *Façade* in April 1926. Lambert also took part, possibly replacing Porter.

5. Christabel McLaren (Lady Aberconway), Walton's confidante and financial supporter, to whom he dedicated his Viola Concerto.

6. Baroness Imma von Doernberg, dedicatee of the First Symphony, in 1940 with Neil McEacharn whom she eventually married.

7. Alice, Lady Wimborne, with Walton, in the painting by Sir John Lavery of a musical evening at Wimborne House, London, in the 1930s.

8. William and Susana Walton, in London in 1949, the year after their marriage.

9. 5 Swan Walk, Chelsea, where Walton first stayed with the Sitwells, sitting 'by the window at the top of the house for long periods, eating blackheart cherries from a paper bag and throwing the stones out of the window'.

10. The Hotel Cappuccini, formerly a monastery, in Amalfi, where Walton first went abroad with the Sitwell brothers in Spring 1920 and subsequently spent many working holidays with them.

11. 2 Carlyle Square, Chelsea (identified by a plaque), where Walton lived with the Sitwells 1919–1932, and where the first private performance of *Façade* was given in January 1922.

12. The Villa Cimbrone, Ravello, where Walton stayed with Alice Wimborne in 1938 and where he wrote much of the Violin Concerto.

13. Siegfried Sassoon, who gave Walton much financial aid, with Stephen Tennant (dedicatee of *Siesta*) in Bavaria in April 1929. Walton, one of the guests, was finishing his Viola Concerto.

14. Dressing-up was a popular activity of the 'Bright Young People'. At Stephen Tennant's home at Wilsford in October 1927 are Zita Jungman, Walton, Cecil Beaton, Tennant, Georgia Sitwell, Baby Jungman and Rex Whistler.

15. Walton with friend, adviser and music editor at OUP, Hubert Foss, in September 1932.

16. Hyam 'Bumps' Greenbaum, conductor, composer and friend to a generation of young composers, who assisted Walton with his earliest film scores.

17. *La Mortella*, Walton's home and water gardens in Ischia, now open to the public.

18. Walton rehearsing the BBC Symphony Orchestra in November 1941 at their war-time home, the Corn Exchange, Bedford. The programme included the first British performance of *Scapino*, and the Violin Concerto, with soloist Henry Holst (standing to Walton's left).

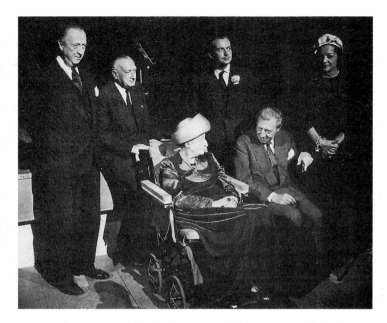

19. Reunited with the Sitwells for Dame Edith's seventy-fifth birthday concert in October 1962 at the Royal Festival Hall, with (left to right) Sacheverell, Edith, Francis, Osbert and Georgia Sitwell.

20. Walton at rehearsal, conducting the London Symphony Orchestra.

21. At Aldeburgh 1966, waiting for the balloon to go up at the conclusion of the Festival.

22. William Walton. A portrait in later life.

7

A Reel Composer

In the summer of 1934, with the first performance of the as-yet unfinished symphony a few months off, Walton broadened his scope by turning temporarily away from the concert hall to film music. Although in Russia Shostakovich had completed nearly half a dozen film scores, and Prokofiev made a notable début that year with *Lieutenant Kijé*, relatively few 'serious' composers in England were then working for the cinema. Those who did tended to be a rather specialised breed, with composers like Louis Levy, Richard Addinsell and John Addison making their names almost exclusively in films. Hubert Bath had been the pioneer, providing the scores for the first British 'talkies', *Kitty* and *Blackmail*, in 1929. Two years later Holst had written his only film score, now lost, and by the time of Walton's involvement, Clarence Raybould, Arthur Benjamin, Eugene Goossens and John Greenwood all had substantial scores to their credit. At the same time in a parallel field, Walter Leigh and Benjamin Britten were working in documentary films for the experimental GPO Film Unit. A few years later Constant Lambert and Lord Berners were both to compose for the cinema.[1]

Ernest Newman was to welcome this change of direction in Walton's career. In his review of the Symphony's first performance, he wrote:

> It is said that he is now going to occupy himself for a time with music for the films. He could do nothing wiser, from the point of view of his future development. I regard it as a sheer impossibility for any man, least of all a man so young as Walton, to go straight on from a work like this first symphony to another big work in any genre, least of all the symphonic. He will do well for some time to keep his hand in with trifles. He will be maturing silently during that time, as Wagner was during those five years between *Lohengrin* and the *Rhinegold* during which he did not write a page

---

[1] Lambert provided the music for the 1940 documentary *Merchant Seamen* and for *Anna Karenina* in 1947. Berners' contributions to the genre were *Halfway House* and *Champagne Charlie* in 1944 and *Nicholas Nickleby* in 1946–47.

of music: for a great artist's development is a matter much more of silent chemical change deep down in the unconscious than of conscious taking thought. It will be time enough for Walton to tackle another emotional and constructional problem of the size of this first symphony of his in three or even five years from now.[2]

Films, hardly the trifles that many people then considered the genre, were to form an important part of Walton's output. His first four, from 1934 until 1938, were all made by the Hungarian-born director Paul Czinner, and starred his wife, the actress Elisabeth Bergner.[3] As a child Czinner had been a violin prodigy, but he was drawn instead to the cinema and made his first film in Vienna in 1919. He rose to prominence in 1924 with his German film *Nju*, a psychological love-triangle drama that starred Elisabeth Bergner, who subsequently took the leading rôle in nearly all his films. In 1933, on the coming to power of Hitler, they both emigrated to England where Czinner directed *The Rise of Catherine the Great* (with his wife and Douglas Fairbanks, Jnr) for Alexander Korda, with the young Muir Mathieson as music director. He turned next, in 1934, to *Escape Me Never*, which was based on a play by Margaret Kennedy,[4] in which Bergner had created quite a stir the year before when she made her English stage appearance, first in Manchester and then London, playing to packed houses. The story is another love triangle centred on Gemma, the mother of an illegitimate baby, who is first looked after by, and eventually marries, a struggling composer (Hugh Sinclair) who becomes involved with another woman. The cast also included Griffith Jones, Penelope Dudley Ward and Leon Quartermain.

Walton was approached at the suggestion of Dallas Bower,[5] who was Czinner's personal assistant on the film and had been sound recordist for

---

2   Ernest Newman, 'William Walton's Symphony: Performance of the Completed Work', *Sunday Times*, 10 November 1935, 5.
3   Paul Czinner (1890–1972) was born in Budapest and in 1933 married Elisabeth Bergner (1897–1986), born in Drohobycz, Galicia, Poland. He had taken a PhD in Vienna in sexual psychology, and this is reflected in the subject matter of many of his films.
4   Margaret Kennedy was more widely known for her novel, *The Constant Nymph*, which was dramatised and produced by Basil Dean in 1926 with incidental music by Eugene Goossens. Elisabeth Bergner starred in its Berlin production. It was filmed twice by Dean, in 1928 (silent version) and 1933–34 (with a revised Goossens score), and later in Hollywood in 1943 (with a score by Korngold). *Escape Me Never* was a sequel to *The Constant Nymph*, and Margaret Kennedy worked on the film script in collaboration with Carl Zuckmayer.
5   Dallas Bower (1907–2000), had a distinguished career in film, radio and television. On the strength of his radio experience, Bower joined British International Pictures in 1929 as a sound recordist. He was the first producer–director for BBC Television, from its first transmission in November 1936 until the war closed down the service. During the war he worked as executive director for the films division of the Ministry of Information and also as a producer for BBC Radio.

Czinner's first film in England, *The Street of Lost Souls*. The associate producer, Richard Norton, had been thinking of using Lambert as his *The Rio Grande* was very popular at the time, while the producer Herbert Wilcox had suggested Vivian Ellis. But Bower, who was a great admirer of the Viola Concerto, pushed forward the name of Walton, whom he had met once casually. Shortly after, Walton came to the Elstree studios with Hyam 'Bumps' Greenbaum. At first he was contracted to write an important ballet sequence, which was filmed at Drury Lane in the first week of December 1934 with the Vic–Wells Ballet Company, with choreography by Frederick Ashton, and with a young Margot Fonteyn among the cast. He gave the impression of not taking it too seriously. Lydia Lopokova, who had danced leading rôles in Ashton's 1931 ballets *Façade* and *The Rio Grande* (originally designated *A Day in a Southern Port*), remembered, 'When they asked Willy and F to compose something à la Massine, W whispered to F, "What they want is bad Russian ballet. Let's do it." '[6] The film rights for this ballet brought him £250, and a piano solo arrangement of the ballet was published by OUP.

Very soon more music was wanted and on 29 November OUP wrote to British and Dominion Films: 'I hope you realise that we are only too anxious for Mr. Walton to complete the music for the film Escape Me Never now that he has written the Russian Ballet for it, and I am trying to set down terms which would be acceptable. . . .'[7] By 21 February 1935 favourable terms had been agreed whereby he would be paid £100 at the end of the month and thereafter £50 a week for 5 weeks. Working in films was proving to be a lucrative venture.

For a first film score Walton's *Escape Me Never* is remarkably accomplished and effective. At first it 'nearly drove me to a lunatic asylum' but 'much to my surprise I soon found myself writing five to ten minutes' music a day without too much difficulty', he later admitted.[8] In completing the orchestration – and a little more – he had help from 'Bumps'.[9] Sidonie Goossens remembers the two working together for films,[10] how they would go through a number of scores in search of ideas.[11] On one occasion (most likely

6   Julie Kavanagh, *Secret Muses: The Life of Frederick Ashton*, Faber & Faber 1996.
7   Letter 29 November 1934 from the Music Editor OUP (Foss) to R. J. Cullen of British & Dominion Films: OUP files.
8   *Sunday Telegraph*, 25 March 1962.
9   Dallas Bower, in conversation with the author, 2 February 1997, spoke of Hyam Greenbaum as being 'absolutely a tower of strength in every conceivable way insofar as Walton was concerned, and a marvellous orchestrator'. In *Escape Me Never* he had screen credits for his part in the orchestration. A letter dated 20 November 1935 in the OUP files makes it clear that the score of *Escape Me Never* was not in Walton's handwriting but in that of the orchestrator's.
10   In conversation with the author, 2 February 1997.
11   Reviewing a recording of the ballet sequence, *Gramophone*, June 1976, 96, Lionel

for the 1938 film *A Stolen Life*) it was Sibelius's *Tempest* music[12] which they turned upside down and managed to extract some theme in their attempt to meet the studio's deadline. 'Bumps' also conducted the studio orchestra on the soundtrack of *Escape Me Never*. The orchestration, which shows much subtlety, calls for a battery of percussion, including cowbells, glockenspiel, tubular bells and vibraphone – hardly conventional. But in this instance music was not to be such a central part of the film's structure as it was in later Walton films. The only substantial section is the two-and-a-half minute opening sequence in which the title music leads into a lyrical Venetian scene with vocal accompaniment. One or two sections (including some popular-styled music) serve only as a background to dialogue, but part of an idyllic pastoral episode is briefly allowed to come to the fore (the 'In the Dolomites' section of the Suite[13]). The 'Russian Ballet' comes much later in the film, when the screen composer is concerned about its production in London. But of the ballet itself, rather more substantial in the Suite than on film, only six tiny sections are heard and seen, in rehearsal and performance – intercut with scenes of Gemma at the hospital after the death of her child. The ballet's yearning 'love theme' is used most effectively for the title music. Walton was also supplied with a Neapolitan folk tune that he was asked to use in the course of the film.

Escape Me Never was first shown at the London Pavilion on 1 April 1935 and scored a considerable success, covering its costs in one West End cinema alone. *The Times* review[14] concentrated almost exclusively on Bergner, and applied Zola's maxim that 'Art is Nature seen through a temperament' to her acting. 'The camera,' it concluded, 'is there to photograph Miss Bergner, and that it does with discretion, skill, and discrimination.'[15] When it opened in America in May, the *New York Times* review[16] somehow managed to credit the music to L. P. Williams (who was in fact the art director) and Wilfred Arnold. Its critic, Andre Sennwald, considered Bergner (who received an Academy Award nomination) 'a miracle of gossamer gracefulness and bewitching humour', but as regards the production he merely commented

Salter suggested that perhaps 'Walton had recently been listening to Borodin's Second Symphony'.

12 Hyam Greenbaum prepared a version of Sibelius's *Tempest* music with reduced orchestration for a television production directed by Dallas Bower. Cecil Gray showed this version to Sibelius, who approved.

13 Suite arranged by Christopher Palmer and recorded on Chandos CHAN 8870. The opening of the second movement might even be an idea later developed as the 'Trumpet Tune' finale to *Music for Children*.

14 2 April 1935.

15 The film's editor was David Lean, who also worked on *As You Like It*, *Dreaming Lips* and *Major Barbara*.

16 24 May 1935.

that the 'brain scoffs at the threadbare machinery.' The film was less successfully remade in America in 1947 with music by Erich Korngold.

In January 1934 the artist and wild-fowl conservationist Peter Scott had
taken his seventy-three-year-old godfather Sir James Barrie to see Miss
Bergner in *Escape Me Never* at The Apollo Theatre. Barrie was enchanted by
her performance, and afterwards he was taken backstage to her dressing-
room where Scott introduced the playwright to her. The outcome of this
meeting was that Barrie broke his long silence in order to write for Bergner
what was to be his last play, casting her in a surprising rôle that she herself
requested, that of the biblical David, the slayer of Goliath. When after some
difficulty on Barrie's part the play was finally written, its production under
C. B. Cochran's management (as *Escape Me Never* had been), initially
planned for London, was delayed by Miss Bergner's film commitments, first
for Shaw's *St Joan* (which never materialised) and then *As You Like It*. In
October 1935 it was announced that the play would open the following
February in Edinburgh, with designs by Augustus John and music by Walton.
But Bergner's sore throat and the late completion of her film caused a change
of date to March. Then, during the final rehearsals, for much of which Barrie
was ill in bed, Bergner found herself in pain. Acute appendicitis was diag-
nosed, and an operation performed. The opening was once again postponed.
Meanwhile, in April Barrie was advising Bergner on the cutting of *As You
Like It*, of which there was a private showing in August. Eventually *The Boy
David* reached the Edinburgh stage on 21 November 1936 for a fortnight's
run before transferring to His Majesty's Theatre, London, on 14 December.
The cast also included Leon Quartermaine (as Ophir, a captain in the army of
Saul), Godfrey Tearle (Saul) and Bobby Rietti (Jonathan). Critically it was a
flop, and it closed on 30 January 1937.[17] If the play quickly disappeared from
the repertoire, the music – which was pre-recorded for the stage – was
allowed a further lease of life when one section of it was used in March of
that year as a *Divertissement*, choreographed by Anthony Tudor, in a television revue devised and produced by Dallas Bower, with Hyam Greenbaum
conducting the BBC TV Orchestra.

At first the quantity of music required for *The Boy David* was uncertain.
Cochran's secretary rang OUP to say that 'Mr. Cochran would like to make
arrangements with Mr. Walton but it is difficult for him to suggest a fee
because he doesn't know how much music there is going to be. In confidence
– Barrie neither understands nor likes music, but he realises that it is necessary to have some. Mr. Cochran doesn't think this will be very much.'[18]
Walton had meanwhile received other offers. In October 1935 Criterion Film

---

[17] A full account of *The Boy David* is given in Denis Mackail, *The Story of J. M. B.*, Peter
Davies 1941, 663–711 *passim*, and in Charles B Cochran, *Cock-a-doodle-do*, Dent
1941, 1–36, which also discusses the aborted *St Joan* film project.
[18] Undated memorandum in the OUP files.

Productions had requested music for a period adventure, *The Amateur Gentleman*. Either realising that working in films and for the stage was a potentially lucrative business or maybe just wanting to put them off, he replied that he might be interested if he were offered £1000. 'The price you have in mind is much too high,' came the reply.[19] Nevertheless, as regards *The Boy David* and *As You Like It* Walton felt that he ought to take a hand in the contractual negotiations himself, and he wrote afterwards to Foss of his mixed success:

> As arranged, I talked to Loring about the Barrie play & after much struggle got what I wanted (pound a performance when & wherever it is performed) but in order to get it I had to repudiate you & take over the whole responsibility of negotiation. I may add that I was told I was a very hard headed & hard hearted business man! Nevertheless I'm informed that I've not done as well as I should do over it – but more specially over the film contract & have been recommended to an agency. . . . The negotiations about 'As You Like It' begin tomorrow & it will be a tricky business & I know from inside information that they were delighted to have got me for such a sum even for arranging only old music.'[20]

In fact for *The Boy David* he was called upon to supply a short overture and introductions to five scenes, totalling about twelve minutes. Only three sections lasting nearly five minutes have survived, on private discs: a bustling sequence based on a repetitive three-note figure on xylophone in 'Eastern style', a plaintive quasi-folk-song appropriately on solo harp in the Dorian mode, and a weary, plodding, march with interruption from agitated brass that anticipates the refugees section in the war-time film score for *The Foreman Went to France*.

In 1935 Walton was also involved in another score for the stage. This was a short ballet, *The First Shoot*, composed for C. B. Cochran's 1936 revue *Follow the Sun*,[21] a show that consisted chiefly of dancing. Meanwhile Osbert Sitwell had had ideas for another ballet called *The Princess Caraboo* in which an escaped slave girl hoodwinked Bath society into believing she was a visiting princess. Intended for Colonel de Basil's Russian ballet, Walton was to write the music. In July, while working at Weston on the Symphony's last movement, he told Foss that he was going to Renishaw 'to discuss this ballet question with these Russian people who are coming also. I

---

19 Richard Addinsell supplied the score for this 1936 film that starred Douglas Fairbanks, Jr.

20 Walton to Foss, 7 March 1936, OUP files.

21 On Diaghilev's death in 1929, Cochran employed some of the Russian company in the miniature ballets that were a feature of his annual revues. Berners' one-act 'fantastic ballet' *Luna Park* with Serge Lifar had been part of Cochran's 1930 revue.

think it is almost as good as settled that I do it.'[22] While this project did not materialise, the two collaborated successfully for Cochran on *The First Shoot*, for which Osbert provided the scenario and Frederick Ashton the choreography. Ashton was already familiar with Walton's music as he had choreographed *Façade* as a ballet for the Camargo Society in 1931. The designer for *The First Shoot* was Cecil Beaton, whom Cochran approached one day over lunch in a Soho restaurant, handing him Osbert's brief synopsis written out on Renishaw notepaper. In his diary Beaton recorded: 'The subject of the work involved the love complications of an Edwardian pheasant shoot. Willie Walton had composed the perversely lyrical music – and this was to be the first of many collaborations with Frederick Ashton.'[23] On 19 October 1935 it was agreed that author and composer would jointly receive £10 a week on the basis of eight performances a week and an advance of £200 on delivery of the complete work in orchestral score. The flimsy story, set in a woodland glade, of a beautiful titled lady (an ex-chorus girl) and her admirer among a circle of fashionable friends has a faint ring of those week-end parties at Stephen Tennant's country home that Beaton and Walton attended, though with the conclusion of the lady being accidentally shot by her admirer any similarity stops there. Sarah Churchill, daughter of Sir Winston, made her stage début as one of the six of Cochran's Young Ladies dressed as a pheasant. (These ladies secretly expressed their dislike of the ballet by renaming it *Swallow the Fun*.) For the show's first two-and-a-half weeks, Ashton had to dance with the leading lady, Claire Luce, because the advertised star, Nick Long, was delayed filming in Hollywood.

Follow the Sun opened first at the Manchester Opera House on 23 December 1935 before going on to The Adelphi on 4 February 1936, its London opening (for which Walton had to supply extra music in the form of an overture) being postponed because of the death of King George V. The show ran until 27 June, from April on a twice-nightly schedule. Foss reported Walton as saying that the ballet was 'a "wow", but the rest of the show has not got a funny line in it'.[24] Ashton thought highly enough of *The First Shoot* to consider reviving it later in America, and *The Times* found this 'mock-ballet of men and pheasants . . . a neat and witty bit of fooling' and rated it one of the three best things of the show. (Some years later Cochran tried unsuccessfully to persuade Walton to collaborate in a light opera called *Big Ben* to a libretto by A. P. Herbert. It was eventually produced in 1946 with music by Vivian Ellis.) The music for *The First Shoot* was then lost but it had a happy reincarnation in 1980 when it was found by Francis Collinson, the

---

22 9 July 1935, Walton to Hubert Foss from Weston, Hubert Foss Archives.
23 *Self Portrait with Friends: The Selected Diaries of Cecil Beaton* edited by Richard Buckle, Pimlico 1979, 46.
24 In a letter from Hubert Foss to his wife Dora, 1 January 1936, Dora Foss, 'Memoirs of Walton'.

conductor of the original performance. Walton had been asked to write a piece for brass band and the re-emergence of this ballet score was 'a god-send'. He re-arranged the music for the Grimethorpe Colliery Band who recorded the work for television[25] at Goldsmiths' College, London on 19 December 1980, conducted by Elgar Howarth whose 'expert advice' Walton acknowledged in the printed score. They took it successfully to the Proms the following year for its first public performance. The nine-minute suite has a disarming tongue-in-cheek air of nonchalance (the third piece is directed 'a tempo di "Hesitation Waltz" '), mixed with an element of what Walton excelled at, parody.

A few days before *Follow the Sun* transferred to London, at Sadler's Wells on 24 January 1936 the Vic–Wells Ballet performed *Siesta*, also choreo-graphed by Ashton, and with Pearl Argyle and Robert Helpmann in this new *pas de deux*. Walton conducted. (At the 1972 Aldeburgh Festival, Ashton devised a new version which was performed as 'a [70th] birthday card for Willie Walton'.) Oxford University Press, feeling very protective for the future of one of its most important composers and concerned for the direc-tions he may be drawn into, informed Lilian Baylis: 'Nowadays he is in exceptionally heavy demand and we have no desire to see him entirely swal-lowed up in writing music for the films and ballets for Mr. Cochran's Young Ladies, in preference to writing further things on the "Facade" and "Siesta" lines. . . .'[26]

But after those two works for the stage Walton did return to films. His next score might well have been for an adaptation of George Bernard Shaw's *St Joan* starring Elisabeth Bergner. In November 1934 Shaw, who had a keen interest in films, had himself worked on a film-script which he handed to Miss Bergner to read. She had taken the lead in Max Reinhardt's acclaimed 1924 stage production in Berlin and Vienna, and Czinner planned to form a syndicate including Twentieth Century Fox and produce a film version of *St Joan* with his wife in the name part. However, he was concerned that the film might offend the Catholic Church, or more seriously that American financial backing would be withdrawn because of the risk of a Catholic boycott, and so he sought the approval of the Church. But Shaw would have no truck with any Catholic entanglements, and by the summer of 1935 as far as he was concerned the film was off.[27] Nevertheless, Miss Bergner did appear as St Joan when the play was produced at the 1938 Malvern Festival.

Instead of *St Joan*, Walton's next film, in 1936 – again at Dallas Bower's suggestion – was his first Shakespeare score which, more importantly, brought him into contact with Laurence Olivier. (Although in an eightieth-

---

25 Tony Palmer's filmed documentary *At the Haunted End of the Day*, ITV.
26 Letter dated 27 January 1936, OUP files.
27 Michael Holroyd, *Bernard Shaw, Vol III (1918–1950): The Lure of Fantasy*, Chatto & Windus 1991, 381–2.

birthday greeting Olivier remembered meeting Walton on the set of *As You Like It*,[28] he seemed to have largely forgotten the name when it was suggested to him for *Henry V*[29] and their strong friendship did not take shape until their collaboration on that film.) Shakespeare in the cinema was then by no means entirely new. The previous year Max Reinhardt had directed James Cagney in *A Midsummer Night's Dream*, and earlier still Mary Pickford and Douglas Fairbanks had been seen in *The Taming of the Shrew*. But these had been Hollywood confections. Olivier had at that time already appeared in a handful of films, but the offer of playing Orlando to Bergner's Rosalind gave him his first leading rôle, whatever doubts he had about the filming of Shakespeare. As it turned out, he disliked working with Bergner[30] and Czinner. Furthermore, at Bergner's insistence Barrie had provided a film adaptation of *As You Like It* with a number of discreet cuts and despite Czinner's assurances to Olivier that the play would not be mutilated, in the end it was reduced to a running time of ninety-six minutes.[31]

Neither Czinner nor Bergner was coming to *As You Like It* for the first time: Czinner had already directed a German version and in 1926 Bergner had appeared in a stage production in Vienna. For this 'million dollar' film version Czinner assembled a strong cast. Besides Bergner and Olivier there was Henry Ainley (the exiled duke), Leon Quartermain (Jacques), Mackenzie Ward (Touchstone), Felix Aylmer (Duke Frederick) and John Laurie (Oliver). Lazare Meerson, designer for the influential French director René Clair, was responsible for the décor (as he had also been for *Escape Me Never*), and Ninette de Valois was called in for the choreography.

As You Like It opened at the Carlton Theatre, Haymarket, on 3 September 1936 to a mixed critical reception. Miss Bergner naturally stole the limelight, but temperamentally she was unsuited to the part. As Roger Manvell has written in *Shakespeare and the Film*,[32] 'Rosalind is a forthright woman, capable, provocative and determined beneath her surface diffidence and charm. Elisabeth Bergner's screen character was exactly the opposite – she derived her charm from depicting an ageless, kittenish quality in women, a kind of self-destructive femininity, half innocent, half knowing, which inevitably led to frustrated infatuations with a tragic outcome.' While one critic referred to her as 'an imp of delicate enchantment', another complained of

28 Michael Kennedy, *Portrait of Walton*, 91.
29 Susana Walton, *Behind the Façade*, 94.
30 Despite Bergner's highly spirited performance there is little on-screen chemistry between the two. For much of the time while Olivier was absent from the studio, playing in *Romeo and Juliet* at the New Theatre (alternating with Gielgud the rôles of Romeo and Mercutio), Dallas Bower fed Bergner Olivier's lines.
31 In his autobiography, *Confessions of an Actor*, Weidenfeld & Nicolson 1982, Orion 1994, Olivier does not even mention *As You like it*.
32 Dent 1971, 31.

her 'inability to stop wriggling'. *The Times* critic,[33] ignoring the music, wrote that she 'soon overcomes the difficulty of her foreign accent and speaks her words with charm and relish, but she underlines them, as she underlines her conception of the character, with a restless and mannered grace'. Regarding the scenery, he commented: 'The fantastic architecture is apt to resemble confectionery and the Forest of Arden, though photographed with an extremely ingenious use of lighting, often looks like a wild garden temporarily assembled at Olympia.' *Sight and Sound* described the Arden set as 'fake flora and genuine fauna prodded in from the wings'. However, despite its defects, *The Times* critic considered it 'a serious attempt to reproduce one of Shakespeare's plays in film' and concluded that it offered promise of further filmed versions.

But Graham Greene, in the *Spectator*,[34] was scornful of this adaptation for the cinema. 'Horns and cuckolds have been heavily censored, the streak of poison which runs through the comedy has been squeezed carefully out between hygienic fingertips, and what is left, apart from Arden and absurd delightful artificial love, is Shakespeare at his falsest, Adam and church bells and good men's feasts and sermons in stone, all the dull didactic unconvincing images. That, I think, is the chief objection to Shakespeare on the screen. . . .' He remarked on 'how the ubiquitous livestock (sheep and cows and hens and rabbits) weary us before the end' and wondered, 'When did English trees, in what is apparently late autumn, bear clusters of white flowers?' Certainly Olivier, despite his grand salary of £600 a week for about thirteen weeks' filming (during the day only; he was Mercutio on stage each evening), was for a while to remain sceptical of the suitability of Shakespeare for the screen. When *As You Like It* went to America in November, Frank Nugent, in the *New York Times*[35] at least commented on 'an original score by William Walton [who] has given it just the proper musical accompaniment'.

One of the most interesting reviews appeared in the October 1936 issue of *World Film News and Television Progress*. Its young contributor was Benjamin Britten (at that time, for a fee of £200, writing his only score for a feature film, *Love From a Stranger*[36]), whose review is worth quoting in full:

That the Directors of 20th Century Fox Film Corporation should have invited one of the 20th century stars of British music to write for one of its biggest productions is very creditable indeed. But the invitation seems to have exhausted their enterprise. His name, perhaps symbolically, is absent

---

33 4 September 1936.
34 *Spectator*, 11 September 1936. Reprinted in Graham Greene, *The Pleasure-Dome: The Collected Film Criticism, 1935–40*, ed. John Russell Taylor, Secker & Warburg 1972, 98 and 100.
35 6 November 1936.
36 Based on a short story, *Philomel Cottage*, by Agatha Christie.

from the programme, and the opportunities he has had for writing serious film music seem negligible.

There is, of course, the Grand Introduction over the credit titles – pompous and heraldic in the traditional manner. There is a Grand Oratorio Finale with full orchestra, based on Elizabethan songs, in which a bunch of Albert Hall contralti is very prominent. Both these are written with great competence, and indeed Walton is incapable of any sort of inefficiency.

But apart from suitable *Waldweben* noises at the beginning of each sequence, which tactfully fade out as the action starts, that is the whole of Walton's contribution to *As you like it*.

One cannot feel that the microphone has entered very deeply into Walton's scoring soul. A large orchestra in which strings are very prominent has been used, and in the accompanying pastoral music one is conscious of the energetic ranks of the London Philharmonic sweating away behind the three-ply trees.

As far as he is allowed, Walton makes one or two musically apt suggestions. The introduction is very neatly dovetailed into the chicken-yard, and Leon Goossens on the oboe mixes very creditably with the Wynadottes. Also a neat and poetic use of the leitmotiv *Rosalind* is to be noted.

But all the music for *As you like it* is not the advance on *Escape Me Never* which we all expected.[37]

Yet, in spite of Britten's reservations, it is an impressive score,[38] once again calling on a wide array of percussion including marimba and tabors (perhaps reminiscent of Elgar's *Falstaff*, a work Walton greatly admired). The expansive title music is very Sibelian – especially in the writing for brass – closer in mood to *Festivo* than the symphonies, while the Forest of Arden, as Britten observed, seems to have called for a few Wagnerian bird-calls and *Forest Murmurs* (as well as a suggestion of 'Daybreak' from Ravel's *Daphnis and Chloe* in the opening of the 'Dreams and Moonlight' sequence). Allusions to Wagner were to occur in later Walton films, while the Sibelius influence is hardly surprising. According to the manuscript, one short sequence, 'Snake Scene', was based 'on a theme by Dr Paul Czinner'. The soundtrack includes four song settings, each presumably using a traditional tune – hence his comment to Foss about 'arranging only old music': *What shall We Have that Kill'd the Deer?* for unaccompanied male voices; *Blow, Blow, Thou Winter Wind* for solo male voice (using Arne's tune unaltered); *There Was a Lover and his Lass* for unaccompanied female voice (tune by Thomas Morley); and *Tell Me Where is Fancy Bred* for solo female voice, verses from *The Merchant of Venice* that he had already set in 1916. *Under the Greenwood Tree*, itself almost a paraphrase of an Elizabethan setting, was not used but was published separately the following year as a solo song. The wedding

37 Donald Mitchell and Philip Reed (eds), *Letters from a Life*, 419–20.
38 Two different suites of music from *As You Like It* have been arranged by Carl Davis and Christopher Palmer respectively, and both have been recorded commercially.

hymn near the end of *As You Like It* fulfils a similar joyous function as the *Agincourt Song* was later to do in *Henry V,* and the script provided Walton with the opportunity to employ one of his favourite devices, the fanfare, which he was to use much in films and elsewhere, either as a fanfare *per se* or as an introduction to another form he was to make peculiarly his own, the march.

A march was in fact his next, impressive composition. On 9 November 1936, with preparations being made for the coronation of Edward VIII, Walton was approached by the BBC to contribute one of several settings 'preferably of a simple nature of suitable poems by contemporary composers like yourself'. These were to form a special series of musical tributes in the hour preceding the Coronation Sunday Service, performed by the BBC Choral Society and the BBC Orchestra 'B' with organ. This invitation met with little enthusiasm, but instead, on the 27 November, Kenneth Wright reported: 'Walton tells me that he would love to be commissioned by the Corporation to write a really fine Symphonic Coronation March.' On 10 December, in the middle of the abdication crisis, it was noted that 'the Walton suggestion of a March is definite', and on 5 March 1937 a fee of forty guineas was agreed. On 11 April John Ireland (who in 1938 dedicated his Piano Trio in E minor to Walton) wrote to Julian Herbage: 'I have seen William's march, it seems good – he has gone back to Italy.' Walton had been invited to conduct the march himself but he told the BBC that he would be abroad at the time of the Coronation. Given the title *Crown Imperial*, it was recorded a month before the ceremony, by the BBC Symphony Orchestra and the recently knighted Adrian Boult. Clarence Raybould conducted a broadcast performance three days before the event, and its public première was on 12 May with Boult directing the 'Coronation Orchestra' in Westminster Abbey. Walton conducted it himself at that year's Proms. With its stirring trio, it proved to be a grand ceremonial work in the true Elgarian tradition.[39] He later spoke of being 'absolutely terrified' while writing it, having been asked for eight minutes of music – quite a long time for a march.[40] In 1963, concerned about its length, he authorised some cuts, although he had already cut *Crown Imperial* when in March 1953 he came to record both the 1937 and 1953 coronation marches with the Philharmonia Orchestra in London's Kingsway Hall, reducing it then from about 8½ minutes to 6¾ minutes by taking out four repeat sections and one small part of the march. He later abbreviated the fanfares at the conclusion for the published reduced version

[39] Wilfred Mellers, writing about Bax's elevation in 1942 to the Master of the King's Music on the death of Walford Davies, commented: 'In lieu of VW, I should have thought that William Walton was the obvious choice, especially considering the depressingly well-meaning self-conscious Elgarizing in which Walton indulges in his own occasional music.' *Studies in Contemporary Music*, Dobson 1947, 182.

[40] Interview with John Amis, BBC broadcast, 17 March 1972.

that is the one generally heard today 'without the repeats as it was originally written'. Second thoughts are not always better and these revisions do rob the march of much of its cumulative grandeur.

Although the title 'Crown Imperial' was taken from a passage in *Henry V*, by coincidence it also appears in William Dunbar's *In Honour of the City of London*, the text that Walton was setting for his major work that year, the 1937 Leeds Festival commission. Why he should have chosen that particular text is a mystery when Sir George Dyson had already set it – somewhat more memorably, one might add – in 1928, a simpler setting that was already very popular with choral societies. (Dyson dropped the words 'of London' for his title, and of Dunbar's seven verses Walton set six and Dyson five.) Walton's work is shorter than *Belshazzar's Feast*, lasting about seventeen minutes and with no soloists, and there were inevitably going to be comparisons made with his Festival success of six years ago. Beecham and Sargent again shared the conducting for the Festival, and on the morning of the second day, 6 October, Sargent directed the première of *In Honour of the City of London*. The following evening Walton himself conducted *Crown Imperial*.

Herbert Thompson, music critic of the *Yorkshire Post* writing for the *Musical Times*, thought that 'the strenuous character of the music lacked relief, and that it would have gained by greater contrast of moods. Considering the strangeness of the idiom, and the fact that the difficulty of many passages seemed almost gratuitous, the choral performance under Dr Sargent's direction was excellent.' Britten, who was at Leeds to hear the UK première of his *Frank Bridge Variations*, thought the Walton 'desperate – typical W. admittedly – but full of mannerisms & frightful lack of invention'.[41] He was also present at Queen's Hall on 1 December 1937 when, in the presence of the Queen, Walton conducted the London première of *In Honour of the City of London* in a programme shared with Boult that also included *Belshazzar's Feast*, John Ireland's *London Overture*, and the first public performance of the latter's *These Things shall Be*. 'I am disappointed with Willy's new piece – I heard it at Leeds & on some records he's got of it – but I hope the new fiddle concerto will be more the goods,' Britten wrote to a friend. 'But by jove, I thought that Belshazzar sounded a masterpiece after all that pretentious tub-thumping, puking sentimentality & really fragrant dishonesty (to say nothing of the gross incompetence of it),' he added, referring to the Ireland work.[42]

Walter Legge, by contrast, saw the concert as 'a triumph of the Elgarian spirit in British music' and 'a vociferous affirmation of the Elgarian manner'. He continued:

41 Donald Mitchell and Philip Reed (eds), *Letters from a Life*, 517.
42 *Ibid.*, 527.

Walton and Ireland are gloriously free from the gentlemanliness of Parry and Stanford, the Delian dreaming, and the market-day modalism of the folk-songists. Musically speaking they are neither gentlemen nor gentlemen-farmers; they are professional musicians who speak the international language of music, albeit personally, when they extol the glories of London. Their music springs, like Elgar's, from the soil and the soul of England. They speak the language not of the Mus.Bac.s or farm-hands but of the nation. . . . Walton, an Oldham man, is more than twenty years [Ireland's] junior, and his more nervous temperament shows clearly the difference between the generations. He conducted the first London performance of *In Honour of the City of London*, which was first given at the Leeds Festival in October, and at once showed up the shortcomings of the first performance and the intrinsic worth that first performance partly obscured.[43]

Nevertheless, partly because of its difficulty and complexity, *In Honour of the City of London* has never gained a firm foothold in the repertoire of choral societies. As Frank Howes put it in his book on the music, when the work was revived in 1962 'the view that the setting was too strenuous for the character of the poem, which calls for something more spacious if no less exuberant, was confirmed. There is too little variety and even the Thames has too much movement in its waters.'[44] The implication that Walton had to choose rather more carefully a text that would match his musical style is endorsed by Christopher Palmer's comment that 'because the Dunbar text is contemplative and poetic rather than narrative or dramatic, Walton found fewer outlets for the type of broad choral effects and wide-ranging invention which ensured *Belshazzar* its immediate and lasting success'.[45]

While much of 1937 was taken up with the Leeds Festival work, there was also his next film collaboration with Czinner, *Dreaming Lips*, of which Czinner had already made a German version with Bergner in 1932 under the title *Der traümende Mund*. This was another play adaptation, this time by Margaret Kennedy of the play *Melo* by Henry Bernstein. In it Bergner was well-suited to the neurotic, selfish Gaby who is married to a musician (Romney Brent) but falls in love with his colleague, a violinist (Raymond Massey). Her plans to leave her husband are thwarted by his serious illness. In the end, worn out by nursing him, she throws herself into the Thames. (Ironically, just before Christmas 1937 Walton himself was the recipient of nursing, being admitted to a London clinic for several days where he underwent a double hernia operation.)

A key scene early in the film is part of a concert in the Queen's Hall which

[43] 'Two British Composers – Walton and Ireland', reprinted in *On and Off the Record*, 55–6.

[44] Frank Howes, *The Music of William Walton*, 175.

[45] Christopher Palmer's notes for the 1991 Chandos recording, CHAN8998.

includes the end of the Tchaikovsky Violin Concerto, an abridged first movement of the Beethoven Concerto and an arrangement for violin and orchestra
of the Waltz from Tchaikovsky's *Serenade for Strings*. Antonio Brosa[46] was
the violinist on the soundtrack, with Boyd Neel visible on screen conducting
the London Symphony Orchestra. In his memoirs Boyd Neel remembered
some of the problems that arose. All the film's music was synchronised in the
studios except for the scene in the Queen's Hall which had to be done with
soloist, orchestra and audience visible. A reproduction of the hall had been
built in the studio and a large number of extras formed the audience. The
pre-recorded music was played back through loudspeakers, and the
performers had to match their movements to the soundtrack.

> For some strange reason nobody had thought of finding out if Massey was
> able to imitate a violinist or not. Someone had been detailed to coach him,
> and we all imagined he was ready for it. Came the entry of the soloist. I
> gave him a big cue – and he just stood there and looked at me. As we were
> not on microphone, I yelled, 'Play!' but by that time the solo had gone by
> several bars. One more attempt was made, with disastrous results. Massey
> said: 'To hell with this thing,' flung the violin on the floor, and rushed from
> the set. 'Cut,' yelled Czinner and pandemonium broke loose. 'Thirty
> minutes' break,' screamed Czinner. Then the awful truth was revealed –
> that Massey was tone-deaf!

With some ingenuity, two orchestral members solved the problem:

> If Massey stood to attention, with his arms held firmly at his sides, one of
> the players would crouch to his right with a bow and the other would
> crouch to his left holding the violin from below. All Massey had to do was
> to keep his chin firmly on the chin rest. The camera would be trained over
> his left shoulder and the audience (including Bergner) could be seen
> ecstatically listening to the concerto.[47]

One further difficulty remained – for the extras in the audience preventing
themselves from laughing at this ridiculous sight of human puppetry.

The soundtrack in fact contains little of the real Walton. The title music is
built largely out of a theme from the Beethoven Concerto (second subject,
first movement) and there is a short sequence of operatic Wagner. Apart from
two dance numbers, a rumba and a tango that may be Walton's, the only
music of any interest is found in a brief passage when the husband is ill and in
the dream sequence that follows, which in mood looks ahead to the ghost

---

46 Antonio Brosa was leader of the Brosa Quartet 1924–38 of which at first Hyam Green-
    baum was second violin (later succeeded by David Wise). The other members were
    Leonard Rubens and Anthony Pini.
47 Boyd Neel, *My Orchestras and Other Adventures: The Memoirs of Boyd Neel*, Univer-
    sity of Toronto 1985, 98–100.

scene in *Hamlet*. The predominance of 'serious' music prompted *The Times* critic[48] to comment perversely that 'the effect of an accompaniment of good music is so unexpectedly delightful that one cannot understand why so easy and profitable a resource should not be more often heard'. The cast also included Joyce Bland, Sydney Fairbrother, Felix Aylmer, Fisher White, Donald Calthrop and Ronald Shiner. The film opened at the London Pavilion on 2 February 1937 and went to America in May. Frank Nugent, discussing the leading rôles in the *New York Times*,[49] wrote that 'those three are the only ones that count: those and a couple of fellows who wrote the score – Beethoven and Tchaikovsky.' This film, which was a flop, could have done nothing to enhance Walton's reputation as a composer of film-music.

A Stolen Life which followed in 1938, again directed by Czinner, was another obvious vehicle for Elisabeth Bergner, here playing twin rôles in a script adapted by Margaret Kennedy from a novel by Karel Benes. The cast also included Michael Redgrave and Wilfred Lawson. Redgrave was then hardly known as a film actor because his first film, Hitchcock's *The Lady Vanishes*, had not been released at the time of his being signed up by Czinner. Here he plays a mountaineer-cum-explorer who meets Martina (Bergner) and they fall in love. But Martina's twin sister Sylvia steals him from her and marries him. When Sylvia is drowned on holiday, Martina takes her place without his realising. Her deception is eventually discovered but all ends happily. *A Stolen Life* was first shown on 18 January 1939 at the Plaza Theatre, London, a charity screening that was attended by Christabel, Lady Aberconway.

In *A Stolen Life* Walton was able to offer a rather more substantial score, about twenty-seven minutes' worth of music. The film opens with music of scenic splendour to match the mountain setting. There is a lengthy sequence of dance music that sounds almost too authentic to be by Walton (although writing for the Savoy Orpheans would have equipped him with the necessary skills). The most dramatic moment is the extensive storm sequence in which Sylvia drowns and it was for this that Walton and Hyam Greenbaum possibly plundered Sibelius's *Tempest* Prelude. Their scavenging may also have produced a short passage, lasting almost a minute, that sounds remarkably like a cross between Berlioz's *Queen Mab* and Mendelssohn's *Midsummer Night's Dream* scherzos. The cinema newsreel of Martina's 'husband's' successful mountaineering expedition in Tibet is accompanied by a brief extract from the *Escape Me Never* ballet with its soaring love theme. Dora Foss thought it 'first class cinema music', adding: 'and by that I mean it is streets ahead in quality of any I've heard',[50] although Walton complained of

[48] 3 February 1937.
[49] 20 May 1937.
[50] Letter from Dora Foss to Hubert Foss, 2 February 1939, Dora Foss, 'Memoirs of Walton'.

not being able to hear most of it. On the soundtrack the BBC Television Orchestra was conducted by Hyam Greenbaum who had been appointed its musical director when the television service started in 1936. The film was remade in 1946 with Bette Davis and music by Max Steiner.

A Stolen Life was Walton's last film for Czinner. With the outbreak of war Czinner went to Hollywood. (In later years he was to turn his attention more to filming opera and ballet.) Elisabeth Bergner did some location shooting in Canada for Michael Powell's 1941 film *49th Parallel* (for which Vaughan Williams supplied the music), but when the Nazi blitz on London started, because of her German upbringing she made it clear that she had no intention of returning to London to complete the studio portions of the film and joined her husband instead. Film director David Lean remembered Bergner as being very talented, '. . . a damned good actress',[51] but in time her very personal style of acting, that lacked the sensuality of a Garbo or a Dietrich, was to seem rather dated.

Walton's last big work before the Second World War, which overlapped *A Stolen Life*, was another commission, the 'new fiddle concerto' alluded to by Britten in December 1937. Jascha Heifetz had asked Walton to write a work for him.[52] Then, by coincidence, in April 1938 the British Council asked him to write a violin concerto to be premièred at the 1939 New York World Fair (though clearly from Britten's comments the work was already on the stocks). The fee of £250 was offered, with a further £100 if he attended the first performance. Bliss, Vaughan Williams and Bax had been approached for works, and realising the considerable prestige that was attached to a commission for both Heifetz and the New York Fair, Walton skilfully engineered the fusion of the two commissions by stipulating that Heifetz should give the first performance. But in order to concentrate on the concerto he had to turn down a tempting offer of 550 guineas from Gabriel Pascal to provide a score for the film *Pygmalion*. As he wrote to Foss: 'It all boils down to this – whether I'm to become a film composer or a real composer' – a reel composer or a real composer, as he might have put it. For a similar reason he also turned down a request from Benny Goodman and Joseph Szigeti for a work for clarinet and violin.[53] The other English works commissioned for the World Fair were Bax's seventh and last symphony, Bliss's grand Piano Concerto and Vaughan

---

51 Kevin Brownlow, *David Lean: A Biography*, A Wyatt Book for St Martin's Press, New York 1996, 95.
52 Spike Hughes claimed a small part in this. In his autobiography *Opening Bars*, 315, he wrote: 'Jascha Heifetz asked me if I knew a young man by the name of Walton with whom he wanted to discuss a violin concerto.' Hughes brought the two together over a lunch of smoked salmon and tournedos at the Berkeley.
53 Goodman and Szigeti instead asked Bartók, who obliged with his *Contrasts* (1938). Also, in an interview for the *Yorkshire Observer*, Walton is quoted as saying: 'Goodman asked me to write a clarinet concerto for him, but the idea fell through owing to the war. I would have been happy to go ahead with it.' 21 December 1942, 2.

Williams' *Five Variants on Dives and Lazarus*. Sir Adrian Boult conducted the New York Philharmonic-Society Orchestra in the Bax, Vaughan Williams and Bliss works at Carnegie Hall in June 1939, but, as it turned out, Walton's concerto was not performed; its première took place later.

Although written for Heifetz and dedicated to him, the concerto was inspired by Alice Wimborne, whose friendship and love had brought about the completion of the symphony three years earlier. The most lyrical of Walton's works, it has a similar emotional warmth to Elgar's Violin Concerto (which also owed something to an Italian holiday) that was written in the same key (B minor) and was also inspired by a lady – another Alice. In Elgar's case it had been Alice Stuart Wortley, the friendship having informed Elgar's Second Symphony as well. In Tony Palmer's 1981 ITV film, *At the Haunted End of the Day*, Walton spoke with much emotion about the writing of his concerto and about *his* Alice:

> Most of it was written at Ravello, near Amalfi, at the Villa Cimbrone where I spent a lot of time with a lady I loved very dearly, Alice Wimborne. . . . Very intelligent, very kind. . . . She was a few years older than me, a grand hostess, very rich and very musical. We had a little room outside the main gate. Alice was very good at making me work and would get very cross if I mucked about. I'd met Alice through the Sitwells, oddly enough. She had a house near Sachie's at Weston and we spent most of the war together there. Then one day after the war she fell ill and the doctor there said she'd got cancer. She was being treated in London by a very eminent old German . . . and he said there was nothing wrong with her at all. . . . Of course in those days I suppose it wasn't easy to find out if you had lung cancer or whatever it was – she had it in the bronchs. . . . It was very painful . . . for everyone concerned. Months . . . six weeks.

It was surely as much for her that he had composed the anthem *Set Me as a Seal upon thine Heart* as for her son, the Honourable Ivor Guest, at whose wedding in Kensington in November 1938 it was first performed.

For advice on writing the concerto Walton turned to the Spanish violinist Antonio Brosa who had been engaged to play on the soundtrack of the film *Dreaming Lips*. Brosa (who gave the first performance of Britten's Violin Concerto in New York in March 1940) remembered his involvement:

> I asked Walton if he had written anything for the violin and he told me he was writing a concerto for Heifetz and I said: 'Oh, that is very interesting. May I see the concerto, please? Would you show it to me?' And he said: 'Well, yes, I could, but as a matter of fact I am very fed up because I do not know very well how to write for the violin,' and I said: 'Well, nowadays you can write anything at all, anything you like, for the violin,' and so eventually he had a copy made. He had written two movements, the first and the second, and he lent it to me and I practised it, and he came home and played it with me and I made a few suggestions and so on, and he wrote to

Heifetz telling him about this and sent him as samples the two movements. Heifetz replied that he was not quite sure that he liked them as Walton wanted them and he suggested that he went to America and worked it out with him. Walton was very upset about this. He said: 'For tuppence I would give it to you.' . . .[54]

Hyam Greenbaum's advice had also been sought. His sister Kyla remembered 'Walton coming to ask Bumps what he thought of his Violin Concerto and Bumps saying that it wasn't up to much because he hadn't got the beginning right and Walton saying, "I'll come back tomorrow and we'll go into it further," just like a student.'[55]

In 1938 Arnold Bax had written for Heifetz a concerto which the violinist effectively rejected and never played, quite possibly because it was not sufficiently virtuosic.[56] Walton made every effort to ensure that his own concerto did not suffer a similar fate. At first he had doubts as to whether Heifetz was the right soloist. As Dora wrote to Hubert Foss in January 1939: 'He says his difficulty is making the last movement elaborate enough for Heifetz to play it. He says he will never write a commissioned work again.'[57] And then in February she reported that 'he feels Heifetz won't do the Concerto – he's a bit "off" Szigeti who "whines" – Kreisler is W's latest idea – a sort of repetition of the Elgar Concerto triumph in his later years. William isn't at all pleased with the last movement – says it wants two months' more work – Brosa not very enthusiastic.' Asked what he might be planning next, he replied that 'he was going to learn composition and start on Chamber music, beginning with a duet, a trio, a quartet and so on, but *not* unaccompanied violin! He is telling Heifetz that if he does it, he (William) will go over any time after Ap. Ist and hold his hand while he learns it etc.'[58]

However, early in March Walton was able to report that Heifetz had cabled 'accept enthusiastically'. At the violinist's suggestion, he sailed to America in May 1939, aboard the *SS Normandie* with Alice Wimborne, so that the solo part, especially the third movement, could be shaped according to Heifetz's liking. Yehudi Menuhin has written that the finished concerto (dated New York 2 June 1939), 'dedicated to Heifetz and edited by him, bears witness to the minuteness of his planning, indicating expressive marks in unusual detail, tiny crescendi and diminuendi on single notes. He strove for a control so complete that each performance would be identical.'[59] But

[54] 'A Conversation with Antonio Brosa', *Royal College of Music Magazine*, Easter 1969, 10.

[55] Carole Rosen, *The Goossens*, 191–2.

[56] Bax withheld his violin concerto from performance until 1943.

[57] 18 January 1939. Dora Foss, 'Memoirs of Walton'.

[58] 4 February 1939. Dora Foss reporting to Hubert Foss after a long telephone conversation with Walton.

[59] Yehudi Menuhin, *Unfinished Journey*, Macdonald & Jane's 1977, 158.

the proposed World Fair première did not take place, not it seems because the work was not ready in time (as some, like Boult in his autobiography,[60] have suggested) but, if Walton's letter to Leslie Heward on 28 March 1939 is to be believed, more for reasons of administrative incompetence: 'As you may have seen I've withdrawn my Concerto from the World's Fair not as is stated because it's unfinished but because Heifetz can't play on the date fixed (the B[ritish] C[ouncil] only let him know about ten days ago!). Heifetz wants the concerto for two years and I would rather stick to him.'[61]

The first performance eventually took place, without the composer present, on 7 December 1939 in Cleveland, with Artur Rodzinski conducting the Cleveland Orchestra. On 15 October Heifetz had received a letter from Walton explaining that, because of the outbreak of war and the difficulties of travelling, there was little chance of him being able to attend the première. He added that there was the possibility of him being called up, and in the meantime he was an ambulance driver for his local Air Raid Precautions unit. Heifetz retained exclusive performing rights for two seasons, taking the concerto to New York with the same performers in February 1941.

The work's first British performance had been planned to take place that same month at Oxford where Walton was to receive his Honorary Doctorate. The soloist was to have been Henry Holst but the performance did not materialise. With the difficulty of obtaining the orchestral parts from America, Richard Temple Savage, the London Philharmonic Orchestra's librarian, had for some time been busy preparing a set, 'sending regular reassuring postcards to Willy at Ashby St. Leger where he was living with the beautiful Lady Wimborne'. (This prompted a mocking Lord Berners to write to Frederick Ashton: 'I hope Constant [Lambert] or Bobby [Helpmann] told you about how we frightened Willie at Oxford where he came to be canonized or whatever it was. He has been getting above himself lately – owing, I presume, to adulation of ecstatic females.'[62]) But on the day of the Oxford concert the parts had not arrived from London and an air-raid on the capital made any contact with the publishers impossible. Savage remembered: 'It was obvious that Willy was bitterly disappointed and had gone out to get quietly drunk. I could see him sitting hiccupping gently during the concert in his doctoral robes while Henry Holst played the Brahms instead.'[63] (Difficulties had been further compounded by Heifetz's copy of the solo part being lost at sea through enemy action – though the precaution of making photostats before sending it had wisely been taken.) The first British performance (which was broadcast) eventually took place on 1 November 1941 in the Royal Albert Hall, with Henry Holst the soloist and Walton conducting the London Phil-

60 Adrian Cedric Boult, *My own Trumpet*, 137.
61 Lewis Foreman (ed.), *From Parry to Britten,* 213–14.
62 Julie Kavanagh, *Secret Muses*, 280–1.
63 Richard Temple Savage, *A Voice from the Pit*, 81 and 89.

harmonic Orchestra. (It was heard again eleven days later in another broad-cast, from the BBC's new war-time venue, the Corn Exchange in Bedford. Henry Holst was again the soloist and Walton this time conducted the BBC Symphony Orchestra in a programme that also included the first British performance of the overture *Scapino*.) One listener to the earlier broadcast was John Ireland who wrote to Edward Clark: 'I expect you listened to the Walton Violin Concerto. He sent me a piano score, though his attitude to me has been unamiable, on the few occasions we have met of late. He is becoming too 'careerist', for me, & I feel the Concerto is strongly tinged with this attitude of mind. But I reserve any definite opinion until I have heard it again on November 12th. One hearing, however, has quite decided me NOT to waste my time in providing material for the glorification of any virtuoso string player.'[64]

It seems extraordinary now to read William McNaught's *Musical Times* review of the first London performance of the Violin Concerto:

> This is a difficult work for the listener. The composer's vocabulary has advanced since his Viola Concerto. It has probably become more chro-matic, if the test be a counting of accidentals; certainly if the test be the impression on the ear . . . there are many solitary clumps of incompatible notes; there is more independence and incongruance among the lines of counterpoint, and the music is very contrapuntal. In short, the technique has been screwed up to a higher pitch.

McNaught felt that the majority of listeners would find difficulty in appre-ciating certain parts of the concerto. When Holst played it again, this time with Boult conducting the London Symphony Orchestra, at the Albert Hall on 27 May 1942, *The Times* critic was left 'still doubtful whether the work as a whole is either so fresh or so original as its predecessor and the symphony'.

Others had no doubts. While Walton had been working on the concerto in Italy, Eugene Goossens and his wife had rented Walton's house in South Eaton Place for five guineas a week. Whatever his feelings had been about the earlier success of the Symphony, he was now full of admiration for the Concerto, about which he wrote from Cincinnati to his parents:

> Willy's concerto is really an amazing piece of work. I know no contempo-rary concerto which could approach it for technical complexity and well-knit structure. It also has great lyric beauty and Heifetz played it for all it's worth. It is one of the hardest things I have ever had to accompany and Jascha and I rehearsed it for five hours at a stretch. Willy is to be congratu-lated on a real 'tour de force', and I think it proves him to be at all odds the most important figure in contemporary 'Young England music'.[65]

---

[64] 'All Souls' Day 1941', Letters to Edward Clark, BL Add. 52256.
[65] 18 November 1940, Carole Rosen, *The Goossens*, 224.

The following February, Goossens and Heifetz made the work's first gramophone recording, with the Cincinnati Symphony Orchestra. This has since remained an important document because by the time Walton himself came to record the work with Heifetz (in July 1950 with the Philharmonia Orchestra[66] in the Abbey Road Studios) – and much later in 1969 with Menuhin – he had subjected it to his customary revision. This involved considerable re-scoring, particularly thinning out the percussion by omitting the bass drum, castanets, glockenspiel and gong. The first performance of these revisions, completed on 30 November 1943, was given in Wolverhampton on 17 January 1944, with Sargent conducting the Liverpool Philharmonic Orchestra and Henry Holst once again the soloist. The Goossens recording is therefore the only one of the original version.

Although of Walton's three string concertos that for the viola is widely rated as the finest, nowhere but in the Violin Concerto has he written music of such gloriously sustained lyricism – matched only, but not surpassed, by passages in *Troilus and Cressida*. The work opens, over a rocking figure first on clarinet and then violas, with two important themes, the first sung by the soloist beneath which, unobtrusively, the solo bassoon announces another with support from the cellos. One of the many memorable moments in the work comes towards the end of the movement when the two themes return, the second now taken up by the solo violin while the other theme is heard on solo flute. Of the frenzied second movement he told Foss: 'Having been bitten by a tarantula a rare & dangerous & unpleasant experience I have celebrated the occasion by the 2nd movement being a kind of tarantella "Presto cappriciosamente alla napolitana". Quite gaga I may say & of doubtful propriety after the 1st movement – however you will be able to judge.'[67] The bravura of the solo writing matches perfectly Heifetz's virtuosic style of performance, even to the brief almost schmaltzy hint of a Neapolitan *serenata notturna* near the close of that movement. The finale is hardly any less virtuosic in its demands. Here again, as in the Viola Concerto, towards the end the soloist recalls the work's opening theme in a fashion similar to the Prokofiev and Elgar violin concertos. And if the Viola Concerto owed a small debt to Prokofiev's First Violin Concerto, then the Violin Concerto owes a similar one to the latter's Third Piano Concerto. The perky 3/4 principal themes in the last movement of each work are remarkably similar. But the most memorable moment is the reappearance in the last movement of the solo violin's long-breathed second subject, on its first appearance directed *a tempo con moto, ma flessible* and now heard on oboes and clarinets while the

---

66 Oddly enough, Heifetz's first public performance of the work in England did not take place until 9 June 1953, at the Royal Festival Hall, with Walton conducting the Philharmonia.

67 *Presto capriccioso alla napolitana* was the direction used. Undated (1938) letter from Walton to Hubert Foss, Foss Archives.

violin spins a lyrical transformation of the movement's opening subject. Heifetz held the work in high regard. Once discussing the Elgar concerto, he remarked: 'A very good work, but the Walton – that's the piece.'[68]

The concerto is a work inspired by both love and surroundings. The medieval-styled Villa Cimbrone, where Walton was staying with Alice Wimborne near Ravello high above Amalfi, has one of the most spectacular views of that coastline across the Gulf of Salerno. He had gone there early in 1938 to recover from his double hernia operation. It was an idyllic setting.[69] The history of the Villa dates back to the eleventh century. In 1904 an Englishman, Lord Grimthorpe, purchased it and had both the buildings and its gardens extensively restored. Walton and Alice had plans of building a house near the Villa, but these were dreams to be shattered by the war.[70] The Violin Concerto, together with *Belshazzar's Feast* and the First Symphony, marked the peak of Walton's achievement before the Second World War. He was thirty-seven. None of his subsequent concert works, despite the emergence of several fine scores, was to repeat those successes or to achieve the same level of excellence.

[68] BBC Radio 3 interview with Itzhak Perlman.

[69] A plaque at the Palazzo records the stay there of Greta Garbo and Leopold Stokowski in February and March 1938.

[70] The Korean violinist Kyung-Wha Chung, who played the Violin Concerto at Walton's 80th birthday concert in the Royal Festival Hall and at a 75th Walton birthday Prom, remembered once playing it in Rome. Walton attended the rehearsal and tears were streaming down his face. On another occasion she asked him why he had written such a difficult work. 'It's not my fault – it's that damn Heifetz!' was his answer. [BBC Radio 3 19 June 2000]

8

Films Again – and Radio

As the art historian Kenneth Clark wrote in his second volume of autobiography: 'At the beginning of the war the Governors of Sadler's Wells decided that it would be a patriotic gesture to close the Ballet down. The sum involved was small enough for Willie Walton and me to provide it; so the ballet remained in being and toured the country, performing new works by Freddie [Ashton] to music chosen and played on the piano by Constant Lambert.'[1]

Walton's first war-time task was for the Vic–Wells Company, orchestrating certain chorale preludes and extracts from the cantatas of J. S. Bach that Lambert had selected for a one-act ballet to be called *The Wise Virgins*. This was not Walton's first arrangement of the music of Bach. In 1931 he had been one of twelve composers to contribute to *A Bach Book for Harriet Cohen*. For this collection of piano pieces he made a free treatment of the chorale prelude *Herzlich thut mich verlangen*. His fellow contributors had been Bantock, Bax, Berners, Bliss, Bridge, Goossens, Howells, Ireland, Lambert, Vaughan Williams and W. G. Whittaker.

For *The Wise Virgins* he used again the same chorale prelude together with seven other pieces of Bach, orchestrating them in a grand manner that bears comparison with Elgar's orchestration of the C minor Fantasia and Fugue, but for a smaller orchestra. The subject, chosen by Frederick Ashton, was the parable of the wise and foolish virgins, and with Ashton's choreography and scenery and costumes by Rex Whistler, the ballet was first staged in London on 24 April 1940 at the Sadler's Wells Theatre with Lambert conducting. Its cast included Michael Soames and Margot Fonteyn. The complete ballet, consisting of nine numbers including a revised repeat, was, although not stated in the programme, dedicated (by Ashton rather than by Walton) to Edith Sitwell. She was delighted. 'It was *most* lovely,' she told Ashton, 'and

---

[1] Kenneth Clark, *The Other Half: A Self-Portrait*, Hamish Hamilton 1977, 46. The accompaniment on tour was actually on two pianos, played by Lambert and the rehearsal pianist, Hilda Gaunt.

170

has a singular youthful innocence which is just like that of the Adorations of the Primitives.' The main set was too heavy to be transported from the Wells, one reason perhaps why this new ballet did not form part of the Vic–Wells' fateful propaganda visit to the Continent in May. The company found itself caught up in the Nazi invasion and had to make a hasty retreat from Holland, leaving behind the scenery, costumes and orchestral parts of several other ballets, an experience that Lambert recalled in his short orchestral piece *Aubade Héroïque*.[2] Walton himself suffered an early war-time loss. In May 1941 his house in South Eaton Place was a casualty of the blitz, and with it his early film music.[3]

The Wise Virgins did not find great favour with either the critics or the public. After the company's return from Holland, it was occasionally teamed up with Lambert's ballet *Apparitions* (using the music of Liszt) and a redesigned *Façade*. Eventually it dropped out of the repertory. Six of its numbers, however, were extracted to form a Suite which Walton recorded with the Sadler's Wells Orchestra in two sessions in July and August 1940.[4]

At about the same time he composed a delightful set of ten piano *Duets for Children* (although originally conceived for solo piano) which he dedicated to the children of his elder brother Noel, adding such playful titles as 'The Three-Legged Race', 'Swing-boats', 'Puppet's Dance' and 'Hop-Scotch'. In May 1940 they were recorded for Columbia by Ilona Kabos and Louis Kentner, and among the early public performances was one given at Caius College, Cambridge in November 1940 when the performers were Patrick Hadley and Angus Morrison. Walton also deftly orchestrated these duets as *Music for Children*, and they were first heard in that form at the Queen's Hall on 16 February 1941, with Basil Cameron conducting the London Philharmonic Orchestra. At the end of the month they were included in an all-Walton composer-conducted broadcast from the BBC Symphony Orchestra's first war-time out-of-town home, Bristol. When in 1949 John Taras devised a ballet, *Devoirs de Vacances*, using the orchestrated *Duets for Children*, Walton promised a *Galop* finale which he then forgot about, the piano score arriving too late for inclusion in the ballet when it was staged at the Théatre des Champs-Elysées, Paris, that November. (Christopher Palmer orchestrated the *Galop* for the 1991 Chandos recording.) *Music for Children* has a charm, simplicity, wit and innocence that draw comparison with Elgar's *Wand of Youth* Suites (that may well have been in Walton's mind) and Fauré's *Dolly* Suite.

---

2   Lambert himself vividly described the episode in a broadcast on 20 May 1940 preserved in the BBC Sound Archives.
3   Walton to Leonard Isaacs, 3 November 1941, BBC Written Archives, Caversham.
4   In April 1944, with the same orchestra, he recorded *Sheep may Safely Graze* on its own in a version with slightly reduced orchestration, for release on a single 78-rpm record. In March 1953 he recorded it yet again, this time with the Philharmonia Orchestra.

Walton had also been commissioned to write an orchestral piece to commemorate the fiftieth anniversary of the Chicago Symphony Orchestra. While he had been in London in July 1938, the orchestra's long-standing conductor Frederick Stock had discussed the commission with Walton, and a contract was signed in June 1939. Walton's initial thoughts were for a work very different from the one he eventually wrote. As he told Foss in September:

> Meanwhile I'm trying not too successfully to get going on this work for Chicago. But I've got quite a good scheme for the work. It is not to be an overture but a suite which I am entitling Varii Capricci. There are to be five pieces, thus:
>
> I   Intrada (full orchestra)
> II   Siciliana (woodwind)
> III   Sarabanda (strings and harp)
> IV   Marcia (brass and percussion)
> V   Gigue (full orchestra)[5]

His mind at this time was full of ideas for works, including this suite, that he detailed in an extraordinary letter to Foss that November with an unabashed literary and linguistic show that one might more readily have ascribed to Lambert:

> Overture 'Bartholomew Fair' for orchestra
> ('I'm not really decided about this title');
> Alba, Pastorela et Serena for String Orchestra
> ('These names are the Provençal ones for Aubade, Pastoral and Serenade');
> Four medieval Latin Lyrics for unaccompanied chorus;
> Däman and Thyrsis (after Giorgione): scene pastorale for oboe solo, strings and harp (in 4 movements);
> Varii Capricci (portraits from the commedia del'arte) for orchestra
> ('This is to be a rather more ambitious work than the original plan I had for it');
> Canti Carnascialeschi (a curtain raiser for Façade);
> String Quartet;
> Amoretti – '. . . this title I shall use as a sort of musical waste-paper basket, into which I shall throw the odds and ends which occur in composing and which in the past I've needlessly discarded! The only thing now is to carry it out which I'm doing by the end of 1940. What a hope![6]

Of these only the String Quartet was to materialise, although he was much later to use the title alone – and not the scheme – of *Varii Capricci*. As for the Chicago work he returned to the idea of an overture, although there was an

---

5   Walton to Hubert Foss, 9 September 1939, quoted in Craggs, *William Walton: A Catalogue*, 79.
6   Walton to Hubert Foss, 7 November 1939, quoted in Craggs, *ibid.*, 79–80.

OUP memo that December to the effect that he was 'anxious to write an orchestral piece with the title *Mosieur Mongo*',[7] a name that derives from Nashe's *Summer's Last Will and Testament* that had itself been the basis for Lambert's choral work of the same name.

In May 1940 he was still contemplating a name for this new work, writing to Foss:

> I am still exercised in my mind about the title for the overture. What do you think of 'The Triumph of Silenus' or '('Twas) Bacchus and his Crew'. I incline to the latter. See Oxford B. of V. p.723 at verse starting 'And as I sat'.[8] Keats. If this and the following veres were quoted it might give enough of a clue without involving one in a 'tone poem'?[9]

In time the resulting work was the brilliant comedy overture, *Scapino*, and his inspiration, as with his other overture, *Portsmouth Point*, came from an etching, in this case one from Jacques Callot's *Balli di Sfessania* of 1622. Scapino is one of the Commedia dell'Arte characters to which Walton may well have been introduced through the work of the artist Gino Severini,[10] who had designed the *Façade* curtain for the 1928 Siena Festival production. Severini's frescoes for the hall of Sir George Sitwell's Italian castle at Montegufoni were of a succession of Commedia dell'Arte figures. The Overture was completed in London on 28 December 1940. Scored for a large orchestra with triple woodwind, cornets, and a full battery of percussion that included Chinese temple blocks, slapsticks and castanets (all removed in the revised version), this far too infrequently played work abounds with the same roguish humour as Bax's *Overture to a Picaresque Comedy* of 1931. It has too an almost Falstaffian swagger after Elgar, but with typically Waltonian vigour. Stock gave the première of *Scapino* in Chicago on 3 April 1941 and Walton himself conducted the first British performance with the BBC Symphony Orchestra at its war-time home of Bedford, on 12 November 1941. Stock recorded the work with his orchestra on 20 November 1941, an important document that preserves the original version before Walton, in 1950, made considerable cuts totalling ninety-four bars as well as slightly reducing the orchestration. The revised version was first heard at the Royal Albert Hall on 13 November 1950 when the conductor was Furtwängler, opening a series of concerts he was giving with the Philharmonia Orchestra. He took it 'at a cautious pace until the coda, when an accelerando came to try

---

7 Craggs, *ibid.*, 80.
8 These verses of Keats from *Endymion* had been set by Gustav Holst in his Choral Symphony.
9 Undated letter to Foss but almost certainly written in May 1940: OUP files.
10 Up till 1951 Severini's designs were used by Walton's publishers, OUP, for the covers of his scores. The cover and endpapers of Edith's anthology *Wheels 1920* were designed by Severini.

the woodwind's equipoise; but the detail in the score and its eloquence emerged lucidly, if not the witty virtuosity of the piece', commented *The Times* critic. But it was with Walton that the orchestra recorded the work in October 1951.

In a 1942 broadcast Boyd Neel played a short extract from *Scapino*, suggesting that it was almost identical with some bars from the last movement of Rimsky-Korsakov's *Scheherazade* (a similarity that has since often been commented upon). Walton was quick to reply: 'The fact is that the extract mentioned is an extension of a theme occurring earlier in the work (towards the end of the first record), and is an actual and intentional quotation from Rossini: it being quite legitimately brought in as a counterpart to the second subject of the overture.' The Rossini quotation was from the second subject of the allegro in the Overture *Tancredi*. Why Rossini? He explained: 'I am inordinately fond of his music and because I hoped it would help to 'point' the character of the piece – Rossini being the most 'Scapinoesque' of composers. It never occurred to me that the quotation would not be obvious to all, still less would it be attributed to the wrong composer! However, in fairness to Rossini as well as myself it should be stated that most people have been able to recognise the quotation and without difficulty.'[11]

Since the outbreak of World War Two the problem had been, as Walton said himself,[12] 'What could I usefully do? I tried driving an ambulance . . . and after I'd run it into the ditch several times they said perhaps you'd better not drive an ambulance. . . .' He couldn't master the knack of double-declutching. On 8 January 1940 he wrote to Eugene Goossens's wife with the discretion required by the official censors: 'The war is just too boring for words, so we won't talk about it anymore. Incidentally I am not driving an ambulance in France as the American press seem to think. They will be giving me the V.C. next! I am driving an ambulance somewhere in the Midlands.'[13] A solution was soon found: 'As I'd written music for films before . . . I was put to work.'

After working in films before the war with Paul Czinner, much of Walton's work during the war was again in films, and his next director was another Hungarian, the more volatile Gabriel Pascal (1894–1954) whose reputation was made (notoriously, one might add) with his film adaptations of plays by George Bernard Shaw. Pascal's first proper meeting with Shaw had been in 1935 when the playwright had been captivated by both Pascal's personality and the fanciful stories he told of his early years.[14] The upshot of

[11] In 'Ralph Hill's Music Article: Rossini and Walton', *Radio Times*, 15 May 1942, 4.
[12] In Tony Palmer, *At the Haunted End of the Day*, ITV.
[13] Carole Rosen, *The Goossens*, 220.
[14] Kenneth Clark, in *The Other Half: A Self-Portrait*, 37–41, has described Pascal as a likeable but 'perfectly shameless' man, 'a sort of Baron Munchausen, who never opened his mouth without telling some obviously untrue story'.

this relationship was that Shaw gave Pascal the film rights to his plays. The first to be made by him was *Pygmalion*, in 1938, with Leslie Howard and Wendy Hiller. (There had already been German and Dutch film versions of *Pygmalion* that were not to Shaw's taste, and in consequence he produced his own film script.) Pascal then approached Walton for the music. But Walton was already too occupied with the violin concerto he had been commissioned for the New York World Fair in October 1939. He had repeatedly to turn down an insistent Pascal who even tempted him with an offer of further films. In the end Honegger provided the film score.

Pygmalion proved a great success, owing in no small measure to the excellent direction of Antony Asquith (together with Leslie Howard), and in 1939 Shaw agreed to Pascal proceeding with a film of his 'parable', *Major Barbara*. (The play was successfully running in London in the early months of the war with Catherine Lacey in the title rôle.) Cusins, a university professor, falls in love with Major Barbara (Wendy Hiller), a Salvation Army preacher whose father, Undershaft (Robert Morley), is an armaments millionaire. Shaw, who had been unhappy with Leslie Heward's casting as Higgins in *Pygmalion*, objected to him as the love-struck Cusins and the part eventually went to Rex Harrison (who was later to become the definitive Higgins in *My Fair Lady*, Lerner and Loewe's musical adaptation of *Pygmalion*). The cast also included Emlyn Williams, Sybil Thorndike, Deborah Kerr, Donald Calthrop, Penelope Dudley Ward and Robert Newton. The costumes were designed by Cecil Beaton. Location shooting began in May 1940 on the Dartington Hall estate in Devon, with some scenes later shot in London and Sheffield. This time Walton was able to accept Pascal's offer and he worked on the score during 1940 and 1941.

Hyam Greenbaum had assisted Walton with the orchestration of at least two of his earlier films, but as conductor of the BBC Variety Orchestra he and his orchestra, like the BBC Symphony Orchestra, had now been evacuated to Bristol on the outbreak of war. His early death in May 1942 brought an end to any further collaboration. For *Major Barbara* in November 1940 Walton now had the help of Roy Douglas, who had already had the experience of working for several film composers. He had orchestrated all Richard Addinsell's music for *Dangerous Moonlight*, released in 1941 with its highly popular *Warsaw Concerto*, and he was to do much work for Walton,[15] and in due course even more for Vaughan Williams. His film work with Walton generally consisted of orchestrating the shorter sections. Walton jotted down the music on 2 or 3 staves for Douglas to orchestrate either according to his directions or as seemed appropriate to his style.

[15] Roy Douglas helped with some of the orchestrations for *Major Barbara*, *Next of Kin* and *Went the Day Well?* He was much involved in preparing for publication the scores of many works (some of them revised versions), including *Troilus and Cressida*. Interview with the author, 23 July 1996.

In 1945 Penguin Books published Shaw's screen version of *Major Barbara*, this representing his idealised script which is slightly longer than Pascal's final version and which diverges in some instances from what eventually emerged on celluloid. In a prefatory note Shaw writes that 'the verses written to fit Rossini's once famous quartet from his *Moses in Egypt* were reset by Mr William Walton for Mr Pascal's film; but I retain my first suggestion partly to explain the constrained versification imposed by Rossini's music; partly because I must not infringe Mr Walton's copyright (Rossini's is extinct); and perhaps mainly because I feel sure that Undershaft was as old-fashioned in his musical taste as he was ultra-modern in his industrial management.' This refers to the scene embodying Shaw's vision of a socialist post-war reconstruction. In Undershaft's Utopian world the employees' social and cultural welfare is well catered for, and Shaw has even foreseen the use of video. 'We have the best orchestras in the world, and the best conductors, and the best singers. We pay them handsomely for one performance, which we televise and record so that we can reproduce it as often as we like.' Shaw was not, it seems, the most realistic of screen writers for in that particular scene he not only asks for the Rossini extract to be viewed on a television set but he specifies that it is to be conducted by none other than Toscanini. As an announcer proclaims: 'For Rossini at his greatest today there is only one conductor: Arturo Toscanini.' And at this point, according to the script, 'Toscanini enters, baton in hand, and takes his place at the conductor's desk . . . , and the quartet and chorus from Rossini's *Moses in Egypt* follows, accompanied by a Wagnerian orchestra.' In the film a compromise clearly had to be made. In place of a performance viewed on a television screen, the strains of Rossini are heard coming from a church. Whatever words are sung they are fairly indistinguishable.

The seven-and-a-half minute sequence of music that includes this scene is of particular interest. Beginning in Undershaft's steel works, the percussive effects accompanying the steel production (cymbal rolls for the showers of sparks, etc.) strive for a realism not unlike those in Mossolov's *The Factory* (or *Iron Foundry*). Prokofiev's ballet *Le Pas d'acier*, first staged in London on 4 July 1927, might well have been known to Walton, its second half depicting life in a Soviet factory with the rhythmic power of machines as they throbbed and hammered with ever-increasing intensity. If the continuation of this sequence in *Major Barbara*, with its nervous energy, is a close prototype for the 'Battle in the Air' section in *The Battle of Britain* film, there is a double irony. Not only was Undershaft manufacturing the weapons of war but the actual filming was done at the time when the Nazi bombing of England had begun. Look-outs were stationed on the studio roof at Denham to keep watch for approaching enemy aircraft so that everyone could if necessary be evacuated to concrete cellars beneath the sound stage.

Shaw, former music critic, was at times present on the set and even suggested to Walton that at one point he added 'the effect of a single trombone sounding G flat quite quietly after the others have stopped, Undershaft pretending to play it. It ought to have the effect of a question mark.'[16] This suggestion was adopted – moderated to E flat – in the Albert Hall scene.

Walton's film score[17] is a fine one, with some affecting love-music, even if his treatment of *Onward Christian Soldiers* in the title music is momentarily reminiscent of Bliss's *Checkmate* (1937). But the film as a whole, in its final cut to a running time of 121 minutes, is not entirely satisfactory. Pascal's desire this time to take overall control of direction resulted in a film that, despite some fine acting and occasional moments of cinematic interest, is over-wordy, laboured and tedious on repeated viewings. Wendy Hiller said of it, 'I saw the finished film once only – I wept with disappointment.'[18] The film overran both its schedule and its budget. Shaw's close involvement, with many rewritings, cuts and transpositions, could not have helped. *Major Barbara* was premièred in Nassau in the presence of the Duke and Duchess of Windsor on 20 March 1941, and it opened in London at the Odeon, Leicester Square on 7 April. In a preview, *The Times* critic[19] thought it 'a freakish film, a mistaken film, but a film with honesty of purpose and some highly amusing moments. . . . It takes [Shaw's characters] out of the confines of intellectual comedy, away from the convention of dialectic cut and thrust, and turns them loose into the vague fluid world of cinematic pseudo-realism where their gestures lose that artificial precision in argument and timing which makes them a delight on the stage. . . .' The film failed to make a profit and Shaw, who had put his royalty payment from *Pygmalion* into it, lost £20,000.

Like his fellow Hungarian, Alexander Korda, Pascal had both a love for the epic and a passion for cinematic detail, both expensive tastes, and his extravagance was to be his undoing in his next Shaw film, *Caesar and Cleopatra* (1945), which earned a reputation as the most expensive failure in British film history and almost terminated Pascal's film career (though he did go on to film Shaw's *Androcles and the Lion* in 1952). Arthur Bliss, who in 1934 had been asked by H. G. Wells to collaborate with him by writing the score for Korda's film *Things to Come*, was similarly invited by Shaw to provide the music for *Caesar and Cleopatra*. He actually started work on it but after meeting Pascal in person he withdrew from the project. 'One look at him made it self-evident that he would never be a sympathetic collaborator,' Bliss later wrote in his autobiography.[20] Pascal turned instead to Georges

---

16 Michael Holroyd, *Bernard Shaw, Vol III*, 477.
17 The autograph score is missing. In 1942, in answer to an enquiry, Walton suggested that Pascal had taken the score and parts with him to America.
18 Michael Holroyd, *Bernard Shaw, Vol III*, 437.
19 2 April 1941.
20 Arthur Bliss, *As I Remember*, 168.

Auric, Walton's film music by that time being allied to Shakespearean rather than Shavian scripts.

Even in the early stages of the war, the government recognised the enormous potential of film for propaganda, and a film division of the Ministry of Information was created by absorbing the GPO Film Unit, famous in pre-war days for its innovative documentaries, which became the Crown Film Unit. A large number of documentary-styled films were produced with scores from such established composers as Constant Lambert, Arnold Bax, Ralph Vaughan Williams, Walter Leigh, Richard Addinsell and William Alwyn. Under the auspices of the MoI, the Forces created their own film units, largely to make instructional films.

On 24 May 1940 Walton wrote to Boult that he was to be appointed Chairman of a Composers' Panel for the MoI's Film Division when it was formed. He wrote as well to Foss: 'It appears that I'm definitely going to be offered the job of general music director of the M.o.I. film unit & though unpaid I think it wisest to accept it. I'm afraid it will involve much more work than I first anticipated, but anyhow one can but see how it works out.'[21] When call-up came in spring 1941 he was exempted from military service and remained attached to the MoI on the condition that he wrote music for films 'of national importance'. It was a position that he did not find disagreeable. As he told Dallas Bower in 1942: 'There is no room for me in the unit as an officer but I think I'm to be made civilian music adviser to the Army Film Unit. . . . I can't say I mind. Also I can say what I think, speak out of turn etc. in my present status. Then I had to remember I was speaking to a general & mind my ps & qs.'[22]

It was not just film music that Walton was expected to produce. He told Foss: 'I've been asked by the M.O.I. "to arrange a simple overture of popular music to run for about 8 mins." I don't know as yet quite what they mean by "popular music" but presume it means things like "Rule Brit." etc. You don't happen to know a volume of popular tunes (non-copyright) upon which I could draw. I suppose it ought to be on the lines of Quilter's Children's Nursery Tunes Overture or VW's Fantasia on Folk Song. It might be a profitable thing to do. Anyhow I've got to do it.'[23] No such work seems to have survived.

The first Director of the MoI Film Division was Kenneth Clark who, with his wife Jane, had known Walton for about ten years. As he remembered: 'In 1940, when I was so much occupied by the Ministry of Information, [William] became for Jane a wonderful standby. I see from her diaries how much she depended on him for the companionship I could not give her. Willie's irreverent and mocking manner (his coté *Scapino*), which he has long

21 Walton to Hubert Foss, n.d., OUP files.
22 Walton to Dallas Bower, n.d., BBC Written Archives, Caversham.
23 Undated letter, OUP files.

ago abandoned, never concealed a north-country good sense and kindness of heart and the warmth of feeling that permeates his music.'[24] However, Susana Walton felt that, far from being a mere standby, another side to William, his fondness for the ladies, came to the fore. She writes of him and Jane having 'a passionate affair' of which Clark was fully aware 'and had once offered to send him and Jane off together'.[25] Apparently he had even offered to finance this, involved as he himself was at that time with Frederick Ashton's sister, Edith, with whom he planned to elope (and at whom, Ashton commented, 'Willie Walton was always making passes').[26] But the presence of Alice Wimborne had put an end to these romantic escapades. At this time Walton is also said to have written some piano pieces for the Clarks' daughter Colette but none of these has survived.

None of the war films that Walton worked on quite falls into the category of pure documentary but each could nevertheless be said to be of national importance for its underlying message or its effectiveness as a morale booster. Certainly the sentiments of *Major Barbara* could hardly be farther from those of three of the next four films he worked on.[27] *Next of Kin, The Foreman Went to France* and *Went the Day Well?*[28] all produced at the Ealing Studios, are essentially propaganda films that were designed, as Charles Barr so aptly put it in his history of the studios,[29] to warn against complacency and amateurishness, a lesson which was seen to be learnt at bitter cost.

The first two of these films overlapped in production. *The Foreman Went to France*, with a narrative by J. B. Priestley and directed by Charles Frend (film editor for *Major Barbara*), was based on the true experience of a certain Melbourne Johns and acknowledges the co-operation of the War Office and the Free French Forces. The foreman of an ammunition factory (Clifford Evans) takes it upon himself, when his superiors seem unconcerned, to go to France to retrieve important machinery before it falls into enemy hands. Set during the period of the fall of France, it deals with fifth columnists, one a French mayor (Robert Morley) and another passing as an English officer (John Williams). It also points an accusing finger at the British obsession with red tape. Constance Cummings plays an American girl involved in the rescue operation while Tommy Trinder (in his first straight rôle) and Gordon Jackson provide the true British elements of humour and

---

24 Kenneth Clark, *The Other Half: A Self Portrait*, 36–7.
25 Susana Walton, *Behind the Façade*, 32 and 213–14.
26 Julie Kavanagh, *Secret Muses*, 293–5.
27 All four films, *Next of Kin, The Foreman Went to France, Went the Day Well?* and *The First of the Few*, were first seen in the same year, 1942.
28 *Next of Kin* and *Went the Day Well?* are discussed at considerable length in Anthony Aldgate and Jeffery Richards, *Britain can Take It: The British Cinema in the Second World War*, Blackwell 1986, with a chapter devoted to each film.
29 Charles Barr, *Ealing Studios*, Studio Vista, revised 1993.

adventurous spirit, with the British soldier emerging, as *The Times* critic[30] put it, as 'something of a natural philosopher and humourist'. Walton provided a thoroughly efficient score, with a memorable fanfare-heralded march for the opening and closing titles and a striking passage depicting the refugees fleeing from the German advance. It is difficult now to appreciate the effect that films such as this had on war-time audiences, but there is no escaping their message and the underlying emotions. Even the French captain's closing words – 'We shall owe everything to your country, monsieur, when France lives again – one day' – can bring a lump to the throat over half a century on. Filmed between August and November 1941 (with Cornwall substituting for the French landscape), *The Foreman Went to France* was first shown on 12 April 1942 at the London Pavilion. Previewing it two days earlier, *The Times* called it 'an outstanding British film'. Other propaganda films showing in London at that time were Harold French's *The Day will Dawn* and Michael Powell's *One of our Aircraft is Missing*. Even in war-time Walton's humour shines through two short sections of the score that are headed *La Ravelese* (with a suggestion of *La Valse*) and *Moto Poulencuo*.

The other film being made at about the same time as *The Foreman Went to France* was *Next of Kin*, directed by Thorold Dickinson[31] who was specially seconded from the Army for the purpose. (He went on to direct *Men of Two Worlds* in 1945, with a score by Bliss.) It began, in December 1940, with a request to Michael Balcon, Head of Ealing Studios, from the War Office's director of military training for an instructional twenty-five minute 'short' on security.[32] However, it soon became apparent that the subject really called for feature-length treatment, and a contract was drawn up on 7 January 1941. It was to be made as cheaply as possible without sacrificing quality. The War Office put up £20,000, Ealing Studios agreeing to cover the balance of the costs which eventually came to £50,000. The opening credits describe it as 'A military training film produced for The Directorate of Army Kinematography by Ealing Studios Limited'. Dickinson called it 'an attempt to take this most unpopular element in the Army, the Security Police, and make its work understandable'. Ealing story supervisor Angus MacPhail and Thorold Dick-

---

30 10 April 1942.
31 In a letter, dated 7 December 1972, to Stewart Craggs (to whom I am indebted for the information), Thorold Dickinson wrote: 'I was naturally delighted when Walton agreed to do the score, and though to him our approach had to be more "music hall" than "opera house" (to reach the widest audience), he disciplined himself and delivered a score that was an object lesson in dignified and appropriate propaganda. Except for a fox trot he had to write which was neither good Walton nor good dance music. I have worked with some superb composers in my time, and I regard Walton as outstandingly professional in coping with the maddening demands of timing and emphasis that a film score demands.'
32 The story of the making of *Next of Kin* is told in more detail by Jeffrey Richards in *Thorold Dickinson: The Man and his Films*, Croom Helm 1986, 93–105.

inson worked together on several drafts of the script until, on 22 April 1941, one finally met with the War Office's approval. The film was shot between 26 July and 24 October. For the battle scenes Dickinson had the use of a battalion of troops from the Royal Worcestershire Regiment, three naval landing craft and their crews, sixty officers of a commando unit, and (for three hours one afternoon) a flight of RAF Spitfires and bombers.

It taught most effectively the lesson of 'careless talk' in war-time. Its opening titles spelt out the message: 'This is the story of how YOU – unwittingly, worked for the Enemy. YOU – without knowing gave him the facts. YOU – in all innocence – helped to write those tragic words THE NEXT OF KIN.' Its first release, in January 1942, was restricted to compulsory audiences of service men and women: to War Office staff at Cheltenham where it was shown five times daily for a week, and then, in February, at the Curzon, the armed forces' cinema in London. Churchill had it withdrawn at the time of the St. Nazaire raid on 28 March 1942, concerned that the film would seriously affect morale if the raid was not a success. Then he became worried about certain aspects of the film and delayed its general release until some of the violence – in effect the number of English dead – had been toned down. Dickinson made a few cuts but even so the long attack sequence as seen today pulls no punches. Much later, he commented on this censorship:

> A more complex case is the bloodshed at the tragic climax of *Next of Kin* which Winston Churchill asked to be toned down. On measuring the fragments removed, none of which lasted one full second, I found that the nausea in the audience was caused by some thirty fragments, each of a few frames, lasting barely twenty seconds in all.[33]

The Cornish town of Mevagissey served as the French port on which the attack is made. When *Next of Kin* eventually opened for release to the general public on 15 May 1942 at both the Carlton and the London Pavilion, where it took over from *The Foreman Went to France*, *The Times* critic[34] questioned the film's delay: 'It is difficult to understand why there should ever have been any discussions as to whether *Next of Kin* should not be shown to the public, [a] film . . . intended to jolt the public into an awareness of the danger of careless talk. A word by an infatuated officer to a strip-tease dancer with an unfortunate taste for cocaine is the first link in a chain of events which leads to so many unnecessary casualties. . . . The Germans are ready to meet an attack which was to have been a surprise. The operation is successful, but the cost is high.'

The film was a success with both the forces for whom it was made and the general public. Michael Balcon considered it 'one of the most important

---

[33] Thorold Dickinson, *A Discovery of Cinema*, OUP 1971, 59.
[34] 14 May 1942.

films made in the life of Ealing' while General Alexander told Dickinson: 'That film was worth a division of troops to the British Army.' The *Sunday Chronicle* called it 'One of the finest pictures ever made', and the *Empire News* said that 'Every man and woman, either in or out of the services, must see *Next of Kin*.' By May the distributors United Artists reported that it was 'one of the best films they have handled from a box-office point of view'. The cast included Mervyn Johns, Stephen Murray, Basil Sydney, Naunton Wayne, Nova Pilbeam, Jack Hawkins and Thora Hird. The musical director was Ernest Irving.[35] The film's running time was about ninety-five minutes and an hour-long radio adaptation, made by Cecil McGivern and including Nova Pilbeam, Stephen Murray and members of the BBC Drama Repertory Company, was broadcast on the Home Service on 6 July 1942 with part of the music from the sound-track being used. For the film's release in America, it was prefaced by a speech by J. Edgar Hoover warning audiences that enemy agents might similarly be at work in the United States. However, the American distributors felt that the film gave quite the wrong image of the British in contrast with the efficiency of the German intelligence network and a further thirty minutes had to be cut, resulting in what Dickinson called 'a total numbing of a vital film.'

Walton worked on *Next of Kin* in December 1941 and once again he turned in an effective score, with a military quick march for title music that dissolves in a typical cinematic cliché into a fragment of *La Marseillaise*, informing the audience that the opening scene is set in France (unnecessarily as it happens because this information has already been conveyed by way of screen titles). Elsewhere there is a lively 'striptease dance' and some passionate string writing for two lovers who meet on the cliff and in a bookshop (ironically the same bookshop from which German spies are operating). Walton was not averse to a little 'borrowing' and at least one of the two foxtrots used in the factory dance scene (that form part of Christopher Palmer's suite *A Wartime Sketchbook*[36]) is certainly not his: the second half of the sequence makes use of Noel Gay and Frank Eyton's *'All Over the Place'* which had recently appeared, in its vocal version sung by Tommy Trinder, in another Ealing film, *Sailors Three* (1940). There are snatches of two further dance tunes in the Café Regale scene. Dallas Bower remembers Walton, with some pleasure, playing to him one of the dance tunes he had written for *Next of Kin* and how he was somewhat taken aback when Bower pointed out that it was almost identical to Ishay Jones's hit of the 1920s called *Spain*. Bower

---

35 Ernest Irving was musical director for *The Next of Kin*, *The Foreman Went to France* and *Went the Day Well?*, in each case recording the soundtrack with the London Philharmonic Orchestra in the Ealing Studios.

36 An eight-movement suite comprising extracts from *The Foreman Went to France*, *The Next of Kin*, *Went the Day Well?* and *The Battle of Britain*, recorded on Chandos CHAN 8870.

even had to get Spike Hughes, a great friend of Walton's,[37] to persuade him to omit it from the score. In a similar fashion the first of the two fox-trots in the dance scene bears some resemblance to *Weary Traveller* from Spike Hughes's innovative jazz ballet *High Yellow* of 1932 (much influenced by Duke Ellington), perhaps a fair exchange as Hughes's 1938 television operetta *Cinderella* had apparently contained a Walton allusion, to the symphony.[38] Walton himself makes a short and just distinguishable appearance in *Next of Kin*, as one of the soldiers seated for a briefing about security.[39]

For his next film, *The First of the Few* made at Denham, Walton produced one of his most memorable scores. After both starring in and directing *Pimpernel Smith*, a patriotic war-time update of the Scarlet Pimpernel theme (with music by John Greenwood), Leslie Howard performed the same dual rôle[40] in this biopic of Reginald J. Mitchell (1895–1937), the designer of the Spitfire. The outline story was written in 1940 by an Australian writer, Henry C. James, with the approval of Mitchell's widow (who also sat through some of the filming to give advice), and from this Miles Malleson and Anatole de Grunwald developed a film scenario. Like *The Foreman Went to France* and *Went the Day Well?*, this is a story told in flashback. At the height of the Battle of Britain, Crisp (David Niven), a former Schneider Trophy pilot now an RAF station commander, relates Mitchell's life story to a group of young pilots. As in *The Foreman Went to France* its story has an underlying theme of one man's struggle against blinkered 'official' attitudes. Just as Melbourne Johns goes it alone when he cannot convince his superiors of the urgency of recovering vital machinery before it falls into enemy hands, so Mitchell first faces opposition to his revolutionary designs and then has to convince government officials of the urgency of arming in the air in the face of the Nazi threat. His late nights working on the Spitfire design take a heavy toll of his health, and the most memorable lines are when Vickers–Supermarine gives the go-ahead to a prototype, telling him: 'This plane of yours; you've got to get it ready in 12 months because that's all the time we are giving you,'

---

37 They first met in 1927 in the Queen's Hall when they shared a score while hearing Elgar's Second Symphony. Hughes remembered the incident in his article 'Nobody Calls Him Willie Now' in *High Fidelity*, Sept. 1960, Vol. 10, No. 9, 43–6, 116–17.

38 Dallas Bower in conversation with the author, 18 February 1997. Bower had been the producer of *Cinderella*, the opera specially written for television, on 13 December 1938 at Alexandra Palace with the composer conducting. When it was broadcast from Bedford on 27 December 1942 on the BBC Home Service with the composer once again conducting, Ralph Hill wrote in *Radio Times*, 25 December 1942, 4, that 'the music is a strong mixture of styles which have been carefully blended into a congruous whole – . . . you will hear an allusion to Walton's Symphony – a personal gesture to Walton' as well as hints of Offenbach, Viennese waltz, Italian opera, Paganini and Mozart. The broadcast has been preserved in the BBC Sound Archives, T5074.

39 At 16 minutes 40 seconds.

40 The rôle of Mitchell was first offered to Robert Donat who could not accept because of contractual reasons.

to which Mitchell grimly replies: 'It'll be ready in 8 months – because that is all the time I can give you.'

Sidney Cole, the supervising editor, arranged a run-through of a rough-cut of the film for Walton. 'Leslie gave me very full instructions to pass on to Willie Walton about his feelings regarding the music. These, after the showing, I dutifully relayed to Walton. He listened carefully, then, observed drily: "I see. Leslie wants a lot of notes!" '[41] Walton enjoyed working with Howard and their association in films might have continued but for Howard's early death when the passenger aircraft in which he was flying home from Lisbon in 1943 was shot down.

The stirring prelude, with its characteristic fanfare opening, is one of Walton's finest marches (and given a splendid performance on the sound-track with Muir Mathieson conducting the London Symphony Orchestra). This leads straight into a tense, agitated prologue, with the European political situation outlined by a sequence of newsreels and, with the threat of the Nazi advance, the music making oblique Wagnerian references to the descent into the Nibelheim (without anvils) from *Das Rheingold* and the Immolation Scene from *Götterdämmerung*, the latter recognisable from its bold descending brass figure. After the prologue, music is used sparingly but to great effect. Interestingly, the Battle of Britain sequence towards the end has no music sound-track, unlike the parallel sequence in the much later film of that name. Together with the title music, the other important episodes are the poignant, lyrical theme with violin solo representing the dying Mitchell and the fugue depicting the Spitfire's factory production (to which piano brings an added piquancy on the sound-track). For this section it was producer–director Adrian Brunel's task to devise a montage sequence, taking a film unit into several aircraft factories producing Spitfires and editing the material into a sort of *ballet mechanique*. Having found a fugue a part solution to his problems with the Symphony in 1935, Walton makes equally effective use of one at this key moment in the film. (These three sections were later skilfully united to form the *'Spitfire' Prelude and Fugue*, the first piece of Walton music to make the jump from the screen to the concert hall.)

From the start the film had the financial backing of Arthur Rank and the official support, through Churchill, of Fighter Command. But it exceeded by several weeks its planned schedule and it wasn't until June 1942 that cutting and editing were fully underway. *The First of the Few* was first shown on 20 August 1942 at the Leicester Square Cinema, appropriately enough in aid of the RAF Benevolent Fund, and has since become the most durable of Walton's 'official' war-time films.

The last of these essentially war-time propaganda films was *Went the Day*

---

41 Ronald Howard, *In Search of my Father: A Portrait of Leslie Howard*, William Kimber 1981, 120.

Well?, made at Ealing in the spring of 1942. Walton was working on the score in the summer, with Roy Douglas's assistance for some of the orchestration, and the film was shown on Sunday 1 November 1942 at the London Pavilion where it faced competition with Noël Coward's *In Which We Serve* which was showing at two London cinemas. If careless talk was the watchword in *Next of Kin*, then complacency and misplaced trust are the messages here. Loosely based on a Graham Greene story that the author had suggested to Cavalcanti in November 1941,[42] it concerns the sleepy English village of Bramley which is invaded by German parachutists passing themselves off as Royal Engineers. The squire of the village (Leslie Banks) turns out to be a quisling and the villagers, at first locked up in the church, eventually defeat the enemy in a battle at the manor house. Excellent direction by the Brazilian Alberto Cavalcanti, a former producer in the GPO Film Unit, makes this a taut realistic action thriller, no film for the faint-hearted. Also in the cast were Basil Sydney, Valerie Taylor, Marie Lohr, Elizabeth Allan, Thora Hird, Mervyn Johns, Frank Lawton, David Farrar, C. V. France and, with War Office permission, men of the Gloucestershire Regiment. Fanfare and march provide the robust title music. Elsewhere music, chiefly militaristic, is used even more sparingly than in *The First of the Few*, with a sinister snatch of march depicting the bogus English soldiers. The waltz from *The First Shoot* appears as radio music acting as cover while the quisling is making Morse contact with the enemy. The inspiration for the theme of the opening march came from trying to fit the film's title to music (a technique he quite likely also used for *The Foreman Went to France*). The march returns for the end titles to provide a moving conclusion. Again, one can only wonder at the disturbing impact this film had on war-time audiences.

In between his film work Walton wrote some incidental music for John Gielgud's production of *Macbeth* that occupied him between Christmas Day 1941 and New Year's Day. It was first staged at the Manchester Opera House on 16 January 1942 before transferring to the Piccadilly Theatre, London on 8 July the same year. The cast included Gwen Frangcon-Davies as Lady Macbeth (to Gielgud's Macbeth) and Leon Quartermaine as Banquo. It ran for four months. As with the score he had supplied for Barrie's *The Boy David* six years earlier, the music for *Macbeth* was pre-recorded for use in the production, Ernest Irving conducting the London Philharmonic Orchestra.[43] In his autobiography, Gielgud remembered the speed with which the music was composed:

One of my great satisfactions in the war years was to persuade William Walton to do the music for *Macbeth*. Naturally it had to be done on records.

---

[42] 'The Lieutenant Died Last', first published in *Collier's Magazine*, 29 June 1940, and reprinted in *The Last Word and Other Stories*, Penguin 1990.

[43] The complete recording, matrices 11950–9 and 12092–3, exists in private hands.

Walton came to the first rehearsal when I was trying to do the scene with the witches, getting them to emphasise the rhythm in the doggerel they have to speak. He listened to this rehearsal for only half an hour and went away. Four weeks later, when we were finishing rehearsals, I was told that the music was ready and could be recorded. I thought it was extraordinary and feared it would not fit properly, so I went up to the big recording studio in Maida Vale and there was a huge orchestra, about fifty pieces. I found that all the witches' scenes had been perfectly timed, exactly to the rhythm of the words, just as I had sketched them out. It took many hours to record – far too long – and, with three hours extra time to pay for, I found myself signing cheques like Ludwig of Bavaria. However, the music was most effective and we took it on tour and used it afterwards for six months in London. I was not so pleased, however, to hear it again some years later, in a production of Thornton Wilder's *The Skin of our Teeth*. As the records belonged to the management, [Hugh] Beaumont had decided to make use of them again.[44]

Inventive as ever, especially with percussion, this time in addition to castanets, gong, bell and wind machine he called for a flexatone.[45] (From the substantial but largely fragmentary score Christopher Palmer extracted two items to form a Fanfare and March, the latter a sinister funereal affair with its steady unrelenting tread.) The designer for *Macbeth* was the young artist Michael Ayrton who was passing through a short but, for him, unpleasant spell in the services. The relationship between producer and designer was at times an uneasy one as an extract from a letter from Gielgud indicates: 'If a man as experienced and brilliant as Walton can show such modesty and collaborate with such complete unselfishness, I feel you could do the same. . . .'[46]

Walton was also involved in an ambitious larger-scale project, a radio production of *Christopher Columbus*. This was planned as a sequel to a radio adaptation of *Alexander Nevsky*, based on Eisenstein's 1938 film and using Prokofiev's score. The script for *Alexander Nevsky*, which came as a result of a government directive calling for a broadcast gesture to the Soviets, was written by Louis MacNeice. Sir Adrian Boult conducted the BBC Symphony Orchestra, Robert Donat took the name part, and the producer was Dallas

---

[44] John Gielgud, *An Actor and his Time*, Sidgwick & Jackson 1979, 186–7.

[45] This instrument, whose effect was somewhat similar to that produced by a theremin, was used by Schoenberg in his Variations Op. 31, first performed in Britain by Boult and the BBC SO on 13 November 1931, and then on 8 February 1933 with Schoenberg conducting the BBC SO. Walton quite likely heard one, if not both, of these performances. (The Variations was one of his choices on the first of his two appearances on BBC Radio's *Desert Island Discs* programme, on 22 July 1965.) Khachaturian used the flexatone in the slow movement of his Piano Concerto (1936).

[46] Letter from Gielgud to Ayrton, 16 May 1942, in Justine Hopkins, *Michael Ayrton: A Biography*, André Deutsch 1994, 66.

Bower. It was broadcast in the Home Service on 8 December 1941,[47] the night after the Japanese attack on Pearl Harbour. There was a repeat performance broadcast on 26 April 1942, this time conducted by Clarence Raybould and with Michael Redgrave standing in for Donat. Walton had listened in to the earlier broadcast and enjoyed it very much. The coincidence of the broadcast of *Alexander Nevsky* and the attack on Pearl Harbour was the spur to another propaganda venture, *Christopher Columbus*, as a tribute to the United States who had now entered the war. As it turned out, *Christopher Columbus* was less overtly propagandist than *Alexander Nevsky* (in which Germany, rather than Teutonic Knights, is repeatedly named as the enemy), but it was planned on a more epic scale.

The use of music in radio drama had become quite a specialised field. Robert Chignell, who had provided scores for several adaptations of H. G. Wells's stories, was regarded as a pioneer in this respect. Since 1937 Benjamin Britten had made a significant contribution, and others like Walter Goehr, Philip Sainton and John Ireland had also been involved. Chignell had died in 1939, and Britten was in America when Bower first approached Walton on 26 January 1942. In an 'official and unofficial letter of exploration' he outlined his plan for *Columbus*, which was a 'development of the Nevsky programme', to be ready for a mid-March performance. He also discreetly mentioned a private charity project (that was not to take place) for which he invited Walton's co-operation – a performance of *Oedipus Rex* in the Royal Albert Hall with Robert Donat as Oedipus. Walton's immediate reaction was: 'This is most irritating – there is nothing I should like better than to accept both propositions.' He continued: 'Unless you get the Corp. to postpone the date to mid-May instead of mid-March I don't see how I can do it, as I'm at the moment doing a film (a boring one only just taken on as a fill-in) for Cavalcanti at Ealing [*Went the Day Well?*]. This should be finished by Feb 23rd at the latest as I have also to do L Howards 'First of the Few' a first-rate one which I start on at once after the Ealing film. It won't I suppose be finished before the end of March.' As an alternative to himself he suggested Alan Rawsthorne – 'he would be best' – although he would have to be got out of the Army.[48] Then there was Benjamin Britten: '[He] is by way of returning [from America] – he may be already back, but I gather he joins the RAF music dept. on landing. Who else is there except the old gang of V[aughan].W[illiams]., J. Ireland, A. Bax, if you want any of them.' He outlined his work over the previous weeks: 'A War Office film [*Next of Kin*] starting on Dec. 2 & finished by the 22nd – 32 mins. music, followed by Macbeth starting on Xmas day & finished on New Year's day 20 mins. And not all of it bad either! in fact Macbeth is pretty good. Then the recording &

---

47 The broadcast has been preserved in the BBC Sound Archives, T3618.
48 Rawsthorne had been given eight weeks' leave to write *The Golden Cockerel* score for a radio production on 27 December 1941.

rehearsing in Manchester. It is only the last day or two that I've had a moment to speak.'[49] (In July 1942 he asked Bower to call in at the Piccadilly Theatre and check the quality of sound reproduction of the music for *Macbeth*.)

Bower replied on the 28th: 'I had given consideration to the idea of using Benjamin Britten, but as there appeared to be a great deal of uncertainty as to whether he was in fact returning, I took no definite steps in the matter. Moreover, my own wish is that you should compose the music for the programme.' Rawsthorne was firmly back in the Army. 'Of the other three names you mention I would consider nobody but V.W. However, considerations of this kind now no longer arise as I am really delighted to think that we shall be working together once again.'

That same day Bower outlined his plans in a BBC internal memorandum, saying that the subject was one he had long been interested in. He had at one stage considered the possibility of using Darius Milhaud's *Christoph Colomb*. (With a libretto by Claudel, it had received its first British performance in January 1937 in the BBC's series of contemporary music concerts.[50]) However, as with *Nevsky*, Louis MacNeice would again supply the script[51] for which Bower suggested using Samuel Eliot Morison's Pulitzer Prize-winning book *Admiral of the Ocean Seas* for its basic outline. Julian Herbage added a note that late April was a likely time when the BBC Symphony Orchestra would be available. An outline sketch of *Christopher Columbus* was sent to Walton who replied on 30 January: 'I am a bit terrified of accepting it, since you know what films are like & I'm worried the Howard film [*First of the Few*] won't be over in time to give this the music it deserves.' He sensed exactly what was required of him: 'The music will have to be good & one can't rely on a quick film extemporisation technique for it, so it will need more time[,] trouble & care', adding as a P.S.: 'I should hate to have to deliver it to the tender mercies of V.W. though on the other hand he might do it rather well, but I must admit it is more up my street.'

On 2 February Boult, no doubt with the problems of the Symphony's completion in mind, scribbled a note of caution to Bower: 'I hope to goodness you will be able to ginger up Walton to get it done in time; it seems to me terribly short notice for a composer.' By 6 March Bower had sent Walton 'the first very rough draft, approximating to about half of the final part', adding the next day: 'I hope it is clearly understood that you should, of course, do no concrete work on Columbus until you are properly commissioned. . . . Immediately the whole script is completed and approved, you will of course be commissioned in the usual way.' Ten days later about two-thirds of the first draft had been completed. Bower wrote in a memo: 'MacNeice

---

49 27 January 1942. This letter and subsequent correspondence relating to *Christopher Columbus* are at the BBC Written Archives Centre, Caversham.
50 A concert performance on 16 January 1937, the composer conducting.
51 Louis MacNeice, *Christopher Columbus: A Radio Play*, Faber & Faber 1944.

and I have discussed the programme at considerable length with Walton, who has proposed a number of excellent ideas. . . . I would like to go ahead and have Walton commissioned to write the music.'

Towards the end of the month Walton wrote that, on returning one day from Denham, he

> started with 'flu the next day & have been in bed till yesterday. It has been the most foul not to say dastardly attack & has left me with double sciatica in the bargain. Nothing was definitely settled at Denham & I've as yet received no footages so 'flu has not stopped that. However I've not, naturally enough, been able to do anything about C.C. either. . . . Now I don't suppose I shall be properly up & doing for another week & at the rate things are moving at Denham I don't think it possible to finish the music for Leslie's picture much before the middle of May, so it is obvious that I can't get C.C. done by the end of May. It is going to take me at least 6 weeks.

He thought as well that the end of May was not a wise time for the production to be broadcast since 'no one listens in at all during double summer time' and again suggested someone else for the job, this time Hely-Hutchinson – 'I know you'll think me dotty but I'm not. . . . He's come on no end of late at this kind of thing, also film music & is extremely good at it.' He continued:

> Actually from my point of view I can't treat C.C. in any way different from a rather superior film. That is, that the music is entirely occasional & is of no use other than what it is meant for & one won't be able to get a suite out of it. Which is just as it should be, otherwise it would probably not fulfil its purpose. That is why I'm against my film music being played by Mr Stanford Robinson or anyone else.[52] Film music is not good film music if it can be used for any other purpose & you've only have got to have heard that concert the other night to realise how true that is. For all the music was as bad as it could be, listened to in cold blood, but probably excellent with the film. So I don't care where Major Barbara is or any other of my films. The music should never be heard without the film.[53]

Bower consulted Muir Mathieson whose view, he told Walton, was 'that by careful handling both *The First of the Few* and *Columbus* should be possible'. On 1 April Walton replied that the film wouldn't be finished before the middle of May and he was still wondering whether 'to put it all off to very much later (Sept.) or whether you get someone else. John Ireland. Hely-Hutchinson or even [with an eye to the date of writing] Loof Lirpa!' But there were further delays with the film and it wasn't until 31 May that he could write 'starting on First of the Few today'. However, on 1 May it was agreed to

---

52 Short programmes of film music were quite frequently broadcast at this time.
53 BBC Written Archives, Caversham.

offer Walton 125 guineas for the broadcasting and recording rights, this being modified to 100 guineas with 25 guineas for each subsequent broadcast.

As if the film scores and *Christopher Columbus* were not enough to be getting on with, he had been asked by Bliss to write a short brass-band work. On 21 March he wrote to Bliss: 'As soon as I'm up from my bed of sickness ('flu is very vicious this year) I'll do your piece as a thanksgiving offering. That is perhaps a rash statement as I've to start on the Leslie Howard film as soon as I'm up & immediately after that I [am] supposed to be do[ing] the music for a play for your august corporation. About 80 mins. music by the end of May & I don't see how it is going to be done. So I hope there is no real hurry for your piece or suite.'[54] On 30 March Bliss thanked him for agreeing to write the work and on 22 April Kenneth Wright sent him a list of the tunes that were to be incorporated in what he suggested should take the form of a 'short march, solo tune, and a short bright final'. Walton wrote back on the 27th: 'I must confess I know precisely nothing about brass bands. So if you could let me have a list of instruments, their compass & characteristics, etc. I should be grateful. I have looked up Grove & Scholes but the information in both is scanty.' From someone who had used brass so effectively in *Belshazzar's Feast*, his plea of total ignorance does not ring entirely true. In the end nothing came of the work.

As there were one or two places in the score of *Christopher Columbus* that called for some church music, on 19 May Bower sent Walton two manuals on plainsong. In the end, however, Walton left that entirely to Leslie Woodgate, conductor of the BBC Choral Society. At the same time it seems that the possibilities of making *Columbus* into a film were being investigated, as a note from M.E.B. (Michael Balcon) to Ernest Irving reads: 'Would you return this script to Walton for me with a very charming letter from you saying how very nice it is to have had the opportunity of reading MacNeice's work but we could not possibly tackle it in a film, and we think it is fairest to say so, particularly in view of Dr Walton's courtesy in letting us see the script etc. etc.' Bower commented disappointedly that 'nothing will make British film producers see the possibility of Christopher Columbus until somebody has produced it and made a fortune thereby'.[55]

By June the date of broadcast had been decided, someone having realised that 12 October would be the 450th anniversary of Columbus's first landfall. On the 13 June Bower informed Boult (who was to conduct) that Walton had 'promised that the score will be available by September Ist'. John Gielgud had been approached and had shown interest in playing Columbus, but the name part was eventually taken by Laurence Olivier who, although attached

---

54 *Ibid.*
55 In 1948 a film *Christopher Columbus* was made, with music by Arthur Bliss, with screenplay by Muriel and Sydney Box and Cyril Roberts. Despite Bower's prophecy, no-one made a fortune.

to the Fleet Air Arm, was doing much war-time radio and film work, including the narration for the film *Malta GC* with music by Bax.

Work on *Christopher Columbus* was now proceeding rapidly. Walton's experience of writing for film music came in handy and he asked Bower to provide him with stop-watch timings of certain sections of the script. The first parts of the score were shown to Herbert Murrill on 28 July and rehearsal dates were fixed. The recording was to be made in the Bedford School Hall, a venue that Bower, 'impressed by its admirable acoustic properties', had wanted from the very start. The final working script was sent to Boult on 19 September.

All-day rehearsals for the cast, choir and orchestra were held on Sunday and Monday 11 and 12 October, but, to Bower's great disappointment, Walton was unable to be present as on the evening of the broadcast he was in North Wales. 'I am, my dear Willie, quite bitterly disappointed that you will not be present at the performance,' Bower had written ten days before the event, 'and I can only hope that there is an adequate radio set in your hotel.' Bower had informed Boult that it was 'singularly unfortunate, but [Walton] is being violently overworked at the moment'.[56] The real reason for Walton's absence was that, because of her declining health, Alice Wimborne was having a rest at Portmeirion and Walton was torn between staying with her and attending the broadcast.

As it turned out, he was able to listen in to the broadcast, though not with great clarity. Afterwards, from the hotel he was staying at in Penrhyndeudraeth, he wrote a letter of congratulations to Bower:

You must be exhausted after the hectic days (or at least I imagine they were) with C.C. I think you came out of it with flying colours & I hope the BBC will be feeling slightly sick at parting with you. In fact I think we all can pat each other on the back. I qualify that as to my part, which I hope was adequate from your point of view & I trust that Louis wasn't dissatisfied.

The transmission here is frightful and full of atmospherics & fading owing to the proximity to rock. The set in any case was poor so I only heard an occasional [..[57]..] but on the whole enough to see that it more or less fitted – in fact what I could gather of the music seemed to me rather good or maybe I'm mistaken.

It was maddening to have Winston's speech buggering things up. But I should like to hope that it was enough of a success for it to be done again & fairly soon.

All the parts that I thought wouldn't come off, came off splendidly as far as one could judge from that rotten machine.[58]

56 19 September 1942.
57 An illegible word.
58 Tuesday [13 October 1942].

In his reply on 14 October Bower wrote that 'Boult worked like a navvy'. He then detailed a number of small cuts that necessarily had to be made, and went on to mention a great disappointment over the casting:

> 'Court' music cut entirely largely because I did not like it and the scene was redundant and we were three minutes overtime on the first Act [the running time was Part One: 55' 19", Part Two: 52' 35"]. Two stanzas of Hedli's song had to go for dramatic reasons. . . . Larry, I think, did me proud. The major irony was the miscasting of Beatriz as a result of being told by our casting office here that Vivien [Leigh, Olivier's wife] would not be available. Having committed myself to Margaret Rawlings, I then found that Vivien was coming to Bedford with Larry as there is no performance of the 'Doctor's Dilemma' on Monday nights. Nothing, of course, could be done about it. But it was pretty sickening to have an actress of that calibre 'on the premises' merely sitting with me in the Control Room and not playing in the entertainment. Moreover, in a private word with Larry, I discovered she would have liked to have done it.

Fitting in the music, he added, 'was fiendishly difficult for me but it worked. I am afraid I had to put in a few repeat bars here and there, but not as you would notice.' And he added a portentous postscript: 'Larry and Vivien are determined to have you for Henry.'

Boult was pleased with the end result and wrote to Bower: 'All my friends are lyrical, & I'm only sorry I shan't hear the playback. It was a *miracle* of organisation on your part.' Leonard Cottrell of the BBC's Features and Drama Department considered the broadcast as 'one of the most moving examples of radio drama which I have heard in ten years of listening'.[59]

The live broadcast had a notable cast that included, in addition to Olivier as Columbus, Robert Speaight, Marius Goring, Stephen Murray, Mark Dignam, Margaret Rawlings, and Gladys Young as Queen Isabella. The score was an impressive one. The opening flourish is unmistakable high-voltage Walton in heroic mood, in fact what a year or so later would become his *Henry V* vein, with some stirring fanfares. There are songs, one with guitar and another, Beatriz's song, an affecting lament with accompaniment of strings, bemoaning Columbus's constant departures and farewells. Interestingly enough, the choral finale contains a brief figure that anticipates the *Hindemith Variations*. Walton's music did for *Christopher Columbus* what Olivier was later ready to acknowledge in the case of *Henry V*: it ensured the success of the production by capturing perfectly in musical terms the mood of the play and by both tightening the dramatic elements and raising the emotional level several notches higher. MacNeice's play had a further lease of life when it was produced, without Walton's music, on 15 July 1944 by Kings' School, Worcester. The broadcast itself, preserved in the BBC Sound

---

[59] Internal memorandum, 13 October 1942.

Archives, was not heard again for nearly thirty years[60] although a shortened ninety-minute version was broadcast on 9 October 1944, also from Bedford School but this time with Clarence Raybould conducting the BBC Symphony Orchestra.

With *Christopher Columbus* behind him and the film *Went the Day Well?* completed, his next score was another ballet. He had meanwhile turned down the request for another Ealing film-score, *The Bells Go Down*, about a London fire-fighting unit during the Blitz. On top of other work in hand, losing his London house during the Blitz was quite likely too close a memory, and in his place to Ernest Irving he recommended Roy Douglas who supplied the score.

The idea for this new ballet, *The Quest*, had come to Frederick Ashton after seeing a particularly fine edition of Spenser's *Faerie Queene* one day when a guest at the home of Doris Langley Moore. She offered to provide a scenario, and he invited John Piper to design the scenery and the costumes. Ashton was on special leave from the RAF, and his first thoughts had been to use the music of Delius but he decided instead to commission a score. While Walton was an obvious choice (Ashton had already choreographed *Façade*, *Siesta* and *The Wise Virgins*), he might have demurred had he foreseen how hard a task it was to be. As his biographer, David Vaughan, has written:

> The ballet was rehearsed on tour. Walton composed very slowly and the music came to Ashton a page or two at a time. Frequently he was obliged to telephone Walton and plead for more music, sometimes only to be told that the composer was stuck. On occasion Ashton had to go to meet a train at the local station to collect pages of manuscript which Walton sent to him via the guard. Still the music did not arrive fast enough and when he got to the finale Ashton had to ask Hilda Gaunt [the rehearsal pianist] to improvise at the appropriate length and tempo and then adjust his choreography to fit when the music finally got there. Not unnaturally the completed ballet showed signs of this peacemeal composition, both musically and choreographically.[61]

Ashton's detailed instructions[62] to Walton gave timings to the quarter-minute for the various sections of music, a pattern of working that would be customary for a composer of film scores. It took him about eight weeks – 'I'm fighting as usual against time to get a ballet for Sadler's Wells ready,' he

---

60 A recording of the broadcast, BBC Sound Archives T28082, was re-broadcast on 8 April 1973. A new production, with Simon Joly conducting the BBC Symphony Orchestra and with Alan Howard in the title rôle, was broadcast on 26 January 1992. A suite from *Christopher Columbus*, arranged by Christopher Palmer, was first heard at the Proms on 28 August 1992, with Barry Wordsworth conducting the BBC Concert Orchestra.

61 David Vaughan, *Frederick Ashton and his Ballets*, 196–7.

62 *Ibid.*, 428–30, where it appears as Appendix C.

wrote on 5 February 1943 – and, with the help of Roy Douglas and Ernest Irving, the orchestration was completed on 29 March (his forty-first birthday).

Frantic preparations for *The Quest* prevented him from making anything more than a token offering to the spectacular *Salute to the Red Army* staged in the Royal Albert Hall on Sunday 21 February 1943 with leading actors and massed choirs, bands and orchestras. Scripted by Louis MacNeice and Basil Dean, it was co-ordinated by the ENSA Musical Council of which Walton was Vice-Chairman.[63] He and Bax provided a fanfare each while Rawsthorne supplied a little extra music. The musical needs of the occasion were otherwise met by exisiting music.[64]

The Quest, lasting just under three-quarters of an hour, opened at the New Theatre, London on 6 April 1943. Among the cast were Robert Helpmann, Margot Fonteyn, and two young dancers being given their first important rôles, Beryl Gray and Moira Shearer. Constant Lambert conducted. Despite some delightful moments including a characteristic Siciliana, a set of variations for the dances of the Seven Deadly Sins and a passacaglia finale, the score is uneven. (Was the Challenge theme in Scene Two with the Saracen Knights intended to hint at an earlier Sadler's Wells success, Bliss's *Checkmate*?) Even Walton himself was uncertain as to its merits. 'It was not much of a success from anyone's point of view, with choreography, scenery or music all suffering from the same causes. I remember having to bribe guards on trains to take a minute or so's music to wherever Freddy happened to be with the ballet . . .,' he recalled.[65] In 1961, after the score had for many years been mislaid and then found, Vilem Tausky, with the composer's co-operation, made a four-movement suite which Walton recorded in 1970. It was not until twenty years later that the complete score was heard again, in a recording subsidised by the William Walton Trust.

The ballet's theme of triumph over adversity – with St George of the Red Cross encountering such obstacles as three Saracen knights and the Seven Deadly Sins during his search for Truth – was suitably patriotic for war-time. But it was not revived. However, another, grander patriotic theme was very soon to demand his attention and lead to an undisputed masterpiece – his score for the film of *Henry V.*

---

63 The Music Council of Entertainment National Service Association (ENSA) was chiefly concerned with bringing good music to the forces and factories. Sir Victor Schuster was Chairman, Walton Vice-Chairman, and Walter Legge liaison officer, becoming its Director of Music in 1942.

64 The performance is described in detail in Basil Dean, *Mind's Eye: An Autobiography, 1927–1972*, Hutchinson 1973, 283–6.

65 Letter to John Warrack, 27 August 1957, quoted in Christopher Palmer's notes for Chandos recording, CHAN 8871.

9

'Terribly dull without the Music . . .'

Up to this point Walton's film scores had all been thoroughly professional jobs which, with the one exception of *The First of the Few*, had little to commend them outside the cinema. But his next three commissions, the Olivier–Shakespeare scores for *Henry V, Hamlet* and *Richard III*, place him in the front rank of film composers with three of the finest scores ever written, scores that are an integral part of the films, each one matching to perfection every action, mood and breath. The first and in many ways the finest film of the three, *Henry V*,[1] was first shown on 22 November 1944 at the Carlton, London in aid of the benevolent funds of the Airborne Forces and Commandos, to whom the film was dedicated. It proved a great success. Its origins, however, go back a few years.

Dallas Bower, who had been an associate producer of the 1936 *As You Like It* film, was, from 1936 to 1939, producer–director for BBC Television. In 1938 he prepared a script of *Henry V* for that new medium.[2] But on the outbreak of war television closed down. However, when Bower was later recalled from the Services and appointed Supervisor of Film Production for the Ministry of Information, he adapted his script for film. But the MoI was only interested in short propaganda films of a documentary nature, so he sold his script to Filippo Del Giudice (1892–1961), an Italian lawyer and refugee who had become managing director of Two Cities Films Ltd (and who, incidentally, had appeared in *The First of the Few*, playing an Italian). Asked if he had anyone in mind for the rôle of Henry, Bower immediately suggested Olivier, a view with which Del Giudice concurred.[3] On April 19 1942 Olivier

---

1 The film was examined in some detail by Harry M. Geduld, *Filmguide to Henry V*, Indiana University Press 1973, and C. Clayton Hutton, *The Making of Henry V*, Chiltern Court, London 1944.
2 Dallas Bower's Shakespeare productions for television had already included *The Taming of the Shrew, Julius Caesar* in Fascist uniforms, and *The Tempest*.
3 Del Giudice and Olivier first met on the opening night of *In which We Serve*, a

took part in a seventy-five-minute radio version of *Henry V,* produced and adapted by Howard Rose. Four days later he was declaiming an extract in a St George's Day 'Battle for Freedom' presentation at the Royal Albert Hall, the closing half-hour of which was broadcast and a part of which was filmed. The play *Henry V* was seen as a clarion call for war-time Britain. Bernard Miles and Michael Powell had even tried to interest Olivier, then serving in the Fleet Air Arm, in taking the name part on stage in battledress. When a filmed version was suggested Olivier, after his experience of *As You Like It,* was not easily persuaded unless he could have complete control which, to Bower's disappointment, meant the overall direction. This he was granted, and although he did not use Bower's script, he nevertheless took him on as associate producer.[4] Walton was the obvious choice of composer, again on Bower's recommendation. The three had just worked together on the radio production of *Christopher Columbus* and even then there had been plans to film *Henry V.* As Bower had told Walton on 14 October 1942: 'Larry and Vivien are determined to have you for Henry,' and twelve days earlier he had written:

> The situation regarding 'Henry V' has become complicated by another matter quite extraneous to it, and I have now to fight yet another private war in order to smooth things out. We appear to be surrounded in this country by past masters in the art of mismanagement. However, I think we shall be in production eventually, but the battle has been an appalling one for me. One has to be quite unrelentless and as tenacious as a lobster.[5]

Henry V was a Two Cities film (as *Hamlet* was also to be), and Del Giudice's financial and distribution link with J. Arthur Rank ensured the essential backing, even when the final cost at £475,000 had exceeded the original planned budget of £300,000. The Ministry of Information, recognising the excellent propaganda value of the film, arranged for Olivier to be seconded from the services.[6] Bower's friendship with John Betjeman, then Press Attaché to the British Embassy in Dublin, facilitated the filming of the Agincourt battle scene in neutral Ireland in Enniskerry, on the estate of Lord Powerscourt, while Bower's contacts in the MoI enabled him to obtain the release of several key actors from their war-time duties to appear in *Henry V.*

Rank–Two Cities film. After his break with Rank, Del Giudice set up Pilgrim Pictures in 1947. But a combination of financial difficulties and ill-health caused him to fold the company two years later. He went to the United States before retiring to Italy in 1952 where he entered a Benedictine monastery. He died in 1961.

4 Bower explained much of the background to *Henry V* in his interview in Brian McFarlane, *An Autobiography of British Cinema by the Actors and Filmmakers who Made It,* Methuen 1997, 80–4.

5 BBC Written Archives, Caversham.

6 Olivier was first asked to star in another propaganda film, *The Demi-Paradise,* for Two Cities.

The large cast included Robert Newton (Pistol), Leslie Banks (Chorus), Esmond Knight (Fluellen), Renée Asherson (Katharine), George Robey (Falstaff), Harcourt Williams (King Charles VI), Max Adrian (Dauphin), Felix Aylmer (Archbishop of Canterbury), Robert Helpmann (Bishop of Ely), Griffith Jones (Earl of Salisbury), John Laurie (English Captain), Russell Thorndike (Duke of Bourbon) and Ernest Thesiger (French Ambassador).

To add the necessary sense of period to his score for *Henry V,* Walton drew on several sources. Tunes from the Fitzwilliam Virginal Book were skilfully reworked for the opening Globe Theatre scene and for the death of Falstaff where he appropriately turned an old drinking song into an affecting passacaglia. Part of the fifteenth-century French tune *'Reveillez-vous, Piccars'* was used as a call-to-arms in the Agincourt battle scene, while another old French tune, the *Agincourt Song*, brought a suitably joyous choral climax. These last two tunes came at the suggestion of Vaughan Williams who had used them in his 1933 overture for brass band, *Henry the Fifth.* Some other suggestions were not taken up. 'Larry knew exactly what he liked and what he wanted,' Walton once said.[7] 'For instance, he'd say: "Now, this is a beautiful tune I've thought of . . . dee da de de da dum. . . ." ' To which he replied, 'Yes, a lovely tune, but it's out of *Meistersinger.*' One suggestion, however, apparently from Olivier, that he dip into Canteloube's *Chants d'Auvergne* for scenes at the French court, landed him in copyright difficulties again. Joseph Canteloube (1879–1957), the collector and arranger of these French folk-songs, had also published them, and once more an out-of-court settlement had to be made. One other suggestion was wisely not adopted, that the music for the Agincourt battle scene be written first and then the scene shot to the music. (In fact a 'guide-track' was recorded on piano by Roy Douglas but never used.) The dramatic centre-piece to *Alexander Nevsky* was the Battle on the Ice, and whether or not it was Prokofiev's music through the broadcast adaptation of *Nevsky* or its aural and visual impact in the Eisenstein film that had influenced Walton, it has a worthy counterpart in the Agincourt scene in *Henry V.* Even Olivier admitted that sequence was 'littered with petty larcenies from our Master of All, Eisenstein'.[8] The filming in Ireland of the fifteen-minute battle sequence occupied a period of thirty-nine days in June and July 1943 (fourteen of which were cancelled because of rain). The remainder of the action was shot at Denham Studios between August and January with the only Technicolor camera in England and work on the music was taken up in earnest. Walton did all the orchestration of *Henry V* himself but Roy Douglas remembered[9] that Walton wrote a part for harpsichord (which Douglas played) in nearly every section so that he could have him close at hand in the studio to advise on the scoring when necessary. (The harpsichord can be

7   In Tony Palmer, *At the Haunted End of the Day*, ITV.
8   Laurence Olivier, *Confessions of an Actor*, 209.
9   Interview with the author, 23 July 1996.

heard at its most effective at the start of the battle charge.) The recording of the music and sound effects was done between 13 March and 20 April.

Right from the film's beginning, as the fluttering flute figure depicts the tumbling Globe playbill, one is aware of an extraordinarily skilful marriage of sound and vision. Even when Henry has raised his troops (and the film's audience) to a fever pitch of excitement in the Siege of Harfleur and St Crispian's Day speeches, Walton matches the mood to perfection with orchestral outbursts that are no less exciting and which carry the action onwards on a tide of emotion. The battle scene called for some special effects. When the volley of arrows did not show up on the Technicolor print, these had to be added afterwards, and the famous twang of their firing was achieved by swishing a long willow switch past the microphone many times and then combining these individual tracks in a quick crescendo and diminuendo.

Olivier was highly appreciative of the music Walton wrote for him. Not only did he give him the final full-screen credit but he openly acknowledged his debt:

> I've always said that if it weren't for the music I don't think *Henry V* would have been a success. That is perfectly sincere, and in case you don't think it is perfectly sincere I will tell you that after he had seen a run-through of the film, naked and innocent of all sound – there was no music, no sound effects as well, he thought to himself, 'Well, I had better do something about this. . . .', and when I thanked him for the music afterwards he said, 'Well, my boy', as he always did, 'I am very glad you showed it to me because I must tell you I did think it was terribly dull without the music'! He had really saved it and he knew that he had saved it too. If ever music was essential and helpful, it was there.[10]

In his autobiography he expressed himself in even stronger terms: 'William Walton's part in the success of the film was unique. Why he has never achieved any Oscars for this or any of my Shakespeare films must remain a prime example of the miasmically mysterious conclusions reached by the award-giving organisations.'[11]

This was obviously music that should not be confined to the cinema alone, and in 1945 Sargent arranged a suite of four extracts for mixed chorus (in the first and last items) and orchestra which Walton premièred on 14 September at that year's Proms. Then in 1963 Muir Mathieson prepared another, purely orchestral suite of five extracts. On the soundtrack Mathieson had conducted the London Symphony Orchestra. Nearly two years after the film's release excerpts from the film score with dialogue were recorded for the gramophone over five sessions between August and November 1946 with Olivier reading

[10] Interview with John Amis in *Portrait of Walton*, BBC Radio 3, broadcast 4 June 1977.
[11] *Confessions of an Actor*, 139.

several parts in addition to King Henry, and Walton conducting the recently formed Philharmonia Orchestra.[12]

When in 1945 a broadcast was heard in Barcelona of three items from *Henry V,* with Mathieson conducting the BBC Northern Orchestra, it brought forward enquiries as to the origin of the prelude. The Spanish press attaché wrote: 'My friends maintain that it is an old Catalan Sardana. My theory is that whilst it closely resembles a Catalan Sardana it is no doubt a piece of Old English music. . . .' Walton settled the matter in a reply to Kenneth Wright: 'The source of the mentioned theme comes from an unexpected one – myself – at least more or less – but certainly not Catalonia. The rhythm is a well-known Elizabethan one, vide Byrd, Farnaby, etc. – but is also common to the Sardana.'[13]

Two of the most compelling movements are delicate miniatures for strings: the passacaglia *The Death of Falstaff* and *Touch her Soft Lips and Part* when Pistol, about to embark for France, bids farewell to his wife, Mistress Quickly. The latter piece might well have been in part Walton's remembrance of Heseltine, so closely does it parallel *Pieds-en-l'air* from the *Capriol Suite.*[14]

In 1942 there had come a request from the Reverend Walter Hussey, Vicar of St Matthew's, Northampton, to compose a work for the Jubilee Festival of his church in September the following year. Walton declined the invitation so Hussey approached Benjamin Britten who responded with *Rejoice in the Lamb.* In February 1944 the work was to be heard again in that church at the unveiling of Henry Moore's sculpture *Madonna and Child.* Britten was to have conducted but he was unable to make the journey because enemy action the night before had destroyed the railway line. Walter Hussey wrote of the occasion: 'By half-past two, the time at which the ceremony was due to start, [Britten] still had not arrived. . . . But William Walton had come over from Ashby St Ledgers. His relations with Britten were somewhat strained at that time, and when I jokingly, and perhaps naughtily, suggested that he should conduct the Cantata, he replied that that would really "put the cap on it"!'[15] When Britten heard of this, he wrote to Hussey: 'I am amused at W. Walton turning up, & to hear that he liked R. in the L., because he doesn't make it a

---

12 Issued first on four 78s (HMV C3583-6), then in 1956 not quite complete on HMV ALP1375, and finally a full CD release as part of EMI's 4-CD set 'The Walton Edition' in 1994.

13 The Sardana was a dance of which Constant Lambert was fond, and he used in his last ballet *Tiresias.*

14 Ian Copley pointed out this similarity in his *The Music of Peter Warlock: A Critical Survey,* Dennis Dobson 1979, 240. He wrote: 'One wonders whether Sir William Walton was haunted by the recollection of it . . . for it has a markedly similar melodic and harmonic fragrance.'

15 Walter Hussey, *Patron of Art,* Weidenfeld & Nicolson 1985, 39–40; also in Donald Mitchell and Philip Reed (eds), *Letters from a Life,* 1188.

secret that he doesn't like my later pieces!'[16] (In 1974, when Hussey was Dean of Chichester Cathedral, Walton dedicated his settings of the *Magnificat* and *Nunc Dimittis* to him.)

The two composers probably first met in July 1937 when they had lunch together, after which Britten wrote: 'He is charming, but I always feel the school relationship with him – he is so obviously the head-prefect of English music, whereas I'm the promising new boy.'[17] Five years earlier, Britten had been much upset when three two-part songs, performed at the first public hearing of any of his music, were criticised as being 'reminiscent in a quite peculiar degree of Walton's latest songs'. (Three Songs from *Façade* had been first heard only two months earlier.) He later countered: 'Anyone who is interested can see for himself that this is silly nonsense. The Walton songs are brilliant and sophisticated in the extreme – mine could scarcely have been more childlike and naïve, with not a trace of parody throughout.'[18]

Britten was less enthusiastic about *Façade* itself. He attended the 1942 Aeolian Hall performance, promoted by Boosey & Hawkes, when it was paired with *Pierrot Lunaire*. Afterwards he wrote to Peter Pears (who was to prove an excellent reciter of *Façade*): 'Friday's do . . . was pretty awful really. Horrible audience, snobby – and stupid. The pieces very faded & Constant Lambert completely inaudible.'[19] Hedli Anderson[20] was the reciter in *Pierrot Lunaire*, and Lambert in *Façade*. Despite Britten's scathing comments the concert was actually very successful – a repeat performance was immediately arranged to take place a month later – and at a party afterwards another side of Walton emerged, at the piano 'doing some very naughty impersonations, notably of Peter Pears singing Britten songs'.[21]

Walton had attended, with Hubert Foss, the first performance of Britten's *A Boy is Born* in December 1934, and he was to be among the audience for

---

16 Donald Mitchell and Philip Reed (eds), *Letters from a Life*, 1188.

17 Humphrey Carpenter, *Benjamin Britten*, 110. On 13 March 1936 Britten accompanied the soprano Sophie Wyss in a broadcast that included Walton's *Daphne* and *Through Gilded Trellises*. In April 1938 Britten and Ashton were invited by Walton to dinner.

18 'Variations on a Critical Theme', *Opera*, March 1952, quoted in Eric Walter White, *Benjamin Britten: His Life and Operas*, Faber & Faber, 1983, 25.

19 Ed. Donald Mitchell and Philip Reed, *Letters from a Life: Selected Letters and Diaries of Benjamin Britten*, 2 vols, 1991, 1055. The BBC producer Dallas Bower also attended and wrote to Walton, 2 June 1942: 'I was unfortunately unable to remain for Façade. I was told it was a good performance, but that the speech was unintelligible due to the inadequacy of the reproduction apparatus.' Nevertheless, *The Times*, under the heading 'Two Freak Works', commented that *Façade* had 'a delightful silliness which pleased an audience that laughed frankly at 20-year-old jokes and appreciated the sharp wit and clear lines of Walton's smaller score'.

20 The wife of Louis MacNeice in whose radio play *Christopher Columbus* (with music by Walton) she took part later that year.

21 Richard Temple Savage, *A Voice from the Pit: Reminiscences of an Orchestral Musician*, David & Charles 1988, 98.

the première of *Peter Grimes* in June 1945. A fortnight later he wrote to Britten: 'I should like to tell you how much I appreciate your quite extraordinary achievement which makes me look forward to your next opera. It is just what English opera wants and it will, I hope, put the whole thing on its feet . . . .'[22] Yet when that same month there were plans for a complete recording of the opera to be made by Decca with the support of the British Council, Walton and Edward Dent voiced disapproval, suggesting that the proposal should be discussed 'at a calmer moment when the wildly hysterical & uncritical eulogies & general "ballyhoo" have somewhat abated, & the true merits of the work can be properly assessed'.[23] When two years later the British Council was approached for financial support for the recording of extracts from Britten's *The Rape of Lucretia*, Walton again demurred, advising four 78-rpm sides as sufficient instead of the proposed sixteen (although sixteen were recorded in due course).

However strained relationships were between the two, Britten had much to be grateful for to Walton who had appeared as witness at his conscientious objector's tribunal in 1942.[24] 'I've never forgotten your noble and generous support of me in a very low moment in the War,' he wrote in December 1963. (At the time he had written to a friend that 'Montagu Slater[25] & William

---

22 Kennedy, *Portrait of Walton*, 131.

23 29 June 1945, John Lucas, *Reggie: The Life of Reginald Goodall*, Julia MacRae Books, 1993, 96 and 221–2. Excerpts from *Peter Grimes* were eventually recorded by Goodall, under the composer's supervision, in 1948 but they were not issued. Donald Mitchell and Philip Reed (*Letters from a Life*, 1269) quote Susana Walton (p. 125) who suggests that Walton had opposed the recording on the grounds that the British Council should support something less commercially successful while, somewhat ambiguously, Humphrey Carpenter (*Benjamin Britten*, 264) seems to suggest that Walton opposed their release in 1948. However, John Lucas, 117–18, states that Britten had been unhappy with Pears's contribution in the recordings and only agreed to their release in 1972 when almost all the recorded sides were transferred to LP. They were transferred to CD in 1993.
  Walton had joined the British Council committee in 1943 replacing H. C. Colles who had died in March. The first work to have been proposed for recording under its auspices was *Belshazzar's Feast* (made in January 1943). When in 1944 a recording of *The Dream of Gerontius* was being mooted, it was Walton who strongly recommended that it be made by Sargent and the Huddersfield Choral Society: Carl Newton, 'The Nightmare of Gerontius', *Elgar Society Journal*, July 1997, 74–89, reprinted in *The Best of Me: A Gerontius Centenary Companion*, ed. Geoffrey Hodgkins, Elgar Editions, 1999.

24 In 1944 Sir Osbert Sitwell raised the question of the conscription of artists in his anti-war tract *A Letter to my Son* which was vigorously contested by the critic James Agate. Even George Orwell weighed into the debate, with Agate at least conceding that 'a wise government will not put a bayonet into the hands of a William Walton, a Constant Lambert, a Clifford Curzon, a Noël Coward, a John Gielgud or a Tommy Trinder'. *The Collected Essays, Journalism and Letters of George Orwell, Vol 3: As I Please (1943–5)*, edited by Sonia Orwell and Ian Angus, Penguin Books 1970, 296–8.

25 Head of Scripts at the MoI and later Britten's librettist for *Peter Grimes*.

Walton were excellent witnesses'.[26]) 'I don't know if I ever told you, but hearing your Viola Concerto & Portsmouth Point (works which I still love dearly) was a great turning point in my musical life. I'd got in a muddle; poor old John Ireland [his RCM teacher] wasn't much help, & I couldn't get on with the 12-tone idea (still can't) – & you showed me the way of being relaxed & fresh, & intensely personal. . . .'[27] While the two were never friends, there was mutual admiration from a distance. With Walton it was a touch of jealousy and that sense of rivalry brought about by another's success. He especially envied Britten his ability – 'not facility, but being able to do it all in his head; like Mozart or Rossini. . . . It's hard work, for me. . . . The trouble is I wasn't properly trained.'[28]

For the latter quarter of 1943 Walton reluctantly served on the BBC Music Advisory Panel, together with John Ireland and Gordon Jacob. One of his duties was to send in reports on recent music broadcasts, but he complained that he did not always have access to a radio and it was officially recorded that he 'did very little work while on the panel'. He resigned at the end of the year and his place was taken by Herbert Howells. Another duty was for the panel to meet with the purpose of reading new scores and recommending them for either performance or rejection. Their comments were recorded. Lennox Berkeley's Sonatina for Violin and Piano drew from Walton the following plea: 'It is to be hoped that not many members of the programme committee will send in works, as it is slightly embarrassing for us to be put in the position of turning them down, as is necessary in this case. No offence meant & I hope none taken!'[29] Gordon Jacob was of a similar opinion, finding 'a depressing air of preciosity. . . . I add my regrets to those of W.W.' He clearly did not allow friendship to flavour his judgement as he rejected also *Seven Poems by Thomas Hardy* set by his friend, publisher and adviser Hubert Foss: 'These settings were not very successful at the time of their first performance and it is doubtful if the value of the music has increased with comparative old age.'[30] He was far more favourably disposed towards Alan Bush's Overture *Resolution*: 'This work is quite definitely to be recommended. Well scored & good lines & the right length, altogether an effective piece,' even though on the same day he could not recommend the same composer's *Freedom on the March* for solo voice, chorus, piano and percussion: 'Freedom,' he felt, 'not to mention the workers, deserves something better than this.'[31]

One reason at least for Walton's reluctance to serve on the Advisory Panel

---

[26] 30 September 1942, Donald Mitchell and Philip Reed (eds), *Letters from a Life*, 1068.
[27] *Ibid.*, 202.
[28] *Sunday Times*, 25 March 1962, 39.
[29] 30 September 1943. BBC Written Archives Centre, Caversham.
[30] *Ibid.*
[31] 14 October 1943.

may be surmised from a letter he wrote to Norman Peterkin on 22 March 1946 when his opinion was sought concerning a new choral and orchestral score by Patrick Hadley, *The Hills*. Should it be offered to the BBC or instead to Sargent and the Huddersfield Choral Society? Hadley had asked Peterkin to elicit Walton's views: 'I have always found him a person of very shrewd instincts and *I should value his opinion, and fancy you would also.*' Isaiah-like came the reply: 'Herewith the judgement of Solomon Walton: Prevarication, it would appear, is becoming second nature to the BBC music dept. under the present regime, & I am inclined to advise that they should be given the "go-by".' 'Wisdom of Walton absolutely correct', Hadley flashed back to Peterkin.[32]

While working on *Henry V,* he had been invited to compose a work to mark the fiftieth anniversary of the Henry Wood Promenade Concerts. On 23 December 1943 Walton wrote to Sir Henry from Ashby St Ledgers: 'Though I can't say I've got very far as yet, I can tell you I am safely launched on a "Te Deum" for chorus & orchestra which I feel would be appropriate for the 50th anniversary of the "Proms". I trust that this will be agreeable to you.'[33] However, by 22 February 1944 he wrote to Julian Herbage that he had decided that he could not proceed with the *Te Deum*. 'Henry V should have been finished six weeks ago – and I need hardly add, through no fault of my own, there is no prospect of it being finished before the end of March.' On 17 March he wrote again: 'The vagaries of Henry V still continue, though at last the date for the final session has been fixed – April 23rd. There is still a great deal of music to write & I can hardly contemplate starting on anything else till it is all out of the way.'[34]

As it turned out, not only did flying bombs put a halt to that season's Promenade Concerts but it was to be Wood's last. He died on 19 August 1944. On 17 January 1945 there came a request from the BBC Concert Manager for a fanfare for the Henry Wood Memorial Concert. Walton reworked for full orchestra the fanfare he had written for the *Salute to the Red Army* pageant in 1943, and with unusual haste the score was received by the BBC nine days later. The revised fanfare was first heard in the Royal Albert Hall on 4 March 1945 when it was played by the combined BBC Symphony, London Philharmonic and London Symphony Orchestras under the baton of Sir Adrian Boult. When a memorial window for Sir Henry Wood was unveiled in St Sepulchre's Church, Holborn on 26 April 1946, Walton composed for it a setting for unaccompanied mixed voices of Masefield's

32 Eric Wetherell, *'Paddy'*, 64–5.
33 Correspondence with Sir H. J. Wood and Lady Jessie Wood, 1943–6, BL Add. MS 56422.
34 BBC Written Archives, Caversham.

Where does the Uttered Music Go?[35] This had not come easily as on 12 January he had written to Jessie Wood that he was having doubts about it. He had changed his mind as to which Masefield poem to set, and even at one stage proposed a string piece instead.

Although he wrote little for solo piano, he agreed to contribute a small piece to a projected album organised by the French Committee of National Liberation. On 16 August 1944 he wrote to Harriet Cohen: 'If you can wait a week or two I can let you have a MS of a Pfte piece which I am supposed to be writing for a Free French Album which is being printed. Heaven alone knows why. It won't matter I hope if I kill two "birds" with one brick – or will it?'[36] On 20 November he wrote to Norman Peterkin (who had by then succeeded Foss at OUP after the latter's resignation): 'I won't want any fee for the Pft. piece for the F[ree]. F[rench].' In the end, however, the volume did not appear as not all the composers who were approached produced a piece.

The coming of peace found Walton in a position of uncertainty. In five years he had written nothing of importance for the concert platform since *Scapino*. His output had consisted almost entirely of film scores. The post-war years would bring him the most difficult challenges, not least to fulfil the expectations of him as one of the leading British composers, a position for which there would be many contenders. There would be the challenge of opera. There would also be the greatest sorrow in his life with the death of Alice Wimborne. But first he took up the threads of a work contemplated in earlier days of peace, another string quartet.

35 First performed by the BBC Chorus, conducted by Leslie Woodgate, who recorded it for HMV (C3503) the following month.
36 Walton to Harriet Cohen, 16 August 1944, written at Ashby St Ledgers, Rugby, Harriet Cohen Papers, BL Deposit 1999/10.

10

Troilus and Ischia

Walton's second (and only published) string quartet, in A minor, was completed in 1946 and dedicated to the film-music conductor Ernest Irving who wrote of its 'lovely slow movement, somewhat unfashionable in these days of atonalism and twelve-tone scales, that will remind many of Brahms and Elgar'.[1] It was clearly a work that had been slow in coming forward since as far back as 3 August 1939 the BBC was writing: 'I wonder whether there were any chance of [Harry] Blech having your long promised Quartet' with a view to placing it in a concert that the Blech Quartet was to give in Paris if a new British work could be included. Then, after the gap of the war, on 7 September 1944 Julian Herbage was enquiring whether 'the magnum opus' was completed or if there was anything new for the BBC symphony concerts that year. Walton's reply was that 'the magnum opus alas is no use for the symphony concert as it happens to be a string quartet', adding somewhat prophetically: 'not that I wouldn't scruple to turn it into a piece for string orch. but I'm afraid it wouldn't sound so good!'[2] And in November he had told Norman Peterkin: 'There is also a 4tet on the way but that will be a little while before complete.'[3]

Although the première was announced for February 1947 in the Wigmore Hall, the work was not in fact heard until a BBC Third Programme broadcast on 4 May 1947 when the performers were the Blech String Quartet. Its first public performance was given the following day by the same artists in the concert hall of Broadcasting House. Irving attended the première: 'I sat beside the lovely lady who I think inspired it, and it now always sounds to me like an elegy.' The source of inspiration was of course Alice Wimborne who at that point had less than a year to live. In hindsight one can only agree with Irving: the *lento*, deeply elegiac, is one of Walton's most tender outpourings.

---

1 Ernest Irving, *Cue for Music*, Dennis Dobson 1959, 173.
2 9 September 1944, BBC Written Archives, Caversham.
3 20 November 1944, OUP files.

The last movement could not be in sharper contrast, opening with those unmistakable lunging, jagged Waltonian rhythms. Something of its character may be surmised from what Irving has written about it: 'I have been told by my enemies that the last movement represents me, quarrelsome, disputatious, didactic and violent; but as I do not admit any of these adjectives, I take a more good-humoured view of the music.'[4]

When twenty-three years later, Neville Marriner, the conductor and founder of the Academy of St Martin-in-the-Fields, asked for a new string work for his orchestra, Walton's inclination was to decline. Composition had always been a very slow process for him, and ideas came even slower. But when Marriner suggested a re-scoring of the quartet for full string orchestra, Walton saw a way through. He could produce what to all intents and purposes would be a new work without having to rely on inspiration for thematic material. There was one further problem. Walton hated the physical labour of writing. But when his good friend Malcolm Arnold offered to come out to Ischia and arrange the whole work under his supervision, all obstacles were cleared away. Arnold himself wrote:

> When I arrived, he had already completed the first two movements and was half-way through the slow movement. This did not surprise me, and the reason for my offer was to give him encouragement to do it himself. However I stayed with him until I had completed the last movement under his supervision, and more or less had a race, meeting for luncheon and dinner and reporting progress. I am sorry to say that he beat me by two days, but after all mine was a quick movement with so many semiquavers.[5]

The new work, known as the Sonata for String Orchestra, received its first performance on 2 March 1972 at Perth during the Academy's visit to Australia. On 27 May it was played at the Bath Festival, and on 11 July it was performed at the City of London Festival.

In the same year that the String Quartet was first heard, 1947, Walton was approached by Yehudi Menuhin for a violin sonata. Menuhin remembered the tragic circumstances of its commissioning.[6] He and his wife Diana had been with Louis Kentner and his wife Griselda (Diana's sister) in Lucerne that September where they met Walton with Alice Wimborne. (The Menuhins had also met up with them earlier that spring in Prague where they dined with David Oistrakh and Dmitri Shostakovich and their respective wives before going to a chamber concert of Shostakovich's music.[7]) Alice's health had

---

4 *Cue for Music*, 173–4.
5 Letter to Stewart Craggs, 3 December 1975, in Stewart R. Craggs, *William Walton: A Catalogue*, 105.
6 In 'Yehudi Menuhin at 80', BBC Radio 3, 30 March 1996.
7 Diana Menuhin, *A Glimpse of Olympus*, Methuen 1996, 304. The occasion was the Prague Festival.

been deteriorating but her London doctor had found nothing wrong so they were on their way to Capri, hoping that the climate would restore her health and spirits. But in Lucerne she was unwell again. Walton took her to a Swiss specialist who diagnosed the worst: cancer of the bronchus. Alice was admitted to a nursing home in Lausanne. Meanwhile Menuhin, who always found Walton 'in good humour, a somewhat self-centred creator, but very entertaining and delightful to be with', had asked for a violin sonata dedicated to the two sisters. Knowing him to be a slow writer, Menuhin, impatient for the work, offered 2,000 francs there and then if he would make a start without delay. Walton, needing money to pay for Alice's treatment, readily accepted. So the two set off for the nearest music shop to purchase manuscript paper. At the front of the shop was a large display with a prominent photograph of Benjamin Britten. Walton's white hand was seen to emerge through the velvet curtain that backed the display, grasp the photograph and turn it face down. The work was not completed until after Alice's death the following year. In two movements and dedicated 'To Diana and Griselda', it was played by Menuhin and Kentner in Zürich on 30 September 1949. According to Menuhin, as an afterthought Walton produced a scherzo which would serve as a middle movement. But there was not time for it to be incorporated into the first performance, so the scherzo was given a life of its own, as the second of Two Pieces for Violin and Piano[8] that Walton dedicated to the Oliviers. The coda of the Sonata was revised before it was heard at the Theatre Royal, Drury Lane on 5 February 1950 with the same performers, who also recorded it in May that year. Reviewing it in *Gramophone*, Alec Robertson called it a 'really beautiful sonata. . . . The architecture is that of a true craftsman, the decoration that of a true artist, and the heart of the matter is that of a man of flesh and blood.'

The first movement, a wistful *allegro tranquillo*, is followed by a Theme and (7) Variations and Coda. Here, to borrow Menuhin's words, is Walton, the 'frank and unabashed sensualist – which is what more refined and intellectualised writers reproach him for'.[9] This beautiful, contemplative work, in essence a love poem – as indeed were the two string concertos that preceded it, has the lyricism of the Violin Concerto at a more relaxed pace. Just as the Quartet was expanded into a work for full string orchestra, so the Sonata has in recent years been orchestrated by Christopher Palmer as a Sonata for Violin and Orchestra and recorded in that form.[10]

---

8   Canzonetta and Scherzetto. According to Louis Kentner, in a letter to Stewart Craggs (*William Walton: A Catalogue*, 101), the Scherzetto began life as one of two piano pieces written for the aborted album organised in 1944 by the French Committee of National Liberation, and Walton then revised it for the Violin Sonata, only ultimately to drop it. The Canzonetta was based on an old troubadour melody.
9   Yehudi Menuhin, *Life Class*, Heinemann 1985, 91.
10 Chandos ABRD1595.

Before Walton started on the Violin Sonata, there had been suggestions earlier that same year from the BBC that he should compose an opera. The première in June 1945 at Sadler's Wells of Britten's *Peter Grimes* had revitalised hopes for British opera and its success might well have stirred Walton to contemplate a medium he had not yet tackled. As John Ireland wrote to a friend after the première, 'Walton was there, with Lady Wimborne. He must have felt rather a draught, I fancy! (Being, so to speak, in the same line of business!!)'[11] Back in 1932, when the idea of creating Glyndebourne was being discussed and the thought of who might write an opera for its opening had arisen, Ernest Newman had suggested Walton as the one person 'who would do a good opera if he could get the right subject'.[12] One wonders what Walton's reactions were to the extraordinary success in the summer of 1935 of the opera *Iernin*, by the twenty-two-year-old Cornishman George Lloyd, which Walton attended.

His first, tentative thoughts towards opera were probably in 1941 when he collaborated with Cecil Gray on the subject of the sixteenth-century Italian composer, Carlo Gesualdo. The suggestion of their collaboration, according to Gray,[13] came from Walton, while the subject was proposed by Gray who had some years earlier joined with Philip Heseltine in writing the composer's biography.[14] With Gesualdo murdering his unfaithful wife, the story had some dramatic focus. Gray, known more as a writer *on* rather than *of* music, had even had ideas of composing the opera himself. Over many years he had periodically been tackling such operatic topics as *Deirdre*, *The Temptation of St Anthony* (both finished in 1937) and *The Women of Troy* (1940), excerpts from which were broadcast from the BBC's war-time Bedford home as a result of some persuasion by Walton and Lambert. When it seemed that Walton might supply the music to Gray's libretto, he completed his part of the collaboration,[15] but Walton, at that time busy with war-time film scores, did not fulfil his share, and Gray left the libretto unset. It had anyway been written with a view to the sort of dramatic treatment that Walton might bring to it, and Gray ultimately felt himself unable to do justice to the subject. There is no evidence of any musical sketches by Walton existing.

Walton's first opera, *Troilus and Cressida*, started as a BBC commission. On 8 February 1947 Victor Hely-Hutchinson, at the end of his term as

11 Muriel V. Searle, *John Ireland: The Man and his Music*, Midas Books 1979, 81.
12 Spike Hughes, *Glyndebourne: A History of the Festival Opera*, David & Charles 1965, 33. Newman's advice was sought while Walton was working on *Troilus and Cressida*. Ernest Irving visited the critic with Walton and afterwards reported that Newman's advice was 'full of wisdom'. *Cue for Music*, 168.
13 Cecil Gray, *Musical Chairs*, 242.
14 Published in 1926 under the title *Carlo Gesualdo: Prince of Venosa: Musician and Murderer*.
15 One side of a fairly lengthy correspondence (from Gray) dealing with the projected opera is in the British Library, Add. MSS 57774–5.

Director of Music, wrote informally to Walton: 'The BBC has decided to commission an opera and would like you to compose it. I do not at all know how you are placed as regards time, but I very much hope that you will be interested in the idea.'[16] In a letter dated 6 March, the fee was fixed at £500 – with £175 for the libretto.

An early candidate for librettist was Dylan Thomas who wrote excitedly to his parents on 12 January 1947:

> Did I tell you about the opera-libretto I have been asked to write? A full-length grand opera for William Walton. I have to turn out a very rough synopsis before I am definitely commissioned. This I hope to do next week. Michael Ayrton, who will do the decor, & I are going, on Wednesday, for a few days, to Gravesend, Tilbury, & all around there, as I want to set the opera in a near-docks area. A very modern tragic opera, in the bombed slums of wharfland. If this ever comes to anything, it will be the biggest English operatic event of the century. Really it will. A whole Covent Garden season in 1949 is contemplated. If, & when, I am commissioned to write the libretto, I shall be able to stop doing any other work & devote about six solid months to it.[17]

Dylan Thomas, whose radio play *Under Milk Wood* was to bring him posthumous fame, was a frequent broadcaster for the BBC, reading his own and others' poems and taking parts in plays. His BBC Engagements Calendar[18] shows that his trip on 14–16 January with Michael Ayrton to Gravesend was also to research for a script on William Hogarth for a General Overseas Service broadcast. However, neither the opera libretto nor the broadcast script was to materialise. The suggestion of Thomas as librettist may well have come from friends such as Edith Sitwell who were concerned at the deterioration in his condition because of alcohol and wanted to find ways by which he could devote himself to 'real work' instead of broadcasting for his daily bread and butter. One cannot but compare the tragic dockland setting of the projected opera with the fishing village of *Peter Grimes* and regret that, as with Thomas's collaboration with Stravinsky at the end of his life, these ideas came to nothing.

Troilus was not Walton's only BBC commission under consideration that year. The Corporation had inaugurated its prestigious Third Programme in September 1946, and on 3 October Walton had been invited to conduct the symphony in the first of the series of Saturday concerts given at People's Palace, London. Kodály conducted his Concerto for Orchestra in the same programme. On 13 February 1947 John Lowe, music organiser for the new programme, wrote to Walton inviting him to write a work for inclusion in a

---

16 This and subsequent BBC correspondence are in the BBC Written Archives, Caversham.

17 *Dylan Thomas: The Collected Letters*, edited by Paul Ferris, Dent 1985, 615.

concert to mark the programme's first anniversary. Lowe followed this up on 3 March with clearer requirements: 'It would be a fine thing if our programme were to begin with quite a short overture by you.' Britten had written an *Occasional Overture* for the opening of the Third Programme, but Walton did not rise to the challenge and no work was forthcoming. Then on 30 September he received a letter from Harman Grisewood, programme planner and soon to become Acting Controller of the Third: 'Before Professor [Gerald] Abraham left the Corporation he wrote to you on the 12th August to ask whether you would care to collaborate in an experimental programme – the setting to music of poems specially commissioned for the Third Programme.' Poems had been commissioned from six poets 'of some standing' and the idea had been to send them – at first without revealing their authorship – to six leading British composers to chose which one they would like to set. But on 1 October Walton telephoned to decline the offer. He was by then busy with his next film for Olivier.

Hamlet, like *Henry V*, had backing from Filippo Del Giudice. The filming of *Hamlet* began in May 1947.[19] By mid-December editing and cutting was under way, and its royal première on 6 May the following year at the Odeon, Leicester Square was attended by almost all the Royal family. *Hamlet* proved an even more immediate commercial success, even though because of its very nature it did not have quite the visual spectacle of *Henry V*, especially having been shot in black and white. Olivier's talk of wanting to shoot it as a series of engravings was only a cover for certain problems he was having. As he later admitted, he was 'in the middle of a bitter row with Technicolor'.[20] But this gave him the chance to make use of deep-focus photography with dramatic effect. More controversial were the interchanging of certain scenes and the textual cuts, of which the most apparent, for reason of length, was dispensing with the characters of Rosencrantz and Guildenstern. Olivier (now Sir Laurence) took with him many of the technicians who had worked on *Henry V*, and the cast included Jean Simmons (Ophelia), Basil Sydney (Claudius), Eileen Herlie (Gertrude), Norman Wooland (Horatio), Felix Aylmer (Polonius), Terence Morgan (Laertes), Peter Cushing (Osric) and Stanley Holloway (Gravedigger).

Walton's score for *Hamlet* is every bit the equal of that for *Henry V* with rather less pastiche. The full tragic import of the plot is graphically portrayed

---

18 *Dylan Thomas: The Broadcasts*, edited by Ralph Maud, Dent 1991, 292.

19 In 1946 there had been tentative plans to make a film of *King Lear*, in which Olivier was appearing on stage that year, but nothing came of that project. Many of those involved in *Hamlet*, including Olivier, Walton and Mathieson, contributed to *The Film Hamlet: A Record of its Production*, edited by Brenda Cross, Saturn Press 1948.

20 Interview with Melvyn Bragg in London Television's *South Bank Show* two-part tribute to Olivier on his seventy-fifth birthday. He had had problems of a different nature with the Technicolor process when making *Henry V*, both with the lighting and the colour printing.

in a prelude of tremendous power.[21] Other memorable moments are the orchestral build-up to the 'To be or not to be' soliloquy, the scenes with Ophelia (the music which Muir Mathieson later extracted to form 'a poem for orchestra, *Hamlet and Ophelia*'), and the Mousetrap play sequence. The brief pirate sea battle even uses a fugue not unlike the one in *The First of the Few*. One noticeable feature of the score is Walton's use of leitmotiv, particularly in the development of the Ophelia motif, with the funereal repetition of its opening phrase at her drowning, and its transformation near the end at Laertes' death. In his article on Film Music in *Grove V*, Hans Keller commented on its skilful use in the Mousetrap scene:

> A score in which the Leitmotiv technique is handled with unfailing and original mastery is Walton's *Hamlet*. . . . Even the best Hollywood composer would just automatically have reused the music from the early backflash showing Claudius's murder, for underlining the corresponding 'murder' in the players' performance: the typical leitmotivic tautology which, among other misuses, has brought the difficult technique into such discredit among sensitive observers. Walton, however, utilises the backflash material in his interpretation of Claudius's reactions to the poisoning of the actor-king, thus impressing upon us, more vividly than the picture itself could possibly do, that the king (Claudius) is overwhelmed by the thought of his own deed.[22]

Extracts from the film soundtrack, on which Muir Mathieson conducted the Philharmonia Orchestra,[23] were very soon released on record (at the time 78-rpm discs). In 1963 Mathieson adapted the music used for the opening and closing titles for concert use as the impressive Funeral March. After completing the score for *Hamlet*, Walton was unusually forthcoming in an article he wrote on the rôle of the film composer and his attitude towards writing for films. This is reprinted as Appendix 3, together with note on *Hamlet* that Mathieson himself contributed.

The première of *Hamlet* took place over a fortnight after the death of Alice Wimborne which had occurred on 19 April 1948. In her will she left Walton £10,000, her car, and her London house, Lowndes Cottage in Belgravia. Alice had been involved in the very early stages of *Troilus and Cressida*,

---

[21] Oddly enough, the soundtrack starts with the sound of the orchestra tuning before launching into the Prelude.

[22] *Grove's Dictionary of Music and Musicians*, Fifth Edition, Vol. 3, Macmillan & Co., 100.

[23] *Penguin Music Magazine*, VII October 1948 included a sixteen-page photographic section entitled *'Hamlet' – The Music is Added* showing the recording sessions at Denham (November–December 1947) and how the music was added to the film. One photograph shows Muir Mathieson with his right arm in a sling as a result of a riding accident, while another shows John Hollingsworth conducting. Although not credited, Hollingsworth was presumably responsible for at least one of the sessions.

helping him search for a suitable subject. On 7 June 1947 she had written to his librettist Christopher Hassall (with whom Walton had already been in contact): 'I wonder, wd Saturday week suit you for luncheon . . . Wd 1 o'clock do as an hour? I believe Claridges is a better bet than the Berkeley if one wants to talk. . . . We are going to have a grand view of all the librettos this weekend.' After that meeting she wrote again to Hassall with that same critical perception and understanding of Walton that had made her such an admirable companion: 'I believe that you should not be perplexed or worried by the unbouncing ball: and equally that he [Walton] should think you quite unmoved by procrastination! so that he doesn't fear being, as it were, pushed into anything because a decision is expected of him. . . . The difficulty is to find the perfect subject. Many that would suit his music have other draw-backs, as a case in point, Byron. For apart from suitability for him the story or plot must be so easy and clear and flowing and scenic. Troilus and C. has got that.'[24] Throughout 1947 and into 1948 the libretto was slowly thrashed out.[25] Despite her increasingly serious illness and the interruption of treatment abroad, Alice's sympathetic hand was there in support of what to Hassall she referred to as 'our child' right up to her death. When that death came in April, Walton was utterly devastated. An attack of jaundice put him in hospital, after which he recuperated on the island of Capri. Only the previous September a planned holiday in Capri with Alice had been interrupted en route by her illness. His companion this time on the journey to Italy was Michael Ayrton[26] with whom he had kept up an irregular friendship since working together on *Macbeth*. Their occasional meetings had often been in London, at the Café Royal or at Pagani's in Great Portland Street, more than likely in the company of their mutual friends, Constant Lambert and Cecil Gray. While on the small boat that took them out to Capri, they found them-selves caught up 'in a storm which came up suddenly and with terrific force . . . jammed with miserable humanity, wet and sick, like a tragic Marx brothers scene. W. & I were not ill and felt like Drake and Hawkins. We prac-tically told each other tales of Trafalgar. . . .'[27] Cecil Gray, who was then living on the island, was another companion on this holiday, as indeed was the Scottish writer Norman Douglas who was also living there. In June

---

24 Extracts from Gilliam Widdicombe's article in *Music and Musicians*, November 1976, 34–5, quoted in Royal Opera House Covent Garden programme booklet for *Troilus and Cressida* the same month.

25 The writing of the libretto for *Troilus and Cressida* has been dealt in greater detail by Michael Kennedy in his *Portrait of Walton* and by Scott Price in ' "A Lost Child": A Study of the Genesis of *Troilus and Cressida*', in *William Walton: Music and Litera-ture*, ed. Stewart Craggs, Ashgate 1999.

26 Michael Ayrton's portrait of a grey, ill-looking Walton, now in the National Portrait Gallery, London, was painted at this time. A post-card reproduction is available.

27 Letter from Michael Ayrton dated 13 May 1948, in Justine Hopkins, *Michael Ayrton*, 135.

Walton was in Rome, exploring the city for a couple of days with Ayrton, and by October he had recovered sufficiently to form part of the British delegation at an international meeting of the Performing Right Society in Buenos Aires.

It had been while working on his first film that someone had suggested that, on top of his initial payment, his income would be considerably increased from performing rights if he were to join the PRS. This he did as an individual, and so it was as a British representative that he found himself at this conference. There he set eyes on a twenty-two-year-old Argentinean girl, Susana Gil, who was working for the British Council. He immediately resolved to marry her. As he himself remembered the occasion:

> The first item there was a conference to meet Mr Peron. He got up and made a speech of which no one understood a word, then all his backers got up and screamed: 'Peron, Peron, Peron.' Then Mr Boosey [Leslie Boosey of the music publishers Boosey & Hawkes] got up and made a speech in reply, and when he finished I said: 'Boosey, Boosey, Boosey.' And that became the cry of the opposition in Buenos Aires for some time, I was told. After that there was a press conference which I had to give and I saw a rather attractive girl in the corner. Of course one of the journalists asked what I thought about Argentinean girls, so I nearly said, Do you see that girl over there, I'm going to marry her, but I controlled myself just in time. Anyhow we met, went off to lunch and I proposed to her the next day. As far as I can remember she said: 'Don't be ridiculous, Dr Walton.' But we got engaged three weeks after that.[28]

Another member of that delegation was the composer Eric Coates who remembered the occasion in his autobiography:

> We saw a good deal of him during the Congress as we were staying in the same hotel in Tucuman. I remember he was in the throes of trying to find inspiration for a violin sonata which was overdue for delivery, and he had a nasty cold and (one thing we had in common) he carried a clinical thermometer about with him. I can still see him sitting with us late into the night, looking the picture of distress, while he opened his heart to us over his inability to choose the right woman to take as his wife. I am rather inclined to think that he had known all along he had made up his mind to marry the attractive South American who is now Lady Walton. But then, William Walton is like his music: quicksilver.[29]

The death of Alice and the lack of permanence in any of his previous relationships may have made him realise that at the age of forty-six it was time that he settled down. But even so the suddenness of his choosing his future

---

[28] *Listener*, 8 August 1968, 173.
[29] Eric Coates, *Suite in Four Movements*, Heinemann 1953, 257.

wife and the persistence with which he relentlessly pursued her are surprising, especially in the face of opposition from Susana's parents who were of Spanish descent. Much to the disapproval of her father (a successful lawyer), they were married in a civil court on 13 December 1948, and the church wedding took place on 20 January. Soon after that they set sail for England, docking at Tilbury on 15 February. Seven days later William was conducting the London Symphony Orchestra, of which he had recently agreed to become President, in *Scapino* and the Viola Concerto in a concert shared with Vaughan Williams.[30]

The married couple lived first in the London house, Lowndes Cottage, that Alice Wimborne had bequeathed to William. One aspect of their union which Susana Walton did not conceal from her biography of her husband was that on their wedding day he had made it quite clear that he refused to have any children. When Susana's inexperience with contraceptive methods left her pregnant, she was faced with the alarming decision of either returning to Buenos Aires or going through the ordeal of a back-street abortion. She chose the latter course, William remaining all the while totally unsympathetic. Susana also tells of one evening at home in London a couple of years later when Malcolm Sargent

> started to abuse William for having married a young woman while not allowing her to have children. William immediately flew into a rage and ejected both Malcolm and me from the house. Malcolm went home, leaving me seated on the steps outside our front door until William's anger had abated and he allowed me in again.[31]

The first work that Walton completed on his return to England in February 1949 was the Violin Sonata for Menuhin. It was only 'after much pleading' on Susana's part that she was taken to Oldham to meet his mother. By October of their first year in England, he was longing for the Italian climate and was looking for somewhere to stay in the Bay of Naples. A chance overhearing at a travel agent's led them to a vacant property on Ischia, the island where he was to make his home for the rest of his life. That autumn the couple drove in their old Bentley to Italy where they stayed first at the castle of Montegufoni with Osbert Sitwell who had already been introduced to Susana, thus bringing to an end several years of coolness between him and Walton. It had not been a clean break from the Sitwell circle as Walton occasionally attended Edith's meetings at the Sesame Club in London when Osbert was also sometimes present. From Montegufoni Susana and William journeyed on to Ischia where they settled into their first home in the coastal

---

30 Humphrey Jennings described the rehearsal and concert in his 'Working Sketches of an Orchestra' in Hubert Foss and Noël Goodwin's *London Symphony: Portrait of an Orchestra*, 240–4.

31 Susana Walton, *Behind the Façade*, 39.

town of Forio. The house they rented, known as the Convento San Francesco, was in poor condition, having been derelict during the war, and needed much attention. Not only was it infested with rats but the roof leaked.

On Ischia Walton took up again the threads of *Troilus and Cressida*. Travel, marriage and the move to Italy had all caused a serious disruption to the opera schedule. In April 1948 the BBC had prepared an announcement to the effect that it had 'commissioned Dr William Walton to write an opera. The libretto has been written by Christopher Hassall in active collaboration with Dr Walton on the theme of *Troilus and Cressida*, but not using Shakespeare's words or following his play. It is 3 acts.' Stanford Robinson, who was in charge of the BBC's Third Programme operatic productions, had suggested as librettist the young actor and lyricist Christopher Hassall, better known for his association with Ivor Novello for whom he wrote the lyrics of a number of shows, among them the popular song *We'll Gather Lilacs*.[32] Ten months later little progress had been made, and in February 1949 Stanford Robinson wrote to Walton: 'Warmest congratulations to you on your marriage. . . . Will this new happiness have the effect of making you finish your opera quick or slower? . . . So far as I can judge you have not actually got down any Act in anything like a final form.' Marriage and his new environment revived his interest in *Troilus*, but many problems and delays lay ahead and its composition was to occupy him on and off for seven years.

Living several months of each year in Ischia did not make working with his librettist at all easy. Much of it was done by correspondence, just as a couple of years earlier J. B. Priestley had worked with Arthur Bliss on his opera *The Olympians*.[33] Christopher Hassall described their working method:

We naturally worked in close collaboration, either by a stream of letters between London and Italy, or together at Sir William's home in Ischia. . . . [He] copied out the initial synopsis so as to examine it the more closely and check on every detail. I then redrafted it and broke it up into numbered sections, and began the actual text on the same pattern, numbers being necessary for easy reference since the work continued by correspondence once the composition of the music began. I kept a pile of envelopes ready stamped and addressed for prompt reply, and our rather extraordinary correspondence over a long period would fill, I should imagine, several volumes. The exact motive or mood at any point was discussed, also the stanza – shape and style of the utterance, for the libretto ranged from meas-

---

32 Hassall had written the lyrics for the songs of all seven of Ivor Novello's musical plays, from *Glamorous Night* (1935) to *King's Rhapsody* (1949). Novello himself wrote the plays and the music. Hassall also worked with Arthur Bliss on the libretto of the latter's TV opera *Tobias and the Angel* (1960) and in the selection of texts for the choral works *The Beatitudes* (1961) and *Mary of Magdala* (1962) which was dedicated 'To the memory of Christopher Hassall, died 25 April 1963'.

33 First performed at the Royal Opera House, Covent Garden, on 29 September 1949.

ured rhyme to free verse (for instance, the passage in hexameter rhythm in Act 1 was not my idea, but was a 'special request'.) Such requests make a task of this kind all the more stimulating.[34]

On 28 March 1949 Walton wrote to Stanford Robinson: 'The opera position is perhaps a little brighter. At last Christopher & I with the help of the producer Otto Erhart have really got the libretto into shape so it only now needs the music. The idea at the moment is to get it ready for the 1951 [Festival of Britain] Exhibition.' He ended the note with a guarded 'We'll see.' But by 4 February 1950 it seems that problems with the libretto were not entirely solved, as he wrote to Steuart Wilson, head of the BBC Music Department: 'Am progressing fairly with my opera, which bristles with difficulties especially libretto ones.' Thirteen days later Steuart Wilson replied:

> I would like to know whether you think that we could do – or that you would like to do – it as a public performance in the RAH or South Bank as a first 'concert' performance with or without narrator, in the way we did Wozzeck, for example. . . . Naturally the BBC are interested and would like to have a 'First Performance', provided that they were assured by you that you were not averse from a studio performance preceding the stage version.

But Walton was steering away from the BBC's idea of a typical Third Programme studio broadcast towards a fully staged production for the première, as he wrote to Wilson on 1 March 1950 in a letter that shows that even at this stage he was harbouring some doubts about the work:

> On the whole I'm not keen about a concert performance of 'Troilus' during 1951. For one thing I don't think it would stand the cold hard light of a concert performance, & it may, with luck, just get away with it on the stage. Though for me, it has progressed fairly well, I've been fairly stuck for the last fortnight & I shall be pleased if I get it finished in sketch by this time next year. I aim for a Cov[ent] Gar[rden] performance about June '52.

Soon the BBC was becoming impatient at the non-appearance of *Troilus*, as an internal memo from the Director-General on 29 September 1950 makes only too clear: 'Is anything happening about the opera we commissioned from Walton? The two years' time limit must be almost twice up now.'[35] Another memo, dated 18 October 1950, reported that the work was 'barely half finished' and that Walton was 'anxious not to have first performance as studio-opera' and that he was 'willing to forego commission fee' [£500] but he was 'nevertheless extremely grateful to the BBC for having in fact commissioned it, thereby forcing him to face up to the task of writing it'.

---

34 'A New Cressida in a New Opera', *Radio Times*, 26 November 1954, 5, and 'And Now – Walton's First Opera', *Music and Musicians*, 1954, 12.
35 Sir William Haley to Basil Nicolls, Director of Home Broadcasting.

However, the recommendation was 'that the commission remains in force and that the commission fee is paid in respect of the first performance despite the fact that it would be a stage performance'. The Director-General deplored the outcome: 'We don't want to negotiate with him.' But this was obviously forgotten when Walton received a knighthood in the Festival of Britain year honours. On offering congratulations, Herbert Murrill, the Head of Music, wrote on 1 January, enquiring if he 'would consider writing us some Festival music for the first of our BBC public concerts in the Festival of Britain series', asking for something 'of about fifteen minutes in length'. But slow progress with *Troilus* made taking on any new commission out of the question, and Walton made no contribution to the Festival of Britain and the representation of his works in London that year was slender. Apart from isolated occasions such as conducting an all-Walton Prom (Second *Façade* Suite, Violin Concerto with Campoli, and *Belshazzar's Feast*) and in Liverpool *Belshazzar's Feast* together with *Façade* (with Edith Sitwell reciting), he was otherwise conspicuously absent from the Festival of Britain.

With the coronation of Queen Elizabeth II in June 1953, Walton had been approached the previous October by John Denison of the Arts Council to contribute to an anthology of unaccompanied choral settings, a collaboration between ten poets and ten composers collectively entitled *A Garland for the Queen*[36] to be performed at the Royal Festival Hall on the eve of the Coronation. A cappella works have not formed a significant part of Walton's oeuvre, and at that time they extended only to his early *Litany*, the *Daily Dispatch* carol, the anthem composed in 1938 for the wedding of Alice Wimborne's son, and the Masefield setting for the unveiling of the Henry Wood window. Perhaps with the struggles over the latter in mind, he turned down the offer, adding: 'You can hardly expect me to say "Yes" when all my best sides [i.e. humour and satire] are verboten – besides I don't want to be accused of making a corner in the Coronation music.'[37]

Yet make a corner he did, with two works that found Walton on top form. The first was the *Coronation Te Deum*, composed for two mixed choruses, two semi-choruses, boys' voices, organ, orchestra and military brass. Conceived on a large scale, this avoided all the defects of *In Honour of the City of London* through its contrasts of texture and volume, alternating the simple and the grand, the penitent and the jubilant. Its first performance was at the Coronation service in Westminster Abbey on 2 June 1953, with Dr William McKie conducting the Coronation Choir and Orchestra.[38] It was music well suited to the acoustics, the bursts of organ punctuating the orches-

---

36 The composers who contributed were Bliss, Bax, Tippett, Vaughan Williams, Berkeley, Ireland, Howells, Finzi, Rawsthorne and Rubbra, the last-named setting words by Christopher Hassall.

37 Neil Tierney, *William Walton*, Robert Hale 1984, 125.

38 A recording of the Coronation Service, including the *Te Deum*, was issued by EMI in

tral commentary, and brass and antiphonal voices reverberating throughout the Abbey. It was completed in – for Walton – record time by December 1952 over a period of two months. Whether it bore any connection with the *Te Deum* that he had abandoned in 1944 one cannot tell, but the chordal progression at the words 'The holy Church' is certainly reminiscent of a passage near the beginning of Kodály's 1936 *Te Deum of Budavár*. The other work, this time a successful Arts Council commission, was the Coronation March *Orb and Sceptre* which caught Walton once again in ceremonial garb, first hinted at in *Belshazzar's Feast* and in the finale to the First Symphony. After the rich panoply of *Crown Imperial*, the joyous exuberance and swagger of *Orb and Sceptre*, dedicated 'To Her Majesty Queen Elizabeth II', seemed to catch perfectly that note of optimism in the dawning of the new Elizabethan era. In both coronation marches he pulled out all the stops. Walton recorded *Orb and Sceptre* with the Philharmonia Orchestra a fortnight before the ceremony.[39] The *Coronation Te Deum* was played at the opening service of the 1953 Three Choirs Festival, and at a Festival concert which began with *Orb and Sceptre*, the *Te Deum* was repeated although it had not been programmed.

In the Coronation year Walton was invited into the Aldeburgh circle as one of six British composers each contributing a variation for strings on the Elizabethan theme known as *Sellinger's Round*. The other composers were Arthur Oldham, Michael Tippett, Lennox Berkeley, Benjamin Britten and Humphrey Searle. The idea for its first performance was that the audience would be invited to guess who wrote which variation. Nobody was successful and Tippett cunningly provided a red herring by beginning and closing his variation with a hint of the passacaglia, *The Death of Falstaff*, from the *Henry V* film music. Walton's began with a round on an inversion of the theme and concluded with the inverted and the original theme in combination. The first performance, which took place in the Aldeburgh Parish Church on 20 June 1953, was conducted by Britten and recorded for commercial release.[40]

In March, Laurence Olivier, going through a difficult period both artistically and personally, had rung William and Susana in Ischia, asking if he could come and stay. 'Wonderful friends that they are,' he wrote in his autobiography, 'they could sense something was wrong and told me to come at once.'[41] But on his arrival he was met with a telegram urging him to return immediately. He later learned the reason: his wife, Vivien Leigh, had had a nervous breakdown. Some weeks later, with Vivien temporarily confined to a

---

1953 on a 3-LP set ALP 1056-8 and reissued on CD in 1997 on EMI 5 66582-2. This CD also includes the first commercial recording of *Orb and Sceptre*.

[39] *Crown Imperial* was recorded at the same session on 18 March 1953. Both were issued in the new LP format while *Orb and Sceptre* was also issued separately on 78 rpm (Columbia LX1583).

[40] Decca LXT2798.

[41] *Confessions of an Actor*, 199.

psychiatric hospital, Olivier escaped the press and photographers that were persistently besieging him and returned to Ischia with Walton. On the boat crossing from Naples to Ischia, Olivier forgot the anonymity he was seeking and signed his autograph for a lady passenger. Very soon the Waltons' house was swarming with press to the extent that if they wanted to go out Olivier had to conceal himself under a rug on the floor of their Bentley. Walton suggested that they would be more likely to find some peace on mainland Italy. So, with the Bentley 'perched grotesquely on the steepest part of the stern of what had been a sailing-ship', Olivier and the Waltons followed in a small fishing-boat. Making a very early start the next morning, the three enjoyed a few days' motoring in Southern Italy, ending up with an evening of *Götterdämmerung* at the Naples opera house. Back in Ischia another telegram summoned Olivier home again. Such hospitality was reciprocated. The Waltons were frequent week-end guests at Olivier's country home, Notley Abbey, in Buckinghamshire, and stayed there in the gardener's cottage on the estate while William was struggling to finish *Troilus and Cressida*.[42]

One sad event in 1953 was the death in May of Hubert Foss, after a stroke, at the age of 54. 'He was always such a staunch supporter,' Walton wrote to Dora with an element of understatement, '& I can never forget what a help he was to me in the early days or for that matter, always.'[43] At the time of his death, Foss had been making plans for a biography of Walton; given his unique position as both publisher and close friend, it is regrettable that it was not accomplished.

In August Walton sailed for the United States where his conducting engagements inevitably included *Belshazzar's Feast*. For the remainder of 1953 and all of the following one he was occupied with *Troilus and Cressida*. The idea for its subject had come to Christopher Hassall after reading a chapter in C. S. Lewis's *The Allegory of Love*. Analysing the character of Cressida (or Criseide), Lewis had written that from the 'fear of loneliness, of old age, of death, of love, and of hostility . . . springs the only positive passion which can be permanent in such a nature, the pitiable longing, more childlike than womanly, for protection, for some strong and stable thing that will hide her away and take the burden from her shoulder.' Was it a similar impulse that had turned Walton's mind to marriage? For his libretto Hassall avoided Shakespeare and turned instead to Chaucer's *Troylus and Criseide*, 'with the order of Chaucer's events rearranged, new details introduced, and the whole compressed within much narrower limits of time, until the latter half of Act

---

[42] *Behind the Façade*, 136. In *My Father Laurence Olivier*, Headline 1992, 185, Tarquin Olivier writes that it was after seeing a run-through at the Denham studios of the final cut of the film *Richard III* that Walton first stayed at Notley Abbey to complete *Troilus and Cressida*. But *Troilus* was staged before *Richard III* was completed.

[43] Letter, 29 May 1953, written from Lowndes Cottage, London, Hubert Foss Archives. Dora Foss died in 1978.

III where the opera bears no relation to the medieval poem. There is nothing of Shakespeare in the libretto, beyond a similarity of situation here and there inevitable in two works derived from the same source.'[44]

Act I opens in the citadel of Troy. Calkas, high priest and father of Cressida, is convinced that further resistance to the besieging Greeks is useless and tries to persuade the people that the Oracle of Delphi has advised surrender. Antenor, a young captain and friend of Troilus, accuses Calkas of being in the pay of the Greeks and sets off on a foray against the enemy. Meanwhile Pandarus, brother of Calkas, overhears Troilus declaring his love to Cressida with little result, and offers to plead his case for him. Shortly he discovers that his brother is deserting to the Greeks. When it is learned that Antenor has been captured, Troilus swears either to retrieve his friend by force or to persuade King Priam, his father, to negotiate an exchange of prisoners.

In Act II Cressida has been invited to supper by Pandarus who cunningly arranges for Troilus to turn up. A storm, depicted by an orchestral passage of passionate intensity, conveniently causes Cressida to stay the night. (Tippett has described how, invited to dine with Walton and Walter Legge, he sat with amazement when 'Willie announced that he was going to include a musical representation of heterosexual copulation . . . and the two of them spent the greater part of the meal working out the rhythmic patterns of sexual intercourse![45])

At dawn the next morning the city is disturbed by drums announcing the approach of the Greek commander Diomede who has come to arrange an exchange of prisoners. Calkas has done the Greeks much service in return for which he asks for his daughter Cressida as his only reward, and she is to be exchanged for Antenor on the authority of the seals of Troy and Greece. When Diomede sees Cressida he is captivated by her beauty. As she prepares to be taken away, Troilus promises to smuggle messages to her through the enemy lines.

Act III opens ten weeks later, during which time Cressida has received no word from Troilus: her servant Evadne, under orders from Calkas, has destroyed all his messages. Meanwhile Diomede, after many advances, asks her to prepare to become Queen of Argos. During an hour of truce, Troilus and Pandarus appear. Seeing Diomede carrying a scarf of Cressida's as a token of her favour, Troilus claims her as his own. Enraged, he attacks Diomede but is stabbed in the back by Calkas. Diomede orders Calkas to return to Troy but declares that Cressida must stay behind as a prisoner. Seizing Troilus's sword, she takes her own life.

---

[44] *William Walton: Troilus and Cressida. Opera in Three Acts: Libretto by Christopher Hassall*, OUP 1954, 4–5.

[45] Michael Tippett, *Those Twentieth Century Blues: An Autobiography*, Hutchinson 1991, 215.

Troilus was one of a number of large-scale British operas to follow in the wake of *Peter Grimes*, nearly all of which were premièred at Covent Garden:[46] Bliss's *The Olympians* (September 1949), Vaughan Williams's *Pilgrim's Progress* (April 1951), Britten's *Billy Budd* (December 1951) and *Gloriana* (June 1953), Lennox Berkeley's *Nelson* (at Sadler's Wells in September 1954), and soon to come, in January 1955, Tippett's *The Midsummer Marriage* (which Walton attended). The first performance of *Troilus and Cressida*, which was broadcast, took place at the Royal Opera House on 3 December 1954 with Richard Lewis[47] (Troilus), Magda Lazlò (Cressida), Peter Pears (Pandarus), Geraint Evans (Antenor) and Frederick Dalberg (Calkas). The producer was George Devine, Hugh Casson designed the scenery,[48] and Sir Malcolm Sargent conducted. It had not been an easy ride to the first night. Richard Temple Savage, bass clarinettist in the Covent Garden orchestra and its librarian, knew from the inside what problems there had been:

> Sargent did not seem well acquainted with the score, he was still an inveterate fiddler and tamperer with other people's works, and he still did not relate well to the singers. He always addressed them by the name of their role in the opera: 'Troilus' for Richard Lewis, 'Pandarus' for Peter Pears and so on. It must have made them feel like mere ciphers, and certainly gave offence. . . . Like the pre-war Italian conductors, he refused to beat unless the orchestra was playing but, whereas in Italian opera it is often a matter of pure recitative, here Sir Malcolm was leaving whole ensembles to fend for themselves without setting a tempo; he would let them start and then join in with the orchestra. Peter Pears came forward at rehearsal and begged him to give them a beat, and he still refused, saying he would feel such a fool, conducting without the orchestra. The acid murmured comments from the pit can be left to the imagination.
>
> As for the alterations, they were legion. Every afternoon after the rehearsal all the material (which was full of inaccuracies anyway as it had not been properly checked by the publishers, and later we had to make a fresh set of parts), had to be carried up four flights to the library, where Walton would join me with the score to look through all Sargent's recommendations and then make alterations which we had to transfer to all the parts. Sargent had a particular aversion to anything written for two harps, and was constantly cutting out bits of the second harp part. One day Walton came upstairs looking particularly disgruntled and suddenly burst out: 'I'm

---

46 Walton himself had strong links with Covent Garden. When for its re-opening in 1946 the Covent Garden Trust had been formed, he was one of its members, together with Kenneth Clark, Edward Dent, Samuel Courtauld and others.

47 Richard Lewis also had a leading rôle, as Mark, in Tippett's opera *The Midsummer Marriage*, premièred at Covent Garden on 27 January 1955.

48 In August 1951, *The Times* had announced that Laurence Olivier would be the producer and Henry Moore the designer.

not making any more alterations. Its my f****** opera and I'm going to write some more for the second harp!' Which he proceeded to do, and this seemed to have the desired effect.[49]

To make matters worse, Sargent, for reasons of vanity, refused to wear glasses, making reading the manuscript score with which he was none too familiar even more difficult. The story goes that Heifetz, after attending a rehearsal, took Sargent aside and applied some professional coercion, suggesting that unless he learnt the score properly his forthcoming tour of the States would be put in jeopardy. Whatever problems there were in rehearsal, the first night was counted a success and the *Daily Express* critic called it 'the proudest hour of British music since the première of Benjamin Britten's *Peter Grimes* nine years ago'. (Walton himself cannot have been too dissatisfied with the performance as in 1960 he wrote to William Glock, then Controller of Music at the BBC, reminding him of the existence of 'an extremely good tape' of the first performance – which had been broadcast, a recording that had been 'successfully smothered by the Third Prog. boys for the last five years or so!'[50])

If the popular press by and large were full of praise for the opera, the work had a mixed reception in the musical journals. The two sides of the critical coin were well represented in *Opera*. Donald Mitchell wrote of 'the antiquity of its music'. A work

> which does not employ a valid contemporary style cannot hope to communicate anything valid to its audience. . . . It was this overwhelming sense of musical unreality which I felt so strongly when listening to *Troilus and Cressida*. Here was a composer who . . . had not even kept up with himself, and who relied in the main on reviving eminent models (Wagner, Strauss, Verdi, Puccini, Walton) as a substitute for genuine composition. . . . Since the Viola Concerto and the Symphony he has progressively relaxed his idiom over the years, and now, it seems from *Troilus and Cressida*, he has abandoned it altogether.

This was a criticism to haunt him in the post-war years. Paul Müller, in the same journal, felt otherwise. He saw *Troilus* as

> a great tragic opera . . . conceived with an admirable instinctive feeling for the stage, and [one which] has absorbed the rich experience of the traditional operatic language. Walton does not raise the problems of opera, he

---

49 'A Voice from the Pit – V', *Opera*, January 1987, 25, reprinted in Richard Temple Savage, *A Voice from the Pit*, 151–2.

50 Letter, 19 September 1960, BBC Written Archives Centre, Caversham. A recording of that first performance exists in the BBC Sound Archives, T30702, and the National Sound Archives, T1401/3BW.

solves them – to the surprise and delight of the public at the Covent Garden
– like one who has had fifty years experience in writing operas.

Similarly, Dyneley Hussey thought that the music showed 'an astonishing
grasp of operatic principles' and that Walton proved himself 'a genuine operatic composer', even suggesting, with reference to the opening to the last act
with its use of vibraphone, that no scene in opera 'has been set with a surer
hand or with such economy for a very long time, perhaps not since the third
act of *Aida* was composed'.[51]

Troilus had seven Covent Garden performances before going to Glasgow,
Edinburgh, Leeds, Manchester and Coventry with Reginald Goodall
conducting, and then coming back to London. Sargent conducted an excerpt
from Act Two at the 1955 Henry Wood Proms. The American première,
which Walton attended, took place in San Francisco on 7 October 1955 with
Richard Lewis and Dorothy Kirsten in the title rôles and Erich Leinsdorf
conducting. On 20 October it was staged by the New York City Opera at the
City Centre, New York, Joseph Rosenstock conducting and Phyllis Curtin
and Jon Crain taking the principal rôles. On 12 January 1956 it opened at La
Scala, Milan, with David Poleri and Dorothy Dow, Nino Sanzogno
conducting. Walton remembered that when he was taken on stage during the
interval he was 'received with boos and cheers and hisses'. He wrote to Peter
Pears: 'The Pandarus there was a disaster, so much so that the trio in the 2nd
Act had to be cut. . . . The first night reception was a riot of hissing & booing
& the Milanese press was foul – in fact I've never seen such a vicious press
for anything. . . .'[52] Susana Walton takes up the story: 'In the last act when
they finally stopped whistling, they had taken off Troilus's sword with which
she was to kill herself. And she went rushing round the whole stage like a hen
looking for corn with her head stuck betwen her toes looking for this sword
instead of killing herself with any old thing. . . . Then somebody threw the
sword in – clatter bang into the middle of the stage – more laughter, more
whistling.'[53] Laurence Olivier attended the second night and wrote home
from Ischia that 'WW's opera was received poorly enough in Milan to place
W. alongside Verdi and Puccini whose first efforts were likewise fated.'[54]

This, the last of Walton's scores to be inspired by love, drew forth some of
his tenderest and most passionate music. Although dedicated 'To my wife', it
must nevertheless have stirred anguished memories of Alice. 'I sweated

---

51 'Walton's "Troilus and Cressida" ', *Music and Letters*, Vol. 36, April 1955, 142 and
   145.
52 Letter of 21 April 1956 quoted in Christopher Headington, *Peter Pears: A Biography*,
   Faber & Faber 1992, 169; the second of only two surviving letters of their correspondence.
53 Tony Palmer, *At the Haunted End of the Day*.
54 Tarquin Olivier, *My Father Laurence Olivier*, 192.

blood over it – in fact it nearly killed me,' he once remarked in an interview.[55] Few pages in his output are lovelier than Cressida's first vocal entry, the accompaniment by turns delicate and agitated. If there are occasional weak moments in the outer acts, Act II is uniformly successful. Here the humour in Pandarus offers emotional relief to the inevitably doomed love affair between Troilus and Cressida that reaches its climax in a powerful orchestral interlude depicting their one night together, an anticipatory Liebestod symbolically set against a storm. Eric Walter White, in his *A History of English Opera*, quotes an example of the librettist's and/or the composer's sense of mischief when, at a climactic point in Act I, Pandarus voices the state of British opera by exclaiming: 'Nothing but royal patronage can save us now!' The word 'Troilus's' was later substituted for 'royal'. Was there mischief too in the several bars at figure 57 that were later cut in which Pandarus sings 'I have much experience in these things' (i.e. love)? The camp character of Pandarus was so evidently designed for Peter Pears, with its occasional Brittenesque phrasing and suggestions of falsetto. On 21 May 1954 Walton had written to Pears:

> I gather that David Webster [General Administrator, Covent Garden] has written you regarding the possibility of your considering to undertake the part of Pandarus in 'Troilus & Cressida'. If he has done so (one can never be sure!) he has done so with my highest approval, and I am hoping that you may find the part worthy of you. If you do I shall be delighted, as I can think of noone who could do it so well, also the relief that this tricky part would be in your safe hands.[56]

In performance Pears proved himself eminently suited to the rôle, despite the fact that he was suffering from a heavy cold or laryngitis and was appearing against his doctor's orders. But he had to withdraw from four of the performances after the première. It was not a part he liked, describing the opera to his biographer as 'a hell of an opera'.[57]

While Walton was fortunate with his Pandarus, he had written the part of Cressida for Elisabeth Schwarzkopf who, much to his disappointment, was never to sing it on stage because, as her husband Walter Legge wrote, 'the text was Ivor Novello-ish and in English'.[58] How magnificently she would have taken on that rôle can be surmised from the extracts she recorded in 1955 with Walton conducting.

In between the first performance and the publication of the vocal score,[59] as was Walton's habit, numerous revisions, deletions and changes were made,

---

[55] *Ibid.*
[56] Quoted in Christopher Headington, *Peter Pears*, 168.
[57] *Ibid.*, 168.
[58] Elisabeth Schwarzkopf, *On and Off the Record.*, 143.
[59] The vocal score, published by OUP in 1954, was largely the work of Roy Douglas who was assisted by Franz Reizenstein for Act III. It took him about 3½ years to complete.

rather more in the case of *Troilus* than in other works. Most of these were minor details, here and there a bar or two was cut to tighten continuity, a line or two of dialogue omitted, some adjustments made to the scoring. Some changes in Act I were more substantial, but Act II remained largely unaltered, and there were only a few changes in Act III.[60] Much more drastic changes were to be made later when Walton further revised the work – or more specifically the rôle of Cressida – to accommodate Janet Baker's mezzo voice.

One person who was not a great admirer of *Troilus* was Vaughan Williams. Ursula Vaughan Williams has written that 'Ralph found that he wanted to hear it more than once, so we saw it a second time.'[61] But according to Roy Douglas (who worked for both William Walton and Vaughan Williams)

> he went to hear it and 'wished he liked it more'. He decided that perhaps more familiarity might breed content, so he asked me to go and play through the vocal score to him. I agreed, and one morning, to an audience of V.W., Ursula [Vaughan Williams], Gerald Finzi, and another friend, Jean Stewart, I played and sang the entire opera. I'm sorry to say that apparently V.W. didn't like *Troilus* any better when he heard it again in the opera house.[62]

In 1952, while *Troilus* was in the process of composition, Christopher Hassall had written a play for that year's Edinburgh Festival and he told Walton that he thought he had found a young actor who was just right for the leading part. 'What's his name?' Walton enquired casually, to which Hassall replied, 'Britton' [i.e. Tony Britton]. 'Oh no!' came the shocked reply. 'Don't tell me he can act too!'[63]

Once *Troilus and Cressida* had been staged, Walton was soon back in the world of films. There were at the same time tentative suggestions for a new ballet. At the end of the Royal Ballet's 1954/5 season, Ninette de Valois announced in her curtain speech that an unspecified three-act ballet by Ashton and Walton would be staged in the following year. *The Tempest* had been suggested as a possible subject but it was soon rejected as Fonteyn was not sympathetic to the rôle of Miranda. *Macbeth* was being seriously considered as an alternative, and Ashton sent Walton a detailed draft synopsis with timings,[64] but he declined as he was then heavily committed to the film score

---

60 The cuts in Act I were some further lines for Calkas (and the chorus's responses) at figure 14, an extra line for the oracle's voice heard through a loudspeaker at 24, and extra bars for Pandarus at 57 and for Cressida at 71. The chief changes in Act III were a shortening of Cressida's solo at 28 and of the orchestral passage at 76. At the première, both Acts II and III ended quietly, instead of fortissimo as printed in the vocal score.

61 Ursula Vaughan Williams, *R.V.W.*, 315.

62 Roy Douglas, *Working with R.V.W.*, OUP 1972, 41.

63 Alan Jefferson, 'Walton – Man and Music', *Music and Musicians*, July 1965, 17.

64 Ashton's draft synopsis and detailed instructions to Walton regarding a score for a

for *Richard III*. Ashton had a change of mind (Fonteyn did not anyway see herself as Lady Macbeth) and turned instead to an earlier idea, the story of the water sprite Ondine (of which Fonteyn approved). For the music Walton quite likely suggested his new near-neighbour on Ischia, Hans Werner Henze, who accepted the commission.[65] *Ondine* was successfully staged at Covent Garden in October 1958. Had Walton accepted there would have been a reunion from pre-war years, as Fonteyn's performance as Ondine was included in the 1959 film *The Royal Ballet*, directed by Paul Czinner.

The filming of the last of the Olivier–Walton trilogy of Shakespeare films, *Richard III* (in Technicolor and VistaVision), came at the request of Alexander Korda (it was in fact one of his last films). As on both previous occasions, Olivier starred and directed (not out of choice but because all the directors he approached were unavailable at the time). 'As usual,' as Olivier himself put it, 'William Walton's music was a life-saver.'[66] Once again there were substantial changes to the text, with whole scenes dispensed with and, instead of opening with the familiar 'Now is the winter of our discontent', the coronation of Edward IV from *Henry VI Part III* was inserted before that soliloquy both to provide an historical framework to the complex political situation and to focus on the film's central image: the crown. Olivier assembled another fine cast that included Claire Bloom (Anne), Ralph Richardson (Buckingham), John Gielgud (Clarence), Cedric Hardwicke (King Edward IV), Stanley Baker (Richmond), Alec Clunes (Hastings) and Andrew Cruickshank (Brackenbury), as well as three who appeared in all three Shakespeare films: Esmond Knight (Ratcliffe), John Laurie (Lovel) and Russell Thorndike (Priest).[67] Bosworth Field was transported to Spain, near Madrid, with Spanish extras for the battle scene. Shooting began in September 1954, and Bernard Hepton, who helped train the Spaniards in the final scene leading up to Richard's death, remembered Olivier bounding down the steps of the twenty-foot camera tower. 'That's good,' he said. 'Just right. Now Willie

---

three-act ballet based on *Macbeth* are reproduced in David Vaughan, *Frederick Ashton*, 434–8. Ashton's requirements, at first for about 75 minutes of music, were revised to 45 minutes before the project was abandoned.

[65] Susana Walton writes that 'unbeknown to Hans, [Walton] suggested to Fred Ashton that he ask Hans to write the music' (*Behind the Façade*, 151). But Ashton's biographer, Julie Kavanagh, disputes this, writing that Henze asked Ashton before the latter's death who dismissed it as 'absolute nonsense'. Henze also adds that were it true, living so close and seeing each almost every day, '[the Waltons] would have told me'. *Secret Muses*, 424–5.

[66] *Confessions of an Actor*, 210.

[67] In all three Shakespeare films Alan Dent was the text editor and Roger Furse the designer.

Walton's got to write some music to this, so could we have them do it all again – in rhythm?'[68]

Richard III had its first showing at the Leicester Square Theatre on 13 December 1955. Walton's score may not be quite the match for either *Henry V* or *Hamlet*, and even he felt that he was repeating himself.[69] Yet the film's murderous plot did not call for the same orchestral brilliance or dramatic effect. Rather more use was made of pastiche to suggest period. The title music (without the opening fanfare that was later added for the concert Prelude) sets off with a bustling figure that leads into a noble Elgarian melody (close relative of the trio in the coronation march *Orb and Sceptre*), these two themes being used in the night-time fanfares before the battle scene to represent respectively the armies of Richard and Henry, Earl of Richmond. Another, poignant theme serves for the unfortunate Queen Anne. When on the death of Edward IV one of the young princes is taken to sanctuary, Walton makes ironic reference to the *Coventry Carol* (a reminder of the slaughter of the innocents by Herod the Great). Something, too, of that dry Waltonian humour emerged later during the recording sessions for *Richard III*. After *Hamlet*, Olivier had apparently asked Walton for 'less austere' music, and Muir Mathieson was amused to find the direction *con prosciuto, agnello e confitura di fragiole* (with ham, lamb and strawberry jam) written on the score.[70] As the film conductor Ernest Irving once remarked:[71] 'Walton's sardonic humour and virtuosity in colourful orchestration [are] assets of the utmost value. He possesses a polite imperturbability which stands him in good stead when faced with unexpected requirements from the directors.' Muir Mathieson conducted the Royal Philharmonic Orchestra on the soundtrack which in pre-video days was rather unusually issued complete on disc in March 1956.[72] The music for the three Olivier-directed Shakespearean films has become widely known through various concert suites, and the films themselves are commercially available on video.

There was another film project that did not materialise. Even before *Richard III* had been screened Olivier was touring Scotland for suitable locations for a film of *Macbeth*. But Korda's death in January 1956 effectively ended hopes for that project, even though two years later Olivier wrote to Eugene Goossens, who was looking for some film work to boost his rather meagre income: 'If *Macbeth* comes off, as I desperately hope it will, I have

---

68 John Cottrell, *Laurence Olivier*, Weidenfeld & Nicolson 1975, Coronet paperback 1977, 278.

69 *Behind the Façade*, 143.

70 Muir Mathieson, BBC Radio, 19 November 1969, BBC Sound Archives LP32648.

71 In 'Film Music', a talk given to the Royal Musical Association on 9 March 1950.

72 On 3 LPs: HMV ALP 1341-3. A single LP of excerpts was issued by RCA Victor: LM 1940. Walton himself recorded with the Philharmonia the Prelude and 'A Shakespearean Suite' as arranged by Mathieson in October 1963.

already committed myself to William Walton, who, as you know, did the music for my three other Shakespeare films.'[73]

Another request of lesser importance came in 1955 when he was asked to provide orchestrations of *The Star-Spangled Banner* and the National Anthem for the Philharmonia Orchestra's tour of the United States that autumn with Karajan. In the event they were not used, although the National Anthem was performed at the Royal Festival Hall before the orchestra embarked on its tour. In January 1965 he was approached by the BBC for the orchestration of *The Star-Spangled Banner* to be used for the BBC Symphony Orchestra's American tour in April with Antal Dorati and Pierre Boulez conducting. Walton replied: 'I have no idea where the MSS of the arrangements of the S.S.B. may be, in fact I had forgotten all about it. Maybe the Philharmonia would know. I should like to think, no doubt misguidedly, that some slightly more important work of mine is included in the programme of the tour!' Although works by Elgar, Tippett, Britten and Vaughan Williams were in the repertoire, there was no Walton.

[73] Carole Rosen, *The Goossens*, 378.

11

'Desperate to find a tune'

After *Richard III*, Walton had a particularly fruitful period that saw the production of four important works, the *Johannesburg Festival Overture*, the Cello Concerto, the *Partita* and the Second Symphony. These works found a new Walton, free from angst and in an unusually relaxed, cheerful mood. The *Johannesburg Festival Overture* was commissioned by Ernest Fleischmann, then musical director of the Johannesburg Festival, for that city's seventieth-anniversary celebrations. It was completed on 31 May 1956 at Ischia and first performed on 25 September with Sargent conducting the South African Broadcasting Symphony Orchestra. Efrem Kurtz and the Liverpool Philharmonic Orchestra gave the first British performance at Liverpool on 13 November. London heard it on 23 January 1957 with Sargent and the BBC Symphony Orchestra. The Overture bursts with energy and memorable themes, and employs as ever a dazzling array of percussion that includes maracas, rumba sticks, xylophone, glockenspiel, castanets and tambourine. Just as Bliss had listened to some field recordings of native African music before composing the score for the 1945 film *Men of Two Worlds*, so Fleischmann had sent Walton some Bantu melodies, suggesting that the Overture should include some African themes. The central percussive section includes at least one theme later identified as being by the African composer and guitarist Mwenda Jean Bosco,[1] and complex African rhythms add a national 'feel'. After the first performance Walton made a few minor alterations including one cut.

The Cello Concerto was a commission from the Russian-born cellist Gregor Piatigorsky. As with Heifetz and the Violin Concerto, there was collaboration between composer and soloist, much of which was necessarily

---

[1] The guitar piece *Masanga* issued commercially on 78 rpm Gallotone GB1586T and in a version for voice and guitar on GB1700T. David Rycroft, 'Melodic Imports and Exports: A By-Product of Recording in Southern Africa', *British Institute of Recorded Sound Bulletin*, No. 3, Winter 1956, 19–21.

done by correspondence, with Walton in Ischia and Piatigorsky often travelling. The work was written between February and October 1956 and first performed on 25 January 1957 in Boston, with Charles Munch conducting the Boston Symphony Orchestra. The same performers recorded the work for RCA. The date of the première was much changed. Originally planned for February 1957, it was brought forward to 7 December, causing Walton to ask the BBC to cancel his Prom date: 'This upsets my plans considerably as now I must complete the work by early Nov. instead of Jan.'[2] However, because of Piatigorsky's illness, the date was eventually put back. The first British performance was at a Royal Philharmonic Society concert at the Royal Festival Hall on 13 February, with Sargent conducting the BBC Symphony Orchestra.[3] For this performance Piatigorsky waived his fee. But he was not entirely happy with the work as it was: 'There was only one question in the entire concerto – the ending of it. I felt that it should end kind of . . . triumphally, very organ-like and large, and he didn't feel like that.'[4] The published ending, a slow diminuendo, effectively mirrors the work's opening without being showy or dramatic. In 1975, at Piatigorsky's request, Walton wrote a new and 'less melancholy'[5] ending which the cellist was never to play as he died the following year. The original ending is the one always played. In the Concerto Walton made use of the vibraphone which he had only previously used in *Troilus and Cressida* and *Escape Me Never*. The first movement, which has a new-found serenity, is followed by a quicksilver scherzo. The last movement, *tema e improvvisazioni* (Walton's favourite 'theme and variations') with two unaccompanied cadenza-like variations, ends as the work began, with the soloist musing against a gently rocking figure. While the emotional impact of this new concerto is at a lower level than those for the viola and violin, the same mastery is much in evidence.

Walton had not attended the Boston première of the Concerto, but he would have been present at its London performance had a serious accident not prevented him. In January he was being driven by Lady Walton from Naples to London when their car ran into a cement lorry near Rome. Both received considerable injuries, Walton breaking his hip and Lady Walton breaking some ribs, an ankle and a wrist. Several weeks of hospitalization in Rome followed.

His next work, the *Partita*, was a commission by the Cleveland Orchestra

---

2   Letter 27 April 1956, BBC Written Archives Centre, Caversham.

3   BBC Transcription Service recording CA2.

4   Piatigorsky speaking in *Portrait of Walton*, BBC Radio 3, broadcast 4 June 1977.

5   As Piatigorsky described the original ending. Michael Kennedy, *Portrait of Walton*, 198. In his Introduction to Craggs' *William Walton: A Catalogue* Christopher Palmer has described (p. 5) the revised ending as involving 'an extra crescendo-diminuendo of the "tick-tock" motif of the first movement – a final flaring up of the sunset'. This ending was played in concert by Raphael Wallfisch before recording the concerto for Chandos in January 1991 but the original version was preferred for the recording.

(the orchestra that had premièred the Violin Concerto) for its fortieth-anniversary celebrations, in fact one of ten works commissioned for the occasion. The other composers approached were Alvin Etler, Paul Creston, Howard Hanson, Peter Mennin, Robert Moevs, Gottfried von Einem, Bohuslav Martinu, Henri Dutilleux and Boris Blacher. In this work Walton was on top form, producing a romp that is sheer delight from beginning to end. As he himself declared in what was for him a rare programme note written especially for the occasion: 'My Partita poses no problems, has no ulterior motive or meaning behind it, and makes no attempt to ponder the imponderables. I have written it in the hope it may be enjoyed straight off, without any preliminary probing into the score. I have also written it with the wonderful players of the Cleveland Orchestra in mind, hoping that they may enjoy playing it.'

Earlier, in his book on Albert Roussel, Norman Demuth had suggested parallels between the French composer's *Suite in F* (1926) and Walton's *Sinfonia Concertante* (c. 1927):

> We feel that the composers might almost be interchanged, save that Roussel would have done differently by the material of the last movements of the *Sinfonia*. Walton has all Roussel's strength and symphonic power, able to curb itself, if need be, or expand to an indefinite length. One does not know to what extent Walton is familiar with Roussel's music or with this particular work, but the more one thinks of the *Suite in F* and the *Sinfonia Concertante*, the stronger the parallel becomes, with the mentioned qualification.[6]

When Walton came to write his *Partita*, there can be little doubt that he knew the *Suite in F* well, for there are striking similarities, especially between the first movements of each work where for a few bars the composers could almost be interchanged. It is as if he had used the Roussel work as a model for his *Partita*, and in the process borrowed one or two thematic elements. Roussel's three movements of *Prélude*, *Sarabande* and *Gigue* are matched by Walton's *Toccata*, *Pastorale Siciliana* and *Giga Burlesca*. When John Amis, in a broadcast interview, pointed out the similarities, Walton put up a smoke screen. 'I don't know that work. . . . I must have a look at it,' he mumbled.[7] Yet this had been one of a number of scores that he had specifically requested Alan Frank of OUP to send him in November 1956. The others were Roussel's Third and Fourth Symphonies, Berlioz's *Roméo et Juliette* and *Nuits d'été*, Prokofiev's Sixth and Seventh Symphonies, and Mahler's Ninth Symphony and *Das Lied von der Erde*.[8]

The *Partita*, dedicated 'To George Szell and the Cleveland Orchestra', was

---

6   Norman Demuth, *Albert Roussel: A Study*, United Music Publishers n.d., 58–9.
7   Interview with John Amis, BBC Radio 3, broadcast 17 March 1972.
8   Kennedy, *Portrait of Walton*, 205–6.

premièred by them in Cleveland on 30 January 1958. Walton himself conducted the British première in Manchester with the Hallé Orchestra on 30 April together with the Cello Concerto, and that orchestra gave its London première under Sir John Barbirolli on 2 May 1958. (Barbirolli took the *Partita* and the Violin Concerto with him on his tour of American orchestras that year.)

The Second Symphony had been commissioned in 1956 by the (Royal) Liverpool Philharmonic Society to mark the 750th anniversary of the granting of a charter to that city. Those who had hoped for a first performance the following year could not have been of the horse- and dog-racing fraternity who study form before placing bets. History seemed almost set to repeat itself. It was not until the end of January 1959 that he had completed the first movement and then a further year elapsed before the second movement was finished (January and February 1960). Then, unhappy with the first movement which he had shown to Szell, he revised it during February and March, and the whole symphony was not completed until 22 July 1960. The première took place, three years later than hoped for, on 2 September 1960 at the opening of the Edinburgh International Festival (where the previous year Walton himself had conducted the First Symphony) with John Pritchard conducting the Royal Liverpool Philharmonic Orchestra.[9] Even after the first performance a few alterations were made to the score. As in the *Partita*, the orchestration included glockenspiel, xylophone, celesta and vibraphone. Like Vaughan Williams in his Eighth Symphony of 1956, Walton was making effective use of 'phones and 'spiels.

In the twenty-five-year gap since his First Symphony appeared, so much had changed in the musical climate and elsewhere. In that intervening period Vaughan Williams, with his Fifth and Sixth Symphonies (1943 and 1947), had contributed two outstanding works, while Bax's line of symphonies had long dried up with the Seventh (1939). Even the future of the symphony as a form of expression was being questioned, and writing a successor to his pre-war musical landmark posed a considerable challenge. Conscious of the difficulties he had experienced with the earlier work, he joked about being stuck in the last movement, of deciding to write the last movement first and performing it without the others. For better or for worse, some habits from scoring for films had stuck with him. Spike Hughes spotted a stopwatch as well as a metronome on his working table, and Roy Douglas observed that some sections of the new symphony (and other works) had been carefully timed.

Inevitably there were those listeners who expected something to match the fire and power of the First Symphony and they were disappointed. As one record reviewer wryly suggested, the trouble with Symphony No. 2 was

---

9 BBC Transcription Service recording 124474.

Symphony No. 1. In his programme note for the work's first Hallé perform-ances[10] John Warrack offered a vigorous apologia:

> Walton, though a personality of strongly drawn and set characteristics, could not expect to remain entirely unaffected by what was going on around him (i.e. Schoenbergian twelve-tone music and other developments such as aleatory or chance music). A man of high intellectual conscious-ness and refined sensibility, his response was defiance – but expressed in a subtle, wholly personal, and by no means hostile, way.

He even suggested that the new work was a great advance on its predecessor:

> The Second Symphony is incomparably lighter, more transparent and im-mediately accessible: the rhythmic vigour and the high-powered thrust of its themes in the outer movements give a sharp definition to its formal outline. These features alone would show it in a more favourable light; but we must also consider the nervous brilliance of its orchestral setting, which refers back to an earlier Walton. While the creative struggle was all too evident in the First, the Second reveals a fluency, indeed a virtuosity of speech. But more: with all its wor[l]dly polish and brilliance, the Symphony must be also considered a contribution to the progress of symphonic thought.

Walton, always a brilliant orchestrator – although he had never had a single formal lesson, nor played in an orchestra as Elgar had – had produced a virtuosic work. The first movement is full of pungent interplay between brass and strings, while the beautiful slow movement finds the composer at his most radiant. In an effort to play the atonalists at their own game, the finale – with its obligatory fugue – is a succession of ten short variations on a boldly proclaimed theme which happens to be a 12-note row. (A little earlier he had used serial techniques in the Coda to the Violin Sonata's Theme and Variations.) He surely appreciated the Symphony at its Edinburgh première being partnered with Berg's Violin Concerto. An old influence returns in the last movement where the solo horn passage in variation 9 is strongly reminis-cent of variation 4 in the 'Theme and Variations' movement of Prokofiev's Third Piano Concerto.

Susana Walton writes of her husband's disappointment at the Symphony's launch, but while it did not create a sensation as its predecessor had done, its reception was not wholly unfriendly. Noël Goodwin, in the *Musical Times*, wrote of it being 'enthusiastically received; it matched expectations but didn't exceed them in a characteristic style that then precluded the sort of impact his First Symphony made twenty-five years ago. I failed to sense much compul-sion of thought behind its facade of a brilliant orchestral technique, as there

---

10 21 and 22 March 1962, Lawrence Leonard conducting.

undeniably was in its predecessor.'[11] With rather more enthusiasm, Frank Howes concluded his (anonymous) review in *The Times* by saying: 'Here at last was something by which to remember this festival.' He well characterised Walton's post-war style by describing the 'unmistakable fingerprints, the electrical discharge of energy in short and rapid figures, the urgent melodies depending largely on the interval of the seventh, the tight but withal clear contrapuntal web, and the mastery of orchestral effect'. Of the performance he wrote that 'the excitement of the piled-up tension in the complex finale was realized so surely as to bring immediate acclamation from the audience'.[12]

Yet, when compared to the trends of contemporary music, Walton's was by certain sections of the critical press now increasingly being seen as outmoded and old-fashioned. Such comments as these of Wilfred Mellers in 1954 are not untypical: 'In some of his later music one deplored a tendency for the elegiac lyricism to relapse into a rather jaded romanticism: a yearning after Elgarian opulence which, in a hard world proffering only dusty answers, convinced neither us nor, one suspects, the composer.'[13] It was against such criticism that others like Robert Layton rose valiantly to his defence:

> Apart from the Elgar [string] concertos, Walton's essays in that medium are undoubtedly the finest works in this country during this present century. This itself is an outstanding achievement, and his output from *Façade* to the new Symphony offers abundant evidence that here is a talent far too prodigious for premature critical dismissal.[14]

However, at its première the Second Symphony did not generate enough interest for EMI to proceed with a planned recording: 'That despised Second Symphony of mine' he called it in interview.[15] The work was not properly appreciated until it was recorded in America in March 1961 by George Szell and the Cleveland Orchestra (who had earlier made a superb recording of the *Partita*). Walton already admired Szell's interpretation as in February he had flown to New York to hear him perform the symphony with his orchestra. On receiving an advance copy of the recording, he was quick to write to Szell from San Felice, Forio d'Ischia:

> This morning I received the record of your recording of my 2nd Symphony, and have already played it several times. Words fail me! It is a quite fantastic and stupendous performance from every point of view. Firstly it is

---

11 *Musical Times*, October 1960, 644.
12 *The Times*, 3 September 1960, reprinted in Frank Howes, *The Music of William Walton*, 41–2.
13 Wilfred Mellers, 'Walton and Twentieth-Century Opera', *Listener*, 25 November 1954, 933.
14 Robert Layton, 'Walton and his Critics', *Listener*, 29 March 1962, 577.
15 *Sunday Times*, 25 March 1962.

absolutely right musically speaking, and the virtuosity of the performance is quite staggering, especially the Fugato; but everything is phrased and balanced in an unbelievable way, for which I must congratulate you and your magnificent orchestra. I can only sink into banality and say that I thank you really and truly from the bottom of my heart, and for once this is not an empty phrase.[16]

So delighted was Walton with Szell's interpretation of the new symphony and other works that on Szell's death in 1970 he amended the dedication of the symphony from 'To the Royal Liverpool Philharmonic Society' to 'Commissioned by the Royal Liverpool Philharmonic Society and re-dedicated to the memory of George Szell'.

San Felice, from where Walton had written to Szell, was his third home on Ischia. The first, the Convento, had been too uncomfortable to serve as any more than a temporary residence. William and Susana's second home for eight years, Casa Cirillo, was another derelict building, a wine cellar that lacked a roof and electricity which they rebuilt and made habitable. Then in 1956 they bought a plot of land near Forio that backed on to the hills, and there, among the lava boulders, they eventually built their final home which they called *La Mortella* (the old name in Ischian dialect for that part of the hill, meaning literally 'the myrtle'). But before building that house, they converted two buildings on the property which, together with three other small houses, they rented to summer visitors as a way of supplementing their income and helping to finance their new home. (In 1958 Ursula and Ralph Vaughan Williams stayed in one of the houses, called *Villa Cristabella*, and Walton lent Vaughan Williams his piano which several men had to transport from house to house.) In 1956 they sold their London house (which had for a while been rented to Olivier) and became tax exiles, now living permanently abroad, but it was to be another six years before their new home was built and ready for them to move into. Susana Walton took particular delight in creating, with the help of the renowned landscape architect Russell Page, a splendid garden which today is open to the public three days a week.

Just before the Second Symphony was completed, Walton produced a cycle of six songs for tenor voice and guitar. The texts were various anonymous sixteenth- and seventeenth-century lyrics that Christopher Hassall selected and these were grouped under the title of *Anon. in Love*. The song-cycle seems to have come at the suggestion of Peter Pears to whom Walton wrote on 21 April 1956: 'I like the idea about the "one-man" opera & I'll see what Christopher [Hassall] thinks. . . . I'm all for some little songs with guitar. . . .'[17] In 1957 Britten had written his *Songs from the Chinese* for Peter

---

[16] Dated 11 May 1962, printed on the record sleeve of Columbia SAX2459.

[17] Christopher Headington, *Peter Pears*, 169.

Pears and the guitarist Julian Bream, and *Anon. in Love* was written for the same artists who gave the first performance in Ipswich on 21 June 1960 as part of that year's Aldeburgh Festival. It was dedicated to one of Walton's hostesses in Suffolk, Lilias Sheepshanks of Eyke. Julian Bream had drawn a diagram of the guitar fingerboard and showed Walton not only how the instrument was played – giving as well some idea of its dynamic range and colour – but also how to write the music down.[18] Walton took this all in and Bream found the guitar writing so good that he asked him to write something for solo guitar. Eleven years later he produced the *Five Bagatelles*.

Anon. in Love catches Walton in Puckish mood. The taxing opening vocal line to 'Fain would I Change that Note' begins on high held C sharp at odds with the firmly placed low B natural in the G major accompaniment which the singer seems almost resolutely to avoid. The second song, 'O Stay, Sweet Love', is gently teasing. While 'Lady, When I Behold the Roses' finds the lover in serious mood, Frank Howes aptly refers to the 'franker sauciness' of 'My Love in her Attire'. This playful mood persists throughout the last two songs. About ten years later he scored the cycle for voice and small orchestra: percussion (one player), harp and strings, preserving the delicacy of the guitar's accompaniment. It was first heard in this form in the Mansion House, London on 21 June 1971 with Robert Tear as soloist, and Harry Blech conducting the London Mozart Players.

Just before *Anon. in Love*, two minor occasional commissions were dispatched in 1959, a Queen's Fanfare for the monarch's entrance at a NATO parliamentary conference on 5 June, and a march for an ABC Television series based on Churchill's 'A History of the English Speaking Peoples'. A more important commission followed, as the dedication reads, 'To celebrate the 125th anniversary of the Huddersfield Choral Society and the 30th year of Sir Malcolm Sargent as its conductor'. This was the eighteen-minute *Gloria*, for three soloists, double mixed chorus and orchestra, first performed at Huddersfield on 24 November 1961 with soloists Marjorie Thomas, Richard Lewis and John Cameron, and the Royal Liverpool Philharmonic Orchestra. (The forces involved are the same as those required for Elgar's *Dream of Gerontius* which was also performed in the same concert.) Sargent also conducted its London première, on 18 January 1962 with the London Philharmonic Choir and Orchestra. The male soloists on that occasion were Ronald Dowd and Owen Brannigan. Frank Howes touched on a sore point when he wrote that 'the trouble with festive commissions is that from the nature of the case they call for something jubilant, and it may well be that these products of the fifties, with the exception of the opera and the concerto, have overdrawn on the strenuous emotions and the tense ejaculatory vein of

---

[18] BBC Radio 3, *Music Weekly*, 28 March 1982.

Walton's style to the detriment of his more lyrical and reflective vein.'[19] The *Gloria* is impressive in its command of voices and orchestra, suitably showy for the commissioned occasion, but ultimately not particularly memorable with its forced jubilation. Together with *In Honour of the City of London*, the *Gloria* has never really made any ground when *Belshazzar's Feast* has invariably been the first choice of choral societies. At the other end of the scale, also completed in 1961, was the unaccompanied carol *What Cheer?* that has found a more frequent place in Christmas carol services.

Four days after the première of the *Gloria*, Walton made a brief appearance at the Royal Festival Hall at one of the humorous Hoffnung Music Festivals to conduct – as the programme stated – an extract from *Belshazzar's Feast*. His appearance was far briefer than his audience expected. With the Festival choir and orchestra arrayed in front of him, with a flick of a fly swat he brought in the shout 'Slain!' – a moment that was delightfully parodied in Joseph Horowitz's *Horrortorio* that followed.

His sixtieth-birthday year brought its round of anniversary concerts and honours. The previous year he had been made Freeman of the borough of Oldham for which he made a rare return to the town of his birth. Now his adopted country of residence appointed him an Accademico Onorario di Santa Cecilia (Roma). In May he made his first visit to Canada, and in June a further visit to the United States where, in Los Angeles, he attended the first American performance of the *Gloria*.

Walton's next commission came from The Worshipful Company of Goldsmiths for the first City of London Festival in 1962. Perhaps encouraged by the success of *Anon. in Love*, he tackled another song-cycle with the texts again selected for him by Christopher Hassall. The poets ranged from Thomas Jordan, Charles Morris, Wordsworth and Blake to Anon. again, each of them relating to some aspect of London, the last the well-known 'Oranges and Lemons'. He had not written for voice and piano since his three Sitwell songs thirty years ago, and he told Alan Frank at OUP: 'I must say I find writing for the pfte very irksome and have spent a lot of time on No 1 which is really for orch.'[20] The cycle of six songs, taking its collective title of *A Song for the Lord Mayor's Table* from the first setting, was first performed on 18 July 1962 by his hoped-for Cressida, Elisabeth Schwarzkopf, with Gerald Moore at the piano. True to his instinct, eight years later Walton provided the cycle with an orchestral accompaniment. Although he called for a small orchestra, he could not resist a range of percussion requiring two players, and this new version was first heard at the City of London Festival on 7 July 1970 sung by Janet Baker, with George Malcolm conducting the English Chamber Orchestra. It was heard again on the last night of that year's Proms with Colin

19 Frank Howes, *The Music of William Walton*, 180.
20 23 February 1962, in Michael Kennedy, *Portrait of Walton*, 218.

Davis conducting and Elizabeth Bainbridge the soloist. This joyous song-cycle, while effective in its original form, is, as one would only expect from a composer more at home with the colours of the orchestra, the more resplendent in its revised dressing.

Another, very different request came from Granada Television for a Prelude and a series of call signs for test transmissions. In the end the call signs were not used but the Prelude, re-orchestrated for wind band by Gilbert Vinter, was recorded for regular transmission. It then became a *Prelude for Orchestra* under which title it received its first performance in 1977 from the Young Musicians' Symphony Orchestra conducted by James Blair. With a fine Elgarian trio, like the other TV-commissioned *March for the History of the English-speaking Peoples*, it is a rather sombre off-shoot of the coronation marches.

Walton was present on 9 October 1962 at a capacity Royal Festival Hall for an event that effectively drew to a close one of the most important episodes in his life. It was a concert to celebrate Dame Edith Sitwell's seventy-fifth birthday. This was almost Edith's last public appearance (she died in December 1964). The concert began with her reading some of her more recent poems. Peter Pears then sang *Still Falls the Rain*, Britten at the last moment being prevented by illness from accompanying him in his own setting. Finally Walton conducted a performance of *Façade*, with Irene Worth and Sebastian Shaw. The occasion reunited Walton with all the Sitwells for the last time, Sir Osbert by then frail and suffering from Parkinson's Disease, and they were photographed together.[21] Although like Osbert frail herself, Edith's critical pen still had plenty of bite. 'Wasn't poor Mr. Shaw *appalling*!' she wrote afterwards to Pears who with Lambert were the only reciters of *Façade* of whom she had really approved. 'At one moment, I and my whole family broke down and had hysterics.'[22] A month later Edith was the subject for the BBC Television programme *This Is your Life* but Walton did not make an appearance. He was now engaged on a work that looked back on another friendship.

In October 1960 Walton had accepted very loosely a commission from the Koussevitzky Foundation for an at first unspecified orchestral work that was soon being discussed as a Concerto Grosso. In December George Szell agreed to giving its world première in Cleveland, although in May 1961 Alan Frank was sounding out Walton about the possibility of its first performance being in England rather than America. In June Szell was asking for further news of the *Suite Concertante* as it was then being referred to, and by December, with Szell pressing for its completion in time for the 1962/3 season, Walton, realising that he would not have it ready in time, was now

---

[21] Osbert died in May 1969; Sacheverell in 1988.
[22] 11 October 1962. Richard Greene (ed.), *Selected Letters*, 444.

thinking of another new work, probably a set of variations, for the 150th anniversary of the Royal Philharmonic Society. 'As a sop' he would offer Szell the American première.

The RPS commission now displaced that from the Koussevitzy Foundation and resulted in one of Walton's finest post-war works. In it he chose to acknowledge his debt to Hindemith in a set of *Variations on a Theme by Hindemith*. If there had been any conscious model it may have been Bliss's *Meditations on a Theme by John Blow* first performed in 1955. In August 1961, OUP sent him a number of Hindemith scores and after some trouble in finding a suitable theme for variation treatment, he wrote to Alan Frank in December: 'I think I've at last decided on the Hindemith theme – the first 36 bars from the slow mov. of the Vlc. Con. . . . I believe it has possibilities – even a tone-row if one put in a D# in the 4th bar!' Work progressed fairly speedily. In January 1963 he was asking Frank for Hindemith's address. 'Now that the end is in sight I think I should write him & send him a score to see how he approves or disapproves my manipulations of his tune – don't you?'[23] On 7 February 1963 he wrote: 'I sent a couple of days ago ps. 95–100 & dispatch today ps. 101–103 (the End!).'[24] Two days later some mocking doubts set in: 'I feel ever so slightly gloomy about the work – the Coda I fear, may sound like the Salvation Army outside the "pub" on a cold & frosty Sun. morn. with a long Sullivanesque & Great Amen at the end.'[25] Almost a fortnight later there was still uncertainty: 'I must confess I find it a trifle dull. I don't think I've got far enough away from the Theme especially the form.'[26]

The whole of Walton's exposition of his 'Tema' follows note for note that of Hindemith's Cello Concerto of 1940, except that the solo cello's line has been distributed between different instruments. There are other interesting parallels: Hindemith's slow movement is itself in variation form, and there are many places in the *Variations* where Walton's and Hindemith's sound worlds are almost indistinguishable.

The work was premièred in the Royal Festival Hall on 8 March 1963, Walton conducting the Royal Philharmonic Orchestra. On 29 July 1963 there was grateful acknowledgement of a private recording of that performance,[27] from one craftsman to another:

Egregio Amico – Finally our criss-cross journeys came to an end and we could sit down in front of the exhaust of our gramophone and play your piece, score before us. Well, we had a half hour of sheer enjoyment. You wrote a beautiful score and we are extremely honoured to find the red

23 Walton to Alan Frank, 20 January 1963, OUP files.
24 Walton to Alan Frank, 7 February 1963, OUP files.
25 Walton to Alan Frank, 9 February 1963, OUP files.
26 Walton to Alan Frank, 15 February 1963, OUP files.
27 The première, which was broadcast, has been issued on CD on Carlton Classics 15656 91782 in the 'BBC Radio Classics' series.

carpet rolled out even on the steps to the back door of fame. I am particularly fond of the honest solidity of workmanship in this score – something that seems almost completely lost nowadays. Let us thank you for your kindness and for the wonderfully touching and artistically convincing manifestation of this kindness (even old Mathis is permitted to peep through the fence, which for a spectre like him seems to be some kind of resurrection after artificial respiration!) – I am glad that George Szell had a great (and well deserved) success with the piece in the States. I also shall put it on my programs as soon as possible. I wrote to the Oxford Press people that this could only be the case during the next season, i.e. starting autumn 1964, since I received the score at a time when all programs for 63/64 were settled and could not be changed. I hope this will be all right with you, and I shall do my best to become a worthy interpreter of WW.[28]

The reference to Mathis concerns a theme in the seventh variation that would seem to be from Hindemith's opera *Mathis der Maler*, a theme that Hindemith himself alluded to in the slow movement of the Cello Concerto (1940) and which Walton had already, no doubt unintentionally, hinted at in his music for *Christopher Columbus*. George Szell was granted US and Canadian premières as well as American exclusivity until February 1964. That year 1964 Szell added the *Hindemith Variations* to his two other impressive Walton recordings.[29]

During the 1960s Walton was once again a member of the BBC's Central Music Advisory Council that also included Tippett, Sargent and Jack Westrup, but his attendance was rare. During that decade he was also involved in much travelling, conducting exclusively his own works. In July 1963 he took *Belshazzar's Feast* (sung in Hebrew) to Jerusalem, Haifa and Tel Aviv. From Israel he flew on to America, conducting first the Chicago Symphony Orchestra at Ravinia Park and then on to New York for another concert. In 1964 he embarked on an extended tour of New Zealand and Australia, the first time he had visited either country, conducting twenty-four concerts between February and May. The highlight of the trip was several performances conducted by Joseph Post of *Troilus and Cressida* at the Adelaide Festival, with Marie Collier and Richard Lewis. On the tour Walton conducted the *Hindemith Variations*, the Cello Concerto, *Façade*, the two symphonies, the Violin Concerto and *Belshazzar's Feast*.[30] He had earlier

---

[28] In Frank Howes, *The Music of William Walton*, 54–5. Sadly, Hindemith was not to conduct the work. He died on 28 December 1963.

[29] Szell's recordings with the Cleveland Orchestra of the *Hindemith Variations*, *Partita* and Second Symphony have been released on CD, Sony MPK 46732.

[30] *Belshazzar's Feast* became very much his 'visiting card' in England, as, for example, at the Bach Choir's all-Walton concert at the Royal Festival Hall in May 1965, in August that year at the Commonwealth Arts Festival, also at the Festival Hall (BBC Transcription Service recording BB29, NSA B1334/1), and in March 1971 at the Royal Albert Hall's Centenary concert.

decided against conducting *Troilus*. 'I think it would be too much of a risk . . . as it would be my first attempt at conducting opera,' he wrote to Alan Frank. 'Presumably they have some capable conductors out there.'[31]

On his return the next composition was an anthem, *The Twelve*, that in its dedication looked back to his musical beginnings: 'To Christ Church, Oxford', adding a further dedication to its then incumbent Dean, Cuthbert Simpson. In the years following his undergraduate days, Oxford had conferred on him an honorary DMus and Christ Church had made him a honorary fellow. The anthem, first sung in Oxford on 16 May 1965 by the choir of Christ Church, was a setting of a text by W. H. Auden, Christopher Hassall having died from a heart attack two years before. Auden was an appropriate collaborator since he, like Walton, had been an undergraduate at Christ Church, and by coincidence after the war had rented a house at Forio in Ischia where for about ten years he was habitually to spend the spring and summer months. Although during the early stages of *Troilus and Cressida* Auden had been engaged on the libretto for Stravinsky's *The Rake's Progress*, because of his proximity on Ischia he had at least been able to offer some help with the last act of *Troilus*.

At about the same time that Walton was working on *The Twelve* and still in choir-boy mood, he composed a *Missa Brevis* for the choir of Coventry Cathedral. In August he conducted the complete *Façade* at its first Promenade performance, with Hermione Gingold and Russell Oberlin as reciters. Towards the end of the year he arranged *The Twelve* for orchestra in time for a broadcast concert on 2 January 1966 to celebrate the 900th anniversary of the foundation of Westminster Abbey. He himself conducted the London Philharmonic Choir and Orchestra in both *The Twelve* and the *Coronation Te Deum*.[32] Later that year Sargent conducted *The Twelve* at the Proms. Despite its short length of about twelve minutes, this tri-partite anthem is of considerable gravity and dramatic effect in its celebration of the apostleship of the twelve disciples, ending in a jubilant fugue of praise in 5/4 time. It can suitably be used as 'an Anthem for the Feast of any Apostle'.

Up till now Walton's health had not given much cause for concern, but during his visit to London for the Westminster Abbey anniversary concert a friend noticed that his breathing became unusually heavy after climbing steps and suggested that he visited a heart specialist. The examination revealed not heart trouble but cancer of the left lung which was straightway operated on in a London clinic. It was hoped that the climate of Ischia would bring about a steady recuperation. A regular smoker, he had already instructed Susana to throw away all his pipes. But after a few months a sharp pain in his left shoulder signalled the return of cancer. He was back in London for intensive

[31] Walton to Alan Frank, 20 January 1963, OUP files.
[32] BBC Sound Archives, T30808; NSA M687-688W.

cobalt ray treatment. The eleven weeks' course, for which he walked daily to the Middlesex Hospital, weakened him considerably. As Susana has written, he was haunted too 'by memories of the agony Alice Wimborne had suffered at the end of her life, . . . how she had gone literally black from lack of oxygen'.[33] When the treatment seemed to be making no improvement, the surgeon decided to double the dose which he promised, if it were not successful, would save him from a long and painful death. Fortunately, it had the desired effect and soon Walton was able to return to Ischia.

The operation and the heat treatment had interrupted work on a one-act comic opera he was writing for the Aldeburgh Festival. It had been commissioned by the Serge Koussevitzky Music Foundation (which had much earlier financed Britten's *Peter Grimes*) and was 'dedicated to the memory of Serge and Natalie Koussevitsky'. Its subject, one of Chekhov's vaudevilles, *The Bear*, had been another suggestion from Peter Pears, possibly a development of the idea for a 'one-man' opera about which they had corresponded. Russian vaudevilles were by and large adaptations of French farces that had originally been musical but from which the music element had in time dwindled away. The plot concerns a pretty widow, Popova, who is mourning the death of her (unfaithful) husband. Smirnov, a landowner, calls to claim settlement of a debt her husband had left. After much banter, argument and abuse, during which they stoop to calling each other names (from which comes the title of the work), they end up facing each other with loaded pistols (he having first to show her how to hold and fire one). But they cannot fire as they have fallen in love.

Walton's librettist was the writer, poet and critic Paul Dehn.[34] This proved to be a happy partnership that might have led to further things had it not been for Dehn's death in 1976. His method of working with Walton was similar to what Christopher Hassall's had been while working on *Troilus*:

> Our collaboration was at first purely postal. While Walton (on Ischia) drafted a reverently pruned version of the play's prose, I (from London) airmailed him two tentative arias in verse. They were acknowledged by a telegram misprinted as only Ischian postmistresses know how:
>
> PLENDID STOP BUT WHY NOT COME AND DISPOSE
> OF BEAR HERE RATR THAN BY CORRESPONDEUCE
> WEATHER ABSOLUTELY DIVANE – WILLIAM
>
> The rest of the libretto was written at the Walton villa in sweltering autumn sunshine. From the outset I thought I had detected in the play occasional

---

33 Susana Walton, *Behind the Façade*, 200.
34 Paul Dehn was the librettist of Lennox Berkeley's *A Dinner Engagement* (1954) and his one-act *Castaway* which shared its première with *The Bear* at the 1967 Aldeburgh Festival. In 1972 he provided words for an additional verse for the three-part song *Put off the Serpent Girdle* discarded during the revisions of *Troilus and Cressida* and now being published for separate performance.

opportunities to accommodate that flair for musical parody which Walton had first unleashed in *Façade*. . . . When the lyrics were done and he had slotted them into a jointly re-edited version of Walton's initial prose-draft, it was he who realised that parody could validly be made the warp, so to speak, of the opera's woof – the woof being purely Waltonian. . . . We sub-titled the opera 'An Extravaganza', which the dictionary defines as 'a wild burlesque or farce; an irregular or fanciful composition'; and Walton, with a muttered 'It's no good pretending it's *The Three Sisters*!', sat down fanci-fully to compose in a music-room which is soundproofed, partly to shut out the stentorian tenor-talent of his head gardener, Antonio, and partly to shut *in* the creative noises made by Walton himself who admits that, among composers, he is the world's worst pianist and the world's second-worst singer.[35]

The Bear, finished on 30 April 1967 at Ischia, was first staged on 3 June at that year's Aldeburgh Festival, in the Jubilee Hall with Monica Sinclair, Norman Lumsden and John Shaw, and the English Chamber Orchestra conducted by James Lockhart (whom Walton then recommended for the vacant position as Musical Director of Welsh National Opera). The same performers recorded the work in the presence of the composer for EMI about two months later after first taking it to London at the Sadler's Wells Theatre. Lasting just under fifty minutes, it reveals the sophisticated side of Walton's *Façade* humour. There are many allusions to, or parodies of, other composers and their works, often more stylistic rather than thematic references, although the opening – that is not far from that comic masterpiece, Puccini's *Gianni Schicchi* – contains in its first bars an unmistakable reference to Britten's *A Midsummer Night's Dream*.[36] Paul Dehn wrote that

> the composer is adamant in refusing to divulge the specific musical sources of these parodies, though the critics (after Aldeburgh and Sadler's Wells performances in 1967) had a high old speculative time identifying them. They are there, like an Elgarian enigma, for the interested listener to probe if he will; and if they are not recognised, they can still be enjoyed as one enjoys the often mystifying herbs that bring character to a soup.[37]

The parodies probably provided more fun for Walton than for the general listener who, with no loss of enjoyment, may not even be aware of them just as when, for example, towards the end of *A Midsummer Night's Dream* Bottom awakes, Britten makes an allusion to Holst's *The Perfect Fool* that has

---

[35] From 1967 record sleeve-note for HMV Angel SAN192, re-printed for Chandos ABT1052.
[36] *The Bear* was paired with *A Midsummer Night's Dream* for the English Chamber Orchestra's performances in Montreal at Expo '67 where, at Britten's instigation, he and Walton met for lunch.
[37] EMI sleeve-note, 1967.

largely gone by unrecognised. But, after his two conflicts with copyright, one parody did trouble Walton. As *The Bear* contained a two bar reference to Strauss's *Salome* it was felt proper to consult the publishers who in turn felt that the composer's heirs should be asked. It started to look as if again some settlement would have to be made, but then Alan Frank wrote to Walton: 'I spoke to Dr Roth whose *private* advice was for us to go ahead as if we had not asked for permission and of course with no acknowledgement. Better not mention it also, so that no comment leaks into the press. I wonder how many people will in fact notice the reference.'[38]

In 1970 Walton conducted *The Bear* for BBC Television and two years later it was staged once more at Aldeburgh for his seventieth-birthday celebrations. Hugely enjoyable, it has since enjoyed regular performances, lending itself well as one half of a double-bill. Characteristically, Walton could not resist calling up an impressive range of percussion that includes the cassa chiara, three blocks, a whip, a rattle, a vibraphone, crotales (a variety of antique cymbal) and bongos.

To the many honours that Walton had received over the years was added in 1967 the Order of Merit. The following year he responded with some difficulty to a commission from the New York Philharmonic Orchestra for its 125th anniversary with the *Capriccio Burlesco*. At first called *Philharmonic Overture N.Y. '68* (and announced as such) it was completed at Ischia on 5 September and its première was conducted by its dedicatee, André Kostelanetz,[39] in New York on 7 December 1968. Colin Davis gave the first London performance at the Royal Festival Hall with the BBC Symphony Orchestra on 5 February 1969. This seven-minute overture is full of Waltonian fireworks but in the final analysis it sounds just a shade too laboured. A criticism raised in some quarters against the post-war works was that Walton was repeating himself and that his style was not advancing with the changing times. Such a viewpoint could be fairly countered by pointing out that those critics were in fact objecting to Walton's *musical language* not having changed – and why should it, any more than a writer or painter, having found his preferred mode of expression, should be expected to shift his ground? Very much aware of this criticism, at the time of his seventieth birthday he argued his case:

> It's always been a nightmare for me, and the more I go on, the more difficult it seems to become. If one's not careful, one tends to be repetitive; an idea comes into your head and you find it's the same one you had ten years ago. Then I envisage the headline 'Walton makes no progress.' I do believe

---

38 Alan Frank to Walton, 10 April 1967, OUP files.
39 Kostelanetz had already recorded *Façade Suite No. 1* in February 1957 and the *Johannesburg Festival Overture* in December 1959, both with the New York Philharmonic, and was to record *Capriccio Burlesco* with his own orchestra in July 1969.

that a composer must stay true to himself. I don't believe in trying to keep up with every change in fashion as Stravinsky did. It's like having your face lifted. I'm sure my critical friends will kill me for saying that, but I'm sure it's true.[40]

Yet recurring features in his works gave rise to the accusation of him just dipping into the same old box of tricks. Tippett remembered how Britten, staying with him in the 1940s and listening to a broadcast of the Violin Concerto, 'with his incredible ear, was able to sit down at the piano immediately afterwards and identify those melodic and harmonic mannerisms that recur in all the Walton scores'.[41] Kenneth Clark felt that after Walton's marriage, having found an ideal retreat on Ischia, 'gradually tension and emotion went out of his life, and then out of his music'.[42] John Amis put it succinctly when he wrote with regard to the later works that 'William's hand had lost nothing of its cunning but the fire had gone out.'[43] Walton himself was only too aware of the problems brought by early success. In 1939, when he was only thirty-seven, he had written: 'Today's white hope is tomorrow's black sheep. I advise all serious composers to die at the age of 37.'[44] A more valid criticism was that his invention now was not always on so high a level. His *Capriccio Burlesco* is a case in point. His friend and publisher Alan Frank, in a record sleeve-note, excused it as 'an elegant and witty trifle, unproblematic and *insouciant* to a degree that is unusual, if not positively indecent, among the formidable tense complexity of most new music of the '60s and '70s. Escapist? Certainly, but executed with irresistible allure.'[45]

In 1968 Walton returned to the world of films after a gap of nearly fourteen years with a commission to write what was to be his penultimate film score, for Guy Hamilton and Harry Saltzman's *The Battle of Britain*. A few years earlier there had been the suggestion that he and Malcolm Arnold should collaborate on David Lean's 1962 epic, *Lawrence of Arabia*. Initially Lean had wanted Arnold, after his Oscar-winning score for *The Bridge on the River Kwai*, while the producer Sam Spiegel had apparently put forward Walton's name. The compromise was that Walton would compose the march and Arnold would write all the dramatic music as well as conducting the final score. One afternoon the two composers sat through a rough cut of the film after having enjoyed rather too good a lunch. Neither was receptive to what they saw and, although Walton felt he needed the money, they decided that it

---

[40] Arnold in conversation with Sheridan Morley, BBC1 East, 25 September 1984. Interview with Alan Blyth in *Radio Times*, 23 March 1972, 15.
[41] Michael Tippett, *Those Twentieth Century Blues*, 214.
[42] *The Other Half*, 192–3.
[43] John Amis, *Amiscellany: My Life, My Music*, Faber & Faber 1985, 190.
[44] Quoted in sleeve-note for Lyrita SRCS49.
[45] *Ibid.* Alan Frank wrote a number of sleeve-notes for EMI recordings of Walton's works.

did not need any music and turned the offer down.[46] Nevertheless, they were to work together on *The Battle of Britain*, but with an outcome that neither of them could have foreseen.

By this time attitudes towards the use of music in films had shifted. Commercial and financial considerations, rather than artistic ones, now seemed to dominate the industry. Just as Bernard Herrmann's score for Alfred Hitchcock's 1966 *Torn Curtain* had been rejected because the studio wanted a catchy title song that would sell thousands of records,[47] so three years later Walton's *Battle of Britain* score, in part orchestrated with the assistance of Malcolm Arnold[48] who conducted the Denham sound-track recording sessions, was rejected by United Artists largely because there was not enough music to fill a planned LP. To conclude this sorry story, without informing Walton (whose name was apparently not known to those in charge of the film's distribution), United Artists then approached another film composer whose name was well known to American studios, Ron Goodwin, asking him to supply a score in place of Walton's. The result was a forgettable bag of film-score clichés. Goodwin himself has told his side of the story:[49]

> The first thing I heard about *The Battle of Britain* was when the producer, Benjamin Fisz, called me and asked me to go and see him in his office in Mayfair. When I got there he said, 'I'd like you to write the score for a film of The Battle of Britain. We commissioned Sir William Walton to write the music for this film' – and I can remember his words quite clearly – 'but you know,' he said, 'he's getting on a bit and he hasn't been able to finish it, and what he's written the Americans don't like anyway, and so I'm going to ask you to write another score.'

Goodwin took legal advice and eventually agreed, on the condition that only his score was used. The matter seemed settled until about a week before the date set for recording his score Harry Saltzman, the executive producer, rang him. He had heard from Laurence Olivier (one of the star-studded cast) who was annoyed that Walton's music was not being used and was demanding that, unless some of it was included, his own name be taken off the film credits. 'We can't afford to upset him,' Saltzman told Goodwin. 'I'll tell you what,' he said, 'the scene that we could use his music in is the Battle in the Air over London. You write your music for that scene and whichever one we like best is the one we'll use.' And as Goodwin said himself, 'I was stupid enough to believe that!'

46 The score was written by Maurice Jarre with orchestrations by Gerard Schurmann.
47 Donald Spoto, *The Life of Alfred Hitchcock*, Collins 1983, 491.
48 Some sections of the score were even expanded and re-scored by Arnold, including the last third of the *Battle in the Air*. See *The Music of Malcolm Arnold: A Catalogue*, compiled by Alan Poulton, Faber Music 1986, 156.
49 In BBC Radio 4, *Cinema 100 – The British Film Studios*, a series of six programmes presented by John Huntley.

So, at the insistence of Olivier one section of Walton's score, the 'Battle in the Air',[50] was retained. These five minutes mark a return to vintage Walton and they form the core of an otherwise routine film that was first shown in London on 15 September 1969. Only later was the remainder of the score retrieved from United Artists, and a twelve-minute suite made by Colin Matthews. This was first performed on 10 May 1985 at Bristol, Carl Davis conducting the Bournemouth Symphony Orchestra. What then emerged was that it also included one of Walton's most glorious marches, a march almost to out-Walton any that he had written before. (Although its première had been announced for the Last Night of the 1969 Proms, two days before the film's opening, in the event it was not played but oddly enough it was used to considerable effect in the film's trailer.) In the trio of the March (and else-where in the score) there are pointed references to Siegfried's horn call, a Wagnerian allusion to match those in *The First of the Few*. In 1990 three back-up reels of tape from the original recordings sessions were recovered from a sound engineer's garage and a number of takes totalling almost twenty-one minutes of music restored for CD release.[51]

His last score for the cinema, also in 1969, was for a film of the National Theatre's production of Chekhov's *Three Sisters*. As it was both directed by and starred Olivier, it seemed only natural that Walton should be turned to for the music. But, while serving its purpose well enough, the score is musically disappointing. The opening titles oddly announce: 'Main musical themes arranged and composed by Sir William Walton O.M.' with 'other arrange-ments by Derek Hudson and Gary Hughes'. But the 'themes' of the three sections of music turn out to be almost exclusively treatments of the Russian National Anthem, Mendelssohn's *Song without Words* Op. 19 No. 1 (a snatch of which is played by one of the characters in an early scene) and, in a dream sequence, a waltz lifted from his short 1935 ballet, *The First Shoot*, the complete score of which was at that time lost. After the first showing of *Three Sisters* in August 1970 in Venice where it had been chosen to represent Britain at the Venice Festival, it came to London in November. With a cast that also included Joan Plowright, Alan Bates, Derek Jacobi, Louise Purnell, Jeanne Watts, Sheila Reid and Ronald Pickup, it preserves Olivier's Old Vic production and his own performance as the old doctor Chebutikin, but it is

---

50 Conducted on the film soundtrack by Malcolm Arnold. Strangely enough, some prints of the film have Walton's march restored to the end titles, but not on the commercial video release.

51 *Battle of Britain Soundtrack*, RCD 10747, a multi-media CD-ROM containing the soundtrack score by Ron Goodwin incorporating Walton's *Battle in the Air*, followed by the restored Walton takes that include an alternative take of *Battle in the Air*. The tape restoration was done by James Fitzpatrick. The CD-ROM also includes a film clip of the complete distributors' trailer for the film.

too stagey to be seen as anything other than a filmed version of a stage production.

In January 1969 Walton was invited to Texas as guest conductor of the Houston Symphony Orchestra. In New York he conducted two concerts with the American Symphony Orchestra and, with his engagements completed, he fulfilled a desire to visit Mexico City. But he caught 'flu there and had to cut short his stay and fly back to London. Later that year he settled down to a new orchestral work, the *Improvisations on an Impromptu of Benjamin Britten*. The theme he chose was the soloist's unaccompanied entry in the third movement, 'Impromptu', of Britten's Piano Concerto. The *Improvisations* came as near as possible to putting a seal on a relationship between the two composers that was at best uneasy, and yet founded on mutual respect – certainly on Walton's part. Tippett tells how, at a lunch organised by Edith Sitwell, Walton had asked him if he had seen Britten's latest opera, *The Rape of Lucretia*, and on hearing that he had not immediately telephoned to Glyndebourne for tickets that afternoon and took him to see it.[52] At the time of Britten's fiftieth birthday in 1963, Walton paid a handsome private tribute to Britten in a letter he wrote on 23 November:

> You must almost by now be suffering from a surfeit of adulation & praise, so I won't add to it. All the same I should like to tell you, that I celebrated your birthday in my own way by playing my favourite works – Spring Symphony – Nocturne & War Requiem – each in its different way a masterwork, particularly the latter – a non-stop masterpiece without blemish – in fact, on a par with the two great Requiems of the 19th century, or for that matter, any other century.
>
> In the last years your music has come to mean more & more to me – it shines out as a beacon (how banal I'm becoming!) in, to me at least, a chaotic & barren musical world & I am sure it does for thousands of others as well.[53]

Although the *Improvisations* had been commissioned by Dr Ralph Dorfman in memory of his first wife, it bore a multiple dedication to the 'San Francisco Symphony Orchestra, Josef Krips, Conductor and Music Director, in memory of Adeline Smith Dorfman'. In June 1967 Walton had been approached by the San Francisco orchestra for a work and at the same time asked to suggest a suitable fee. Five thousand dollars for 12–15 minutes of music, came the business-like reply. He approached the work with some reluctance, however. He wrote to Alan Frank:

> Yes, I suppose you had better sign the new agreement on my behalf – but make it a work around 15 mins. But anyone will be lucky to get anything,

52 Michael Tippett, *Those Twentieth Century Blues*, 189.
53 Donald Mitchell and Philip Reed (eds), *Letters from a Life*, 202.

judging by the way this overture [*Capriccio Burlesco*] is working out. It will, I fear have to be burn't & I must make a restart. It's too bad even for A[ndré]. K[ostelanetz]. In fact, I [am] most depressed & seem to find it almost impossible to find a good idea.[54]

Variation form was in many ways the easiest one to adopt and the work was temporarily known as *Elegiac Variations*. But on what theme? Alan Frank kept up kind but gentle pressure by reminding him: 'You should know that Joe Krips is retiring from the San Francisco Symphony Orchestra at the end of the 1969/70 season (and being replaced by Ozawa). This means that if by any chance you do get around to writing the Elegiac Variations and not in time for 1968/9, it would be his last season, which might be a rather good thing.'[55] In time he hit upon the theme from Britten's Piano Concerto and in September 1968 he wrote to Britten, asking his permission to use the theme in variation form, just as Britten himself had done. (In the Concerto the 'Impromptu' is a passacaglia with seven variations: Walton treats the theme to five improvisations.) Over a week later Britten replied warmly: 'Of course you may "vary" that tune in the 3rd movement of the Pft. Concerto – with the greatest pleasure. Perhaps it will be my way of going down into the future! – anyway, I feel very honoured.'[56] As a person who always kept a watchful eye on financial matters, Walton was disgusted to learn that Britten's publishers were expecting payment for his use of the theme. 'Not that it will soften their hearts,' he wrote to Alan Frank, 'you could however tell B. & H. that Schott's allowed me to use the theme of the H[indemith]. Vars. for nowt – & it's about 3 times as long as Ben's. Anyhow perhaps it will be as well before doing anything for me to see if I'm going to finish the piece or not!'[57]

Walton was now increasingly seeing new works in terms of timed lengths. 'I've dispatched another 10ps of the Vars.,' he wrote to Alan Frank in October 1969. 'We are now about halfway having reached 6' – 10" including the Theme! So there's only 6 or so [minutes] to go, but of course it becomes more difficult to deal as one proceeds. There is only one interval in the whole theme & we are all sick of that already. However we'll see.'[58] In November the title was changed to *Improvisations on an Impromptu of Benjamin Britten* and the first performance was given by its dedicatees in San Francisco on 14 January 1970. It was first heard in Britain at the Snape Maltings on 27 June 1970 when Charles Groves conducted the Royal Liverpool Philharmonic Orchestra.[59] Krips took it to the Royal Festival Hall, London on 20 October 1970 with the London Philharmonic Orchestra. Although it was included in

54 Walton to Alan Frank, 29 December 1967, OUP files.
55 Alan Frank to Walton, 13 May 1968, OUP files.
56 Benjamin Britten to Walton, 22 September 1968, OUP files.
57 Walton to Alan Frank, 31 October 1968, OUP files.
58 Walton to Alan Frank, 21 October 1969, OUP files.
59 A recording of this performance exists in the BBC Sound Archives, T33626.

Walton's seventieth-birthday Festival Hall concert two years later, it has not found its way into the more general repertoire. No work of Walton can be dismissed out of hand, and the *Improvisations*, as one might expect, has many pages of brilliance. Indeed, Walton turns Britten's theme, that John Evans has described as 'a somewhat curious invention of rising and falling scales in intervals of augmented seconds and semitones',[60] into a thing of mystery and fascination. Yet the work as a whole lacks the variety of the *Hindemith Variations*, its coda sounding forced and hollow. Could it be that the warmth of friendship between two composers so evident in the *Hindemith Variations* is here noticeable by its absence?

In 1970, as well as contributing a Theme (for Variations) for Cello Solo towards a musical anthology entitled 'Music for a Prince' (Charles), he fulfilled Julian Bream's wish by writing something for solo guitar. Using the fingerboard plan that he had been given for *Anon. in Love*, he produced the *Five Bagatelles for Guitar* of which Bream considered the guitar writing to be even more imaginative and mature than that of the song-cycle. Malcolm Arnold, who was staying over Christmas at Ischia, observed Walton's painfully slow progress with the *Bagatelles*. All he had down on paper were six notes of the first *Bagatelle* that were just the open notes of the guitar. A week or so later he had got no further. 'You know, I've been worrying about this very much,' he remarked one day. 'I'm wondering if when he begins they'll think he's tuning the bloody thing up.'[61] Walton later added a dedication on the manuscript 'to Malcolm Arnold, with admiration and affection for his 50th birthday' (1971). The following year Arnold returned the compliment by dedicating his overture *The Fair Field* to 'William Walton with the greatest esteem and affection'. His Seventh Symphony, completed in 1973, was partly written while staying at Ischia. The two composers had much in common, both in character and musically. As Piers Burton-Page, Arnold's biographer, has pointed out, 'they shared the trials of writing film music; they loved Italy, Italians and Italian food; each had flirted with jazz, as well as with Schoenberg; and they regarded humour as a distinctly plausible musical ingredient'. The rogue in *Scapino* was well matched by the cheeky street urchin in Arnold's overture *Beckus the Dandipratt*, first performed in 1946.

As the creative process became more arduous and inspiration rarer, it was easier to rework existing works, and so he re-scored *A Song for the Lord Mayor's Table* and *Anon. in Love* for orchestra, and, with Arnold's assistance, he turned his String Quartet into the *Sonata for Strings*. In the same way, to fulfil a commission from the Greater London Council for the twenty-fifth

---

60 'The Concertos', in *The Britten Companion*, edited by Christopher Palmer, Faber & Faber 1984, 413.

61 Malcolm Arnold in interview with John Amis in *Portrait of Walton*, BBC Radio 3, broadcast 4 June 1977. In BBC 2's *A Portrait of Malcolm Arnold* (1990). Arnold was insistent that there were six *Bagatelles*, but only five were published.

anniversary of the opening of the Royal Festival Hall, the *Bagatelles* became the *Varii Capricci* for orchestra[62] which André Previn and the London Symphony Orchestra premièred in that hall on 4 May 1976. This time new to the percussion line-up are claves (two cylindrical hardwood sticks), noticeable in the restful central *Alla Cubana* movement that also contains one of Walton's most beguiling tunes. Two lively movements frame three slower ones in siesta mood. Walton subsequently rewrote the last movement by lengthening it and effectively doubling its duration.[63]

The remainder of his new works in the 1970s was a handful of fanfares and several short choral works, either unaccompanied or with organ: the Christmas carol *All This Time* (1970); a *Jubilate Deo* written for the 1972 English Bach Festival; a short *Birthday Greeting to Herbert Howells* (an eight-bar greeting in short score only for his eightieth birthday, completed on 22 September 1972 with the message: 'Many Happy Returns! This I fear is a very inadequate return for your beautiful "grace" at No. 10 for my 70th!'); an *Anniversary Fanfare* for EMI's seventy-fifth anniversary concert in 1973; the motet *Cantico del Sole* commissioned by Lady Mayer (wife of Sir Robert) for the 1974 Cork International Choral Festival; a *Magnificat* and *Nunc Dimittis* for the 900th anniversary of Chichester Cathedral; a television *Fanfare* to mark the opening of the National Theatre in 1976; a *Roaring Fanfare* for the inauguration of the Lion Terraces at London Zoo in 1976; an *Antiphon* for St. Paul's Church, Rochester, New York; another Christmas carol, *King Herod and the Cock* (1977) that charms with its simplicity and was first heard at the traditional King's College Chapel Christmas Eve Festival of Nine Lessons and Carols that year; title music for BBC TV's series of Shakespeare plays (1977); and a hundredth-birthday *Salute to Sir Robert Mayer* (1979).

Spring 1971 brought more travelling when, at the invitation of the London Symphony Orchestra, he joined Previn and the LSO on the first part of their tour of Russia and the Far East, with performances under Previn of the First Symphony in Leningrad and Moscow. Ever since making his outstanding recording of the First Symphony in 1966, Previn had become one of Walton's most devoted champions. Walton's seventieth birthday the following year was widely celebrated. One of the highlights was the Festival Hall concert, again

---

62 Walton had wanted Ashton to devise a ballet using the *Bagatelles*, but Ashton had been hesitant. Under some pressure to provide a new work for the *Britain Salutes New York* Festival at the Metropolitan Opera House in 1983, he eventually choreographed *Varii Capricci* 'out of friendship for Willie', with David Hockney's set based on Walton's garden at Ischia. 'But then he went and died on me,' having only a few hours earlier completed a short nine-bar coda at Ashton's request.

63 The revised finale was first heard in a broadcast from Cardiff, recorded by Owain Arwel Hughes conducting the BBC Welsh Symphony Orchestra on 28 January 1981, but not relayed until 21 July.

with Previn and the LSO, on the eve of the actual day.[64] Before the concert started, Previn announced from the rostrum that he and the orchestra had been promised a Third Symphony. Then followed six musical birthday telegrams, from Richard Rodney Bennett, Malcolm Arnold, Thea Musgrave, Nicholas Maw, Robert Simpson and Peter Maxwell Davies. Each composer, apart from Richard Rodney Bennett, conducted a minute-long treatment of 'Happy Birthday' that contained humorous allusions to one or other of Walton's better-known works. The concert proper then continued with the *Improvisations*, the Viola Concerto (with Menuhin), and – inevitably – *Belshazzar's Feast*. Walton restricted his conducting to the Viola Concerto. As he said himself, conducting *Belshazzar's Feast* in London for his previous birthday

> nearly knocked me flat, so I decided this time to confine myself to some of the less exacting pieces. It's not just the problem of keeping all those forces together. It's also the question of keeping oneself going, and at 70 I think that sort of work is best left to a younger man. Besides, I've only got one lung and it's too tough for me.[65]

Previn and the LSO went into the EMI studios the next day to record *Belshazzar* for release with the *Improvisations* which had been committed to tape almost a fortnight earlier.

On the birthday itself a dinner party was given at 10 Downing Street by the Prime Minister, Edward Heath.[66] Later that year, on 28 July, Walton was fêted at Aldeburgh with performances of *The Bear* and a staging by the Royal Ballet of *Siesta* and *Façade*, both choreographed by Frederick Ashton and the latter danced for the first time to the Sitwell verses which were recited by Peter Pears. In September an all-Walton Promenade concert was especially notable for the inclusion of Act II from *Troilus and Cressida*, Previn conducting.

Over the years Walton had conducted authoritative recordings of his own works for the gramophone, and in April 1970 he had made his last studio appearance, for the enterprising Lyrita company.[67] In 1973 he made his last public conducting appearance when he directed a fiftieth-anniversary performance of *Façade* at the Aeolian Hall on 12 June with soloists Mary

---

64 The whole concert was broadcast live by BBC Radio 3 and the first half was shown on BBC 2 on 2 April.

65 Interview with Alan Blyth, *Radio Times*, 23 March 1972, 15.

66 The guests included Queen Elizabeth the Queen Mother, Arthur Bliss, Benjamin Britten, Kenneth Clark, Lord Goodman, Herbert Howells, Henry Moore, Laurence Olivier, Lionel Tertis, and three people whose concern had been his health: Dr. Jean Shanks, John Hunt (his London general practitioner) and Sir Thomas Sellers who had operated on him.

67 *Scapino*, *The Quest* Suite, *Sinfonia Concertante* (with Peter Katin), *Capriccio Burlesco*, *Portsmouth Point*, *Siesta* and *Music for Children*, all reissued on SRCD224.

Thomas and Derek Hammond-Stroud, and members of the London Sinfonietta. But the most important project of that decade was the revival in 1976 at Covent Garden of *Troilus and Cressida*. The opera, with some revisions and cuts, had already been revived at Covent Garden on 23 April 1963. On that occasion Marie Collier sang Cressida, André Turp Troilus and John Lanigan Pandarus, and once again it was conducted by Sargent (who died in 1967). But ten years later Walton was much taken by the singing of Janet Baker and, with her in mind, he revised the part of Cressida to accommodate her mezzo voice – which involved in many places transposing down the vocal line as well as reshaping it, and making further changes elsewhere. The result of all the revisions made since the publication of the vocal score in 1954 was to reduce the overall time from about 144 minutes to 126 minutes.[68]

It had been on his way to see the 1963 production of *Troilus* that Christopher Hassall collapsed and died. As if *Troilus* were fated, just before rehearsals were due to start in 1976, André Previn, who was to have conducted, had to withdraw because of bursitis. Lawrence Foster gallantly stepped into the gap. EMI, who were going to record the performances 'live' for release on LP, quibbled over the choice of Troilus, but eventually a fine cast, that included Richard Cassilly, Gerald English, Benjamin Luxon and Richard Van Allan, was assembled. The first of six performances was on 12 November 1976. While the singing and playing did much to redeem the opera, the production was let down by sets that spoke only too clearly of tight budgets. Nevertheless, interviewed on BBC Radio 3, Walton seemed delighted: 'It was a very special evening for me because I've been waiting for the last twenty years and more to get this opera vindicated. Of course, Janet Baker to me is so beautiful on the stage, and the way she acts and moves is really wonderful, and her singing is divine: there is no other word for it. And it just made me cry.' Janet Baker for her part remembered Walton's 'tremendously child-like gratitude for the fact that the piece was going on and for the fact that the opera house was full for it'.[69]

What alarmed many of those who saw Walton attending the performances of *Troilus* was how frail he had become. 'At the end he could hardly stand on his feet, and twice lost his balance and fell on the floor of the hotel.'[70] At a celebratory meal after the final performance he collapsed. His doctor, fearing a mild stroke, recommended a brain scan.[71] An examination revealed instead

---

68 The most substantial revisions were cuts in Act I from pages 29 to 37 (vocal score), a long passage with Calkas followed by the voice of the oracle, and from pages 107 to 110, abbreviating the report of Antenor's capture. Opera North's production in 1995 restored the original soprano rôle and reinstated a few cuts, adding about four minutes to the running time. Opera North also recorded the work for Chandos Records Ltd.

69 BBC Radio 3, *Music Weekly*, 28 March 1992.

70 Susana Walton, *Behind the Façade*, 223.

71 Reviewing Michael Kennedy's *Portrait of Walton* in *Music and Musicians*, October

that his blood circulation had become severely restricted. He returned to Ischia for a long period of rest under Susana's careful supervision.

Composition was made increasingly difficult in his last years by failing eyesight, and as ever, as he wrote to his publisher and friend Alan Frank, 'I'm desperate to find a tune'. He had lost much weight and cataracts in his eyes made it necessary for him to use a powerful magnifying glass when working on a score. But he did not give up. Several projects were considered and rejected, among them the Third Symphony on which little more than a start had been made, and a request in 1977 for a piece for concert band for the American Bandmasters Association. In 1979 there came a request that revived hope. It was for an *a cappella* work to be performed at the 1982 Llandaff Festival. 'I feel it may be just the thing to "turn me on",' he wrote to Christopher Morris of OUP on 2 March. The commission fee was £3,000. Christopher Cory, artistic director of the Festival, was anxious to receive the work, but he had his hopes slightly dampened at the start when Walton wrote to him: 'What really worries me is the impasse I seem to have reached with my composing, but I am counting on the Llandaff commission to set me off again.'[72] Walton felt that a Latin text would be more suitable and Cory suggested three odes by Horace for which he provided English translations of his own. By August 1980 Walton felt inclined to set the translations rather than the originals: 'I think it would be a help to my getting going.' But by December, Morris was writing to Cory: 'Sir William telephoned last night to say that he made no progress with Horace, in spite of your lucid translations. He said he now feels like doing something more festive and hankered after the 150th Psalm. I said it would have to be accompanied and suggested brass, which clearly appealed to him.'[73] However, in October 1981 Morris had to inform Roy Bohana of the Welsh Arts Council: 'I feel very unsure about the commission. William is struggling to write a work for the Washington National Symphony and has only completed a few minutes of music. The first performance of this work was supposed to have been on the 15th September and has now been postponed until the end of January.'[74]

The orchestral work on which he was labouring with such difficulty was for the distinguished Russian cellist and conductor Mstislav Rostropovich. The two had met in Russia and at Aldeburgh and became good friends. Walton reminded Rostropovich that while he had played the cello concertos

1989, 49, Lewis Foreman wrote: 'I was told by an eminent neurologist [Dr Michael Kremer] that brain scans taken in the last years of Walton's life showed that the centre of the brain was completely hollow. It was a triumph of personality, said the famous doctor admiringly, that Walton was still able to compose at all.'

[72] Christopher Cory to Christopher Morris, 3 April 1979, quoting from a letter he had received from Walton, OUP files.

[73] 10 December 1980, OUP files.

[74] 12 October 1981, OUP files.

of most composers he had not played his. So they struck a deal that if Walton were to write for him a new work, the cellist would play both the new and 'the old one'. It was not a concerto that he eventually wrote for Rostropovich but instead from 1979 until 1980 he worked on a six-minute *Passacaglia* for solo cello that, after some delay, was first played at the Royal Festival Hall on 16 March 1982 by its dedicatee who sadly seems never to have fulfilled the other half of his bargain. Nevertheless, for him and the National Symphony Orchestra of Washington DC,[75] Walton wrote a taut 5½-minute *Prologo e Fantasia* that its dedicatees premièred at the Royal Festival Hall on 20 February 1982. Walton was there to hear it. An unattributed note on the score provides a useful description of the work:

> There are three sections. The first forms the *Prologo (Lento maestoso)*, its mood slightly reminiscent of the French Overture. The *Fantasia* opens briskly with characteristic Waltonian energy, and leads, after a climax, into the thematically connected final section *Fuga finta* (or 'make-believe fugue'). Opening enigmatically with only shadowy reference to implied counterpoint, the material is gathered together in a majestic chordal conclusion.

In this, his last work (and – barring the *Varii Capricci* – his only original orchestral work in thirteen years since the *Britten Improvisations* of 1969), Scapino lurks among the bar lines, the 'false fugue' being the last flash of Waltonian humour. Considering the struggle he had to complete even a very short work, he must have realised that the *Stabat Mater* promised for the Huddersfield Choral Society's 150th anniversary in 1986 would remain an unfulfilled hope.

In 1980 there was talk of ITV's *South Bank Show* commissioning the playright, humourist and fellow northerner Alan Bennett to produce a libretto for a companion piece to *The Bear* for performance at Aldeburgh in 1982 and with a television broadcast produced by Tony Palmer. This was even mentioned by Roy Plomley in the course of Walton's second *Desert Island Discs* appearance in April 1982 – 'it's very difficult to find the right subjects and he [i.e. Alan Bennett] is a very good person – I think I could collaborate with him very well'.[76] But it came to nothing. However, in 1981 ITV's *South Bank Show* presented Tony Palmer's long and probing film profile of Walton, then approaching eighty, calling it (after *Troilus and Cressida*) *'At the Haunted End of the Day'* and with Walton himself as the chief contributor and narrator. His eightieth birthday was marked on the actual day by a

---

[75] During the last months of his life, Britten had also been working on a work for Rostropovich and the Washington orchestra: a setting for solo quartet, chorus and orchestra of Edith Sitwell's *Praise We Great Men*. It was left unfinished at his death in December 1976.

[76] Interviewed by Roy Plomley in BBC's *Desert Island Discs*, 2 April 1982.

concert given by Previn and the Philharmonia Orchestra[77] at the Royal Festival Hall. Walton was there to hear his own arrangement of the National Anthem, his *Anniversary Fanfare* that led straight into *Orb and Sceptre*, the Violin Concerto with Kyung-Wha Chung, and *Belshazzar's Feast*. The concert was simultaneously broadcast on BBC 2 and Radio 3. After a round of celebrations and visiting friends, Walton was on the point of flying back to Ischia when he was taken ill again and put into intensive care for a week. When he was well enough to do so, he returned home for further birthday celebrations.

Then in July he was involved in Tony Palmer's epic twelve-hour television serialisation, *Wagner*.[78] Richard Burton played the composer while Olivier and his two fellow theatrical knights, Gielgud and Richardson, were wily courtiers. But the most unexpected contribution came from Walton, making a very brief speaking appearance as Friedrich August II of Saxony, filmed in front of a backdrop set up on their terrace at home with Lady Walton on screen at his side. For someone who had done so much for films, it was appropriate that his last association with that medium should be to appear in one.

He died on 8 March 1983, three weeks short of his eighty-first birthday. He had awakened early that morning and found breathing difficult. The doctor was called and, after giving him a mild injection, was in the process of writing out a prescription for an oxygen cylinder when, in Susana's words, 'William was shaken by a slight tremor, and died.'[79]

*

Walton was cremated in Florence, chosen in compliance with Italian law because it happened to be the nearest town that permitted the cremation of a person who had died elsewhere. His ashes were returned to Ischia where they were interred under a large rock, high up in the garden. A memorial stone was unveiled at Westminster Abbey on 20 July 1983 during a Thanksgiving Service that appropriately included an organ improvisation by Henry Ley who, with Thomas Strong, had been the first to recognise the young Walton's talents at Oxford. Today the William Walton Trust perpetuates his memory through the sponsoring of recordings and performances of his music as well as by instituting an Arts Centre at his home, *La Mortella*, for the benefit of young musicians. Somewhat improbably, his manuscripts were sold to Frederick Koch of New York and form part of the Koch Collection at Yale University, USA.

---

[77] The birthday concert had originally been booked for the London Symphony Orchestra who, nearer the time, found that they had to fulfil their Barbican season of concerts, so the Philharmonia took their place.

[78] A shortened version had a brief cinema release.

[79] *Ibid.*, 231.

Unlike many composers in the years following their death, Walton's music did not suffer any serious eclipse. Some works may have dipped below the horizon, but the key works retained their place in the repertoire. The European rather than parochial English elements that make up his musical language may be one reason for their endurance. As Percy Grainger[80] commented: 'When I hear the Walton Viola Concerto I hear something that sounds lik[e]able & is somewhat tinted with Englishness – but (for me) it is not England itself.'[81] Nine of his orchestral works and one chamber work had, after all, received their first hearings abroad.[82] His self-concealment in Ischia had made him more private a composer than most. His occasional conducting appearances apart, his innate shyness and a certain insecurity contributed to this. Nevertheless, like many other composers when on the rostrum, such as Bliss, Elgar, Britten, Arnold and Vaughan Williams, he had the knack of getting to the heart of his own music with 'no nonsense and no frills' performances. The flautist Gerald Jackson commented: 'Completely "one of the boys", with a wry sense of humour, I feel that he conducts his own music as well as anyone else, with the possible exception of Sargent, who of course introduced and always makes a big thing of *Belshazzar's Feast*.'[83] At the 1933 Proms Felix Aprahamian listened to *Façade Suite No. 1* 'conducted by its long and lanky composer in his usual slick and square manner',[84] and Bernard Shore, from his desk as principal viola in the BBC Symphony Orchestra, provided a useful sketch of Walton the conductor in his earlier years:

William Walton restricts his appearances before an orchestra to performances of his own works, which he conducts with adequate skill and complete absence of fuss. Though his stick technique is probably not the result of any very intense application, it takes him through a maze of intricate bars – 7/4, 15/8, 4/2, 3/8, 2/6, or whatever they may be – with the easy nonchalance of a guide discoursing on the places of interest from a charabanc. Pale of face but extremely calm, he never gets rattled. Not in the least dictatorial or fidgety over his own work, he is quite able to give an excel-

---

80 Walton was one of several composers of whom Grainger took colour photographs for display in his museum in Melbourne as part of his thesis that blue eyes were a sign of creativity.
81 Letter to Balfour Gardiner, 27 September 1941, in *The All-Round Man: Selected Letters of Percy Grainger, 1914–1961*, ed. Malcolm Gillies and David Pear, Oxford 1994, 175–6.
82 *Façade* Suite No. 2, *Portsmouth Point*, Violin Concerto, *Scapino*, Cello Concerto, *Johannesburg Festival Overture*, *Partita*, *Capriccio Burlesco*, *Improvisations on an Impromptu of Benjamin Britten* and Violin Sonata.
83 Gerald Jackson, *First Flute*, 62.
84 Diary entry, in Barrie Hall, *The Proms and the Men who Made Them*, George Allen & Unwin 1981, 92.

lent performance, though he is not a conductor of the calibre of Lambert or Bliss.[85]

In a sixtieth-birthday interview he conceded with some pride: 'I think I conduct my own music as well as anyone else now – except George Szell.'[86]

Conducting apart, however, he could rarely be drawn into the public arena. In July 1944 the BBC tried unsuccessfully to persuade him to participate in a musical quiz for *Music Magazine*, and four years later he declined a request to appear in a fifteen-minute 'Brains Trust' programme to answer questions on music in the theatre. 'I might add that I doubt if I ever could be induced to face the microphone!' he replied. (The fact that his fellow panellists were to have been Britten and Tippett quite likely influenced his decision.) Whenever he was persuaded to permit an interview he tended to be reticent, revealing little – almost, it seems, to the point of concealment. This shyness, this reserve was more than likely the result of his years of living with the Sitwells whose conversational elegance and brilliance he could not match. There was almost certainly some truth in Stephen Tennant's suggestion that they had 'swamped his personality'. Although their protégé, he was neither treated as nor allowed to be their equal, and the inadequacy that he felt when he wrote to Harriet Cohen of his 'limited literary talents' quite likely hindered his self-expression in oral communication as well as in letter-writing. He had the sardonic wit but none of the eloquence that his inter-war friends like Cecil Gray, Philip Heseltine and Constant Lambert had possessed. His character was channelled instead through music. But even there the writer and critic Peter Pirie has suggested that he used the *Scapino* element in his music – 'dodging, equivocal, elusive, ambiguous' – as a means of escape. Pirie continued: 'It would almost seem that Walton has borrowed technical devices in order to conceal something vulnerable. . . . But if he remains entirely elusive (and I believe his weaknesses come from concealment of his essential personality rather than from lack of it) he is lost.'[87] Thus Scapino can be seen as another façade.

His upbringing, his social background and his education had been handicaps rather than assets. He lacked the poetic sensibility of a Britten, the intellectuality of a Tippett, and the morality of a Vaughan Williams. His large-scale choral works are showy and impressive, but the profundity of Vaughan Williams's *Sancta Civitas* and *Dona Nobis Pacem*, the literary intellect behind Elgar's *Falstaff* and the religious fervour of his *Dream of Gerontius*, and the searching pacifism of Britten's *War Requiem* and Tippett's *A Child of our Time*, for example, are on a level far removed from the

---

85 Bernard Shore, *The Orchestra Speaks*, Longmans 1938, 145.
86 *Sunday Times*, 25 March 1962.
87 Peter Pirie, 'Scapino: The Development of William Walton', *Musical Times*, April 1964, 258–9.

'occasional' mood of his *Gloria* and *In Honour of the City of London*. *Belshazzar's Feast* is a masterpiece of sheer (almost visual) drama rather than a work that challenge one's very being in the way that great works do. While *Façade* epitomised the flippant 1920s so wittily and so cleverly, and the First Symphony caught the dissonant mood of the brittle Thirties with such force, no later work of his captured the spirit of successive decades. He surely felt these limitations, aware as much of what he had *not* written as of what he had, and of what had been expected from him. Friends spoke of the failure of *Troilus and Cressida* to establish itself as haunting him for the rest of his life.

His insecurity shows in the difficulties he had with each new work, often his doubts and uncertainties about their quality, even doubts about his own ability, his having to turn to others for advice and help, and his constant revising of works. He could not, unlike Elgar, permit a work to go into print before the test of performance. Hardly a major score of his escaped the most rigorous revision. Very few of his works had an easy journey from conception to first performance, and for a good many of them there were delays in their arrival. He continued to sense that his lack of formal training was a handicap and indeed acknowledged as much in a sixtieth-birthday interview,[88] although Susana Walton writes of him countering such suggestions with the statement of Hindemith's that 'the most conspicuous misconception in our educational method is that composers can be fabricated by training'.[89] There can be little doubt that the change in the musical climate after the Second World War added considerably to his insecurity. Gone were the days when he and Lambert were regarded as the 'white hopes' of British music. Up to 1939, his position in British music had seemed unassailable, but there were to be many pretenders to the throne. It was the pre-war rather than the later works that kept his name in the public eye at a time when musical languages were changing dramatically. Yet if he felt keenly his pre-eminent position in English music being overtaken by a new generation of composers, this did not impair his respect for and interest in his younger contemporaries:

> I admire tremendously Britten's *Serenade* and *Nocturne*, Tippett's *Midsummer Marriage*, Rawsthorne's concertos and Arnold's Second Symphony, to mention only a few works. Nor am I indifferent to the many gifted composers who express themselves in the 12-tone technique, for instance Henze, and I possess nearly all the available records of this school. All the same, I don't feel the necessity to try to compose in this idiom myself.[90]

When he heard Hindemith's oratorio *Das Unaufhörliche* in Zürich, he wrote to Edward Clark of a magnificent performance – 'a terrific work'. On

---

88 Interview with J. W. Lambert, *Sunday Times*, 25 March 1962.
89 From Hindemith's 1949 Harvard lecture, quoted in *Behind the Façade*, 190–1.
90 *Sunday Telegraph*, 25 March 1962.

23 March 1934 he congratulated Clark on programming Berg's *Wozzeck* – 'I very much hope it will be given again soon' – and Edgard Varèse – 'which I consider another feather in your cap'. His suggestions on looking through draft programmes for the BBC's 1940/1 season with its French accent showed other sympathies: Charpentier's *Mediterranean Suite*, inviting Jean Françaix to write a work, and 'the mention of Gounod makes me long to include the Wind Symphony'. He added generously: 'Also perhaps there ought to be some songs by B Britten included.'[91]

He enjoyed meeting composers like Luigi Nono and Hans Werner Henze[92] and he kept abreast of the modern in music through gramophone records, generally avoiding the radio. He had no interest in the later Stravinsky – 'I don't like his idiom any more. . . . I think he has gone misguidingly into something he didn't really understand – I mean that Mr Craft[93] understood, but *he* didn't understand. . . . I don't think he's a serialist by instinct – he is by *Craft*', he added with punning implied capitalisation.[94] According to David Horner, he disparaged *The Rake's Progress*. 'Willie told me chiefly in words of one syllable what he thought of the Stravinsky–Auden opera,' David wrote to Christabel in 1951.[95] But he singled out *Oedipus Rex*, *Symphony of Psalms* and *Les Noces* as marvellous works, adding: 'It's rather extraordinary that all the choral works appeal to me more than things like *Petroushka*', although in 1965 he did choose *Pulcinella* as the first of his *Desert Island Discs* to remind him of his youth, of Diaghilev and of meeting Stravinsky for the first time.

As a heterosexual who all his life, when not involved in musical pursuits, had spent much of his time in chasing women, Walton must have felt keenly that his own sexuality set him apart from many of his contemporaries. Tippett, a homosexual, was of the opinion that Walton had associated himself too closely with a circle of composers who were anti-Britten and 'entertained absurd fantasies about a homosexual conspiracy in music, led by Britten and Pears'. One morning, at a rehearsal for one of the BBC's Winter Proms at the Royal Albert Hall, he challenged him: 'Introducing myself, I said, "You know, you can't be Ben, I can't be Ben, we none of us can be each other: so

---

91 2 March 1940. Letters to Edward Clark, BL Add. 52257 fols 139–148b.
92 On both occasions when he was the guest on BBC Radio's *Desert Island Discs*, in 1965 and 1982, he chose Hans Werner Henze's *Five Neapolitan Songs* as one of his eight discs.
93 Robert Craft, American conductor who was a close friend and interpreter of Stravinsky with whom he collaborated on recordings and a series of published conversations and memoirs.
94 Interview with Hans Keller, BBC Radio 3, 28 March 1972.
95 30 October 1951. Letters of Lady Aberconway, BL Add. 70837A. David Horner maliciously continued: 'It reminded me of the occasion when that stupid Alice Wimborne went round telling everyone how bad "Peter Grimes" was. He shd. cultivate a large and generous heart.'

isn't it time you stopped all this nonsense about a conspiracy?" It seemed to bring him to his senses. At any rate, from this first meeting onwards we became firm friends and remained so until the end of his life.' And yet, as Tippett has written, 'Willie never lost his sense of rivalry with Ben.'[96] He remembered an occasion when he and Walton were being driven home after a concert in Brighton. 'On the way back, sitting in the front of the car next to Susana, who was driving, he let out a great cry, saying, "Everyone is queer and I'm just normal, so my music will never succeed." '[97] Even making some allowances for exaggeration, for someone who in the 1920s and 1930s had moved among a considerable number of eminent figures in music and the arts who were homosexual – and sometimes blatantly so – this may well be something with which he found it hard to come to terms.

Throughout his life there had been a strong dependence on others. It was only in 1948, with the death of Alice Wimborne, that those strings of dependence were cut, and his marriage later that year to Susana Gil must have come as a life-line to someone who found himself suddenly adrift. It was in some ways fortunate that she was completely non-musical. Her care and devotion saw to his material needs, and the skill she lavished on their home and garden provided him with a refuge from the musical world to which select friends like Laurence Olivier and Malcolm Arnold could be admitted. On their visits to England she enjoyed the entrée into British society that their marriage opened up.

As Susana Walton was ready to admit, William had learned how to use people. When she was asked if he had regretted not having had Auden as librettist for *Troilus and Cressida* instead of Christopher Hassall, her reply was frank: 'William was too wise. He could bully Christopher but he could never bully Auden, so he only used Auden as far as he needed him. He would never have asked him to do a libretto for him. I think that William used Christopher as he did most people who came into his life.' (Auden was additionally a good friend of and collaborator with Britten in a number of works.) And when pressed as to whether he had used her too, she was equally frank: 'Absolutely, all the time. One was a commodity. I adored William. William was the most entrancing person alive, but he used you. You knew it and there was no use in being offended because it was for a purpose. So I provided the frame for his life.'[98]

Right from his Oxford days Walton had been extremely fortunate in his contact with people through whose help (and financial assistance) he was

---

96 Walton's wry sense of humour would surely have seen some irony in there being a recording of a quartet by Walton played by a Britten Quartet (Collins Classics 1280–2; Regis RRC1015) – but not the other way round.
97 Michael Tippett, *Those Twentieth Century Blues*, 214.
98 Interview with Humphrey Burton in an interval talk during the broadcast of Opera North's production of *Troilus and Cressida*, BBC Radio 3, 2 February 1995.

able to make his way. Many responded readily to his temperament and enjoyed his often barbed humour. His publisher, Hubert Foss, was 'enchanted by Willie's airy nonchalance, amused by the shafts of lightning and acid which would suddenly illuminate his conversation'.[99] After attending a concert at the Central Hall, Westminster at which a piece by the South African-born composer Priaulx Rainier was played, he commented: 'I really think Miss Rainier must have barbed-wire underwear!'[100] In his correspondence, too, he rarely missed an opportunity to make some caustic comment about a rival composer or musician. Alan Frank observed in a radio programme: 'He can't resist injecting quite a good deal of spice into his correspondence, not entirely free from indiscretion. He speaks his mind with Lancastrian shrewdness and directness and the sharp remarks come as a surprise from so quiet and seemingly so reserved a personality.'[101] In BBC Television's *Late Night Line-Up* programme he matched the naïveté of a question with a blunt answer. To Joan Bakewell's enquiry 'Sir William, I understand that you wrote a lot of popular music in the 30s. Why did you do this?' came the immediate reply 'For the money, of course!'

Not all who knew him found him easy to deal with or appreciated his shafts of acid. Roy Douglas, who for many years worked closely with both Walton and Vaughan Williams in the preparation of their scores for publication by OUP and is a great admirer of both composers' works, is in no doubt as to which of the two was the easier to work with. Walton seemed to lack Vaughan Williams's humanity and generosity of spirit, and Norman Peterkin of OUP told an interesting story that pinpoints the difference:

> While [Vaughan Williams] was with me, Walton arrived at Soho Square, as usual not having warned me. The showroom girls told him I was engaged with V.W., and reported later that Walton remarked, 'I suppose the old buffer is going to monopolise him all morning'. He then sent through a message that he would come back in half an hour to see me. He had apparently been waiting a few minutes when I took V.W. out. I left them talking together, and afterwards heard that when V.W. learned Walton had been waiting to see me apologised to him for keeping me engaged. According to the girls, V.W. was far nicer to W, than W was to him, and W is not considered to be a gentleman I gather!' Walton came in my room remarking 'Well, the old pussy cat has gone at last'.[102]

Walton was not generally an admirer of Vaughan Williams and claimed that

---

99 Dora Foss, 'Memoirs of Walton'.
100 Remembered by Tippett in *Those Twentieth Century Blues*, 119.
101 'Four English Composers', BBC Radio 3, January 1977.
102 Letter from Norman Peterkin to Humphrey Milford, 27 April 1942, in *An Extraordinary Performance*, 71–2. Milford's reply was 'You know my views about Walton, which agree with those of your Showroom Girls' (p. 72).

he could not get ecstatic about a folk tune. 'There's no overwhelming reason why modern English music should chew a straw, wear a smock-frock, and travel by stage-coach. Folk tunes, like peas, bureaucrats, and Chinamen, are all the same,' he is reported as saying.[103]

Ursula Strebi, managing director of the English Chamber Orchestra, made an interesting comparison with another touchy individual, Benjamin Britten, when she wrote: 'Willie Walton, for example, who was an entirely different character, you had to handle *very* carefully. He was very suspicious and thin-skinned, and could be very difficult. And while there were things about Willie which I think were entirely admirable, I don't think I would ever have hit it off with him as well as I did with Ben.'[104]

If there was an occasionally prickly exterior, with all the support, financial and otherwise that he received from many friends, Walton was not unmindful of the needs of others, and Elisabeth Lutyens warmly acknowledged his generosity:

> William was the single most beneficent influence on music and his fellow composers whilst still living in England. There was not a 'good musical cause' he would not stick his neck out to support; there was not a colleague he would not stretch out an encouraging hand to. Music as a whole, and so many composers, have reason to be grateful for his generosity and toler-ance. He was the best of company, devoid of that 'safety first' cautious respectability of the middle classes.[105]

Walton had had reason to be grateful to Elisabeth's husband, Edward Clark, and when she asked Walton for an introduction to Muir Mathieson in the hope of receiving some work in films,

> William, who is as quick to respond as his music is to register, replied, 'Of course I will; but I'll do more than that. Write any work you like, dedicate it to me and I'll give you £100.'[106]

This, she wrote, gave her courage in her darkest hour. The resulting work was the scena *The Pit*. On 7 May 1945 the promised cheque arrived with the covering note: 'Here is my effort at playing Paganini to your Berlioz.' (Berlioz was a composer he much admired, an enthusiasm he shared with Dallas Bower, Michael Ayrton, Cecil Gray and Humphrey Searle.)

---

103 Interview with Charles Stuart, *Yorkshire Observer*, 21 December 1942, 2. Walton would not have been pleased to hear Sir Adrian Boult refer to Vaughan Williams as 'the undisputed leader of English musical life' in a 75th birthday tribute broadcast on 12 October 1947. [*Boult on Music*, Toccata Press 1981, 63]
104 Humphrey Carpenter, *Benjamin Britten*, 416–17.
105 Elisabeth Lutyens, *A Goldfish Bowl*, Cassell 1972, 148–9.
106 *A Goldfish Bowl*, 148.

Humphrey Searle experienced Walton's kindness. In his autobiography he has written:

> Sir Hugh Allen was taking an interest in my compositions at the time; he did not pretend to understand modern music, and said: 'Show them to a really modern composer'. He gave me an introduction to William Walton, then a leading composer, with Constant Lambert, of the younger generation. Britten was only just beginning to be heard of, and Rawsthorne and Tippett had not yet appeared on the scene. Walton was very kind; he looked at my songs and an overture which I had sketched out and gave me encouragement, which was what I needed. He did not pretend to know much about twelve-note music [but] there was no-one in England to whom I could turn for knowledge of that subject. . . . For my composition lessons at the college Walton had suggested that I should study with John Ireland.[107]

Another young composer to receive help from Walton was John Veale, who had been greatly impressed by the First Symphony. Even Tippett found Walton 'always very generous to me and I loved his sardonic humour',[108] while Spike Hughes wrote of his 'sharp-edged witticism – not so much malice as a delight in teasing . . . his natural quick-wittedness, his intense physical vigour and masculinity, the strong romantic streak, his sense of fun and horror of pomposity'.[109] This vigour did have its limitations: Dora Foss found when he first stayed with her and her husband that 'Willie was allergic to physical exercise in any form' and a walk she took him on completely exhausted him. On his next visit, however, he was persuaded to play tennis.[110]

Edith Sitwell, too, observed physical aspects of Walton's character. She described the Walton she first met as 'a very tall young man, slim, but extremely muscular. This latter trait was not understood immediately by unfortunates who had aroused his wrath.'[111] Even Sachie was to learn this to his cost after 'an awful fight with poor Willie' outside their house when William forgot his promise to leave Sachie alone with Georgia and 'stayed on and would not leave'. Sachie came off worst with a black eye.[112] Osbert remarked on his 'manual dexterity: he could do almost anything with his hands, and by his ingenuity, so that often, for example, I would, when a key was lost, ask him to pick a lock for me'.[113] Both Edith and Osbert recalled a curious episode concening something rather larger than a lock or key. As Edith explained it:

---

107 *Quadrille with a Raven: Memoirs by Humphrey Searle*, unpublished, Internet.
108 Michael Tippett, *Those Twentieth Century Blues*, 214.
109 'Nobody Calls Him Willie Now', 116–17.
110 Dora Foss, 'Memoirs of Walton'.
111 *Sunday Times*, 18 March 1962.
112 Sarah Bradford, *Splendours and Miseries*, 147, June 1925.
113 Osbert Sitwell, *Laughter in the Next Room*, 176 (188).

At one time, William composed in the stables. Then it was thought that the piano must be moved upstairs. Throughout the morning, men in green baize aprons attempted this operation, unsuccessfully. In the afternoon Sacheverell, my sister-in-law and I went for a drive, leaving William at home, composing. On our return, we found to our astonishment that the piano had made its way upstairs and was in the drawing room. 'How on earth did you manage that?' asked Sacheverell. 'Quite easy. I just used a piece of string.' said William.[114]

If composition for him was a difficult and arduous process, the finished works betray no sign of this whatsoever. Each score has that same Waltonian certainty of touch, directness, strength and energy. At an early age he had created such a name for himself that he never lacked commissions. In fact scarcely a work of his did not come at the instigation or request of one person or musical body. Rather than works being inspired from within, it seems that they had to be encouraged from without. Even so, he maintained a regular composer's timetable. Even in his later years he disciplined himself to doing some composition every day, however pitifully small the result would often be. While staying with him in Ischia, Malcolm Arnold observed his daily routine: up at 8 a.m. and working solidly till 1 p.m., then lunch and a rest. Then he would fetch the mail from the gate-house down the garden, have a pot of tea with Susana, followed by another two hours' work. Friends like Arnold noticed his anxiety, that he would be 'terribly self-critical' and would often think 'in terms of rewriting. He gets in a terrible worry – he gets in the state of a person immediately before a concert.'[115] Alan Frank spoke of Walton suffering from waves of depression, and of how he was kept going entirely by Susana.

Like all great composers Walton created a style that was instantly recognisable. It was a style readily imitated, particularly in the medium to which he made such a significant contribution – films. For London Television's *South Bank Show* tribute to Sir Laurence Olivier on his seventy-fifth birthday, Stephen Oliver provided a brilliant score that was rightly Waltonian to its core. When permission was refused to use the Prelude to *Richard III* for the title music to the BBC TV 1988 Falklands war drama *Tumbledown*, Richard Hartley turned in a very effective pastiche (or near copy) of the Prelude, and in the title music for the 1969 film *Mosquito Squadron* Frank Cordell inserted a march that might have been chippings from the Walton work-bench. His music left its mark on a number of composers, such as Gerald Finzi (moments in his *Magnificat* and his choral magnum opus *Inti-*

---

114 Edith Sitwell, 'Young William Walton Comes to Town', *Sunday Times*, 18 March 1962. Osbert tells the story in *Laughter in the Next Room*, 176–7 (188–9).
115 Malcolm Arnold in interview with John Amis in *Portrait of Walton*, BBC Radio 3, broadcast 4 June 1977.

mations of Immortality)[116] and William Mathias (in his brilliant percussive orchestration), although such an extrovert style as Walton's could make the difference between influence and mere imitation a very fine line. It is a curious fact that while Walton's virtuosic scoring for the orchestra may invite comparison among British composers with Elgar, neither of them had any formal musical education. It is all the more remarkable that, unlike Elgar, Walton had not enjoyed the great benefit of learning 'from the inside' as an orchestral player.

Walton was among the last of the major composers whose music appealed directly to the heart of the music public at large. Towards the end of his life in a rare moment of self-analysis he admitted: 'I think I could have done it better than I have done. I am a disappointment to myself if you really want to know, musically speaking. I am disappointed in myself – I don't say necessarily that the works are disappointing, but I think I could have done better if I had thought about it. Rather sad really.'[117] It is, happily, a view that few would share.

---

116 Stephen Banfield, in *Sensibility and English Song*, CUP 1985, Vol. I, 283, observed that 'the more intense aspects of his harmonic language are considerably indebted to his contemporary William Walton'.
117 *Kaleidoscope* memorial programme.

Appendix 1. Lambert on Walton

One

Fresh Hand; New Talent; Vital Touch
Brief record of William Walton, composer of 'Portsmouth Point' and a score or two besides

Boston Evening Transcript   Saturday 27 November 1926

Though only twenty-four years old, William Walton is undoubtedly one of the most important composers in England today. The presence of such a figure is all the more encouraging when we consider how the startling renaissance in British music which took place at the beginning of the century seemed, in the years immediately following the war, to be already relapsing into a premature old age. The causes of this decay were not far to seek and lay chiefly in the increasingly narrow and provincial outlook of the composers of that time who were, for the most part, depressingly reminiscent of a mongrel chasing its own not too interesting tail.

Walton from the first resolutely set his face against the pseudo-archaic and fabricated 'nationalism' which has proved such a 'cul-de-sac' to nine British composers out of ten and did not scorn to derive what benefit he could from the most advanced experiments of the day, whether in Central Europe, France or America. Eclecticism (the bugbear of such purely party leaders as Jean Cocteau) may be a pitfall for the weak-minded but to anyone whose character is strong enough for him to emerge from each successive phase with his personality intact it is a most valuable quality and through the experience its possession gives him a composer such as Walton approaches his work with a freedom of outlook and a sureness of touch which might well do credit to an older man. Though Walton does not consider as thoroughly representative those works which are prior to *Portsmouth Point* it is necessary, if one is to give more than a profile portrait of the composer, to examine the more important of his early works as through them we may get a valuable insight not only into the composer's present style but also into his future tendencies.

The first work which commands our attention is a quartet for pianoforte and strings, written at Oxford when Walton was only fifteen. Though a remarkable technical achievement for a boy of that age, the quartet shows us

267

the composer very much in the chrysalis stage. The first movement is pleasant but uneventful, with occasional touches of Ravel and Vaughan Williams, and it is not until we come to the eloquent and lyrical slow movement that we feel that the composer has anything important to say; this is followed by a finale of astonishing energy that gives in its development ample presage of Walton's next phase in which he was strongly attracted to the savage intellectuality of the Central European school.

The principal compositions of this period are a string quartet and a toccata for violin and pianoforte, both making considerable demands upon the virtuosity of the performers. In examining the carefully wrought score of the string quartet one feels, as is so often the case when confronted with works emanating either directly or indirectly from Vienna, that the undoubted skill and energy expended on them might have been spent more profitably, perhaps, on some purely intellectual rather than musical task. The toccata for violin and piano, a rhapsodical work showing traces of the influence of Bartók and even Sorabji, has to my mind a greater and more genuine vitality than the string quartet and contains at least one excellent passage – an emotional middle section in which the lyrical quality we noticed in the piano quartet makes a welcome reappearance though cast this time in a severer mould.

Walton's next phase, though it puzzled some of his friends, was not really surprising. Small wonder that, surfeited with the intellectuality of Schönberg he should turn with a sigh of relief towards Gershwin. For more than a year he did nothing but study jazz, writing and scoring fox-trots for the Savoy Orpheus Band and working at a monumentally planned concerto, for two pianofortes, jazz band and orchestra. So great, indeed, was his obsession with ragtime that even when writing incidental music for Lytton Strachey's Chinese melodrama, *The Son of Heaven*, he was unable to prevent some unmistakable touches of Gershwin from entering the score! Although the concerto was finished and about to be performed, Walton suddenly abandoned the jazz style in a fit of disgust, rightly realising that the virtues of ragtime, its pungent timbres and intriguing syncopation are more that handicapped by the deadly monotony of the four-square phrases, the inevitable harmonic clichés stolen from Debussy and Delius, the trite nostalgia of the whole atmosphere.

For some little while Walton wrote nothing but it was clearly a case of 'reculer pour mieux sauter' for in his next work, the brilliant overture *Portsmouth Point*, he quite suddenly and emphatically attains real self expression for the first time in his career. We can see now that his excursions into atonality and jazz were in the nature of mental exercises, studies in a foreign language that enabled him to speak his own tongue with greater knowledge and conviction.

Here, if you like, is English music, English as the *Water Music* of Handel or as the hornpipes of Purcell, English as the point by Rowlandson from which the title is taken. The clear air is unclouded by the least suspicion of Celtic Twilight and the sparkling gaiety is undimmed by any pretentious moralising. Wisely refraining from striking the deeper note the composer has nevertheless succeeded in producing a work of profundity, if we use that word as it might be applied to a Scarlatti sonata or a rondo by Haydn. Though lasting only a few minutes this overture is one of the most sustained efforts I know for unlike so many modern works where the utmost ingenuity on the part of the composer cannot disguise the fact that the piece is a mere pot-pourri of fragmentary scraps of material, *Portsmouth Point* has a clear and sweeping line that is only too rare in contemporary music. Though some attempt may be made to analyse the overture as sonata form the impression we receive is of one breathless section, an effect in no way mitigated by the profusion of themes, which take their place in the order of things like so many sudden views of the sea from the window of an express train. Techni-cally speaking we may notice the influence of jazz on the exhilarating synco-pation of the tunes, but nothing could be further removed from the soulful chromaticisms of the jazz-composer than the rollicking high spirits of this work. Since then Walton has written a charming idyll for small orchestra en-titled *Siesta* to which one might apply the epithet 'Mendelssohnian' were it not that the texture is mainly contrapuntal.

I have purposely avoided speaking of *Façade* until the last, for though it gives us the composer at his best and most typical, it is so linked with the poetry of Miss Edith Sitwell that a few words of explanation may be neces-sary. When at Oxford, Walton met Sacheverell Sitwell, the youngest of the brilliant trio of poets (whose work needs no introduction to the United States), and since then he has been closely associated with the family. They were quick to realise that no other composer could so well supply the musical equivalent of what has been well described as 'the hallucinated vision, the glassily clear technique, the curiously profound wit' of Edith Sitwell's poems. An entertainment was devised in which twenty or thirty of the poems were recited through a megaphone – 'sensa expressione' – but with every precision and variety of rhythm to the accompaniment of flute, clarinet, trumpet, saxophone, 'cello and battery.' The orchestra was placed behind a screen painted to resemble a gigantic mask, through the mouth of which came the megaphone. Since its first performance *Façade* has been completely remoulded and it is most interesting to compare the two different versions. In the first Walton did little more than provide a frame for Edith Sitwell's remarkable poems; there was a running commentary of peculiar timbres whose appeal was to the nerves rather than to the musical reason. In the second version the music is for the most part on equal terms with the poetry; each movement is classically formed, and without losing any of its individuality the whole entertainment has become more straightforward and popular. Mr Ernest Newman, in his review of the second performance of *Façade*, said: 'Here is obviously a humorous musical talent of the first order

. . . the deft workmanship, especially in the orchestration, made the heart of the listening musician glad.'

The magic of *Façade* is extraordinarily varied – strident hornpipe polkas are placed side by side with charming little pastorales – nocturnes – an 1860 valse prepares the way for a Swiss yodelling song where William Tell is heard in the style of Honegger – an English music hall song is transformed into a languorous tango from which we are led by a rapid cadenza for the voice into a pasodoblé of riotous vulgarity: the fantastic conceptions of Miss Sitwell's verses are imbued with an uncanny reality by the manner of their presentation.

Walton has just finished an orchestral suite based on *Façade* and it will be interesting to see how the music stands by itself: he has kept fairly closely to the rhythm and form of the poems except in the finale – a Tarantella in which the original material has been considerably expanded into a brilliant burlesque of the 'Mediterranean' style.

To conclude, we may safely say that Walton has already given proof of such vitality and fecundity of imagination that the musical world will look forward to his next important work with eagerness; one can form little idea of his future development save that of all modern composers he is the least likely to remain in a groove.

Two

Some Angles of the Compleat Walton
Constant Lambert writes a lively literary overture to the Walton Prom to be broadcast on Tuesday
Radio Times 7 August 1936

I find it increasingly difficult to write about the music of William Walton. Not that my admiration for his music has in any way declined. Far from it. Walton is one of the few composers of recent years who have not disappointed their admirers. But with each succeeding work he has become not only more personal but more strictly musical with the result that the critic is offered less and less of an 'angle' on which to base his criticism. His symphony, for example, his latest work, evokes no pictorial or literary associations, nor does it bear the label of any particular school or tendency. It is just a symphony, and one cannot really pay it a greater compliment when asked 'What is Walton's symphony like?', than to say, 'Oh, it's a very good symphony'. After all, that is what we say of the classical symphonies. The moment we start speaking of aesthetic-cum-political tendencies it is usually a sign that the music, though interesting, is not completely satisfying in itself.

This, indeed, is true of the earlier works of Walton himself, when the composer though gifted with a remarkably powerful musical personality for his years was only discovering this personality by a rather restless survey of the principal post-war tendencies.

The piano quartet, his first work (an astonishing achievement for a boy of sixteen), is eclectic in style, written for the most part in the rhapsodic pastoral manner of the 'English Musical Renaissance' but deviating from it as far as Elgar on the one hand, Stravinsky on the other. Like many an opus one it foreshadows the composer's later development more vividly than the works that immediately succeed it. Of these the most important is the string quartet – a work that first brought the composer into prominence when it was chosen for the 1923 International Festival of Contemporary Music at a time when Walton was quite unknown in his own country. It is rather a dour work written in the then fashionable Central European or 'International Pioneer' idiom.

A short while afterwards we find him writing and scoring fox-trots for the Savoy Orpheans. Although he has never produced any symphonic jazz, Walton has demonstrably been influenced by the rhythms of modern dance music, while the necessity of writing in a popular idiom had a salutary effect in clarifying his melodic line. This new sureness of technique was displayed in the overture *Portsmouth Point*, the first work of his to get established in the repertoire and the first work of his that can be described as typical Walton.

Written in 1925–26 it received its first performances as an interlude at the Diaghilev ballet and it has many of the qualities one associates with the Diaghilev ballets of that time; breezy diatonic tunes supported by a very free use of diatonic discords, restless syncopated rhythms and clean but rather acid scoring. *Portsmouth Point*, however, has both more personality and more ability than the other works of its type and has deservedly outlasted them.

The same period also produced the second version of *Façade*, which, as most people know, was an entertainment for speaking voice and six instru-mentalists. The poems were by Edith Sitwell and were spoken through a megaphone from behind a curtain. In the original version, which dates from his Central European period, the instruments were mainly occupied by complicated arabesques and the melodic interest was slight – the second version, however, is one good tune after another and each number is a gem of stylisation or parody. What distinguishes Walton's parodies from the comic polkas and waltzes of Stravinsky or Milhaud is that he can 'guy' a type of music and yet write good music at the same time. The waltz in *Façade* is an excellent waltz, the tarantella is an excellent tarantella. Theirs is not the obvious humour of a lampoon but the far more subtle humour of a Beerbohm parody. They are not only like the originals but ridiculously like. The orches-tral suite consists of five of the most popular numbers minus the voice part and expanded for medium orchestra. *Portsmouth Point* and *Façade* gave the public the impression that Walton was primarily a witty composer, an English rival to the post-war Parisians.

The *Sinfonia Concertante* for piano and orchestra soon corrected this impression. Although the first and last movements still had a slight flavour of the Diaghilev twenties, the slow movement showed an entirely new side to Walton's talent and is one of the finest pages in modern music.

The concerto for viola which followed is consistently successful throughout, and although the symphony is a more weighty and important work there are many who feel that the viola concerto is his most poetic achievement. Whereas the *Sinfonia Concertante* was an eighteenth-century type concerto with the soloist on equal terms with the orchestra, the viola concerto is a nineteenth-century type concerto with the soloist as romantic hero. But it is noteworthy that Walton did not throw over the classical paraphernalia of the earlier work merely because the mood was more romantic this time. He is not one of those composers who proceed by a series of violent reactions. Nor does he repeat himself. He incorporates in each succeeding work what has been of value in the style of the preceding works. Thus in the viola concerto the romantic peroration represents a new angle to his character, but the scherzo is a continuation of the style established in *Portsmouth Point* though considerably subtilised on this occasion. Similarly in the symphony, the tragic first movement reveals a new aspect of Walton's character but the finale represents a continuation of the massive and festal style of *Belshazzar's Feast*. Even more striking is the fact that the slow movement in spite of its epic scale recalls in mood an early number from *Façade*, 'By the Lake'.

It is this capacity to build logically upon his foundations which distinguishes Walton from his contemporaries, and gives us hope that he may be able to lead modern music out of its present impasse.

Most modern composers can be divided into two classes. There are those who change their style with each succeeding work, like Walton in his early days, and there are those who concentrate so intensely on their own personal tics and mannerisms that all their works sound the same. Walton is one of the few who have been able to steer a middle course. His works are varied in physical texture and formal conception, but consistent in their emotional and intellectual approach.

Portsmouth Point, which opens this week's concert, is recognisably by the same composer as the symphony which ends it, but what progress, technical, intellectual, and emotional has been made in ten years that separate the two! I can think of no other composer of Walton's generation who has shown anything like this artistic progress, and no modern composer of any generation who could provide a 'one-man' programme at once so varied and so satisfying.

Appendix 2. Walton on Lambert

Constant Lambert
(In memoriam 21 August 1951)
Reprinted from
Selections from the BBC Programme 'Music Magazine',
chosen and edited by
Anna Instone and Julian Herbage,
Rockliff Publishing Corporation Ltd., 1953

My earliest memories of my musical life in London are connected with my friend Constant Lambert. He had been one of my closest friends for nearly thirty years. When I first met him he was still a student at the Royal College of Music. He had gone there with a scholarship for piano playing, but his natural bent for composition soon intervened and became his first study, under the direction of Dr Vaughan Williams and R. O. Morris.

It was towards the end of his days at the College that I met him, when I went to hear a performance of two settings of Sacheverell Sitwell's poems for soprano, flute and harp. More or less at the same time he made his mark as a budding young conductor when he directed a Suite he had arranged from Glinka's *Ruslan and Ludmilla*. That here was a versatile talent was unmistakable.

He was, as a young man, of strikingly handsome and distinguished appearance and with a most pronounced personality which he carried with him to the end of his days.

His taste in music for so young a man was very unusual. He did not really like the classics, or indeed ever come to care for them, but preferred more the highways and byways of music; the Elizabethans, Purcell, Scarlatti, the Russian school – particularly Glinka and Moussorgsky – and amongst the French composers he had a particular predilection for Debussy and Erik Satie. He was one of the earliest Sibelius enthusiasts, and while still a student at the College conducted the slow movement of the Fourth Symphony. He was also one of the earliest admirers of Duke Ellington, and I can recall going night after night with him to hear Florence Mills, that great coloured singer, and to hear Will Vodery's band in Mr Cochran's revue *Dover Street to Dixie*, all of which left its mark when he came to write *The Rio Grande*, the Piano Sonata, the Concerto for piano and seven instruments and the *Elegiac Blues* in memory of Florence Mills.

273

He was later to become a champion of the music of Liszt and Berlioz and, amongst others, Van Dieren.

It was when still a student that his friend Edmund Dulac brought Lambert to the notice of Diaghilev. This unique spotter of talent immediately recognised Lambert's capabilities and commissioned a ballet, *Romeo and Juliet*. Here was Constant's knowledge of Russian music to stand him in good stead. So much so that Diaghilev would not believe that Constant had not some Russian blood in his veins, and it was one of Constant's rare boasts that he was one of the very few who had played piano duets with Diaghilev.

To show Constant's independence of mind, even at so young an age and at such a crucial moment in his career, he did not hesitate to have a bitter quarrel with Diaghilev about the scenery of the ballet. Constant had been working on this ballet with the painter Christopher Wood,[1] and was disappointed and horrified when Diaghilev determined that the surrealist painters Ernst and Miro should do the décor. They did not speak for some years, but were eventually reconciled in what turned out to be Diaghilev's last season at Covent Garden, when he invited Constant to conduct his *Music for Orchestra* as an interlude during the season.

In spite of the fame which *The Rio Grande* brought him, it was still difficult for Constant to earn a living as a composer, so he became the music critic to the *Sunday Referee*. This, however, was not entirely unfruitful. Messrs. Faber and Faber, struck by the brilliance of his criticisms, commissioned him to write a book on music, the outcome of which was the now almost classic volume *Music Ho!*

With the award of the Collett Scholarship, he was again enabled to devote himself to composition, and he produced what is, to my mind, his masterpiece, *Summer's Last Will and Testament*, a work of remarkable beauty and originality, but even today not really appreciated at its true worth.

It was during this time that the Camargo Society, which ultimately became the Sadler's Wells Ballet, was founded. Constant devoted himself heart and soul to this, and, in fact, threw overboard almost all his other activities in its favour. I am sure that his eminent collaborators in this project, Ninette de Valois, Freddie Ashton and Bobbie Helpmann, will agree with me that without Constant's enthusiasm and knowledge, not only of music but of choreography and décor, and his instinct for the theatre, the whole project might have fallen to the ground. Indeed, it may be that he will be best remembered by this, his great contribution to the theatre of our time.

I have left unsaid so many things that I have wanted to say of his companionship, his charm, his lively and amusing conversation, his abilities as a

---

1 Christopher Wood (1901–30) made a pencil sketch of Walton in 1925 (Magdalen Street Gallery, Cambridge), reproduced in Alan Jenkins *The Twenties*, Heinemann 1974, 145, and three portraits of Lambert, the finest of which (1926), in oils, is in the National Portrait Gallery.

conductor, and also as an arranger and orchestrator of other composers' work, of his limericks, his wit and the numerous other facets of this unique character.

Constant's last work, the ballet *Tiresias*, showed that his gifts were by no means exhausted, but only dormant. The tragedy lies in the fact that he should have been cut off just as he was abandoning his outside activities and returning to what, after all, was his true vocation – that of a composer.

Appendix 3. Walton on Films

Music for Shakespearean Films

Sir William Walton[1]

Writing music for the screen is undoubtedly a specialised job. To begin with, the composer is rightly disciplined in his work by the time factor. For example, in *Hamlet* (as in all other films) my first contact with the production was the arrival of the script. This meant that I could obtain at least some idea of the treatment envisaged by the producer–director, in translating this monumental work into celluloid. An occasional visit to the film set also gave me some impressions of how the project was coming along.

The real work, however, begins when the picture is complete – complete, that is, in what is called the rough cut. It is only at this stage that the full atmosphere and dramatic impact of the screen play can be seen. However much a composer may examine the scenario, he can never grasp all those little individual touches which a director adds while he is shooting the picture. Then, again, there is this time business. After I have seen the film with the director and music director, the editor passes me a typewritten sheet giving the exact timings of each section of the film to which music will be fitted. For example, a sequence may call for 1 minute 23 seconds of music; 1 minute 24 seconds is too long, and 1 minute 22 seconds is too short. This means that a composer must, right from the start, adjust his approach to the composition. In writing for the concert hall, he can work out his ideas to suit himself. His symphony may run for 20, 30, or 50 minutes. Not so in films. The form and content of the music is governed absolutely by the exacting requirements of the pictures on the screen.

There seems to be an idea among film people that a composer can turn out pages and pages of fully orchestrated manuscript just on the spur of the moment. The sort of things that happen is that the unfortunate writer comes to the studio, is shown the film, finds that there is a total of 50 minutes of

---

[1] *Film/TV Music* 15:20 Spring 1956, and included in James L. Limbacher, *Film Music: from Violins to Video*, Scarecrow Press 1974, 128–31. This is a much-expanded version of Walton's article, 'The Music of Hamlet', in *The Film Hamlet: A Record of its Production*, ed. Brenda Cross, Saturn Press 1948, 61–2.

music required, and some bright spark in the music office says, 'That's lovely. We can book the orchestra in two weeks' time, and get the whole thing in the bag.' Frankly, two weeks is no earthly use for 50 minutes' music, as anyone who has attempted full scale composition will know. I think that composers as a whole should decry this bad aspect of film-making and see if some arrangement cannot be made whereby the composer is guaranteed a certain reasonable time in which to deliver his score, and I myself always insist on this.

In the case of *Hamlet*, I received every consideration from Laurence Olivier, and the film unit, in that the music recording dates were spread over a month, thus giving ample time to consider the results of each of the recording days' work, and allowing time for discussion before proceeding to the next music section. The closest collaboration was maintained between Olivier and myself, and some of my musical ideas were evolved from suggestions from him.

The value to a film of its musical score rests chiefly in the creation of mood, atmosphere, and the sense of period. When the enormous task of re-imagining a Shakespearean drama in terms of the screen has been achieved, these three qualities, which must be common to all film music, appear in high relief.

In the case of 'mood' I would quote as an example the incidental musical effects in Hamlet's soliloquies which varied their orchestral colour according to the shifts of his thought. For 'atmosphere' take the music of rejoicing after the victory of Agincourt in *Henry V*, which also illustrates the power to evoke a sense of historical period in a special way, for the contemporary Agincourt hymn which has been handed down to us was adapted to my purpose. Indeed the atmosphere of human feeling and the evocation of a past time are often combined, or made to blend from one to the other without any abruptness of transition. At the entry of the players in *Hamlet* I took the chance to suggest the musical idiom of the time by using a small sub-section of the orchestra (two violas, cello, oboe, cor anglais, bassoon, harpsichord) and then proceeded to make my comment on the action in my own personal idiom.

In a film the visual effect is of course predominant, and the music subserves the visual sequences, providing a subtle form of punctuation – lines can seem to have been given the emphasis of italics, exclamation marks added to details of stage 'business', phrases of the action broken into paragraphs, and the turning of the page at a crossfade or cut can be helped by music's power to summarise the immediate past or heighten expectation of what is to come. The analogy with printer's typography is useful, but beyond this, music offers orchestral 'colour' to the mind's ear in such a way that at every stage it confirms and reinforces the colour on the screen which is engaging the eye.

The composer in the cinema is the servant of the eye; in the Opera House he is of course the dominating partner. There everyone, beginning with the librettist, must serve him and the needs of the ear. In the film world, however, from the first stage called the 'rough-cut' where the composer first sees the visual images that his work must reinforce, an opera composer finds his controlling position usurped. He works in the service of a director. Since proportion is as important in music as in any other of the arts, the film composer, no longer his own master, is to a great extent at the mercy of his director.

A close and delicate collaboration is essential for the film must be served, but music must not be asked to do what it should not or cannot. After a while the composer who stays the pace acquires what has been called 'the stop-watch mentality', a quality which I have heard deplored; but I am quite certain the habit, a particularly strict form of self-discipline, does a composer far more good than harm when he is working on his own for his own ends. Within or outside the cinema every second counts.

A film composer must have confidence in his director or collaboration will break down. In my three major Shakespearean films I have been particu-larly blessed in working with a director who knew precisely what he wanted at any given point not only in quantity but in kind. Laurence Olivier under-stands the composer's problems. He has a genius for thinking up ways of adding to them, or increasing those that already exist, but he never demands the impossible, and his challenges have invariably led me to be grateful in the end. In the deployment of his visual resources he is himself a dramatist and though a composer's task is never anything but difficult, the confidence inspired by such a director has certainly made things far easier than they might have been.

If the musical aspect of the battle sequences in *Henry V* and *Richard III*, for instance, is considered helpful to the general effect, that is due to an unusually complex and close collaboration of sound and screen from one bar or visual movement to the next, the outcome of much patience and exercise of technique certainly, but above all, I think, the fruit of mutual confidence and esteem.

Recording the Music

Muir Mathieson[2]

My work on a picture such as *Hamlet* begins with the arrival in the Music Department of the final shooting script. This is immediately read through, and a note made of the more obvious points at which music will occur – trumpet calls, for example, and scenes showing musicians or, possibly,

---

2 Included in *The Film Hamlet: A Record of its Production*, 61–2.

unusual instruments. Close contact is maintained with the composer from now on, and any specialised items discussed with the director and the producer. After all the preliminary work has been completed, the film goes on the floor, the Music Department arranging any 'playbacks' required for shooting, advising if necessary on musical or choral scenes in the film as they arise throughout production.

Immediately the first 'rough cut' of the picture is put together, a screening is arranged for the composer, editor, director and myself. We are seeing the film in its final form, except for minor alterations, to decide where music is required and what form it should take. When these matters have been thrashed out, the film editor prepares a complete time sheet of all the sections requiring music, which is passed over to the composer, in this case, William Walton.

For *Hamlet*, the Philharmonia Orchestra of London assembled in the Music Theatre of Denham Studios on the days agreed upon the recording, and the work of translating the composer's score on to the sound-track went ahead. The music was recorded in short sections in much the same way as the individual shots in the picture, though the music sections usually covered several shots for greater effect.

Altogether there are about 50 minutes of music in Hamlet, and it took several days to record. The composer, Laurence Olivier and the film editor attended all the music sessions. The recording was made by the music mixer, Ted Drake (who was responsible for the layout of the microphones and the 'balance' of the orchestra) and by Kenneth Rawkins, who was in charge of the film and disc recording equipment.

I have recorded many of Walton's film scores, and believe him to have excelled himself in the case of *Hamlet*. He has a tremendous dramatic sense, and the music for the two other Olivier Shakespearean productions must surely augur well for his first opera. A single instance from the score of *Hamlet* will perhaps be sufficient to illustrate the extraordinary ingenuity Walton brings into his screen writing, making his one of the famous names in film music all over the world. This example is taken from the players' scene.

The arrival of the Court is heralded by trumpet calls and a superb march theme which appears to keep step with the retinue as they take their places around the King's dais. Then the players make their entry, accompanied by a small group of musicians. For this, Walton hints at the idiom of the period, and uses an orchestra of two violas, cello, oboe, cor anglais, bassoon and harpsichord. He opens with a sarabande, music in slow three-in-a-measure dance time often encountered in seventeenth- and eighteenth-century music, and follows this with a slower, sinister passage for the entry of the poisoner.

As the camera moves round to show the reactions of the audience, and particularly of the King, the stage music dissolves into the Players theme, which is taken up by the full symphony orchestra [of about 50 players], as the dramatic undercurrent of the scene, and the tension of the Court, rises.

The camera, from its circular tracking orbit, returns to the Players, and the music reverts to the quiet accompaniment of the play. The actor-king has been poisoned; the King can no longer stand the strain. ('The play's the thing, Wherein to catch the conscience of the king.') The full power of the orchestra rises up, swamping the soft sounds of the cello, oboe and harpsichord, and ends in a tremendous chord, as the King roars out, 'Give me some light.'

William Walton's score was a constant delight to record, being so perfect in detail and sure in its dramatic conception. It will certainly prove the perfect complement to a great subject.

Appendix 4. The Façade *Poems*

The table (overleaf) charts the evolution of *Façade*, from its first performance to its final published version with later additions, and shows the constant revision, re-ordering, rejection and addition of the poems used. The titles in bold type are those used in the definitive published *Façade* score, while those in italics were revived to be incorporated in either *Façade Revived* or *Façade 2*. The years in question refer to the following performances:

1922	24 January	Carlyle Square	First (private) performance with Edith Sitwell
1923	12 June	Aeolian Hall	First public performance with Edith Sitwell
1926	27 April	New Chenil Galleries	Second public performance
1926	29 June	New Chenil Galleries	First performance with Constant Lambert alone
1928	14 Sept.	Siena	First European performance(s) with C. Lambert
1929	28 Nov.	New Chenil Galleries	Decca Recording (excerpts) with E.S. and C.L.

Walton conducted all the above performances

1930	3 March	Central Hall, Westminster	First complete broadcast with E.S. and C.L., cond. Heward
1942	29 May	Aeolian Hall	Definitive version with C. L., cond. Walton
1951			Published score
1977	25 March	Plaisterers' Hall, London	*Façade Revived* with Richard Baker, cond. Mackerras
1979	19 June	The Maltings	First performance of *Façade 2* with Peter Pears, cond. Bedford

The following symbols are used in the first column of the table:

+   Published 1932 in version for voice and piano.
1 or 2   Orchestrated for First or Second Suite respectively (2-3 denotes third movement of Second Suite). In these Suites, *Tarantella* was renamed *Tarantella-Sevillana* with several changes made, and *Long Steel Grass* became *Noche Espagnole*.

Table 1. The incidence and ordering of poems through different performances of Façade

	1922	1923	1926	1926	1928	1929	1930	1942	1951	1977	1979
[Fanfare] 2-1	✓	✓	✓	✓	✓	✓			✓	✓	
[Overture]	✓	✓	✓								
Dame Souris Trotte (Madam Mouse Trots)	1										
The Octogenarian	2	5	11	15							4
Aubade	3	10[b?]	16	10						4	5
The Wind's Bastinado	4	22	14							7	2
Said King Pompey	5	9	6	9						8	8
[Interlude]	✓										
Jumbo's Lullaby	6	3	12	18	7			8	7		
Small Talk I & II	7	7	4								
Rose Castles (Water Party)	8	19									7
(Introduction and) **Hornpipe**	9	21	1	1	1			1	1		
Long Steel Grass 2-4	10	13	17	16	16	E.S.	13	4	4		
(Trio for Two Cats and a Trombone)											
(When) Sir Beelzebub	11	27	26	14	22		12	21	21		
Switchback	12	6	10								
Bank Holiday I & II	13										
Springing Jack	14										
En Famille	15	20	2	2				2	2		
Mariner Man	16	18	3	3				3	3		
Gardener Janus catches a Naiad		1									6
Clown Argheb's Song		2									
Trams		4	13								

	1	2	3	4	(source)	5	6	7	8
By the Lake	8	5	8	8		5	10	11	
Serenade	10a?								
Herodiade's Flea (Came the Great Popinjay)	11							2	1
Through Gilded Trellises +	12	18	17	18		14	5	5	2
A Man from a far countree	14	8	21	14	E.S.	8	11	10	
Daphne +	15	7	20	13		7			1
Country Dance 2-3	16	9	22	15		9	12	12	
Gone Dry	17								
The (White) Owl	23							6	
Dark Song	24								
Fox-trot: Old Sir Faulk + 2-6	25	15	11	4	C.L.	3	9	20	
Ass-Face	26								
Tango–Pasodoble (I do Like . . . the Seaside) 1-4	19	19	19		C.L.	15	6	6	3
Valse (Daisy and Lily) 1-2	20	5	10		C.L.	4	17	16	
Polka 1-1	21	7	12		C.L.	1	16	13	
(Swiss) Jodelling Song 1-3	22	6	11		E.S.	11	13	17	
Scotch Rhapsody 2-2	23	4	3		C.L.	10	7	18	
Something lies beyond the scene	24	23	21			20	15		
Four in the Morning	25	13	5			2	19	14	
March		12	17						
Tarantella 1-5		24	20		C.L.	6	18	9	5
Mazurka		25							
Popular Song 2-5			6		C.L.	17	15	19	
Black Mrs Behemoth			9		E.S.	16	14	8	
The last galop	18				18				3
No. of poems used	16	28?	26	25	11	22	18	21	8

The Publication of the Poems

As a generic term, the word *Façade* can be misleading, referring as it does both to the Entertainment and to Edith Sitwell's collection of poems. It is further complicated by the fact that not all Edith's poems under that heading were used in the Entertainment, neither did all the poems that were set to music come from *Façade*.

The printed programme for the first private performance of the Walton–Sitwell *Façade* in Janaury 1922 contained the texts of the sixteen poems set. The private printing in February 1922 of the anthology entitled *Façade* (The Favil Press, Kensington, with a frontispiece by Severini) was a limited edition of 150 numbered copies. It consisted of two groups of poems, five under the heading of *Winter*, the remaining nine under *Façade*. Nine of the poems in this edition had been used at the première a week or so earlier, and one, *Through Gilded Trellises*, was to be included in the first public performance of *Façade* in 1923. They were:

from *Winter*:   *En Famille*
from *Façade*:   *Long Steel Grass* (*Trio for Cats and a Trombone*),
               Madame Mouse Trots, Through Gilded Trellises,
               Said King Pompey, The Octogenarian, Sailors Come
               (changed to *Hornpipe*), *The Wind's Bastinado, Jumbo Asleep*
               (*Jumbo's Lullaby*), *When Sir Beelzebub*

Of these, *En Famille* had first appeared in *The Chapbook* July 1920, and *Long Steel Grass* in the *Saturday Westminster Gazette* of 3 September 1921.

Another six of the remaining seven poems used in the first private performance had seen earlier publication. *Aubade* had appeared in the *Saturday Westminster Gazette* of 2 October 1920. The others had come from two earlier anthologies. *Clowns' Houses* (Blackwell 1918) included *Mariner Man* (or *Mariner-Men* as it was named). *The Wooden Pegasus* (Blackwell 1920) included four poems set in the 1922 performance, all of which had been previously published in such periodicals as *Wheels*, *Oxford & Cambridge Miscellany* and *Arts and Letters*: *Switchback, Bank Holiday I & II, Small Talk I & II* and *Springing Jack* (No. 14 of *Fifteen Bucolic Poems*), as well as one to be used in the first public performance: *Trams*, revised since its appearance in an even earlier anthology, *Twentieth Century Harlequinade* (Blackwell 1916).

Most of the above poems and nine new ones reached a wider circulation in the anthology *Bucolic Comedies*, published by Duckworth on 24 April 1923, about a fortnight before the public première. In this volume of fifty-one poems, nineteen came under the heading *Façade*. Their titles were:

Père Amelot, The Wind's Bastinado *, Lullaby for Jumbo *,
Trio for Two Cats and a Trombone *, Dame Souris Trotte *, Dark Song *,
Fête Galante, The Owl *, Alone, Fading Slow and Furred in the Snow,
Said King Pompey the Emperor's Ape *, The Sky Was of Cinnamon, Ass-
Face *, The Octogenarian Leaned from his Window *, Said the Noctambulo
Herodiade's Flea *, Water Party *, Hornpipe *, Sir Beelzebub *

The thirteen titles with an asterisk are those that were set to music and used in either the first private performance or the public première, or both. With the inclusion of *Water Party* all the poems used in the first private performance had by then been published.

Of the remaining poems in that anthology that were used in the Entertainment, five came from the group of *Nineteen Bucolic Poems*, these being *Aubade, Fox Trot (Old Sir Faulk), Gardener Janus Catches a Naiad, Clown Argheb's Song* and *Country Dance*. (Two other titles that might suggest themselves as suitable candidates, *Cacophony for Clarinet* and *The Five Musicians*, were not set.) *En Famille* was appearing in print again, while *By the Lake* from the group *Spleen* was one of the five poems seeing first publication.

Three poems first heard at the public première in 1923 appeared in Edith's long poem *The Sleeping Beauty* (Duckworth 1924): *Daphne* (pp. 70–1), *A Man From a Far Countree* (p. 72) and *Through Gilded Trellises* (pp. 74–5). Four poems from her *Troy Park* anthology (Alfred Knopf 1925) were included in the 1926 and 1928 performances: *I do Like to Be Beside the Seaside (Tango–Pasodoble), Something Lies Beyond the Scene, Four in the Morning* and *Black Mrs Behemoth*, together with a snatch of *Scotch Rhapsody* (p. 75). *Valse* and *Polka*, that had first appeared in *Vogue*, were printed, together with *Aubade* and *Tarantella*, in the programme for the second Aeolian Hall performance on 29 June 1926.

Of the forty-four titles listed in the table above, twenty-three appeared in *The Canticle of the Rose* (R. & R. Black 1949), twenty-nine were printed in *Façade and Other Poems* (Duckworth 1950) and thirty-three in *Collected Poems* (The Vanguard Press 1954).

The text of *Gone Dry*, found in one of Edith's notebooks in the Harry Ransom Humanities Research Center at Austin, Texas was the subject of an article by Neil Ritchie in the Autumn 1999 issue of the *Book Collector* ('Bibliographical Notes & Queries, Note 570, "Gone Dry": An Unpublished *Façade* Poem', 459–61). *Jodelling Song* and *Mazurka* derived from *Prelude to a Fairy Tale* in *Rustic Elegies* (1927). The text of *March* was printed in the facsimile edition of *Façade 2* (OUP 1979). *Popular Song* received a special printing on its own near the time of its first hearing in September 1928 in Siena.

A copy of the programme for the first public performance of *Façade* had long eluded Walton researchers until one turned up in auction in 1998.

Besides settling the question of which poems were used and in what order, the recently discovered programme poses one problem. With the poems divided into eight numbered groups and therein listed by letter (e.g. III a, b, c), IV a is identified as *Serenade/The Octogenarian* (printed over two lines). It is not clear whether *Serenade* is a setting of a poem, possibly the similarly named one that appeared in the *Daily Mirror* in November 1913 and subsequently in both Edith's first printed volume, *The Mother* (1915) and *The Wooden Pegasus* (1920), and *Collected Poems* (1957). If this is so, why, unlike all the others on the programme, was it bracketed with another poem and not listed separately? At six lines it is shorter than any poem set in *Façade* and could have led without a break into *The Octogenarian*. Was the *Daily Express* critic including the *Overture* when reporting '28 items on the programme'? If not, the *Serenade* would bring the number of poems up to that total. Or was it a piece of music without voice that has since been lost, as Neil Ritchie interprets Helen Rootham's review of the concert for *The New Age* of 21 June 1923? For the first Chenil Galleries performance, the second half of the programme began after an interval with a *Fanfare* (presumably a repeat of the opening *Fanfare*) followed by an Introduction that led into *The Octogenarian*. Could the *Serenade* have been a musical link like the Introduction that was later reduced to the brief flourish that now precedes the poem in *Façade 2?* The puzzle remains.

Author's note: Acknowledgement is made to Richard Fifoot's *A Bibliography of Edith, Osbert and Sacheverell Sitwell* (second edition, revised, Archon Books 1971) which has been invaluable in compiling this appendix.

The Music

Following the burning of the Maltings concert hall in 1969, Walton allowed the *Façade* manuscripts to be auctioned for the Snape Rebuilding Fund. Most of the manuscripts are held today in either the Humanities Research Center, University of Texas, Austin, USA or the Beinecke Library, Yale University, USA as part of the Frederick R. Koch Collection that includes most of the Walton manuscripts. A few *Façade* manuscripts are held in private hands. The settings that remain untraced are: *The Wind's Bastinado, Small Talk II, Switchback, Bank Holiday I & II* and *Springing Jack* (all used in the first private performance); *Trams, Gone Dry* and *Ass Face* (from the first public performance); and *Mazurka* (1926).

An enterprising CD issued in 1993 on the Discover label (DICD 920125) includes all forty-four poems except *Gone Dry* and *Serenade*, either as set by Walton or, in the absence of the score, read without music. The reciter Pamela Hunter is accompanied by the Melologos Ensemble, conducted by Silveer van den Broeck.

Appendix 5. Reviews of Façade

1. *Evening Standard* 13 June 1923

Metrics through the Megaphone

In the afternoon, at the Aeolian Hall,
Through a megaphone we heard Edith bawl,
Pink and white face, cut down the middle
Another face, black; a man with a fiddle;
Her brother's voice, dark blue in a void
Behind a black mask that looked annoyed.
People rising like pig-snouted fishes
To the newest bait thrown by those whose wish is
To be fresh as the crisp young lettuces green.
(Buns for the bears of Sheba's queen!)
Flutes and trumpets and such ripe sounds
Like an ape that's choking with coffee grounds;
Flat-sided noises with braided hair
Cropped as close as from here to there.
Clapping poets in rows like cheeses; –
'Shall we slide on the Caspian when it freezes?'
And the negro said: 'See how they come
At a flick of my clouded crystal thumb.'

Present-day poets are sometimes accused of blowing their own trumpets. Miss Edith Sitwell, with the originality that marks her work (and that of her gifted brothers, Osbert and Sacheverell), prefers the megaphone. She used the megaphone, which – again with the touch of originality – she called a Sengerphone, for the better dissemination of her poems at a curious entertainment, entitled 'Façade', at the Aeolian Hall, yesterday afternoon.

Some people were a little puzzled by this title. They could only conclude that it referred to the scenic setting, which again, was distinctly original. On an arrangement of yellow curtains and pillars there appeared two painted faces. The charm of the centre and larger face, blushing a delicate pink on one cheek, and of a deathly whiteness (with apprehension) on the other, was a little spoiled by the total absence of nose or lips. These features were replaced by the Sengerphone, which resembled the larger end of an immature megaphone.

Below and to the right of this so charming countenance there was another, similarly equipped. It was black, but not comely. Through it another voice 'off' – believed to be that of Mr Osbert Sitwell – announced the various items from her works recited by the Sengerphonist. The latter was aided by a small concealed orchestra of six unsynchronised instruments and a 'percussion' which, under the direction of Mr W T Walton, produced appropriate music and noises.

The audience seemed a little cold at first; the first sign of real emotion was when three members of the audience went out hurriedly – presumably to weep in the vestibule – at the conclusion of the affecting 'Lullaby for Jumbo', which begins:

> Jumbo asleep!
> Grey leaves thick furred
> As his ears, keep
> Conversations blurred.

It is possible, of course, that they left out of chagrin because they were unable to answer the question with which the poem closes:

> And why should the spined flowers
> Red as a soldier,
> Make Don Pasquito
> Seem still mouldier?

Why, indeed?

Gradually, under the influence of Miss Sitwell's fervent chanting of her exotic lines, the audience became attuned to the spirit of the Sengerphonist, as was shown by the enthusiasm that followed the sonorous rendering of a 'Trio for Two Cats and a Trombone.'[1]

2. *Vogue July 1923*

"Façade": A New Entertainment

Mr W T Walton's Music Provides a Decorative
Accompaniment to Miss Edith Sitwell's Poems
by Gerald Cumberland[2]

'You will meet strange people,' announced Mr Osbert Sitwell; 'Queen Victoria and Venus, Circe and Lord Tennyson.' Was this, as they say, a threat or a

---

[1] K. K., *Evening Standard*, 13 June 1923, 3.
[2] His real name was Charles Kenyon.

promise? Mr Edmund Gosse, a not inconspicuous figure in the Aeolian Hall on the afternoon of June 12th, did not flinch, though Mr Sitwell's words must have disturbed him not a little. To us of a younger generation the announcement was rich with promise; for not even now are we tired of being very rude to the Albert Memorial, the Crystal Palace and the dingy ideals of that perilous period. So, wide-eyed, we waited to see the curtain by Mr Frank Dobson, which, the programme seemed to hint, would be the prelude to Miss Edith Sitwell's poems and Mr W T Walton's music.

And, in due time, that curtain was revealed to us. It achieved its destiny. It surprised and held us; it prophesied to us dimly the nature of the things to come. An enormous female face looked down upon us: a face with a low forehead, fat cheeks strangely coloured, and a look that signified its owner was, so to speak, perfectly at home. From her open mouth issued a sengerphone pointed – oh, so thrillingly! – in our direction. By the side of the lady's face a mask was painted; into the mask's mouth another, but smaller, sengerphone was inserted. Behind the former, as it soon transpired, Miss Edith Sitwell was stationed, her clever head full of her strangely disturbing poetry; from behind the latter Mr Osbert Sitwell guided us through the charming programme.

During the entire course of the entertainment we were permitted to see nothing save Mr Dobson's curtain, Miss Sitwell reciting and her musicians playing in tantalising concealment. It was an attempt at the elimination of personality. The ordinary professional reciter was accused by Mr Osbert Sitwell of using poetry for the exploitation of his own personality, of indulging in hysterical pathos and hysterical charm. Miss Sitwell half spoke, half shouted, her poems in strict monotone, emphasising the metre rather than the rhythm, and permitting her voice no expressiveness save on rare occasions when, because of its unexpectedness and because of the sudden relief it afforded, it had a deeply, emotional effect. Her voice, beautiful in tone, full, resonant and clear, could, without effort, be heard above the decorative din of the music. It was only by variations in the speed of her delivery that she sought to give additional expressiveness to her words; her command of a fluid rubato was consummate; and though I failed sometimes to follow her in the application of her method, I have no doubt that my failure was due to the novelty and the daring of that method. Sometimes she spoke with the rushing rapidity that Bernhardt used to give us twenty years ago in scenes of angry passion, at other times she dropped heavily on a word, remained upon it, giving it a static emphasis. Many of the poems she recited are familiar to me, but her interpretation of them disclosed implications that previously had not been apparent. To this hour I am by no means sure what some of her poems mean; but if I do not understand their beauty, I divine it, and for that reason am all the more attracted, drawn, seduced.

Mr Walton's music was clever. It had intuition, it understood the words. Its office seemed to be to sprinkle jewels and flowers with an apt hand on the pathway of Miss Sitwell's poetry. Only once did I observe it to fail, and it failed by becoming obvious. The introduction of a few bars of hornpipe music was like underlining a phrase with the thick of one's thumb. Miss Sitwell never crosses her t's or dots her i's; and it was distressing, for the moment, to hear Mr Walton doing it for her. Need I say that the audience mistook Mr Walton's error of judgement for a stroke of genius? At last, in that familiar hornpipe music, it heard something it could understand. It demanded it again. The only scrap of Mr Walton's music that was not his own was precisely the scrap that pleased his hearers most. I shudder to contemplate what would have happened had Miss Sitwell quoted a couplet from Tennyson. The little orchestra of flute, clarinet, saxophone, trumpet, violoncello and percussion instruments played with airy delicacy and occasional pomp.

Miss Sitwell, then, has discovered and tried a new method of interpretation. The experiment was well worth making; but I am inclined to think that her success was in no small measure due to the strangeness and beauty of her poetry. Her bizarre work demands a bizarre setting, a bizarre delivery. No other poetry known to me would survive this particular kind of presentation. But the brittle loveliness of Miss Sitwell's work, its kaleidoscopic colour, its ellipses so full of imagination, and its darting cleverness are all enhanced by this deliberately sought artificiality. For the new method *is* artificial. Mr Osbert Sitwell warned the audience that if it liked the entertainment there was no occasion for it to spoil the new method by copying it. There is no need to fear any imitation of this very interesting art. Mr J C Squire's chaste muse, for example, would be shattered to bits by Miss Sitwell's sengerphone, and Mr Edward Shanks' little wings would break at its first blast.

And the audience? Did the audience succeed? Well, it did its best. But it came ill-prepared. A previous knowledge of Miss Sitwell's work would have helped it to an understanding; but, being without that knowledge, it applauded often in the wrong place, spoiling picture after picture by its anxiety to assert and prove its enthusiasm. For a full appreciation of Miss Sitwell's poetry one must have a mind both alert and sensitive:

> For only the gay hosannas of flowers
> Sound, loud as brass bands, in those heavenly bowers.

Not all who visited the Aeolian Hall the other day heard the brazen call of the tiger-lily or saw the gleaming purple of the nightingale's song.[3]

---

[3] July 1923, Vol. 62, No. 13, 36 and 70.

Appendix 6. List of Works

The information given for each work in this chronological list is as follows:

1. publisher and year of publication, where applicable;
2. work number (preceded by the letter C) following the classification in Stewart Craggs' *William Walton: A Catalogue* (to which the reader is referred for further information);
3. first performance (in some cases first European/ United Kingdom/ London/ public/ private/ broadcast performance, etc.);
4. a selective list of recordings.

The short list of recordings includes those made by Walton himself, together with any other historical issue of special interest: for example, those made by the original artists or the first (or only) recording of a particular work. In such cases details of both the initial and more recent releases are given. For each work at least one representative modern recording on CD (with the catalogue number in italics) has also been given. The inclusion of any recording in this list does not, of course, ensure its current availability. The quantity of fine recordings now available on CD makes any selection difficult. Beside EMI's 4-CD set *The Walton Edition* with the composer conducting (on CHS 5 65003-2, all items of which are included in the list below, with many of them also re-issued separately), the reader is referred to the complete Chandos series of recordings (many of which have also been included), those on the super-budget label Naxos, the three Decca CDs made by Andrew Litton and the Bournemouth Symphony Orchestra, and many others. A number of recordings of live performances of particular interest (the premières of *Troilus and Cressida* and the Cello Concerto, the war-time broadcast of *Christopher Columbus*, etc.) are held in the National Sound Archive in the British Library and can be heard by special request.

In compiling this list, both Stewart Craggs' *William Walton: A Catalogue* and Alan Poulton's *Sir William Walton: A Discography* have been invaluable. Where there has been any difference in the recording dates, the information given in the sleeve-notes for the latest releases has generally been followed.

As regards the printed music, Oxford University Press is issuing a complete William Walton Edition. The first volume, the definitive version of the Symphony No. 1, was launched in 1998.

1916

A Litany (Phineas Fletcher) Motet for unacc. mixed chorus. OUP 1930 C1
   Recordings:
>   1.   St. John's College Choir, Cambridge, George Guest. Argo ZRG5340.
>   2.   Christ Church Cathedral Choir, Oxford, Simon Preston. 1971. Argo
>   ZRG725
>   3.   Trinity College Choir, Cambridge, Richard Marlow. 25–7 June 1988.
>   *Conifer CDCF164*

Tell Me Where is Fancy Bred (Shakespeare) Song for soprano and tenor, 3 violins
       and piano C2

Choral Prelude for Organ on 'Wheatley' C3 39 bars

The Forsaken Merman (Matthew Arnold) Cantata for soprano and tenor, double
       female chorus and orchestra C4 – unperformed

1917

Valse in C minor for piano C5

1918

Child's Song (A. C. Swinburne) for voice and piano
Love Laid his Sleepless Head (Swinburne) for voice and piano
A Lyke-wake Song (Swinburne) for voice and piano
The Winds (Swinburne) for voice and piano. Curwen 1921; OUP 1985 C6
   Recordings:
>   1.   Yvonne Kenny and Malcolm Martineau. 2–4 May 1992. *Etcetera
>   KTC1140*
>   2.   Felicity Lott and Graham Johnson. *Collins 14932*

1919

Quartet for Piano and Strings C7
——— revised 1921 after score had been lost. Stainer & Bell 1924
   Fp: Liverpool. 19 September 1924. McCullagh String Quartet, J.E. Wallace (pno.)
   FLon.p: Aeolian Hall, London. 30 October 1929. Pierre Tas, James Lockyer,
       John Gabalfa, Gordon Bryan (pno.)
   Recordings:
>   1.   Reginald Paul Piano Quartet. 1939. Decca AX238-41
>   2.   Robert Masters Piano Quartet. November 1954. Argo RG48
——— further small revisions 1974–75 for republication. OUP 1976
   Recordings:
>   1.   John McCabe and English String Quartet. 1986. *Meridian CDE84139*
>   2.   Gabrieli String Quartet. *CHAN8999*

1920

Tritons (William Drummond) for voice and piano. Curwen 1921; OUP 1985 C8
   Recordings:
>   1.   Yvonne Kenny and Malcolm Martineau. 2–4 May 1992. *Etcetera
>   KTC1140*
>   2.   Felicity Lott and Graham Johnson. *Collins 14932*

The Passionate Shepherd (Christopher Marlowe) Song for tenor and ten
    instruments (whereabouts unknown) C9 – unperformed

1921

Dr Syntax Pedagogic overture for full orchestra (lost) C10 – unperformed
Quartet (No. 1) for Strings in two movements (lost) C11
    Fp: London. 4 March 1921. Pennington String Quartet
    ——— revised c.1922 with addition of third movement. OUP hire
    Fp: RCM London. 5 July 1923. McCullagh String Quartet
    FEur.p: ISCM Festival Salzburg. 4 August 1923. McCullagh String Quartet
    Recording: Gabrieli String Quartet. 30–1 October 1990. *CHAN8944*
[Revision of **Quartet for Piano and Strings** C7]

1922

Façade (Edith Sitwell): An Entertainment for reciter and chamber ensemble C12
    Fpriv.p: 2 Carlyle Square, London, 24 January 1922. Edith Sitwell,
        William Walton
    Fpub.p: Aeolian Hall, London, 12 June 1923. Edith Sitwell, William Walton
    ——— definitive version performed 1942 and published OUP 1951
    Recordings:
        1. [11 numbers only] Edith Sitwell, Constant Lambert, ensemble, William
            Walton. 28 November 1929. Decca T124/5; *Symposium 1203*;
            Claremont CD GSE 78-50-65
        2. [without *Tarantella*] Edith Sitwell, David Horner, ensemble, Frederick
            Prausnitz. 21 January 1949. Columbia 72806/9D; *Sony SMK 46685*
        3. Edith Sitwell, Peter Pears, English Opera Group Ensemble, Anthony
            Collins. July/August 1954. Decca LXT2977; *425 661-2*
        4. Peggy Ashcroft, Paul Scofield, members of London Sinfonietta,
            William Walton. 5–7 May 1969 (voices added to the music later). Argo
            ZRG649; *Belart 450 36-2*.
        5. [*Façade 1* and *2*] Susana Walton, Richard Baker, members of City of
            London Sinfonia, Richard Hickox. 19–21 March 1990. *CHAN 8869*
        6. ['Complete version'] Pamela Hunter, Melologos Ensemble. 8–10
            March 1993. *Discover DICD 920125*
    ——— eight unpublished numbers assembled as **Façade Revived** 1977 (q.v.)
    ——— revision of above as **Façade 2** 1979 (q.v.)
    ——— **Ballet** (based on Entertainment) 1972 C12a
    Fp: The Maltings, Snape. 28 July 1972. Peter Pears (narrator), David Taylor
    ——— **First Suite for Orchestra** (5 movements) 1926. OUP 1936 C12c
    Fp: Lyceum Theatre, London. 3 December 1926. Lyceum Orchestra, William
        Walton
    ——— **Ballet** (based on First Orchestral Suite) 1929 C12d
    Fp: Hagen, Westphalia. 22 September 1929. Georg Lippert
    ——— **Second Suite for Orchestra** (6 movements) 1938. OUP C12e
    Fp: New York. 30 March 1938. New York Philharmonic-Symphony Orchestra,
        John Barbirolli
    FLon.p: Queen's Hall. 10 September 1938. BBC Symphony Orchestra, Henry
        Wood

Recordings (Suite No. 1 and **No. 2** combined, with the order of movements changed):
  1. [order: 6,1,3,2,4,10,8,7,5,9,11] London Philharmonic Orchestra, William Walton. 5 March 1936 and 25 October 1938. HMV C2836-7 and C3042; *EMI CDH 7 63381-2*
  2. [order: 6,1,3,2,4,8,10,7,5,9,11] Philharmonia Orchestra, Constant Lambert. 27 September 1950. Columbia DX1734-6; Columbia 33SX1003
  3. [order: 6,7,2,4,3,8,1,9,10,11,5] Philharmonia Orchestra, William Walton. 20 April 1955 and 26 March 1957. Columbia 33C1054; *EMI CHS 5 65003-2*
[Revision of **Quartet (No 1) for Strings** C11]

1923
Toccata for Violin and Piano C13
  Fp: London. 12 May 1925. K. Goldsmith and Angus Morrison
  Recording: [incomplete] Kenneth Sillito, Hamish Milne. 11–12 January 1992. *Chandos CHAN9292*

1924
Fantasia Concertante for two pianos, jazz band and orchestra (unfinished and lost) C14
Bucolic Comedies (Edith Sitwell) Five songs, three with instrumental accomp. (lost) C15
——— revised as **Three Songs** (1932, q.v.) C26

1925
A Son of Heaven (Lytton Strachey) Incidental music (lost) C16
  Fp: Scala Theatre, London. 12 July 1925. William Walton
Portsmouth Point Overture for full orchestra. OUP 1928 C17
  Fp: Zürich. 22 June 1926. Tonhalle Orchestra, Volkmar Andreae
  FLon.p: His Majesty's Theatre. 28 June 1926. Eugene Goossens
  Recordings:
  1. New English Symphony Orchestra, Anthony Bernard. 1935. Decca M94
  2. BBC Symphony Orchestra, Adrian Boult. 12 June 1936. HMV DA1540; *VAIA 1067-2*
  3. Minneapolis Symphony Orchestra, Dimitri Mitropoulos. 1947. Columbia 12755D
  4. Philharmonia Orchestra, William Walton. 21 March 1953. Columbia 33C1016; *EMI CHS 5 65003-2*
  5. London Philharmonic Orchestra, William Walton. 15 April 1970. Lyrita SRCS47; *SRCD224*
——— arranged for small orchestra by Constant Lambert C17a
  Fp: Savoy Theatre, London. 6 June 1932. Camargo Society, Constant Lambert (with Spike Hughes' *High Yellow*)

Recording: London Philharmonic Orchestra, Jan Latham-Koenig. 12 November 1991. *CHAN 9148*
————— arranged for piano duet by composer OUP 1927 C17b

1926
Siesta for small orchestra OUP 1929 C19
   Fp: Aeolian Hall, London. 24 November 1926. Aeolian Chamber Orchestra, William Walton
   Recording: London Philharmonic Orchestra, William Walton. 25 October 1938. HMV C3042; *EMI CDH 7 63381-2*
————— arranged for piano 4 hands by composer OUP 1928 C19a
————— **Ballet** 1936 C19c
   Fp: Sadler's Wells Theatre, London. 24 January 1936. Vic–Wells Ballet, William Walton
————— revised 1962 OUP 1963
   Recording: London Philharmonic Orchestra, William Walton. 15 April 1970. Lyrita SRCS47; *SRCD224*
Orchestration of Lambert's *Romeo and Juliet* C18
Orchestration of numbers in Berners' *The Triumph of Neptune* C20

1927
Sinfonia Concertante for orchestra with piano 'continuo'[1] OUP 1928 C21
   Fp: Queen's Hall, London. 5 January 1928. York Bowen (piano)
       Royal Philharmonic (Society) Orchestra, William Walton
   Recordings:
     1. Kathryn Stott, Royal Philharmonic Orchestra, Vernon Handley. 10–12 July 1989. *Conifer CDCF 175*
     2. London Philharmonic Orchestra, Jan Latham-Koenig. 12 November 1991. *CHAN 9148*
————— revised 1943 OUP 1953
   Fp: Liverpool. 9 February 1944, Cyril Smith (piano). Liverpool Philharmonic Orchestra, Malcolm Sargent
   Recordings:
     1. Phyllis Sellick, City of Birmingham Orchestra, William Walton. 8 August 1945. HMV C3478-80; *EMI CDH 7 63828-2*; *Avid AMSC604*
     2. Peter Katin, London Symphony Orchestra, William Walton. 14 April 1970. Lyrita SRCS49; *SRCD224*
————— arranged for 2 pianos by composer OUP 1928 C21a

---

[1] A manuscript of the *Sinfonia Concertante* is now part of the Koch Foundation's Walton collection at Yale University (with the first movement apparently not in Walton's hand). However, in December 1999 an autograph manuscript of an earlier version, differing in some details from the published edition, came up for auction at Sotheby's (*Sotheby's: Printed and Manuscript Music [Auction Catalogue]* London, 9 December 1999, Lot 263, pp. 265–6). It is now in the Koch Collection, Yale University, USA.

1929

Concerto for Viola and Orchestra OUP 1930 C22

Fp: Queen's Hall, London. 3 October 1929. Paul Hindemith, Henry Wood
 Symphony Orchestra, William Walton

Recordings:

1. Frederick Riddle, London Symphony Orchestra, William Walton.
   6 December 1937. Decca X199-201; *Dutton CDAX 8003*
2. William Primrose, Philharmonia Orchestra, William Walton. 22–3 July
   1946. HMV DB6309-11; *EMI CDH 7 63828-2*; *Pearl GEMMCD9252*;
   Avid AMSC604
3. William Primrose, Royal Philharmonic Orchestra, Malcolm Sargent.
   1954. Philips ABL3045

——— revised 1961 OUP 1964

Fp: Royal Festival Hall, London. 18 January 1962. John Coulling (viola), London
 Philharmonic Orchestra, Malcolm Sargent

Recording: Yehudi Menuhin, New Philharmonia Orchestra, William Walton.
 9–11 October 1968. HMV ASD2542; *EMI CHS 5 65003-2*; *EMI
 CDM565005-2*

1931

Belshazzar's Feast (Bible arr. Osbert Sitwell) Cantata for baritone solo, double
 mixed chorus and orchestra OUP 1931 C23

Fp: Town Hall, Leeds. 8 October 1931. Dennis Noble, Leeds Festival Chorus,
 London Symphony Orchestra, Malcolm Sargent

FLon.p: Queen's Hall. 25 November 1931. Stuart Robertson, National Chorus,
 BBC Symphony Orchestra, Adrian Boult

Recording:

 Dennis Noble, Huddersfield Choral Society, Liverpool Philharmonic
 Orchestra, William Walton. 3 and 10 January 1943. HMV C3330-34; *EMI
 CDH 7 63381-2*

——— revised 1948 OUP 1957

Recordings:

1. Dennis Noble, London Philharmonic Choir and Philharmonic
   Promenade Orchestra, Adrian Boult. 10 December 1953. Nixa
   NLP904; *Pye PVCD 8394*
2. James Milligan, Huddersfield Choral Society, Royal Liverpool
   Philharmonic Orchestra, Malcolm Sargent. 27 February and 1–2 March
   1958. HMV ALP1628; *EMI CHS 7 63376-2*
3. Donald Bell, Philharmonia Chorus and Orchestra, William Walton. 2–5
   February 1959. Columbia 33CX1679 (SAX2319); *EMI CHS 5
   65003-2*; *EMI CDM565004-2*
4. John Shirley-Quirk, London Symphony Chorus and Orchestra, André
   Previn. 29–30 March 1972. EMI SAN324; *CDM 7 64723-2*
5. [*'Slain!'* only] Hoffnung Festival Choral Society, William Walton. pub.
   perf. 28 November 1961. Columbia 33CX1785; *EMI CMS 7 63302-2*

Make We Joy in this Feast Old English Carol for unacc. mixed chorus OUP 1932
 C24
Recordings:
 1. New College Choir, Oxford, David Lumsden. 1962. Alpha ADV001
 2. Christ Church Cathedral Choir, Oxford, Simon Preston. 1971. Argo
 ZRG725
 3. Trinity College Choir, Cambridge, Richard Marlow. 25–7 June 1988.
 Conifer CDCF164
Choral Prelude 'Herzlich Thut Mich Verlangen' (Bach arr. Walton) for piano
 OUP 1932 C25
Fp: Queen's Hall, London. 17 October 1932. Harriet Cohen

1932
Three Songs (Edith Sitwell): *Daphne, Through Gilded Trellises, Old Sir Faulk* for
 voice and piano OUP 1932 C26, revision of **Bucolic Comedies** (Edith
 Sitwell) Five songs (1924) C15
Fp: Wigmore Hall, London. 10 October 1932. Dora Stevens and Hubert Foss
Recordings:
 1. Dora Stevens and Hubert Foss. 20 March 1940. Decca M489-90;
 Dutton CDAX 8003
 2. Felicity Lott and Graham Johnson. *Collins 14932*

1934
Symphony No. 1 for full orchestra. OUP 1936 C27
 Fp (three movements): Queen's Hall, London. 3 December 1934. London
 Symphony Orchestra, Hamilton Harty
 Fp (complete): Queen's Hall, London. 6 November 1935. BBC Symphony
 Orchestra, Hamilton Harty
Recordings:
 1. London Symphony Orchestra, Hamilton Harty. 10–11 December 1935.
 Decca X108-113; *Dutton CDAX 8003*
 2. Philharmonia Orchestra, William Walton. 17–18 October 1951. HMV
 ALP1027; *EMI CHS 5 65003-2; EMI CDM565004-2*
 3. Philharmonic Promenade Orchestra, Adrian Boult. 16 August 1956.
 Pye GGC4008; *PVCD 8377*
 4. London Symphony Orchestra, André Previn. 26–7 August 1966. RCA
 RB6691 (SB6691); *GD87830*
 5. New Philharmonia Orchestra, Malcolm Sargent. 18–22 October 1966.
 HMV ASD2299; *5 68026-2*

1935
Escape Me Never Film music C28
 Fp: London Pavilion. 1 April 1935 (soundtrack conducted by Hyam Greenbaum)
 Recording: [Ballet sequence only] National Philharmonic Orchestra, Bernard
 Herrmann. 5–6 November 1975. Decca PFS4363; *421261-2DA*
 ———— **Suite** arranged by Christopher Palmer (4 sections)
 Recording: Academy of St Martin-in-the-Fields, Neville Marriner. 2–3 March
 1990. *CHAN8870*

The First Shoot Ballet music C29
    Fp: Opera House, Manchester. 23 December 1935. Francis Collinson
    FLon.p: The Adelphi Theatre. 4 February 1936
———— arranged for brass band 1980 OUP 1986 C29b
    Fp: Goldsmiths' College, London. 19 December 1980 (recording for TV).
        Grimethorpe Colliery Band, Elgar Howarth.
    Fpub.p: Royal Albert Hall Proms, London. 7 September 1981. Grimethorpe
        Colliery Band, Elgar Howarth
    Recordings:
        1. London Collegiate Brass, James Stobart. *CRD3444*
        2. [orch. Christopher Palmer] London Philharmonic Orchestra, Bryden
           Thomson. 8–21 January 1991. *CHAN8968*

1936

As You Like It (Shakespeare) Film music C31
    Fp: Carlton Theatre, London. 3 September 1936 (soundtrack conducted by Efrem
        Kurtz)
    Recording: Commercial release of film on video and DVD
———— **Suite** arranged by Carl Davis (8 sections) C31a
    Recording: London Philharmonic Chorus and Orchestra, Carl Davis. 27 March
        and 6 and 25 May 1986. *EMI CDC 7 47944-2*
———— **Suite** arranged by Christopher Palmer (5 continuous sections) C31b
    Recordings:
        1. Chorus, Academy of St Martin-in-the-Fields, Neville Marriner. 8–11
           November 1989. *CHAN8842*
        2. Chorus, RTE Concert Orchestra, Andrew Penny. 11–12 January 1995.
           Naxos 8.553344
———— **Under the Greenwood Tree** (not used in film) for solo voice and piano
    OUP 1937 C31c
    Recording: Felicity Lott and Graham Johnson. *Collins 14932*
———— **Under the Greenwood Tree** arr. for unison voices OUP 1937 C31c
The Boy David (J. M. Barrie) Incidental music (lost) C30
    Fp: King's Theatre, Edinburgh. 21 November 1936 (music pre-recorded;
        conductor uncertain)
    FLon.p: His Majesty's Theatre. 14 December 1936

1937

Crown Imperial Coronation march for full orchestra OUP 1937 C32
    Fb/cast.p: 9 May 1937. BBC Symphony Orchestra, Clarence Raybould
    Fpub.p: Westminster Abbey, London. 12 May 1937. Coronation Orchestra,
        Adrian Boult
    Recordings:
        1. BBC Symphony Orchestra, Adrian Boult. 16 April 1937. HMV
           DB3164; *VAIA 1067-2*
        2. London Philharmonic Orchestra, Adrian Boult. 10 October 1976. EMI
           ASD3388; *CDM5 65584-2*
        3. City of Birmingham Symphony Orchestra, Louis Frémaux. 18–19
           September 1976. HMV ASD3348; *EMI CDM 7 64201-2*
———— revised with cuts 1963 OUP 1967

Recordings:
1. Philharmonia Orchestra, William Walton. 18 March 1953. Columbia 33C1016; *EMI CHS 5 65003-2*
2. Royal Liverpool Philharmonic Orchestra, Charles Groves. 1–2 June 1969. Columbia TWO272; *EMI CDM 7 63369-2*
—————— arranged for piano by composer OUP 1937 C32g

In Honour of the City of London (William Dunbar) Cantata for mixed chorus and orchestra OUP 1937 C33
Fp: Town Hall, Leeds. 6 October 1937. Leeds Festival Chorus, London Philharmonic Orchestra, Malcolm Sargent
FLon.p: Queen's Hall, London. 1 December 1937. BBC Choral Society, BBC Symphony Orchestra, William Walton
Recordings:
1. London Symphony Chorus and Orchestra, Richard Hickox. 19 September 1984. *EMI CDC 7 49496-2*
2. Bach Choir, Philharmonia, David Willcocks. 26–7 April 1991. *CHAN8998*

Dreaming Lips Film music (lost) C34
Fp: London Pavilion. 2 February 1937
Recordings: Commercial video

1938

Set Me as a Seal upon Thine Lips (Song of Solomon) Anthem for unacc. mixed chorus OUP 1938 C35
Fp: Kensington, London. 22 November 1938. St. Mary Abbots Church Choir, F. G. Shuttleworth
Recordings:
1. St. John's College Choir, Cambridge, George Guest. 1958 Mirrosonic DRE1006
2. Christ Church Cathedral Choir, Oxford, Simon Preston. 1971. Argo ZRG725
3. Trinity College Choir, Cambridge, Richard Marlow. 25–7 June 1988. *Conifer CDCF164*

A Stolen Life Film music (lost) C36
Fp: The Plaza Theatre, London. 18 January 1939 (soundtrack conducted by Hyam Greenbaum)

1939

Concerto for Violin and Orchestra C37
Fp: Cleveland (Ohio), USA. 7 December 1939. Jascha Heifetz, Cleveland Orchestra, Artur Rodzinski
F.Eng.p: Royal Albert Hall, London. 1 November 1941. Henry Holst, London Philharmonic Orchestra, William Walton
Recording:
Jascha Heifetz, Cincinnati Symphony Orchestra, Eugene Goossens. 18 February 1941. HMV DB5953-5; *Biddulph WHL016*; in *RCA 09026 61778-2*; *Avid AMSC604*; *Naxos 8.110939*
—————— revised 1943 OUP 1945

Fp: Wolverhampton 17 January 1944. Henry Holst, Liverpool Philharmonic Orchestra, Malcolm Sargent
Recordings:
1. Jascha Heifetz, Philharmonia Orchestra, William Walton. 26–7 July 1950. HMV DB21257-9; *RCA Victor GDB87966*; in *RCA 09026 61778-2*
2. Yehudi Menuhin, London Symphony Orchestra, William Walton. 12–15 July 1969. HMV ASD2542; *EMI CHS 5 65003-2*; *EMI CDM565005-2*

1940
The Wise Virgins Ballet in one act C38
Fp: Sadler's Wells Theatre, London. 24 April 1940. Sadler's Wells Orchestra, Constant Lambert
——— **Suite** (6 movements) OUP 1942 C38a
Recordings:
1. Sadler's Wells Orchestra, William Walton. 24 July and 8 August 1940. HMV C3178-9; *EMI CHS 5 65003-2*
2. [*Sheep may Safely Graze* only] Sadler's Wells Orchestra, William Walton. 26 April 1944. HMV B9380
3. [*Sheep may Safely Graze* only] Philharmonia Orchestra, William Walton. 21 March 1953. Columbia 33C1016; *EMI CHS 5 65003-2*
4. London Philharmonic Orchestra, Bryden Thomson. 6–7 March 1990. *CHAN8871*

Duets for Children for piano duet OUP 1940 C39
Recordings:
1. Ilona Kabos and Louis Kentner. 7 May 1940. Columbia DX972-3
2. Rhonda Gillespie and Robert Weatherburn. *AVMCD1022*
——— arranged for orchestra 1941 as **Music for Children** OUP 1941 C39a
Fp: Queen's Hall, London. 16 February 1941. London Philharmonic Orchestra, Basil Cameron
Recording:
London Philharmonic Orchestra, William Walton. 15 April 1970. Lyrita SRCS50; *SRCD224*

Scapino Comedy Overture for full orchestra OUP C40
Fp: Chicago 3 April 1941. Chicago Symphony Orchestra, Frederick Stock
FEng.p: Corn Exchange, Bedford. 12 November 1941. BBC Symphony Orchestra, William Walton
FLon.p: Royal Albert Hall. 13 December 1941. London Philharmonic Orchestra, William Walton
Recording:
Chicago Symphony Orchestra, Frederick Stock. 20 November 1941. Columbia LX931; *Biddulph WHL021/2*
——— revised 1950 OUP 1950
Fp: Royal Albert Hall, London. 13 November 1950. Philharmonia Orchestra, Wilhelm Furtwängler
Recordings:
1. Philharmonia Orchestra, William Walton. 19 October 1951. HMV DB21499; *EMI CDH 7 63381-2*

2. London Symphony Orchestra, William Walton. 13–14 April 1970. Lyrita SRCS49; *SRCD224*
3. Bournemouth Symphony Orchestra, Andrew Litton. March 1994. *Decca 444 114-2*

1941

[Revision of **Duets for Children** as **Music for Children** C39a]

Major Barbara (G. B. Shaw) Film music C41

> **Fp**: Nassau. 20 March 1941 (soundtrack conducted by Muir Mathieson)
> **FLon.p**: The Odeon, Leicester Square. 7 April 1941
> **Recording**: Commercial video

———— **Suite: A Shavian Sequence** arranged by Christopher Palmer (4 continuous sections) C41a

> **Recording**: Academy of St Martin-in-the-Fields, Neville Marriner. 8–11 November 1989. *CHAN8841*

Next of Kin Film music C42

> **Fpriv.p**: War Office, Cheltenham/Curzon Theatre, London. January/February 1942 (soundtrack conducted by Ernest Irving)
> **Fpub.p**: Carlton and London Pavilion. 15 May 1942
> **Recordings**:
> 1. Commercial video
> 2. [Extracts: in *A Wartime Sketchbook* arr. Christopher Palmer] Academy of St Martin-in-the-Fields, Neville Marriner. 2–3 March 1990. *CHAN8870*

1942

Macbeth (Shakespeare) Incidental music C43

> **Fp**: Opera House, Manchester. 16 January 1942 (music pre-recorded; conducted by Ernest Irving)
> **FLon.p**: Piccadilly Theatre. 8 July 1942
> **Recording**: [*Fanfare* and *March* only] Academy of St Martin-in-the-Fields, Neville Marriner. 8–11 November 1989. *CHAN8841*

The Foreman Went to France Film music C44

> **Fp**: London Pavilion. 12 April 1942 (soundtrack conducted by Muir Mathieson)
> **Recordings**:
> 1. Commercial video (US as *Somewhere in France*)
> 2. [Extracts: in *A Wartime Sketchbook* arr. Christopher Palmer] Academy of St Martin-in-the-Fields, Neville Marriner. 2–3 March 1990. *CHAN8870*

The First of the Few Film music C45

> **Fp**: Leicester Square Cinema, London. 20 August 1942 (soundtrack conducted by Muir Mathieson)
> **Recording**: Commercial video (US as *Spitfire*)

———— **Spitfire Prelude and Fugue** OUP 1961 **C45a**

> **Fp**: Liverpool. 2 January 1943. Liverpool Philharmonic Orchestra, William Walton

Recordings:
1. Hallé Orchestra, William Walton. 24 June 1943. HMV C3359; *EMI CDH 7 63381-2*
2. Philharmonia Orchestra, William Walton. 16 October 1963. HMV SXLP30139: *EMI CHS 5 65003-2*; *EMI CDM565007-2*

Christopher Columbus (Louis MacNeice) Incidental music for radio play for speakers, three solo voices, chorus and full orchestra C46
    Fp: Bedford. 12 October 1942. Cast with BBC Chorus and BBC Symphony Orchestra, Adrian Boult [BBC Archive recording]
———— **Suite** for soloists, chorus and orchestra arranged by Christopher Palmer (3 sections) C46a
    Fp: Royal Albert Hall, London. 28 August 1992. Judith Howarth, Arthur Davies, BBC Singers, BBC Concert Orchestra, Barry Wordsworth
    Recording: Linda Finnie, Arthur Davies, Westminster Singers, City of London Sinfonia, Richard Hickox. 11–12 October 1989. *CHAN8824*
———— **Beatriz's Song** OUP 1974 C46b
    Recording: Felicity Lott and Graham Johnson. *Collins 14932*

Went the Day Well? Film music C47
    Fp: London Pavilion. 1 November 1942 (soundtrack conducted by Ernest Irving)
    Recording: [Extracts: in *A Wartime Sketchbook* arranged by Christopher Palmer] Academy of St Martin-in-the-Fields, Neville Marriner. 2–3 March 1990. *CHAN8870*

1943

Fanfare (Salute to the Red Army) for brass and timpani C48
    Fp: Royal Albert Hall, London. 21 February 1943. Malcolm Sargent
———— Revised as **Memorial Fanfare for Henry Wood** for full orchestra 1945 C48a
    Fp: Royal Albert Hall, London. 4 March 1945. Combined BBC, London Philharmonic and London Symphony Orchestras, Adrian Boult

The Quest Ballet in five scenes C49
    Fp: New Theatre, London. 6 April 1943. Sadler's Wells Orchestra, Constant Lambert
    Recording: London Philharmonic Orchestra, Bryden Thomson. 6–7 March 1990. *CHAN8871*
———— **Suite** arranged by Vilem Tausky 1961 (4 sections) OUP 1962 C49a
    Recording: London Symphony Orchestra, William Walton. 13–14 April 1970. Lyrita SRCS49; *SRCD224*

[Revision of **Sinfonia Concertante** C21]
[Revision of **Violin Concerto** C37]

1944

Henry V (Shakespeare) Film music C50
    Fp: Carlton, London. 22 November 1944 (soundtrack conducted by Muir Mathieson)
    Recordings:
1. Commercial video and DVD
2. [Selected Scenes] Laurence Olivier, chorus, Philharmonia Orchestra,

William Walton. 27–8 August, 12–13 October and 13 November 1946. HMV C3583-6; *EMI CHS 5 65003-2*; *EMI CDM565007-2*

———— **Suite** arranged by Malcolm Sargent for chorus and orchestra 1945 (4 sections) C50a

Fp: Royal Albert Hall, London 14 September 1945. BBC Choral Society, Croydon Philharmonic Society, BBC Symphony Orchestra, William Walton.

Recordings:

[*Two Pieces for Strings* only] Philharmonia String Orchestra, William Walton. 12 October 1945. HMV C3480; *EMI CDH 7 63381-2*

———— **Suite** arranged by Muir Mathieson for orchestra alone 1963 (5 sections) OUP 1964 C50b

Recording: Philharmonia Orchestra, William Walton. 15 October 1963. Columbia 33CX1883 (SAX2527); *EMI CHS 5 65003-2*; *EMI CDM565007-2*

———— **Suite: Henry V – A Shakespeare Scenario** arranged by Christopher Palmer for speaker, chorus and orchestra (8 sections) C50c

Fp: Royal Festival Hall, London. 11 May 1990. Christopher Plummer, chorus, Academy of St Martin-in-the-Fields, Neville Marriner

Recordings:

1. above artists. 14–15 May 1990. *CHAN8892*
2. Michael Sheen and Anton Lesser, RTE Concert Orchestra, Andrew Penny. 11–12 January 1995. *Naxos 8.553343*

Contribution to the Projected Free French Album for solo piano C51

1945

[Revision of **Fanfare (Salute to the Red Army)** C48 as **Memorial Fanfare for Henry Wood** for full orchestra 1945]

1946

Where does the Uttered Music Go? (Masefield) for unacc. mixed chorus OUP 1947 C52

Fp: St Sepulchre's Church, Holborn, London. 26 April 1946. BBC Chorus and Theatre Revue Chorus, Leslie Woodgate

Recordings:

1. BBC Chorus, Leslie Woodgate. 13 June 1946. HMV C3503
2. Trinity College Choir, Cambridge, Richard Marlow. 25–7 June 1988. *Conifer CDCF164*

Quartet (No. 2) for Strings OUP 1947 C53

Fb/cast.p: Broadcasting House, London. 4 May 1947. Blech String Quartet
Fpub.p: Broadcasting House, London. 5 May 1947. Blech String Quartet
Recordings:

1. Hollywood String Quartet. 1949. Capitol P8054
2. English String Quartet. 1986. *Meridian CDE84139*

———— re-scored for strings as **Sonata for Strings** 1971 OUP 1973 C53a

Fp: Perth, Western Australia. 2 March 1972. Academy of St Martin-in-the-Fields, Neville Marriner

FUKp: Bath. 27 May 1972. Academy of St Martin-in-the-Fields, Neville Marriner

Recordings:
1. Academy of St Martin-in-the-Fields, Neville Marriner. October 1972 and May 1973. Argo ZRG711
2. Strings of London Philharmonic Orchestra, Jan Lathan-Koenig. 28–9 March 1992. *CHAN9106*

1947

Hamlet (Shakespeare) Film music C54

Fp: Odeon, Leicester Square, London. 6 May 1948 (soundtrack conducted by Muir Mathieson)

Recordings:
1. Commercial video and DVD
2. [excerpts from soundtrack] Laurence Olivier, Philharmonia Orchestra, Muir Mathieson. 8 April 1948. HMV C3755-7; RCA LSB4104

────── **Funeral March** adapted by Muir Mathieson 1963 OUP 1963 C54a

Recording: Philharmonia Orchestra, William Walton. 15 October 1963. Columbia 33CX1883 (SAX2527); *EMI CHS 5 65003-2*

────── **Hamlet and Ophelia: A Poem for Orchestra** adapted Muir Mathieson 1967 OUP 1968 C54b

Recording: Academy of St Martin-in-the-Fields, Neville Marriner. 8–11 November 1989. *CHAN8842*

────── **Suite: Hamlet – A Shakespeare Scenario** arranged by Christopher Palmer for speaker and orchestra (9 sections) C54c

Recordings:
1. John Gielgud, Academy of St Martin-in-the-Fields, Neville Marriner. 8–11 November 1989. *CHAN8842*
2. Michael Sheen, RTE Concert Orchestra, Andrew Penny. 11–12 January 1995. *Naxos 8.553344*

1948

[Revision of **Belshazzar's Feast** C23]

1949

Sonata for Violin and Piano C55

Fp: Zürich. 30 September 1949. Yehudi Menuhin and Louis Kentner

────── revised OUP 1950

Fp: Theatre Royal, Drury Lane, London. 5 February 1950. Yehudi Menuhin and Louis Kentner

Recordings:
1. Yehudi Menuhin and Louis Kentner. 8 May 1950. HMV DB21156-8; *EMI CDM5 66122-2*
2. Kenneth Sillito, Hamish Milne. 7–8 November 1993. *Chandos CHAN9292*

Two Pieces for Violin and Piano: Canzonetta and Scherzetto OUP 1951 C56

Fp [**Scherzetto** only]: possibly Zürich. 30 September 1949. Yehudi Menuhin and Louis Kentner

F.Lon.p: Broadcasting House. 27 September 1950. Frederick Grinke and Ernest Lush

Recording: Kenneth Sillito, Hamish Milne. 29 May 1991. *Chandos CHAN9292*

1950

[Revision of **Scapino** Comedy Overture C40]

[Revision of **Sonata for Violin and Piano** C55 OUP 1950]

1951

'Happy Birthday to You' (for Mary Curtis Bok Zimbalist) 9 bars only C57

1952

Coronation Te Deum for two mixed choruses, two semi-choruses, boys' voices, organ, orchestra and military brass OUP 1953 C58

Fp: Westminster Abbey, London (Coronation service). 2 June 1953. Coronation Choir and Orchestra, William McKie

Fpub.p: Royal Albert Hall. 25 July 1953. BBC Symphony Orchestra, Malcolm Sargent

Recordings:

1. Commercial release of Coronation Service. HMV ALP1056-8; *EMI 5 66582-2*
2. City of Birmingham Chorus and Symphony Orchestra, Louis Frémaux. 18–19 September 1976. HMV ASD3348; *EMI CDM 7 64201-2*
3. Bach Choir, Philharmonia, David Willcocks. 6–8 April 1989. *CHAN8760*

Orb and Sceptre Coronation march for full orchestra OUP hire C59

Fpub.p: Westminster Abbey, London (Coronation service). 2 June 1953. Coronation Orchestra, Adrian Boult

Recordings:

1. Philharmonia Orchestra, William Walton. 18 March 1953. *EMI CHS 5 65003-2*; *5 66582-2*
2. City of Birmingham Symphony Orchestra, Louis Frémaux. 18–19 September 1976. HMV ASD3348; *EMI CDM 7 64201-2*
3. London Philharmonic Orchestra, Adrian Boult. 10 October 1976. EMI ASD3388; *CDM5 65584-2*

1953

The National Anthem arranged for full orchestra OUP 1987 C60

Fp: Royal Opera House, Covent Garden, London. 8 June 1953. Covent Garden Orchestra, John Pritchard

Variation on an Elizabethan Theme (Sellinger's Round) for string orchestra Boosey & Hawkes hire C61

Fp: Aldeburgh 20 June 1953. Aldeburgh Festival Orchestra, Benjamin Britten

Recording: Commercial release of first performance. Decca LXT2798

FLon.p: Wigmore Hall. 29 May 1957. Collegium Musicum Londini, John Minchinton

1954

Troilus and Cressida (libretto by Christopher Hassall) Opera in three acts OUP
1954 C62
> **Fp**: Royal Opera House, Covent Garden, London. 3 December 1954. Malcolm
> Sargent [BBC Archives]
> **Recording**: [excerpts] Richard Lewis, Elisabeth Schwarzkopf, Monica Sinclair,
> Peter Pears, Philharmonia Orchestra, William Walton. 18–20 April and 16
> May 1955. Columbia 33CX1313; *EMI 7 64199-2*

——— revised with alterations and cuts
> **Fp**: Royal Opera House, Covent Garden, London. 23 April 1963. Malcolm
> Sargent
> **Recording**: [excerpt from Act II only] Marie Collier, Peter Pears, Orchestra of
> Royal Opera House, Covent Garden, William Walton. 26–7 February 1968.
> Decca SET392-3; *EMI 7 64199-2*

——— revised with part of Cressida amended to suit a mezzo-soprano (Janet Baker)
OUP 1980
> **Fp**: Royal Opera House, Covent Garden, London. 12 November 1976. Lawrence
> Foster
> **Recording**: Richard Cassilly, Janet Baker, Gerald English, Orchestra of Royal
> Opera House, Covent Garden, Lawrence Foster. Live recordings 12, 17, 27
> and 30 November 1976. EMI SLS997; *CMS 5 65550-2*

——— original 1954 (soprano) score with revisions of 1972–76
> **Fpub.p**: Grand Theatre, Leeds. 14 January 1995. Judith Howarth, Arthur Davies,
> Nigel Robson, English Northern Philharmonia, Richard Hickox
> **Recording**: artists as above. 19–25 January 1995. *CHAN9370-1*

1955

Richard III (Shakespeare) Film music C63
> **Fp**: Leicester Square Theatre, London. 13 December 1955 (soundtrack
> conducted by Muir Mathieson)
> **Recordings**:
> > 1. Commercial video
> > 2. [Complete soundtrack] Laurence Olivier, Royal Philharmonic
> >   Orchestra, Muir Mathieson. February–March 1955. HMV ALP1341-3;
> >   [highlights only] RCA LM1940

——— **Prelude and Suite** (6 sections) arranged by Muir Mathieson 1963 OUP
1964 C63a and c
> **Recording**: Philharmonia Orchestra, William Walton 15–16 October 1963.
> Columbia 33CX1883 (SAX2527); *EMI CHS 5 65003-2*; *EMI
> CDM565007-2*

——— **Suite: Richard III – A Shakespeare Scenario** arranged by Christopher
Palmer for speaker and orchestra (9 sections) C63d
> **Recording**: John Gielgud, Academy of St Martin-in-the-Fields, Neville Marriner.
> 8–11 November 1989. *CHAN8841*

The Star-Spangled Banner arranged for full orchestra C64
God Save the Queen arranged for full orchestra C64
> **Fp**: Royal Festival Hall, London. 18 October 1955. Philharmonia Orchestra,
> Herbert von Karajan

———— revised with chorus

Fp: Royal Festival Hall, London. 29 March 1982. Philharmonia Chorus and
Orchestra, André Previn

1956

Concerto for Cello and Orchestra OUP 1957 C65

Fp: Boston, USA. 25 January 1957. Gregor Piatigorsky, Boston Symphony
Orchestra, Charles Munch [National Sound Archives]

FEng.p: Royal Festival Hall, London. 13 February 1957. Gregor Piatigorsky,
BBC Symphony Orchestra, Malcolm Sargent [BBC Archives]

Recordings:
1. Gregor Piatigorsky, Boston Symphony Orchestra, Charles Munch.
   1957. RCA RB16027; *74321 29248-2*
2. Pierre Fournier, Royal Philharmonic Orchestra, William Walton. pub.
   perf. 12 August 1959 Edinburgh Festival. *ARLA66*
3. Paul Tortelier, Bournemouth Symphony Orchestra, Paavo Berglund.
   7–8 January 1973. HMV ASD2924; *EMI 5 73371-2*

———— revised with new ending 1975 (now not used)

Johannesburg Festival Overture for full orchestra OUP 1958 C66

Fp: Johannesburg, Republic of South Africa. 25 September 1956. South African
Broadcasting Symphony Orchestra, Malcolm Sargent

FEng.p: Liverpool. 13 November 1956. Liverpool Philharmonic Orchestra,
Efrem Kurtz

FLon.p: Royal Festival Hall. 23 January 1957. BBC Symphony Orchestra,
Malcolm Sargent

Recording: Philharmonia Orchestra, William Walton. 26 March 1957. Columbia
33C1054; *EMI CHS 5 65003-2*

1957

Partita for Orchestra OUP 1958 C67

Fp: Cleveland (Ohio), USA. 30 January 1958. Cleveland Orchestra, George Szell

FEng.p : Manchester. 30 April 1958. Hallé Orchestra, William Walton

FLon.p: Royal Festival Hall. 2 May 1958. Hallé Orchestra, John Barbirolli

Recordings:
1. Philharmonia Orchestra, William Walton. 6 and 16 February 1959.
   Columbia SAX2319; *EMI CHS 5 65003-2*; *EMI CDM565005-2*
2. Cleveland Orchestra, George Szell. 1959. Columbia SAX2459; *Sony
   MPK46732*
3. Hallé Orchestra, John Barbirolli. pub. perf. 8 August 1969. *BBC
   BBCL4013-2*

1959

A Queen's Fanfare for brass OUP 1972 C69

Fp: Westminster Hall, London. 5 June 1959

Recordings:
1. Locke Brass Consort, James Stobart. *CHAN6573*
2. Philharmonia Brass, David Willcocks. 26–7 April 1991. *CHAN8998*

March: A History of the English Speaking Peoples for orchestra OUP hire C70
    Fp: (recording) Elstree Studios. 25 May 1959. London Symphony Orchestra,
        William Walton
    Recording: London Philharmonic Chorus and Orchestra, Carl Davis. 27 March
        and 6 and 25 May 1986. *EMI CDC 7 47944-2*

Anon. in Love (anonymous sixteenth- and seventeenth-century lyrics selected by
        Christopher Hassall) six songs for tenor voice and guitar OUP 1960 C71
    Fp: Ipswich. 21 June 1960. Peter Pears and Julian Bream
    Recordings:
        1. Peter Pears and Julian Bream. RCA RB6621; *09026 61583-2*
        2. Martyn Hill and Craig Ogden. *Collins 14932*
———— arranged for tenor voice, percussion, harp and strings OUP hire 1971 C71a
    Fp: The Mansion House, London. 21 June 1971. Robert Tear, London Mozart
        Players, Harry Blech
    Recording: Martyn Hill, City of London Sinfonia, Richard Hickox. 11–12
        October 1989. *CHAN8824*

1960

Symphony No. 2 for full orchestra OUP 1960 C68
    Fp: Usher Hall, Edinburgh. 2 September 1960, Royal Liverpool Philharmonic
        Orchestra, John Pritchard [BBC Archives]
    FLon.p: Royal Festival Hall. 23 November 1960, Royal Liverpool Philharmonic
        Orchestra, John Pritchard
    Recordings:
        1. Cleveland Orchestra, George Szell. 2 and 24 March 1961. Columbia
            SAX2459; *Sony MPK46732*
        2. London Symphony Orchestra, André Previn. 12 February 1973. EMI
            ASD2990; *5 73371-2*

1961

Gloria for contralto, tenor and bass soloists, double mixed chorus and orchestra
        OUP 1961 C72
    Fp: Huddersfield. 24 November 1961. Marjorie Thomas, Richard Lewis, John
        Cameron, Huddersfield Choral Society, Royal Liverpool Philharmonic
        Orchestra, Malcolm Sargent
    FLon.p: Royal Festival Hall. 18 January 1962. Marjorie Thomas, Ronald Dowd,
        Owen Brannigan, London Philharmonic Choir and Orchestra, Malcolm
        Sargent
    Recordings:
        1. Barbara Robotham, Anthony Rolfe Johnson, Brain Rayner Cook, City
            of Birmingham Chorus and Symphony Orchestra, Louis Frémaux.
            18–19 September 1976. HMV ASD3348; *EMI CDM 7 64201-2*
        2. Ameral Gunson, Neil Mackie, Stephen Roberts, Bach Choir,
            Philharmonia, David Willcocks. 6–8 April 1989. *CHAN8760*

What Cheer? (Christmas carol) for unacc. mixed chorus OUP 1961 C73
    Recording: Trinity College Choir, Cambridge, Richard Marlow. 25–7 June 1988.
        Conifer CDCF164
[Revision of **Viola Concerto** C22]

1962

A Song for the Lord Mayor's Table (various texts selected by Christopher Hassall)
Cycle of six songs for soprano and piano OUP 1963 C74
Fp: Goldsmiths' Hall, London. 18 July 1962. Elizabeth Schwarzkopf and Gerald
Moore
Recordings:
1. Heather Harper, Paul Hamburger. L'Oiseau-Lyre SOL331
2. Sarah Walker, Roger Vignoles. *Hyperion CDA66165*
───── arranged for soprano and small orchestra 1970 OUP hire C74a
Fp: The Mansion House, London. 7 July 1970. Janet Baker, English Chamber
Orchestra, George Malcolm
Recording: Jill Gomez, City of London Sinfonia, Richard Hickox. 11–12
October 1989. *CHAN8824*
Granada TV Music for orchestra C75
───── **Prelude for Orchestra** C75a
Fp: St John's, Smith Square, London. 25 June 1977. Young Musicians' Symphony
Orchestra, James Blair.
Recording: London Philharmonic Orchestra, Bryden Thomson. 8–21 January
1991. *CHAN8968*
[Revision of **Siesta** C19]

1963

Variations on a Theme by Hindemith for orchestra OUP 1963 C76
Fp: Royal Festival Hall, London. 8 March 1963. Royal Philharmonic Orchestra,
William Walton
Recordings:
1. Commercial release of first performance. *Carlton 15656 91782*
2. Cleveland Orchestra, George Szell. 1964. *Sony MPK46732*
[Revision of **Crown Imperial** C32 OUP 1967]

1965

The Twelve (W. H. Auden) Anthem for mixed chorus and organ OUP 1966 C77
Fp: Christ Church Cathedral, Oxford. 16 May 1965. Sydney Watson
Recording: Trinity College Choir, Cambridge, Richard Marlow. 25–27 June
1988. *Conifer CDCF164*
───── arranged for soloists, choir and orchestra 1965 OUP hire C77a
Fp: Westminster Abbey, London. 2 January 1966. Ann Dowdall, Shirley Minty,
Robert Tear, Maurice Wakeham, London Philharmonic Choir and
Orchestra, William Walton
Recording: Soloists, Westminster Singers, City of London Sinfonia, Richard
Hickox. 11–12 October 1989. *CHAN8824*

1966

Missa Brevis (Book of Common Prayer) for double mixed chorus and organ OUP
1966 C78
Recordings:
1. Christ Church Cathedral, Oxford, Simon Preston. 1971. Argo ZRG725

 2. Trinity College Choir, Cambridge, Richard Marlow. 25–27 June 1988.
    Conifer CDCF164

1967
The Bear (Paul Dehn, after Chekhov) An extravaganza in one act for three soloists
    and orchestra VS OUP 1968; FS OUP 1977 C79
 Fp: Aldeburgh. 3 June 1967. Monica Sinclair, Norman Lumsden, John Shaw,
    English Chamber Orchestra, James Lockhart
 FLon.p: Sadler's Wells Theatre. 12 July 1967. Performers as above
 Recordings:
  1. artists as above 30 July – 2 August 1967. EMI SAN192; *CZS57398-2*
  2. Daphne Harris, Gregory Yurisich, Noel Mangin, Melbourne Symphony
     Orchestra, Vanco Cavdarski. 1977. Chandos ABR1052
  3. Della Jones, Alan Opie, John Shirley-Quirk, Northern Sinfonia,
     Richard Hickox. 1992. *CHAN9245*

1968
Capriccio Burlesco for orchestra OUP 1969 C80
 Fp: New York, USA. 7 December 1968. New York Philharmonic Orchestra,
    André Kostelanetz
 FLon.p: Royal Festival Hall. 5 February 1969. BBC Symphony Orchestra, Colin
    Davis
 Recordings:
  1. André Kostelanetz and his orchestra 23 July 1969. *Sony SMK58931*
  2. London Symphony Orchestra, William Walton. 13–14 April 1970.
     Lyrita SRCS49; *SRCD224*
  3. London Philharmonic Orchestra, Bryden Thomson. 8–21 January 1991.
     CHAN8968

1969
The Battle of Britain film music C81
 Fp: [*Battle in the Air* only] Dominion Cinema, London. 15 September 1969
 Recordings:
  1. Commercial video [including *Battle in the Air* only]. Studio orchestra,
     Malcolm Arnold
  2. [*Battle in the Air* only] Studio orchestra, Malcolm Arnold. United
     Artists UAS29019
  2. ['complete' takes for soundtrack, and trailer video] Studio orchestra,
     Malcolm Arnold. *RCD 10747*
——— **Suite** arranged by Colin Matthews 1985 (6 sections) OUP C81a
 Fp: Bristol. 10 May 1985. Bournemouth Symphony Orchestra, Carl Davis
 FLon.p: The Barbican. 10 May 1985. Bournemouth Symphony Orchestra, Carl
    Davis
 Recordings:
  1. London Philharmonic Orchestra, Carl Davis. 27 March and 6 and 25
     May 1986. *EMI CDC 7 47944-2*
  2. Academy of St Martin-in-the-Fields, Neville Marriner. 2–3 March
     1990. *CHAN8870*

Improvisations on an Impromptu of Benjamin Britten for full orchestra OUP
1970 C82
>   **Fp**: San Francisco, USA. 14 January 1970. San Francisco Symphony Orchestra,
>   Josef Krips
>   **FEng.p**: The Maltings, Snape. 27 June 1970. Royal Liverpool Philharmonic
>   Orchestra, Charles Groves [BBC Archives]
>   **FLon.p**: Royal Festival Hall. 20 October 1970. London Philharmonic Orchestra,
>   Josef Krips
>   **Recordings**:
>>   1.   London Symphony Orchestra, André Previn. 16 May 1972. EMI
>>   SAN324; *CDM 7 64723-2*
>>   2.   London Philharmonic Orchestra, Bryden Thomson. 18–20 January
>>   1991. *CHAN 8959*

Three Sisters (Chekhov) Film music C83
>   **Fp**: Venice. 26 August 1970 (soundtrack conducted by Marc Wilkinson)
>   **Recording**: Commercial video
> ——— **Suite** arranged by Christopher Palmer (3 sections)
>   **Recording**: Academy of St Martin-in-the-Fields, Neville Marriner. 2–3 March
>   1990. *CHAN8870*

1970

All This Time (anon. sixteenth-century) for unacc. mixed chorus OUP 1970 C84
>   **Recordings**:
>>   1.   Christ Church Cathedral Choir, Oxford, Simon Preston. 1971. Argo
>>   ZRG725
>>   2.   Trinity College Choir, Cambridge, Richard Marlow. 25–27 June 1988.
>>   *Conifer CDCF164*

Theme (for Variations) for Cello Solo: part of *Music for a Prince* with 14
>   contributors OUP C85
>   **Fp**: Rome. 29 April 1985. Antonio Lysy

[Arrangement of **A Song for the Lord Mayor's Table** C74 for soprano and small
>   orchestra OUP hire C74a]

1971

Five Bagatelles for Guitar (ed. Julian Bream) OUP 1974 C86
>   **Fp** (complete): Bath. 27 May 1972. Julian Bream
>   **FLon.p**: Queen Elizabeth Hall. 21 January 1973. Julian Bream
>   **Recording**: Julian Bream. February 1973. RCA SB6876; *09026 61595-2*
> ——— transcribed for orchestra as **Varii Capricci** 1976 C86a
>   **Fp**: Royal Festival Hall, London. 4 May 1976. London Symphony Orchestra,
>   André Previn
> ——— revised version OUP 1978 C86a
>   **Fp**: Cardiff. 28 January 1981. BBC Welsh Symphony Orchestra, Owain Arwel
>   Hughes
>   **Recording**: London Philharmonic Orchestra, Bryden Thomson. 23–24 February
>   1990. *CHAN8862*
> ——— **Ballet** C86b
>   **Fp**: Metropolitan Opera House, New York, USA. 19 April 1983.

[Re-scoring of **String Quartet** (No. 2) C53 as **Sonata for Strings** C53a]
[Re-scoring of **Anon. in Love** C71 for small orchestra]

1972
Jubilate Deo for double mixed chorus and organ OUP 1973 C87
    Fp: Christ Church Cathedral, Oxford. 22 April 1972. Simon Preston
    Recordings:
        1. Christ Church Cathedral Choir, Oxford, Simon Preston. 1971. Argo
          ZRG725
        2. Trinity College Choir, Cambridge, Richard Marlow. 25–27 June 1988.
          Conifer CDCF164
Birthday Greeting to Herbert Howells C88 eight bars in short score only

1973
Anniversary Fanfare for brass and percussion OUP 1975 C89
    Fp: Royal Festival Hall, London. 29 November 1973. Kneller Hall trumpeters,
      Rodney Bashford
    Recording: Philharmonia Brass, David Willcocks. 26–27 April 1991. *CHAN8998*

1974
Cantico del Sole (St Francis of Assisi) Motet for unacc. mixed chorus OUP 1974
    C90
    Fp: University College, Cork. 25 April 1974. BBC Northern Singers, Stephen
      Wilkinson
    FEng.p: BBC Studios, Manchester. 14 September 1974. BBC Northern Singers,
      Stephen Wilkinson
    FLon.p: Queen Elizabeth Hall. 23 September 1974. Louis Halsey Singers, Louis
      Halsey
    Recordings:
        1. BBC Northern Singers, Stephen Wilkinson. Abbey LPB798
        2. Trinity College Choir, Cambridge, Richard Marlow. 25–27 June 1988.
          Conifer CDCF164
Magnificat and Nunc Dimittis for mixed chorus and organ OUP 1975 C91
    Fp: Chichester Cathedral. 14 June 1975. Chichester Cathedral Choir, John Birch
    Recordings:
        1. Chichester Cathedral Choir, John Birch. July 1976. Abbey LPB770.
        2. Trinity College Choir, Cambridge, Richard Marlow. 25–27 June 1988.
          Conifer CDCF164
Fanfare for the National [Theatre] for brass and percussion C92
    Fp: [recording] Wembley, London. 1 April 1976. Band of the Life Guards, Harry
      Rabinowitz [several revised versions followed]
[Revision of ending to **Cello Concerto** C65]

1975
[Further revision of **Quartet for Piano and Strings** C7 prior to republication. OUP
    1976]

1976

Roaring Fanfare for brass and percussion C93
  Fp: London Zoo. 3 June 1976. Kneller Hall trumpeters, Trevor Platts
[Orchestration of **Five Bagatelles for Guitar** C86 as **Varii Capricci** C86a]
[Revision of **Troilus and Cressida** C62 1972–76, with part of Cressida amended to
    suit a mezzo-soprano OUP 1980]

1977

Façade Revived
  Fp: London. 25 March 1977. Richard Baker, English Bach Festival Ensemble,
    Charles Mackerras
——— revision of above as **Façade 2: A Further Entertainment** 1979 OUP
  Fp: The Maltings, Snape. 19 June 1979. Peter Pears, ensemble, Steuart Bedford
  Recordings:
    1. [*Façade 1* and *2*] Cathy Berberian, Robert Tear, ensemble, Steuart
        Bedford. 28–9 June 1979. OUP201
    2. [*Façade 1* and *2*] Susana Walton, Richard Baker, members of City of
        London Sinfonia, Richard Hickox. 19–21 March 1990. *CHAN 8869*
Antiphon (George Herbert) Anthem for mixed chorus and organ OUP 1978 C94
  Fp: St Paul's Church, New York, USA. 20 November 1977. St Paul's Church
    Choir, David Fetler
  Recording: Trinity College Choir, Cambridge, Richard Marlow. 25–27 June
    1988. *Conifer CDCF164*
King Herod and the Cock (trad.) Christmas carol for unacc. mixed voices OUP
    1978 C95
  Fp: King's College Chapel, Cambridge. 24 December 1977. King's College
    Choir, Philip Ledger
  Recording: Trinity College Choir, Cambridge, Richard Marlow. 25–27 June
    1988. *Conifer CDCF164*
Title Music for BBC TV Shakespeare Series for woodwind, brass and percussion
    C96
  Fp: (recording) BBCTV studios. 26 January 1978. Members of English National
    Opera Orchestra, David Lloyd-Jones

1978

[Revision of **Varii Capricci** OUP 1978 C86a]

1979

Salute to Sir Robert Mayer on his 100th Birthday for 12 trumpets C97
  Fp: Royal Festival Hall, London. 5 June 1979. Twelve ILEA trumpeters
[**Façade 2** – revision of **Façade Revived** 1977]

1980

Passacaglia for cello solo OUP 1982 C98
  Fp: Royal Festival Hall, London. 16 March 1982. Mstislav Rostropovich
  Recording: Raphael Wallfisch. 28 January 1986. Chandos ABRD1209;
    CHAN8959

[**The First Shoot** C29 arranged for brass band]

1981
A Birthday Fanfare for 7 trumpets and percussion OUP 1983 C99
    Fp (private): Recklinghausen. 10 October 1981. Members of Westphalia
        Symphony Orchestra, Karl Rickenbacher
    FLon.p: Royal Albert Hall. 7 June 1982. Kneller Hall trumpeters, G. E. Evans

1982
Prologo e Fantasia for orchestra OUP 1984 C100
    Fp: Royal Festival Hall, London. 20 February 1982. National Symphony
        Orchestra of Washington, Mstislav Rostropovich
    Recording: London Philharmonic Orchestra, Bryden Thomson. 8–21 January
        1991. *CHAN8968*

Bibliography

Publications primarily about Walton

Cox, David, 'William Walton', in *The Symphony Volume Two: Elgar to the Present Day*, ed. Robert Simpson, Penguin Books 1967

Craggs, Stewart, *William Walton: A Thematic Catalogue of his Musical Works*, OUP 1977 (with 'William Walton: A Critical Appreciation' by Michael Kennedy), revised as: *William Walton: A Catalogue*, OUP 1990 (with an Introduction by Christopher Palmer)

——— *William Walton: A Source Book*, Scolar Press 1993

——— (ed.), *William Walton: Music and Literature*, Ashgate 1999 (Alan Cuckston: 'The Songs'; John Coggrave: 'Sacred Music'; Kevin McBeath: '*Façade* – "a Noise like Amber" '; Michael Kennedy: 'Belshazzar and the BBC Bureaucracy: The Origins of a Masterpiece'; Robert Meikle: 'The Symphonies and Concertos'; Stephen Lloyd: 'Film Music'; Zelda Lawrence-Curran: ' "All the things that might have been": *Christopher Columbus*'; Scott Price: ' "A Lost Child": A Study of the Genesis of *Troilus and Cressida*'; Lyndon Jenkins: 'The Recorded Works'; Lewis Foreman: 'Walton's Words')

Driver, Paul, ' "Facade" Revisited', *Tempo*, September 1980, 3–9

Foss, Dora, 'Memoirs of Walton' (unpublished), part of the Hubert Foss Archives in the private possession of Mrs Diana Sparkes

Goddard, Scott, 'William Walton', in *The Concerto*, ed. Ralph Hill, Penguin Books 1952

Howes, Frank, *The Music of William Walton*, Vols. 1 and 2, 'The Musical Pilgrim' series, OUP 1942

——— *The Music of William Walton*, OUP 1965, second edition 1974

Kennedy, Michael, *Portrait of Walton*, OUP 1990, revised edition Clarendon Press 1998

Mason, Colin, 'William Walton', in *British Music of our Time*, ed. A. L. Bacharach, Penguin Books 1946; new edition 1951

Palmer, Christopher, Sleeve-notes to the Chandos Walton Edition of recordings 1990–92

Poulton, Alan, *The Recorded Works of Sir William Walton: A Discography*, Bravura 1980

Smith, Carolyn J., *William Walton: A Bio-Bibliography* (No. 18), Greenwood Press 1988

Tierney, Neil, *William Walton: His Life and Music*, Robert Hale 1984

Walton, Susana, *Behind the Façade*, OUP 1988

Walton, Sir William, 'My Life in Music', *Sunday Telegraph* 25 March 1962

On the Sitwells

Bradford, Sarah, *Splendours and Miseries: A Life of Sacheverell Sitwell*, Farrar Straus Giroux 1993

Fifoot, Richard, *A Bibliography of Edith, Osbert and Sacheverell Sitwell*, 1963, second edition, revised, Archon Books 1971

Glendinning, Victoria, *Edith Sitwell – A Unicorn among Lions*, Weidenfeld & Nicolson 1981, Phoenix Paperback 1993

Pearson, John, *Façades: Edith, Osbert and Sacheverell Sitwell*, Macmillan 1978, Fontana Paperbacks 1980

Salter, Elizabeth, *Edith Sitwell*, Oresko Books Ltd 1979

Sitwell, Edith, *Bucolic Comedies*, Duckworth 1923, New Readers' Library edition 1927

——— *The Sleeping Beauty*, Duckworth 1924

——— *Troy Park*, Alfred A. Knopf, New York 1925

——— *Selected Poems: Edith Sitwell* (Penguin Poets), a selection by the author with 'Some Notes on my own Poetry', Penguin 1952

——— *Collected Poems*, with 'Some Notes on my own Poetry', Macmillan 1957

——— *Taken Care Of – An Autobiography*, Hutchinson 1965

——— *Edith Sitwell: Selected Letters*, ed. John Lehmann and Derek Parker, Macmillan 1970

——— *Selected Letters of Edith Sitwell*, ed. Richard Greene, Virago Press 1997, revised 1998

Sitwell, Osbert, *Great Morning*, Macmillan 1948, The Reprint Society 1949

——— *Laughter in the Next Room*, Macmillan 1949, St Martin's Library (paperback) edition 1958

——— *Tales my Father Taught Me*, Hutchinson 1962, Readers Union edition 1963

——— *Queen Mary and Others*, Michael Joseph 1974

Sitwell, Osbert, and Sacheverell Sitwell, *All at Sea: A Social Tragedy in Three Acts for First Class Passengers Only*, Duckworth 1927

Skipwith, Joanna (ed.), *The Sitwells and the Arts of the 1920s and 1930s*, Catalogue for the National Portrait Gallery exhibition 14 October 1994 to 22 January 1995, National Portrait Gallery Publications 1994, reprinted 1996

Ziegler, Philip, *Osbert Sitwell*, Chatto & Windus 1998

On Other Friends, Contemporaries, etc.

Aberconway, Christabel, *A Wiser Woman? A Book of Memories*, Hutchinson 1966

Acton, Harold, *Memoirs of an Aesthete*, Metheun 1948

Amis, John, *Amiscellany: My Life, My Music*, Faber & Faber 1985

Amory, Mark, *Lord Berners: The Last Eccentric*, Chatto & Windus 1998

The Music of Malcolm Arnold: A Catalogue, compiled by Alan Poulton, Faber Music 1986

Beaton, Cecil, *The Wandering Years: Diaries, 1922–1939*, Weidenfeld & Nicolson 1961

——— *Self Portrait with Friends: The Selected Diaries of Cecil Beaton*, ed. Richard Buckle, Pimlico 1979

Bennett, Arnold, *The Journals of Arnold Bennett*, selected and edited by Frank Swinnerton, Penguin Books 1954

Berners, Lord, *Far from the Madding War*, Constable & Co. 1941

——— *Count Omega*, Constable & Co. 1941

——— *Collected Tales and Fantasies*, Turtle Point Press and Helen Mark Books, New York 1999

——— *The Girls of Radcliff Hall*, private publication 1937; reprint Asphodel 1999; new edition ed. John Byrne, Cygnet Press 2000

Bliss, Arthur, *As I Remember*, Faber & Faber 1970

Boult, Adrian, *My own Trumpet*, Hamish Hamilton 1973

Britten, Benjamin, *Letters from a Life: Selected Letters and Diaries of Benjamin Britten*, ed. Donald Mitchell and Philip Reed, 2 vols, 1991

Burton-Page, Piers, *Philharmonic Concerto: The Life and Music of Sir Malcolm Arnold*, Methuen 1994

Campbell, Roy, *Light on a Dark Horse: An Autobiography (1901–1935)*, Hollis & Carter 1951

Carpenter, Humphrey, *Benjamin Britten: A Biography*, Faber & Faber 1992

Clark, Kenneth, *The Other Half: A Self-Portrait*, Hamish Hamilton 1977

Coates, Eric, *Suite in Four Movements*, Heinemann 1953

Cochran, Charles B., *Cock-A-Doodle-Do*, Dent 1941

——— *Showman Looks on*, Dent 1945

Cohen, Harriet, *A Bundle of Time: The Memoirs of Harriet Cohen*, Faber & Faber 1969

Copley, Ian, *The Music of Peter Warlock: A Critical Survey*, Dennis Dobson 1979

Cottrell, John, *Laurence Olivier*, Weidenfeld & Nicolson 1975, Coronet paperback 1977

Coward, Noël, *Collected Sketches and Lyrics by Noël Coward*, Hutchinson 1931

——— *The Noël Coward Diaries* ed. Graham Payne and Sheridan Morley, Weidenfeld & Nicolson 1982

——— *Noël Coward: Autobiography*, issued in one volume, Mandarin 1992 (first published as *Present Indicative* [1937] and *Future Indefinite* [1954])

Craft, Robert, *Expositions and Developments*, Faber 1962

Dalton, David, *Playing the Viola: Conversations with William Primrose*, OUP 1988

Demuth, Norman, *Albert Roussel: A Study*, United Music Publishers n.d.

Douglas, Roy, *Working with R.V.W.*, OUP 1972

Foreman, Lewis, *Bax: A Composer and his Times*, Scolar Press 1983, revised 1988

Gielgud, John, *An Actor and his Time*, Sidgwick & Jackson 1979

Goossens, Eugene, *Overture and Beginners: A Musical Autobiography*, Methuen 1951

Gray, Cecil, *Peter Warlock: A Memoir of Philip Heseltine*, Jonathan Cape 1934, 1938

———— *Musical Chairs or Between Two Stools: An Autobiography*, Home & Van Thal 1948

Gray, Pauline, *Cecil Gray – His Life and Notebooks*, Thames 1989

Greer, David (ed.), *Hamilton Harty: His Life and Music*, Blackstaff Press 1978

Harries, Meirion, and Susie Harries, *A Pilgrim Soul: The Life and Work of Elisabeth Lutyens*, Michael Joseph 1989, Faber & Faber n.d.

Headington, Christopher, *Peter Pears: A Biography*, Faber & Faber 1992

Hindemith, Paul, *Selected Letters of Paul Hindemith*, edited and translated from the German by Geoffrey Skelton, Yale 1995

Hinnells, Duncan, *An Extraordinary Performance: Hubert Foss, Music Publishing, and the Oxford University Press*, OUP 1998

Hoare, Philip, *Serious Pleasures: The Life of Stephen Tennant*, Hamish Hamilton 1990

Holden, Anthony, *Olivier*, Weidenfeld & Nicolson 1988, Sphere paperback 1989

Holroyd, Michael, *Bernard Shaw, Vol III (1918–1950): The Lure of Fantasy*, Chatto & Windus 1991

———— *Lytton Strachey – The New Biography*, Chatto & Windus, 1994

Hopkins, Justine, *Michael Ayrton: A Biography*, André Deutsch 1994

Howard, Ronald, *In Search of my Father: A Portrait of Leslie Howard*, William Kimber 1981

Hughes, Spike, *Opening Bars – Beginning an Autobiography by Spike Hughes*, Pilot Press 1946

———— *Second Movement – Continuing the Autobiography of Spike Hughes*, Museum Press 1951

Irving, Ernest, *Cue for Music*, Dennis Dobson 19599 September 1944

Jablonski, Edward, *Gershwin: A Biography*, Simon & Schuster 1988

Jackson, Gerald, *First Flute*, Dent 1968

Kennedy, Michael, *Adrian Boult*, Hamish Hamilton 1987, Papermac 1989

Constant Lambert, 1905–1951, South London Art Gallery exhibition souvenir, 1976

Lewis, Wyndham, *Blasting and Bombardiering: An Autobiography (1914–1926)*, Eyre & Spottiswoode 1937, revised edition Calder 1982

Lucas, John, *Reggie: The Life of Reginald Goodall*, Julia MacRae Books, 1993

Lutyens, Elisabeth, *A Goldfish Bowl*, Cassell 1972

Mackail, Denis, *The Story of J. M. B.*, Peter Davies 1941

MacNeice, Louis, *Christopher Columbus: A Radio Play*, Faber & Faber 1944

Maine, Basil, *Twang with our Music*, Epworth Press 1957

Menuhin, Diana, *A Glimpse of Olympus*, Methuen 1996

Menuhin, Yehudi, *Unfinished Journey*, Macdonald & Jane's 1977

Morley, Sheridan, *A Talent to Amuse: A Biography of Noël Coward*, Heinemann 1969, Penguin Books 1974, revised 1975

Motion, Andrew, *The Lamberts: George, Constant and Kit*, Chatto & Windus 1986, Hogarth Press 1987

Neel, Boyd, *My Orchestras and Other Adventures: The Memoirs of Boyd Neel*, University of Toronto 1985

Olivier, Edith, *Edith Olivier: From her Journals (1924–48)*, ed. Penelope Middleboe, Weidenfeld & Nicolson 1989

Olivier, Laurence, *Confessions of an Actor*, Weidenfeld & Nicolson 1982, Orion 1994

Palmer, Christopher, *Delius: Portrait of a Cosmopolitan*, Duckworth 1976

———— *Herbert Howells – A Celebration*, Thames Publishing 1996 (revised edition of *Herbert Howells – A Centenary Celebration*, Thames Publishing 1992)

Quennell, Peter, *The Marble Foot: An Autobiography, 1915–1938*, Collins 1976

Rapoport, Paul (ed.), *Sorabji – A Critical Celebration*, Scolar Press 1992

Roberts, John Stuart, *Siegfried Sassoon*, Richard Cohen Books 1999

Rosen, Carole, *The Goossens: A Musical Century*, André Deutsch 1993

Sassoon, Siegfried, *Siegfried's Journey, 1916–1920*, Faber & Faber 1945

———— *Siegfried Sassoon Diaries, 1920–22* ed. Rupert Hart-Davis, Faber & Faber 1981

———— *Siegfried Sassoon Diaries, 1923–25*, ed. Rupert Hart-Davis, Faber & Faber 1985

Savage, Richard Temple, *A Voice from the Pit: Reminiscences of an Orchestral Musician*, David & Charles 1988

Schwarzkopf, Elisabeth, *On and Off the Record: A Memoir of Walter Legge*, Faber & Faber, 1982

Searle, Humphrey, *Quadrille with a Raven: Memoirs*, 1982 Internet

Shead, Richard, *Constant Lambert*, Simon Publications 1973

Skelton, Geoffrey, *Paul Hindemith: The Man Behind the Music: A biography*, Victor Gollancz 1977

Smith, Barry, *Peter Warlock: The Life of Philip Heseltine*, OUP 1994

Stravinsky, Vera, and Robert Craft, *Stravinsky in Pictures and Documents*, Simon & Schuster, 1978

Tertis, Lionel, *My Viola and I: A Complete Autobiography*, Paul Elek 1974

Thomas, Dylan, *Dylan Thomas: The Collected Letters*, ed. Paul Ferris, Dent 1985

Tippett, Michael, *Those Twentieth Century Blues: An Autobiography*, Hutchinson 1991

Vaughan Williams, Ursula, *R. V. W. – A Biography of Ralph Vaughan Williams*, OUP 1964

Vickers, Hugo, *Cecil Beaton: The Authorized Biography*, Weidenfeld & Nicolson 1985

Wetherell, Eric, *'Paddy': The Life and Music of Patrick Hadley*, Thames Publishing 1997

Whistler, Laurence, *The Laughter and the Urn: The Life of Rex Whistler*, Weidenfeld & Nicolson 1985

White, Eric Walter, *Benjamin Britten: His Life and Operas*, Faber & Faber, 1983

Wilson, Jean Moorcroft, *Siegfried Sassoon: The Making of a War Poet. A Biography, 1886–1918*, Duckworth 1998

Woolf, Virginia, *Collected Letters III*, Hogarth Press 1994

On Cinema

Aldgate, Anthony, and Jeffery Richards, *Britain can Take It: The British Cinema in the Second World War*, Blackwell 1986

Barr, Charles, *Ealing Studios*, Studio Vista 1977, revised 1993 and 1995

Brownlow, Kevin, *David Lean: A Biography*, A Wyatt Book for St Martin's Press 1996

Cross, Brenda (ed.), *The Film HAMLET: A Record of its Production*, Saturn Press 1948 (including Sir Laurence Olivier: 'An Essay in Hamlet'; William Walton: 'The Music of Hamlet'; Muir Mathieson: 'Recording the Music')

Geduld, Harry M., *Filmguide to Henry V*, Indiana University Press 1973

Hutton, C. Clayton, *The Making of Henry V*, Chiltern Court 1944

Limbacher, James L., *Film Music: From Violins to Video*, Scarecrow Press 1974

McFarlane, Brian, *An Autobiography of British Cinema by the Actors and Film-makers who Made It*, Methuen 1997

Manvell, Roger, 'The Film of Hamlet', *The Penguin Film Review* 8 January 1949, 16–24

——— *Shakespeare and the Film*, Dent 1971

Richards, Jeffrey, *Thorold Dickinson: The Man and his Films*, Croom Helm 1986

On Diaghilev, Ballet, etc.

Beaumont, Cyril W., *The Diaghilev Ballet in London – A Personal Record*, Putnam 1940, first illustrated version 1945

——— *The Sadler's Wells Ballet: A Detailed Account of Works in the Permanent Repertory with Critical Notes*, C. W. Beaumont 1946, revised and enlarged 1947

Buckle, Richard, *Diaghilev*, Weidenfeld & Nicolson 1979

Gala Performance: A Record of The Sadler's Wells Ballet over Twenty-Five Years, ed. Arnold Haskell, Mark Bonham Carter and Michael Wood, Collins 1955

Kavanagh, Julie, *Secret Muses: The Life of Frederick Ashton*, Faber & Faber 1996

Lifar, Serge, *Serge Diaghilev: His Life, his Work, his Legend. An Intimate Biography*, G. P. Putnam's Sons 1940

Vaughan, David, *Frederick Ashton and his Ballets*, A. & C. Black 1977

On Music in General

Banfield, Stephen, *Sensibility and English Song: Critical Studies of the Early Twentieth Century*, 2 vols, CUP 1985

Brook, Donald, *Composers' Gallery*, Rockliff 1946

Cox, David, *The Henry Wood Proms*, BBC 1980

Demuth, Norman, *Musical Trends in the 20th Century*, Rockliff 1952

Foreman, Lewis (ed.), *From Parry to Britten: British Music in Letters, 1900–1945*, Batsford 1987

Foss, Hubert, and Noël Goodwin, *London Symphony – Portrait of an Orchestra*, Naldrett Press 1954

Hall, Barrie, *The Proms and the Men who Made Them*, George Allen & Unwin 1981

Howes, Frank, *The English Musical Renaissance*, Secker & Warburg 1966

Hughes, Spike, *Glyndebourne: A History of the Festival Opera*, David & Charles 1965

Kennedy, Michael, *The Hallé Tradition: A Century of Music*, Manchester University Press 1960

Kenyon, Nicholas, *The BBC Symphony Orchestra: The First Fifty Years, 1930–1980*, BBC 1981

Mellers, Wilfred, *Studies in Contemporary Music*, Dobson 1947

Newman, Ernest, *Essays from the World of Music* selected by Felix Aprahamian, Volume One, John Calder 1956

Parker, Maurice (compiler), *Sir Thomas Beecham Bart, C.H. (1879–1961): A Calendar of his Concert and Theatrical Performances*, privately circulated 1985, with *Supplement 2* compiled by Tony Benson, 1998 (replacing the original, April 1990)

Pearton, Maurice, *The LSO at 70: A History of the Orchestra*, Victor Gollancz 1974

Pettitt, Stephen J., *Philharmonia Orchestra: A Record of Achievement, 1945–1985*, Robert Hale 1985

Schafer, Murray, *British Composers in Interview*, Faber & Faber 1963

Searle, Humphrey, and Robert Layton, *Twentieth Century Composers, Vol. III: Britain, Scandinavia and the Netherlands*, Holt, Rinehart & Winston 1972

Shore, Bernard, *The Orchestra Speaks*, Longmans 1948

———— *Sixteen Symphonies*, Longmans 1949

Index